Gustave Nébié, Chinyere Emeka-Anuna,
Felix Fofana N'Zue, Enrique Delamonica (Eds.)

Child Poverty and Social Protection
in Central and Western Africa

CROP International Poverty Studies

Edited by Thomas Pogge

1   *Maria Petmesidou, Enrique Delamónica, Christos Papatheodorou,
        and Aldrie Henry-Lee (Eds.)*
        Child Poverty, Youth (Un)Employment, and Social Inclusion
        ISBN 978-3-8382-0912-8

2   *Alberto Minujin, Mónica González Contró, and Raúl Mercer (Eds.)*
        Tackling Child Poverty in Latin America
        Rights and Social Protection in Unequal Societies
        ISBN 978-3-8382-0917-3

3   *Mariano Féliz and Aaron L. Rosenberg (Eds.)*
        The Political Economy of Poverty and Social Transformations
        of the Global South
        ISBN 978-3-8382-0914-2

4   *Chris Tapscott, Tor Halvorsen, and Teresita Cruz-Del Rosario (Eds.)*
        The Democratic Developmental State: North-South Perspectives
        ISBN 978-3-8382-0915-9

5   *Enrique Delamonica, Gustave Nébié, Chinyere Emeka-Anuna, and Felix
        Fofana N'Zue (Eds.)*
        Child Poverty and Social Protection in Central and Western Africa
        ISBN 978-3-8382-1176-3

Gustave Nébié, Chinyere Emeka-Anuna,
Felix Fofana N'Zue, Enrique Delamonica (Eds.)

CHILD POVERTY AND SOCIAL PROTECTION IN CENTRAL AND WESTERN AFRICA

ibidem
Verlag

Bibliographic information published by the Deutsche Nationalbibliothek
Die Deutsche Nationalbibliothek lists this publication in the Deutsche
Nationalbibliografie; detailed bibliographic data are available in the Internet at
http://dnb.d-nb.de.

Bibliografische Information der Deutschen Nationalbibliothek
Die Deutsche Nationalbibliothek verzeichnet diese Publikation in der Deutschen Nationalbibliografie;
detaillierte bibliografische Daten sind im Internet über http://dnb.d-nb.de abrufbar.

Cover image: © copyright 2020 by Cornelia C. Walther.

ISBN-13: 978-3-8382-1176-3

© *ibidem*-Verlag, Stuttgart 2020
copyright © GRIP, 2020

Printed in the United States of America

About CROP

CROP, the Comparative Research Programme on Poverty, was initiated in 1992, and the CROP Secretariat was officially opened in June 1993 by the Director General of UNESCO, Dr Frederico Mayor. The CROP network comprises scholars engaged in poverty-related research across a variety of academic disciplines and has been coordinated by the CROP Secretariat at the University of Bergen, Norway.

The CROP series on *International Studies in Poverty Research* presents expert research and essential analyses of different aspects of poverty worldwide. By promoting a fuller understanding of the nature, extent, depth, distribution, trends, causes and effects of poverty, this series has contributed to knowledge concerning the reduction and eradication of poverty at global, regional, national and local levels.

From CROP to GRIP

After a process of re-thinking CROP, 2019 marked the beginning of a transition from CROP to GRIP the Global Research Programme on Inequality. GRIP is a radically interdisciplinary research programme that views inequality as both a fundamental challenge to human well-being and as an impediment to achieving the ambitions of the 2030 Agenda. It aims to facilitate collaboration across disciplines and knowledge systems to promote critical, diverse and inter-disciplinary research on inequality. GRIP will continue to build on the successful collaboration between the University of Bergen and the International Science Council that was developed through the former Comparative Research Programme on Poverty.

For more information contact:

GRIP Secretariat
Faculty of Social Sciences
University of Bergen
PO Box 7802
5020 Bergen, Norway.
E-mail: gripinequality@uib.no
Web: www.gripinequality.org

For more information about CROP and previous publications in this series, please visit www.crop.org.

CONTENTS

Gustave Nébié, Chinyere Emeka-Anuna, Felix Fofana N'Zue,
and Enrique Delamonica

INTRODUCTION

Gustave Nébié, Chinyere Emeka-Anuna, Felix Fofana N'Zue, and Enrique Delamonica

BACKGROUND

According to a path-breaking study commissioned by UNICEF in 2003, child poverty in Sub-Saharan Africa (in particular, Central and Western Africa) was extremely high (Gordon et al., 2003). Fortunately, the situation has improved in many countries since then. This is in part due to the expansion of social protection. However, given the rate of population growth, the decline in the incidence of child poverty is too low to make a dent in the total number of children living in poverty. It also seems that the reduction in child poverty has occurred in areas and among groups that are relatively close to those who are better off. Thus, inequalities, social exclusion, and the depth of poverty might have increased. Moreover, this takes place in a context where social protection is still limited and fragmented in most countries.

Thus, the International Labour Organization (ILO), Economic Community of West African States (ECOWAS), Equity for Children, the Comparative Research Programme on Poverty (CROP) of the International Science Council, and UNICEF, all collaborated to organize a workshop inviting scholars, civil society representatives, and practitioners to discuss these issues and pathways forward. This workshop intended to further understand the trends of child poverty, its distribution, and how social protection has contributed, or not, to its decline in Central and Western Africa during the last 10-15 years. The organizers asked participants to explore the types and limitations of social protection in the region, as well as its accomplishments. Other policies that can help to reduce child poverty, improve well-being, promote child protection, and address inequities were also to be investigated.

Consequently, a three-day Conference on child poverty and social protection in Central and Western Africa was held at the ECOWAS Commission, Abuja, Nigeria, from 23 to 25 May 2016. A total of 21 papers (addressing a given country or comparing across countries) were presented by participants from 14 countries (mostly from the region but also from other African countries, Asia, Europe, and the Americas). The presentations addressed questions about the trends, distribution, and depth of child poverty. They also dealt with social protection policies, and their role to mitigate and eliminate child poverty. Experiences from other regions were shared, as well as different analyses of the impact of social protection policies in emergencies and economic crises. There was also substantive discussion about the potential role of social protection to help prevent the abuse, exploitation and neglect of children. The presentations relied on a mixture of methodologies and a truly inter-disciplinary discussion ensued.

The workshop succeeded in engendering dialogue among academics, activists and policy makers. Thus, it was agreed that the papers with the most salient points and that generated the most debate (roughly half of them) were worth collecting in this volume. These papers, now chapters, cover 15 countries, maintaining roughly the three-to-one ratio between Francophone and Anglophone countries that exists in the region. At the end of the conference a communiqué was prepared, and it is reproduced in the Annex.

DEFINITION OF CENTRAL AND WESTERN AFRICA

The title of the conference, and of this book, explicitly mentions "Central and Western Africa". However, there is no clear definitive list of which countries are or should be included. Is this a purely arbitrary (colonial/neo-colonial) construct?

According to the Economic Community of West African States (ECOWAS), its 15 member states "have both cultural and geopolitical ties and shared common interests".[1] However, it also recognizes that contemporary boundaries partly reflect the ones imposed in colonial times[2]. Consequently, they cut across ethnic and cultural lines, separating groups and communities between two or more states.

Moreover, ECOWAS is not the only regional body. There is also the Economic Community of Central African States (ECCAS) and regional central banks (Bank of Central African States, BEAC, and, Central Bank of

---

[1]   www.ecowas.int, last accessed October 25, 2018.
[2]   Emanating from the 1884 conference held in Berlin.

West African States, BCEAO). Table 1 shows that there is no one-to-one correspondence between countries belonging to one or another organization. These regional entities overlap. Table 1 also displays the way countries are classified by international organizations. Again, there is overlap, but no unanimity about the contours of the region.

Table 1:   Countries in Central and Western Africa: classification by international agencies and participation in regional bodies

	ILO	ECOWAS	ECCAS	UNICEF	BEAC	BCEAO
Benin	1	1		1		1
Burkina Faso	1	1		1		1
Cabo Verde	1	1		1		
Cameroon	1		1	1	1	
Central African Republic	1		1	1	1	
Chad	1		1	1	1	
Congo, Dem. Rep.	1		1	1		
Congo, Rep.	1		1	1	1	
Côte d'Ivoire	1	1		1		1
Equatorial Guinea	1		1	1	1	
Gabon	1		1	1	1	
Gambia, The	1	1		1		
Ghana	1	1		1		
Guinea	1	1		1		
Guinea-Bissau	1	1		1		1
Liberia	1	1		1		
Mali	1	1		1		1
Mauritania	1			1		
Niger	1	1		1		1
Nigeria	1	1		1		
São Tomé & Príncipe	1		1	1		
Senegal	1	1		1		1
Sierra Leone	1	1		1		
Togo	1	1		1		1

Source: Website of each organization
Note: ECCAS also includes Angola, Burundi, and Rwanda, which are not included as part of Central and Western Africa by any other entities.

This is not to say that the region is conceived as such only since (recent) colonial times. Several kingdoms and empires as well as trading routes[3] and peoples have ebbed and flowed for centuries, such as the Akan, Benin, Dagomba, Dyula, Fulani, Ghana, Hausa-Bakwari, Kanem, Kongo, Kuba, Songhai, and Wolof (to name a few). These kingdoms covered large swathes of the territory now labelled West and Central Africa. This variety gives the region a shared common past and a unique blend of cultures.

In addition, there is a linguistic distinctiveness. Despite the hundreds of languages (actual ones, not dialects), spoken in the region, they mostly share a common ancestry and syntactical structure. They belong to the group known as Niger-Congo languages (Greenberg, 1970, Sebeok, 1971, and Bendor-Samuel and Hartell, 1989).

Although these languages span all the way from Dakar – the westernmost point of the African continent – to Cape Horn in South Africa, a natural border with what is usually considered Eastern Africa exists, the Great Rift Valley[4]. However, as with all borders, this too is permeable. Thus, throughout history, similarly to the situation now, there have been links across this border and beyond. Nevertheless, geographically, culturally, linguistically, and historically, it is possible to speak of a Central and Western Africa region. Chapter 2 by Nébié further explores institutional and political commonalities and differences across the countries in the region in order to elucidate the policy context for social protection expansion and child poverty reduction.

SOCIAL PROTECTION: BRIEF HISTORICAL EVOLUTION, CHARACTERISTICS AND THE SITUATION IN CENTRAL AND WESTERN AFRICA

Origins of Social Protection

Social protection has origins at least as far back as the Guilds in Northern Europe during the Middle Ages and Zakat in Islam. Guilds were linked to work trades, and usually provided at least disability and widowhood support. They functioned almost as a pension or insurance. Zakat instructs the contribution of a percentage of income to support the needy, similar to a tax to finance welfare interventions.

---

3   Some even mentioned by Herodotus.
4   Although in Central Africa it splits into two branches.

As the European feudal system was disintegrating, several Poor Laws were enacted during the reign of Queen Elizabeth I of England. The one from 1601 capped a succession of Poor Laws, which had begun in 1563. These laws attempted to deal with increasing poverty due to structural social and economic changes. The relevance of the 1601 Poor Law resides in setting up a national system of "poor relief" as opposed to one based on local governments.[5]

By the 1800s, with the Second Industrial Revolution in full swing, additional developments took place. In the United States, an approach aimed at avoiding destitution among the "deserving" poor was adopted to support orphans, widows, and disabled veterans in the aftermath of the Civil War of the 1860s (Skocpol, 1992).

In contrast, in Western Europe, with German Chancellor Bismarck in the lead, a more generous approach was put in place, although it was limited to formal workers. It provided compensation to workers during illness, accident insurance and pensions.[6]

In the 1930s, with the western world in the grip of the Great Depression, social security interventions were put in place in many countries, in particular unemployment insurance. After World War II, and with economic recovery, these programmes were expanded, providing social protection "from the cradle to the grave".[7] In the Scandinavian countries, which had also started the inception of social protection (including housing subsidies) before World War II, the welfare state reached its most advanced development and coverage.[8]

It is not surprising, then, that social protection was enshrined in the 1948 Universal Declaration of Human Rights (Arts 22, 23, and 25). Since then, it has been included in the International Covenant on Economic, Social, and Cultural Rights (ICESCR, Arts. 9 and 10); the Convention of the Rights of the Child (CRC, Arts. 26 and 27); the Convention on the

---

[5] The relief depended on the "type of poor" (e.g. idle poor, deserving poor, etc). For the "non-deserving", the relief consisted of prison-like forced labor or forced removal to their town of origin (in particular after the Law of Settlement and Removal of 1662).

[6] This is a divergence in social policy models among the rich countries that continues to this day (Esping Andersen, 1990).

[7] Partly guided by the 1942 Beveridge report in the UK as reported by Marshall (1950).

[8] This fact, however, does not mean there are no limits or challenges in their implementation or impact (Therborn, 1987).

Elimination of Discrimination Against Women (CEDAW, Arts. 11 and 14); the Convention on the Rights of People with Disability (CRPD, Art. 28); and the Declaration on the Rights of Indigenous Peoples (DRIP, Arts. 21).[9]

More recently, in 2012, the ILO Social Protection Floors Recommendation Number 202 established a Tripartite (governments, private sector, and labour unions) agreement for a minimum set of social protection interventions to be provided to all citizens in all countries. The set includes pensions, essential health care (including maternity care), basic income security for families with children, and minimum income for adults in case of sickness, unemployment, maternity and disability.[10]

Social Protection Floors (SPFs) are nationally defined sets of basic social security guarantees, which secure protection aimed at preventing or alleviating poverty, vulnerability, and social exclusion.[11] As part of the efforts to pull the world out of the financial crisis of 2007-09, the Social Protection Floor was taken up as a core element of the United Nations response.

Thus, social protection has evolved into a human right. It aims to prevent and eliminate poverty throughout the life cycle. Social protection includes preventive, protective, promotive, and transformative interventions (Mkandawire, 2004), such as child and family benefits, unemployment insurance, employment injury benefits, health insurance (including for maternity), benefits for orphans and widow(er)s and for people with disability, and, old-age pensions. This, clearly, does not mean that social protection can or should solve all problems faced by families and children. Nevertheless, particularly in contexts with high and very high poverty, it is important to explore the contours and the connections between social protection and other actions required to protect children. This is examined in Chapter 10 by Derby et al. for Ghana, and in Chapter 9 by Skelton and Plaisir, for Burkina Faso, Central African Republic, and Democratic Republic of Congo.

---

[9] All these Conventions can be found at the website of the Office of the High Commissioner for Human Rights (www.ohchr.org). There are also regional human rights instruments that include Social Protection (e.g. Arab Charter on Human Rights, Art 36).

[10] It is recognized that implementing all these elements may take time. Thus, progressive realization, which requires plans and milestones, is needed in accordance with the International Covenant on Economic, Social and Cultural Rights and the Limburg Principles.

[11] ILO (2011)

In summary, social protection programmes guarantee access to necessary goods and services, such as essential health care, maternity care, nutrition, education, and childcare. These programmes can also provide income security throughout the life cycle. Social protection can be financed via contributory schemes such as social insurance, or non-contributory social assistance, where taxes are the source of the funding. There are also important linkages between social protection and the prevention of, and response to, crises and emergencies. Chapter 7 by Abdu investigates this issue in the context of the Ebola crisis in Sierra Leone.

What about Africa?

Formal African relief systems date back to ancient Egypt under the Pharaohs (World Bank 1990). In general, though, there were few formal institutions for social protection outside of Ethiopia and Islamic West Africa. In the savannah kingdoms of central Africa, the level of institutional care was higher than anywhere on the continent. There appears to have been no tradition of begging, but there is evidence that secret societies cared for struggling individuals. People turned to chiefs for assistance. Kuba kings kept huge storehouses, while Bemba chiefs "were expected to maintain food reserves against scarcity and to support those too old or young to provide for themselves" (Iliffe 1987:58-9).

In most areas, vulnerability was addressed through family networks. Most communities and families draw on a range of social protection mechanisms based on extended family and community ties in the face of shocks and chronic poverty. Kinship-based support systems provide access to economic assistance, reproductive care and psychosocial support. Long-standing socio-cultural practices often create a moral responsibility to help less-fortunate family members through cash and/or in-kind transfers.

Traditional community-based systems of risk pooling are based on the rule of "generalized reciprocity," which has been often formulated in anthropological literature: "in a community where everyone is likely to find himself in difficulties from time to time (...) he who is in need today receives help from him who may be in like need tomorrow" (Evans-Pritchard, 1940: 85). The basic logic underlying these schemes is that of "a collective disaster-avoidance strategy whereby the participants form a long-term 'partnership reservoir' which can be tapped in times of stress" (Platteau, 1991: 143).

Community-based and family-based social protection systems still play a crucial role in mitigating social risks and human vulnerability in Africa. These informal social protection systems are not confined only to rural areas but reach out into peri-urban and urban areas as well, partly by maintained urban-rural linkages (Von Braun, 1991). However, these traditional solidarity mechanisms and safety nets appear to be eroding in recent years, underscoring the importance of strengthening the formal social protection system.

Characteristics of Social Protection Implementation

Social protection has several complementary objectives. It provides care for children, including those who survive neglect and exploitation, orphans, and children whose parents are monetary-poor. Social protection also provides insurance against external shocks (e.g. disability pension). It also levels the playing field, for example by establishing education grants for children in monetary-poor families. In addition, it reduces monetary poverty, addressing the right to a minimum standard of living, particularly through the use of cash transfers. Moreover, it promotes social integration and inclusion by lowering inequalities in terms of both income and access to basic social services.

The above description also portrays social protection as a system that covers individuals throughout their life cycle. For babies there is free health care, for slightly older children there is nutrition support. For even older children and youth, there is support to access education and for working adults there is unemployment insurance. For elderly persons there are pensions and for everyone, there is health insurance. In a nutshell, a social protection system is universal, not just for the poor.

Thus, it is important to think of social protection as an integrated system of interventions and programmes. It can be envisaged as consisting of four pillars: 1) monetary and in-kind social transfers; 2) programmes to ensure access to services; 3) social support and care services; and 4) legislation and regulation for equity.[12]

---

[12]   Several authors and agencies provide different, but very similar, classifications. A summary was provided in Minujin et al. (2007). This text follows the one

In implementing social protection schemes and benefits, different approaches are often used. They include universal benefit schemes, social insurance schemes, social assistance schemes, negative income tax schemes, public employment schemes, and employment support schemes. With a combination of interventions, maximum impact can be achieved.

Monetary and in-kind social transfers, can include, among others: birth grants; universal child allowances; employment of last resort programmes; disability benefits; sick leave; maternal or parental benefits; climate-related insurance; unemployment benefits; and cash- or food-for-work schemes, particularly in emergency settings. With this diversity of approaches, it is important to realize what the objectives of these interventions are. For instance, in Figure 1, (where the vertical line represents income and the poverty line is shown for reference), the light part of each bar signifies the pre-intervention income and the dark portion at the top of the bar indicates the supplement provided by the social protection programme. Thus, if the objective is to eliminate monetary poverty (first column), the intervention has to ensure that the post-intervention income surpasses the poverty line. This is not the case for the second column, which represents a programme intending to (only) reduce monetary poverty or reduce the depth of poverty. Other interventions (e.g. a universal child grant) are not associated with the poverty line (third column). In the fourth column, there are no light and dark parts. It is all shaded. This could be the case when the social protection interventions provide income, which would not have been there otherwise (e.g. unemployment insurance). This could (or not) surpass the poverty line.

presented in UNICEF (2012), which is currently being updated but not radically changed.

Figure 1:   Objectives and impact of transfers

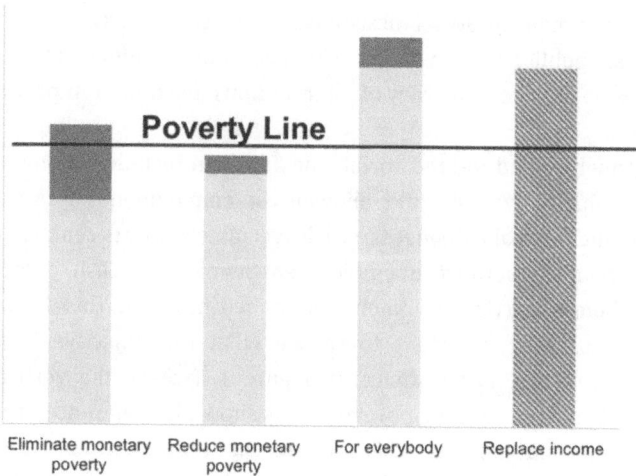

| Eliminate monetary poverty | Reduce monetary poverty | For everybody | Replace income |

Programmes to ensure access to services include the abolishing of user fees for services; housing allowances; subsidies for water and sanitation; scholarships for adolescents (to avoid school drop-out); school feeding; food vouchers or food assistance; health insurance, and other programmes. A key point to remember across these interventions is that although social protection does not supply these services, it assists families to access them.

Social support and care services, on the other hand, may involve actual provision of goods or services. This is the case, for example, of home-based care (e.g. children with disabilities or affected by HIV/AIDS), support for children separated from parents, children who survive violence, or care of children while parents work or study. Providing assistive devices would also fall in this category. Another very important element in this pillar is capacity building. This includes awareness-raising, empowering and training of beneficiaries in order that they know what they are entitled to, and helping people access and navigate the system to claim the benefits that they are due.

Legislation and regulation for equity would ensure that legal and policy frameworks should be put in place to provide overarching guidance in designing and implementing the social protection programmes. They ensure that social protection schemes and programmes are nationally owned and sustainable as well as equitable. This includes, among other issues: maternity protection (including breastfeeding promotion) and special programmes to access education or other services (e.g. children with disabilities). It could also encompass legislation against discrimination as well as inheritance rights.

A crucial element to facilitate integration is the presence of a single registry of beneficiaries.[13] A single registry system promotes integration as well as efficiency by helping to avoid unnecessary duplication. It can also help to increase effectiveness by coordinating the delivery of all the different types of benefits that families or individuals facing several risks simultaneously may require.

Figure 2 illustrates another aspect of an integrated social protection system. It shows vertical and horizontal integration on the utilization and provision sides. Vertical integration on the utilization side refers to the coordination of activities (including crossing over of beneficiaries) along the life cycle as they grow older. Horizontal integration on the utilization side harmonizes the assistance to different groups in need of simultaneous interventions. For instance, a rural widow with a disability may require benefits from various programmes such as agricultural extension, survivor benefit and subsidies to acquire assistive devices (or receive them directly in-kind). Vertical integration on the provision side synchronizes activities across the various layers of the state structure. This is particularly important in federal countries or those with advanced decentralization/devolution of social sector responsibilities. Horizontal integration deals with the coordination of activities across ministries, departments, and other government units or organizations delivering the various programmes and interventions.

---

13   This is different from a social register, which could be stigmatizing and (mis)used to engage in narrow targeting, which is inimical to the universalistic approach of Social Protection (Kidd, 2017).

Figure 2:   Social protection systems and axes of disparities

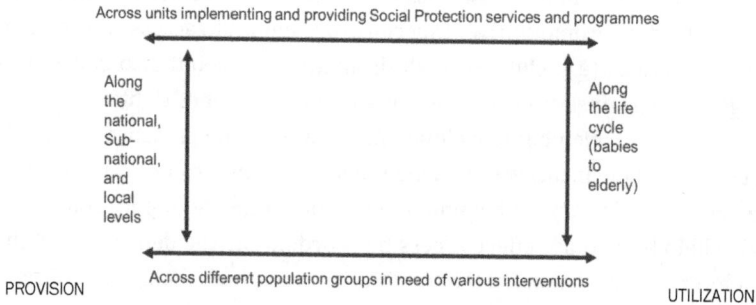

Across units implementing and providing Social Protection services and programmes

Along
the
national,
Sub-
national,
and
local
levels

Along
the life
cycle
(babies
to
elderly)

Across different population groups in need of various interventions

PROVISION

UTILIZATION

Source: adapted from Cecchini and Martinez (2011)

There are further issues to consider in the design, implementation and monitoring of social protection interventions. These pertain to gender, ethnicity, and disability. For example, when designing interventions for childcare it is important to avoid reproducing gender division of labour stereotypes. In addition, nutrition supplementation should consider culturally appropriate food, and assistive devices should enhance dignity. Gender and other stereotypes in public work programmes should be avoided. There should be consultation and outreach during programme implementation and monitoring, which should include disaggregated data and participatory evaluation.

Mapping Social Protection in Central and Western Africa

African countries have repeatedly asserted the imperative to expand social protection in the continent even before a specific target was included in the UN Sustainable Development Goals (SDGs). For example, the Livingston Call for Action of 2006 and the African Union Agenda 2063 of 2013 both emphasize social protection.

In terms of the UN targets, SDG 1.3 calls for nationally appropriate social protection systems for all. Other SDGs targets also implicate social protection, particularly in terms of universal health care (SDG 3.8), gender equality (SDG 5.4), decent work and economic growth (SDG 8.5) and equality (SDG 10.4).

According to the World Social Protection Report, 2017-19 (ILO, 2017)—the most recent and comprehensive global review of the status of social protection—only 17.8 percent of the African population are covered by at least one social protection such as cash benefit. As with all averages, there is much inter-country variation. There are also large differentials by age. For instance, 29.6 percent of Africa's elderly benefit from a pension. However, Botswana, Cabo Verde, Lesotho, Mauritius and Namibia have achieved (or are close to achieving) universal pension coverage. On the other hand, the unemployed workers and persons with disabilities are lagging far behind.

In terms of the specific interventions for children, Figure 3 portrays the situation of Africa in the global context. Social protection coverage is the lowest in the world, standing at half of the world average.

Figure 3:   Percentage of children and households receiving child and family benefits, by region, latest available year

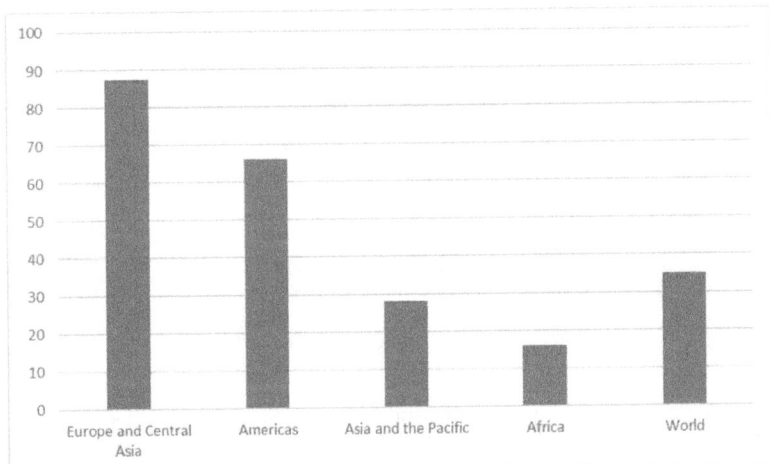

Source: ILO (2017)

Figure 4 shows that, by and large, regions with a larger proportion of children invest less in the social protection programmes that benefit them and their families. This is one of the reasons why, as it is discussed below, the pace of child poverty reduction has been too slow in Central and Western Africa. Low taxation and insufficient public resources compromise the possibility of channelling the benefits of economic growth through social policy in general and social protection in particular (Nébié 2017). One of the reasons why this happens is because interventions are not universal. Another element constraining opportunities for child poverty reduction are inequities and inequalities.

Vandemoortele in Chapter 1 of this volume writes about some of the limitations imposed on social protection by inequalities. Asogwa in Chapter 11 analyses the benefit incidence of public investments in the social sectors in Nigeria.

Figure 4: Percentage of children in the total population and share of GDP spent on social protection interventions for children and families

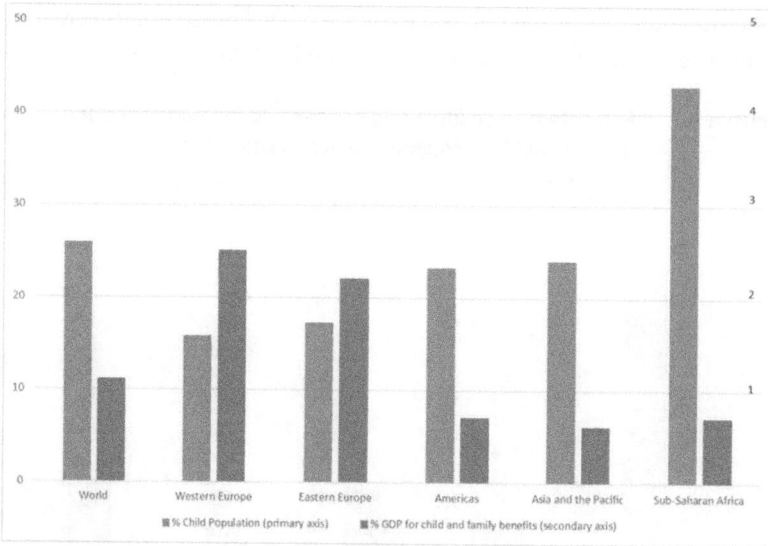

Source: ILO, 2017
Note: Western Europe includes Northern and Southern Europe as well. Not all developing regions and sub-regions are shown. Only children up to age 14 have been included. Social protection expenditures exclude health.

In Table 2 the different elements in the Social Protection Floor and their rate of coverage in Central and Western African countries are shown. First and foremost, it is clear that the information available is not sufficient, as most cells are empty.

Table 2:   Social protection coverage

	% of Population covered by at least one benefit (1)	% children covered by social protection benefits (2)	% women covered by maternity benefits (3)	% persons with disabilities receiving benefits (4)	% of older persons receiving a pension (5)
Benin					9.7
Burkina Faso	7.6		0.4	0.1	2.7
Cabo Verde	30.4	31.5			85.8
Cameroon	8.7	0.4	0.6	0.1	13.0
Central African Rep.					
Chad					1.6
Congo, Dem. Rep.	14.1	1.3			15.0
Congo, Rep.					22.1
Côte d'Ivoire					7.7
Equatorial Guinea					
Gabon					38.8
Gambia	6.1				17.0
Ghana	18.3	5.6	41.7		33.3
Guinea					8.8
Guinea-Bissau					6.2
Liberia					
Mali		5.4		0.6	2.7
Mauritania					9.3
Niger	20.6	4.2			5.8
Nigeria	4.4			0.1	7.8
São Tomé & Príncipe					52.5
Senegal		4.0			23.5
Sierra Leone					0.9
Togo					10.9
Africa	17.8	15.9	15.8	n.a	29.6
World	45.2	34.9	41.1	27.8	67.9

Source: ILO, 2017

Notes:
(1) Proportion of the total population receiving benefits from at least one (contributory or non-contributory) benefit or actively contributing to at least one social security scheme (SDG indicator 1.3.1 (a)).
(2) Ratio of children/households receiving child benefits to the total number of children/households with children.
(3) Ratio of women receiving maternity benefits to women giving birth in the same year (estimation based on age-specific fertility rates published in the UN World Population Prospects or on the number of live births corrected by the share of twin and triplet births).
(4) Ratio of persons receiving disability benefits to persons with severe disabilities. The latter is calculated as the product of prevalence of disability ratios (published for each country group by the World Health Organization) and each country's population.
(5) Ratio of persons above statutory retirement age receiving an old-age pension (including contributory and non-contributory) to persons above statutory retirement age.

In the first column, Cabo Verde is shown to have managed to cover a third of its population with at least one social protection benefit.[14] This is almost double the African average, but it is still below the world average of almost half of the population. Most countries in the region struggle to cover more than 15 percent of their citizens.

Coverage of families with children with a child grant or similar child-focused benefits does not fare much better (column 2). Cabo Verde (almost a third of the children) and Cameroon (just above 40 percent) are above the African average (15.9 percent). Cameroon is even a bit higher than the global average of 35 percent. Most countries cover barely 5 percent of their children.[15]

Information about coverage of mothers with newborns is paltry – there are data from only five countries (third column). In three of these, coverage is less than 1 percent. However, in Cabo Verde it is about 10 percent and in Ghana about 4 in 10 mothers are covered, roughly equal to the world-wide average.

Most countries provide pensions for the elderly (last column). This is, obviously, very important for the persons in that age bracket and they

---

[14]   This includes population contributing to at least one social security programme or receiving benefits from at least one programme (either contributory or non-contributory).

[15]   Moreover, while most of them are contributory (employment based), the programmes in Gambia, Ghana, Liberia, Nigeria, São Tomé and Sierra Leone are not based on legislation (and they are not employment related) or there is no information about their legal status.

have a right to a pension during old age. In addition, it is good for children, as several studies from around the world have shown that a substantial part of the pensions directed towards the elderly are used to provide for their grandchildren. Only Cabo Verde (85.8 percent) surpasses the world average of almost two-thirds of coverage of the elderly population. Three countries (Congo, Gabon, São Tomé and Príncipe) have a coverage higher than the Africa-wide average—almost a third of the elderly. Half of the countries with documented data are in the single digits of coverage.

Most of these interventions are nationally developed and financed. However, some are supported with donor financing and sometimes are "encouraged" by international agencies (Deacon 2013, Mkandawire 2015). The table does not cover the myriad, small-scale "pilot" projects run by national or international Non-Governmental Organisations (NGOs). This lack of coherent data can create problems such as lack of coordination, duplication, uneven (and consequently unfair) benefits in different locations, lack of capacity and plans to scale-up towards universality, inconsistent selection criteria, etc.

In addition, about half of the countries have ratified ILO social security conventions covering children and mothers. Some have done this around the time of independence. In 1964 the Central African Republic (CAR) approved convention 118 (1962), covering both mothers and children, and stipulating equal treatment of nationals and non-nationals. In the same year, CAR also committed to about half of the main interventions in Table 2, but the other ones are not covered yet.[16] Similarly, in 1967 Guinea ratified convention 118 for mothers and children along with all other provisions except for unemployment and disability. In 1968 and 1966, respectively, Mauritania and Niger ratified convention 102 (1952), which deals with minimum standards of social security, but only committed to a few other provisions. In addition, Mauritania ratified convention 118 the same year. However, in Mauritania both conventions have been used only to cover children and

---

16 Coverage of the other interventions are also important for children (e.g. unemployment benefits help parents take care of their children when they lose their jobs). Also, as mentioned above, pensions that go to the elderly are often spent on their grandchildren. Nevertheless, this brief summary does not address issues such as the gender bias in some maternity and leave benefits or the risks associated with community-based health care (which could be unsustainable if risks are not spread through large populations).

not maternity. In 1962, Senegal ratified convention 102 only to cover children, mothers and employment injury. In 2017 they also ratified convention 183 (of 1952)[17] protecting maternity benefits.

The delayed ratification seems to be a pattern, followed by other countries. Benin (in 2012), Burkina Faso (in 2013), Mali (in 2008), and São Tomé (in 2017) also ratified convention 183 but only for maternity benefits. In contrast, other countries ratified more than one convention and expanded coverage. Chad ratified convention 102 for children and a few other categories (but not maternity) in 2015. In 1987, Cabo Verde ratified convention 118 for all types of interventions except unemployment insurance. The same year, the Democratic Republic of Congo (DRC) ratified convention 102. More recently, in 2013, Togo ratified the same convention for mothers, children, and a few other interventions.

Table 3 portrays additional evidence about the low coverage of social protection in the region. It deals with the deficit in health care coverage. Sadly, for the majority of countries more than 90 percent of the citizens lack coverage. Notable exceptions are Cabo Verde, Gambia and Ghana. Even in countries which are doing relatively better than the rest, there are wide disparities between the urban and rural populations, with the latter much less protected than the former.

This lack of coverage is reflected in the high out-of-pocket expenditures burdening families. Although the quantitative information in the table cannot show it, it is known that health care expenditures are uncertain and often catastrophic. The impact of this uncertainty can be very high stress and/or situations where health care is completely unaffordable thus resulting in avoidable death of family members.

---

[17]   Unlike conventions 102 and 118 which entered into force within a few years after ratification, the date of entry into force for convention 183 was the year 2000, almost half a century after it was written.

Table 3: Health care coverage and out of pocket expenditure (as a percentage of total national health expenditure)

	Total Legal health care coverage deficit	Urban Legal health care coverage deficit	Rural Legal health care coverage deficit	Year	Total out of pocket expenditure	Urban out of pocket expenditure	Rural out of pocket expenditure	Year
Benin	91.0	87.2	94.0	2009	44.5	48.5	41.3	2008
Burkina Faso	99.0	99.0	99.0	2010	32.9	36.2	31.8	2009
Cabo Verde	35.0	27.9	46.5	2010	21.8	31.0	6.8	2007
Cameroon	98.0	-	-	2009	66.1	91.6	38.9	2007
Central African Republic	94.0	94.6	93.6	2010	-	-	-	-
Chad	-	-	-	-	72.7	45.2	80.4	2003
Congo, Dem. Rep.	90.0	82.1	94.0	2000	33.4	37.0	33.2	2004
Congo, Rep.	-	-	-	-	37.2	49.4	16.4	2005
Côte d'Ivoire	98.8	98.6	99.0	2008	56.5	67.4	45.3	2008
Equatorial Guinea	-	-	-	-	-	-	-	-
Gabon	42.4	40.6	53.6	2011	20.4	28.8	9.4	2003
Gambia, The	0.1	0.1	0.1	2011	27.7	35.3	19.8	2006
Ghana	26.1	4.5	48.8	2010	62.6	71.4	57.9	2007
Guinea	99.8	99.6	99.9	2010	-	-	-	-
Guinea-Bissau	98.4	-	-	2011	24.6	29.1	20.4	2007
Liberia	-	-	-	-	58.9	62.6	56.9	2006
Mali	98.8	97.6	98.4	2008	33.2	30.8	34.9	2004
Mauritania	90.4	89.4	97.2	2009	60.5	40.6	64.7	2007
Niger	96.9	95.7	97.1	2003	70.5	69.9	71.2	2009
Nigeria	97.8	97.0	95.8	2008	56.2	77.4	21.4	2000
São Tomé and Principe	97.9	97.3	98.8	2009	35.4	50.8	24.2	2005
Senegal	79.9	69.1	87.4	2007	77.4	99.0	59.8	2003
Sierra Leone	100.0	100.0	100.0	2008	45.7	58.1	45.0	2006
Togo	96.0	93.9	97.3	2010	-	-	-	-

Source: ILO (2017)

It could be argued that one of the reasons for the lack of social protection coverage is lack of national financial resources. However, this is belied by the (albeit limited) evidence in Figure 5. It shows the variation among countries in Central and Western Africa regarding the proportion of children covered by child or family benefits.[18] The same (very low) coverage of 5 percent of children is demonstrated in countries with 500, 1000, or 1500 US$ per capita income. This means that resources could be doubled or tripled without any effect at all on the provision of child benefits. That there are other drivers and barriers are further confirmed by countries enjoying three to eight times the level of coverage with the same (low) per capita income.

Figure 5:   Percentage of children covered by social protection in countries with different level of per capita income

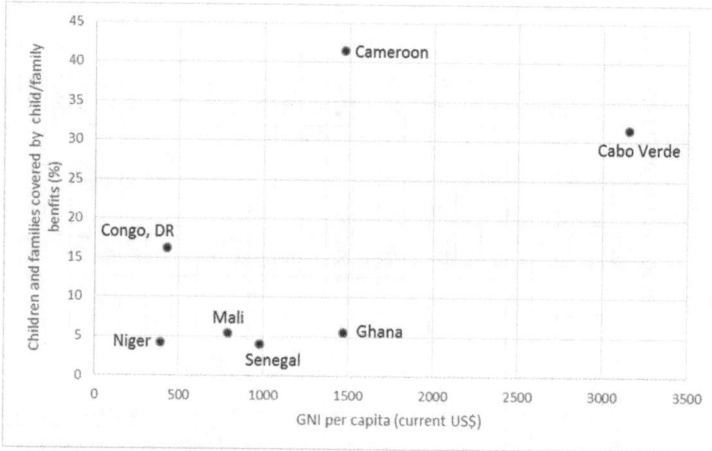

Sources: ILO (2017) and World Bank World Development Indicators database. Accessed: 30 August 2018

[18] Even if lack of financial resources were the issue, the international community, in particular the richer countries, also have an obligation to contribute under several international conventions (e.g. General Comment number 3 on the International Covenant on Economic, Social and Cultural Rights), agreements and commitments, including the "promise" to allocate 0.7% of their total income for ODA (Pearson, 1969), the Monterrey Consensus (United Nations, 2003), and the Addis Ababa Action Agenda (United Nations, 2015). Additionally, financial resources should be complemented with human and material resources, which are still nonetheless lacking. The international community also has an obligation in terms of technical assistance.

Other estimates show that social protection is affordable in all countries, even the poorest ones. Figure 6 shows that in more than 60 developing countries a universal pension would cost less than 1 percent of total output, and in another 40 countries it would cost between 1 - 2 percent. A universal pension requires more than 2 percent of total income in fewer than 10 countries.

Figure 6:   Countries classified according to the percentage of GDP required to provide a universal pension

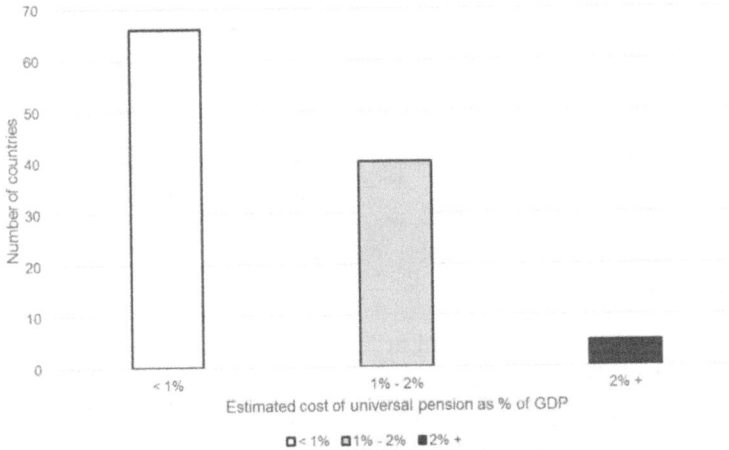

Source: Knox-Vydmanov (2011) using a universal old-age pension for people over 65.

In Figure 7, various elements of social protection have been costed for four countries in Central and Western Africa. Except for universal basic health care, they usually cost less than 1.5 percent of total output.

Figure 7:   Estimated cost of various social protection elements (% of total output)

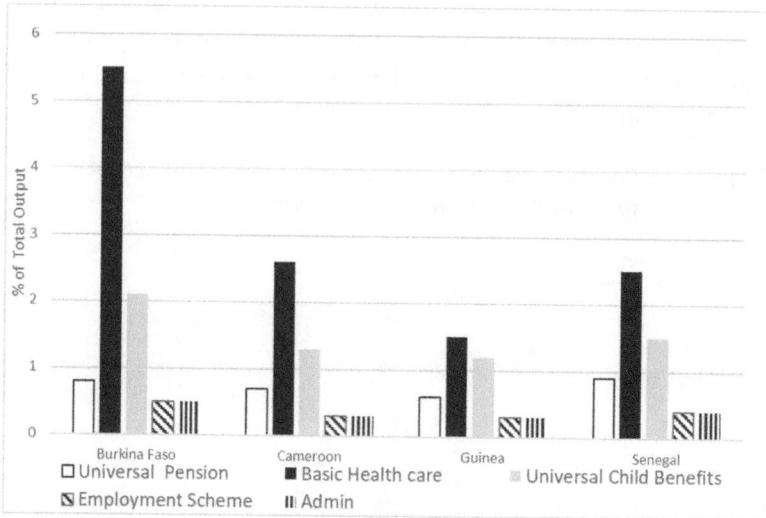

Source: ILO (2008)

Similar conclusions are arrived at by reviewing several cost estimates produced by ILO as well as the International Monetary Fund (IMF), the United Nations Department of Economic and Social Affairs (UN DESA), UNICEF and many others.[19] Some of these cost estimates can be replicated or adjusted for alternative assumptions in the web-based ILO costing tool.

Thus, the question to ask is not if social protection is affordable. The question is whether NOT investing in social protection is affordable.

CHILD POVERTY IN CENTRAL AND WESTERN AFRICA

Why Child Poverty?

It has been well understood for several decades that children experience poverty differently from adults (Boyden, et al., 2012; Jones and Sumner, 2011; Lyytikäinen et al., 2006; Minujin et al., 2006; Nieuwenhuys, 1994; and Wordsworth et al., 2005). When measuring national averages, it is possible to observe improvements in access to health care, household income, and literacy campaigns, yet children are still not taken to clinics,

---

[19]   ILO (2011).

children are exploited or neglected, and children are not going to school. As children make up almost half of the population in Central and Western Africa, unless child poverty is specifically measured, policy makers may be lulled into believing much progress is made to reduce poverty, when in reality half of the population is stagnating or worse off.[20]

This is one of the main reasons why the SDGs have set up a target (1.2.2) to measure poverty and specifically to measure child poverty. It states that the goal is to measure the "proportion of men, women and children of all ages living in poverty in all its dimensions according to national definitions".[21] Moreover, the target explicitly mentions that this measurement should be multidimensional.

The so-called "international" poverty line ("a dollar a day") is not aligned with the actual cost of a minimum basket of goods and services in most Central and Western African countries (even when taking Purchasing Power Parity (PPP) conversations into account). Thus, for national planning and policy design, the national poverty lines should be used.

However, while it is important to note the amount of resources available in the household in which the child lives, child poverty must be conceptualized and measured directly. This means that in order to have a general assessment of the opportunities children could theoretically have to satisfy material needs and attain a minimum standard of living, it is useful to estimate the proportion of children living in households with income/consumption below the poverty line. However, this is not enough to understand child poverty.

Household income could surpass the poverty line because children beg in the streets or are engaged in hazardous work; household income could increase because parents work extremely long hours, leaving children abandoned, neglected, and without any adult supervision, comfort, or guidance. Household income may be above the poverty line, yet if social services are not available (e.g. in rural areas), the above-the-poverty-line household income would not change the situation of children, who would still be left without schooling or health care.

Thus, child poverty should be measured directly. How is this done in practice?

---

[20]   The issue is not to pit children against adults. It is only to recognize the specificity of the rights of children and, thus, the need to have child poverty explicitly measured as such and then combined with overall poverty.

[21]   https://sustainabledevelopment-uk.github.io/1-2-2/.

Measuring Child Poverty

The measurement should be aligned with the concept that child poverty is not about lack of income but deprivations of children's rights. In this respect, the literature on human rights and poverty (Hunt et al., 2002, OHCHR, 2012) is very clear: not all rights violations constitute poverty – only those clearly associated with material shortcoming or deprivation. In other words, when discussing poverty from a human rights perspective, the deprivation or violation of certain rights constitutes poverty, i.e. it makes the person poor. This is independent of income. Thus, it is not that multidimensional poverty is a proxy or a substitute or a marker or cause or a consequence of lack of income. The deprivation in these dimensions is what makes the child poor.

Child poverty could be either a cause or a consequence of monetary poverty, but it could also be both at once. In addition, monetary poverty could be a cause or consequence of child poverty. There are intricate feedback loops between the two in the short term as well as in the long run across generations. The important issue, is that child poverty is not measured just because it could be a cause or a consequence of monetary poverty. It is measured because it is important in and of itself and it directly affects children today, independently of any possible causal relationship with their parents' income. Consequently, its correct measurement is crucial for proper policy design.

As a result, three basic principles should guide the practice of measuring multidimensional child poverty. These principles are based on the conceptual definition based on human rights and have been validated from global practice.

Firstly, the dimensions are only those rights considered constitutive of poverty. These are clearly associated with material shortcoming and/or the absence of public goods and services that are needed to satisfy basic human needs.[22] In other words, not everything that is bad that happens to children constitutes in or is poverty. In particular, child poverty is about material deprivation, not inappropriate behaviour.[23]

---

[22]   Thus, there is a relationship between the human rights approach to poverty and the earlier literature on basic needs (ILO, 1976, Morris, 1978, Streeten et al., 1981).

[23]   For example, violence against children (which occurs even among the wealthiest households all over the world) is a child rights violation that does not constitute poverty as it is not determined by lack of material resources. Early and preventable child deaths do not constitute poverty either. Also, improper handwashing is a bad

Secondly, all rights are equally important. This means that there should be no differentials in weighting the different dimensions. This is congruent with the capabilities approach. As Dixon and Nussbaum (2012) express it: "A Capabilities Approach is generally committed to the equal protection of rights for all up to a certain threshold. Any trade-off that leaves some people below this threshold will thus be a clear failure of basic justice under a Capabilities Approach". Weighting the dimensions is equivalent to providing an exact numerical value to trade-off one right for another one (e.g. it would be tantamount to say that health is 3.14 times more important than nutrition). This leads to the distinct possibility that children suffering from three or even four constitutive rights violations would not be considered poor, a clear failure of basic justice.

Thirdly, child poverty is about the experience of the whole child. This means, on the one hand, that child poverty ought to be measured at the child level, and all the dimensions must be assessed simultaneously for the same child. Consequently, it cannot be estimated using different sources of information. On the other hand, it means that all children under the age of 18 should be counted, and total estimates for all children should be calculated.

While following these basic principles, it is possible for estimates across countries to be flexible in order to adjust them to national priorities. This would also include participatory processes to ensure communities' and families' (including children's) voices about how they experience poverty and the items that should be included in its measurement. This approach is described in Chapter 3 by Nandy and Pomati, looking at child poverty in Benin, Gabon, Guinea, Liberia, and Mali.

However, there are international standards for flexible country estimates of child poverty (see the appendix to this chapter). These are the thresholds used consistently throughout the chapters that provide child poverty evidence. The same standards are used in Figure 8a, which shows the incidence of child poverty for all countries in Central and Western Africa for which data are available for two points in time (circa 2000 and 2015), while in Figure 8b the estimates for which there is only one point in time are presented.

---

habit. However, it does not constitute poverty (while lack of access to water or to sanitation is a material deprivation that constitutes poverty). Similarly, when a child is not breastfed, it is not due to material deprivation but (usually) due to lack of knowledge or cultural barriers, so no breastfeeding does not constitute poverty.

Figure 8a: Child poverty trends in Central and Western Africa: Countries
with two data points c. 2000 (in black) and 2015 (in white)

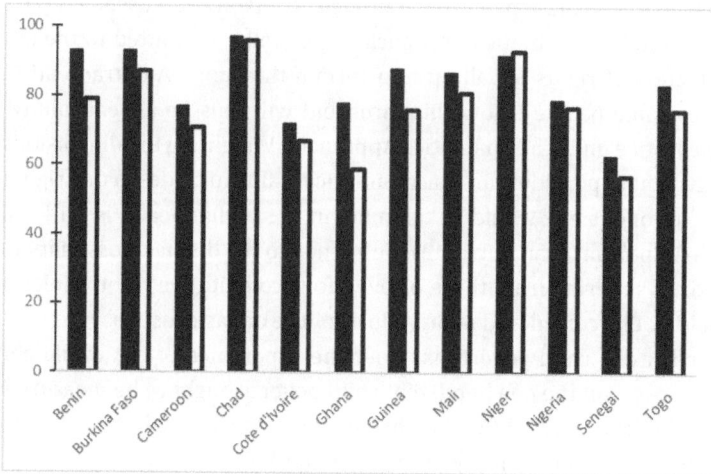

Figure 8b: Child poverty trends in Central and Western Africa: Countries
with only one data point c. 2000 (in black) and 2015 (in white)

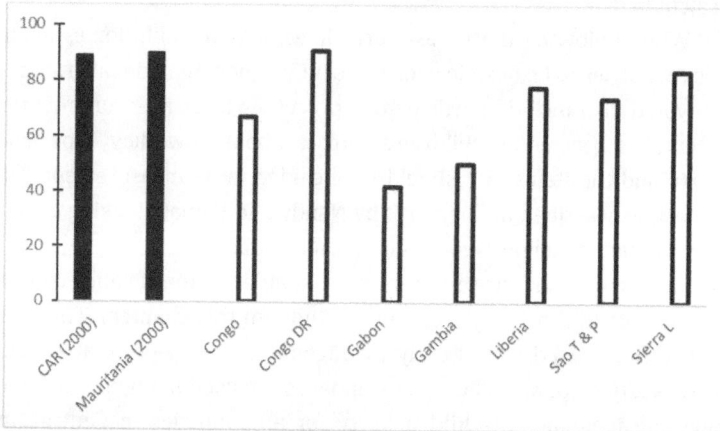

Source: Multiple Indicator Cluster Surveys (MICS) and Demographic Health Surveys
(DHS).

Two conclusions clearly come out of these graphs. Child poverty is very
high in the region. The lowest recorded estimate (for Gabon) is about 4
out of 10 children. In the majority of countries, it is double that level.
Secondly, for all but one of the 12 countries with at least two points in
time, child poverty is estimated at the same or lower level than 10-15

years ago.[24] The only exception is Niger, where it has risen. However, the observed increase is not statistically significant.

While the above-mentioned standards ensure comparability across countries, there is (and should be) room for flexibility and adaption to different contexts. Nevertheless, adaptation should always be upwards; countries may deem the threshold is too low to properly describe child poverty, but they cannot say that some group of people (e.g., in rural areas or ethnic minorities) are less deserving than the rest of the population so their thresholds are lower. Moreover, adjusting the thresholds, which allows for sensitivity exercises, and cross tabulation with monetary poverty, provide very important and informative analysis and a fuller description of child poverty. Chapter 4 in this volume by Cid Martinez addresses thresholds in Cameroon, Côte d'Ivoire, and Nigeria, while Chapter 5 by Hague et al. combines and analysis of child poverty with monetary poverty in Ghana.

Time Trends

Moreover, the trends of child poverty are not related to economic growth. Figure 9 is a scatter diagram showing the lack of association between accumulated economic growth (real per capita income increase between the years 2000 and 2012 – horizontal axis) and the reduction in child poverty (percentage points reduction of the incidence of child poverty – vertical axis) for the 12 countries in the region with estimates of child poverty for at least two points in time. Five countries are highlighted. Niger, where per capita income doubled but child poverty is stagnant, the slight change in incidence being within the margin of error of the estimates. In Nigeria and Chad, income grew five-fold without any changes in child poverty. In Togo and Senegal, where child poverty declined by 10 percent (a statistically significant change), per capita income doubled or increased by 60 percent (respectively). Chapter 8 in this volume by Kielem assesses the power of social protection policies in mitigating the impact of the economic downturn on child poverty in Togo during part of this period.

---

[24]   For some countries, the decline is within the margin of error so the reduction cannot be said to be statistically significant.

Figure 9:   Child poverty changes and accumulated economic growth

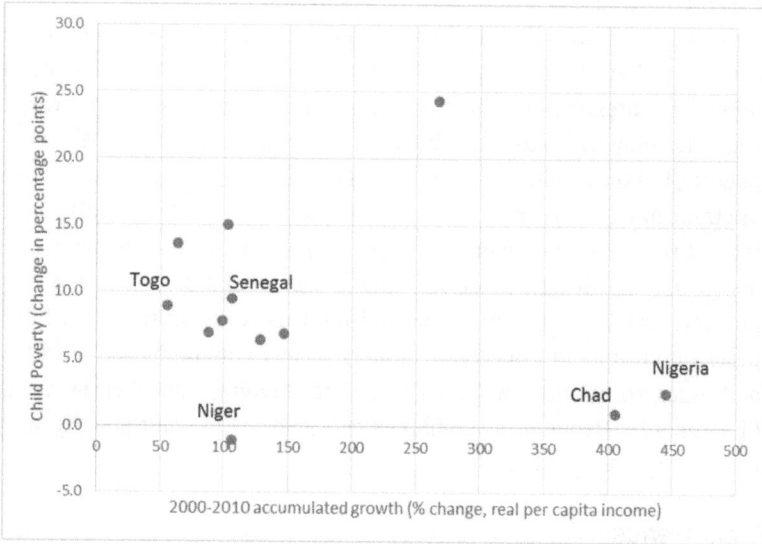

Source: MICS and DHS for Child Poverty and World Bank World Development
Indicators database. Accessed 30 August 2018.

This result should not be surprising. It is similar to what is found
regarding monetary poverty. In Table 4, the 12 countries with at least two
child poverty observations are listed. These countries also have at least
two estimates of monetary poverty since the year 2000.[25] For each, where
2-3 monetary poverty measures exist, the accumulated per capita income
growth rate is calculated. There are 26 "inter-poverty-measurement"
periods.[26] Out of these 26 episodes, 5 correspond to cases where
monetary poverty increased. Although one of them is not statistically
significant, they all occurred in periods where income per capita
increased between 27 and 166 percent. In three of the cases per capita
income nearly doubled, or surpassed that mark, while monetary poverty
increased.

---

[25]   The selection of these 12 countries responds to the need to maintain comparability
        with the Child Poverty trends. Nevertheless, if all Central and Western African
        countries with data were taken into account, the results would be similar.

[26]   This is different from growth-spells analysis and the periods are determined by
        the existence of monetary poverty measurement and not by peaks and troughs of
        the business cycle. Nevertheless, it is illuminating to analyze the relationship
        between economic growth and poverty reduction (or lack thereof).

In 12 of the remaining 21 episodes, the change in monetary poverty was less than 5 percentage points. They are not statistically significant. Using the approximation developed by EUROSTAT (2013) and without taking into account the possibility of the margin of error in estimating the poverty line itself, it is possible that in only two or three of the cases there are statistically significant changes. This is a very conservative estimate.

In some of these episodes, the accumulated increase in per capita income increased significantly – there are cases where it doubled or nearly tripled the baseline value. Concomitantly, the growth elasticity of poverty reduction (estimated only based on the 21 cases where monetary poverty declined) only averages 0.2 with a maximum value of 0.6. This is very far from the purported one-to-one ratio described as "growth is good for the poor". Clearly, much more than rapid growth is needed to make a dent on monetary poverty.

Table 4:   Monetary poverty reduction episodes and economic growth

	1st period	2nd period	Total range
Benin			27.0
2006 -2011*			1.0
Burkina Faso	96.4	23.6	142.9
2003-2009-2014	4.4	6.6	11.0
Cameroon	73.8	33.6	132.3
2001-2007-2014	0.3	2.4	2.7
Chad			368.4
2002-2011			8.1
Côte d'Ivoire	92.9	138.0	166.1
2002-2008-2015	-10.5	2.6	-7.9
Ghana			231.9
2005-2012			7.7
Guinea	27.3	50.0	90.9
2002-2007-2012	-3.9	-2.2	-6.1
Mali	63.3	36.7	123.3
2001-2006-2009	8.1	3.9	12.0
Niger			16.7
2011-2014			4.4
Nigeria			182.9
2003-2009			2.4
Senegal	52.9	34.6	105.9
2000-2005-2010	6.9	1.6	8.5
Togo	18.4	20.0	42.1
2006-2011-2015	3.0	3.6	6.6

Note: Accumulated change in monetary poverty per time period.
Source: World Bank Development Indicators database.

Child Poverty and Other Child Rights Violations

In addition, an advantage of circumscribing child poverty estimates to only the rights that constitute poverty allows for further analysis of the correlation of child poverty and other problems affecting children. This could not be done if child poverty estimates included all dimensions of well-being.[27] Similarly, it is important to be able to link the specific

---

[27]   Another way to look at this issue is to separate monetary poverty, multi-dimensional (material) poverty, and non-material (relational, capabilities, or quality of life) poverty as some authors have suggested recently (Lister, 2004; Redmond, 2014; Spicker, 2017; Trani and Biggeri, 2013).

experience of child poverty to other issues like exposure to national disasters, as it is explained in chapter 6 by Gregr.

For instance, in Figure 10 it can be observed there is no correlation between children suffering violent punishment (measured in terms of physical violence such as shaking, slapping, hitting in the head, or beating repeatedly), and whether they are poor or not. Moreover, the depth of poverty is not relevant either, as the seemingly lower incidence of physical punishment for the children suffering six deprivations is not statistically significant.[28]

Figure 10:   Percentage of children suffering from physical violence for disciplinary purposes, according to the number of deprivations (incidence and depth of poverty)

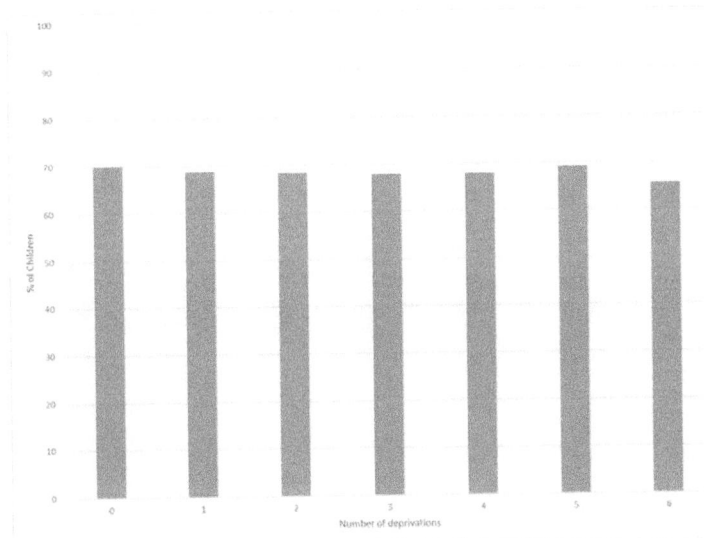

Source: MICS and DHS (various years).

On the other hand, child poverty is a major factor influencing birth registration. As registration of birth is a universal human right in itself, and also a pre-cursor to many other rights such as nationality and access to health services, this is significant. In Figure 10, there is a significant

---

[28]   These results are consistent with other regions and countries when violence against children is assessed by quintiles or for urban and rural areas (UNICEF, 2010 and 2017).

difference between poor and not-poor children whose births are registered. Moreover, there is also a steep gradient. This means the deeper child poverty is, measured by the number of deprivations suffered by children, the lower the probability of being registered. This effect seems to plateau at three or four simultaneous deprivations, meaning the poorest of the poor (see also chapter 4).

Figure 11:   Percentage of children whose births are registered, according to the number of deprivations (incidence and depth of poverty)

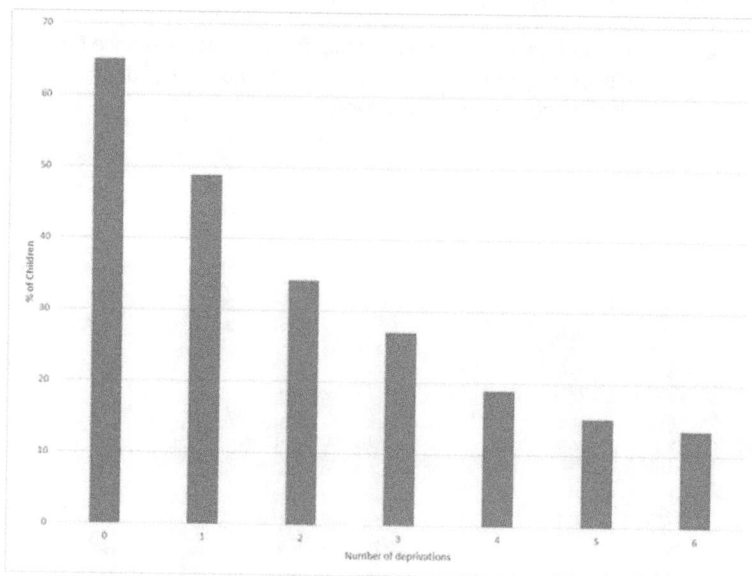

Source: MICS and DHS (various years)

The impact of child poverty and the salience of the depth of child poverty is even starker when analysing child marriage. This is the case both for girls that are forced to marry before 15 or 18 years of age, as seen in Figure 12, which is measured in the same nationally representative MICS and DHS household surveys.

Figure 12:   Percentage of girls forced to be married before age 15,
according to the number of deprivations (incidence and depth
of poverty)

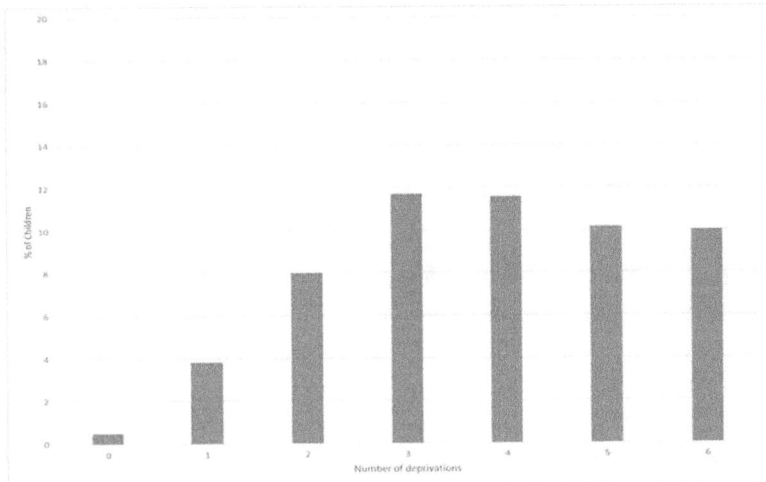

Source: MICS and DHS (various years)

Child labour, as it can be seen in Figure 13, is also heavily influenced by
the incidence and depth of child poverty.

Figure 13:   Percentage of children engaged in child labour, according to the
number of deprivations (incidence and depth of poverty)

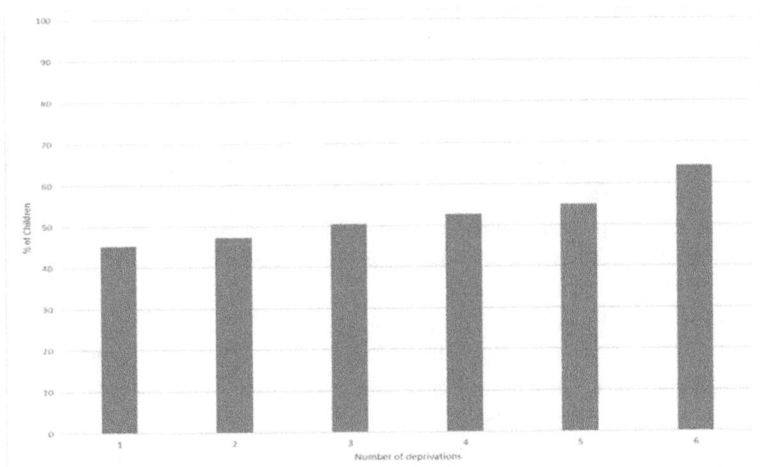

Source: MICS and DHS (various years)

It is evident that if child poverty is not addressed properly, it leads to more abuses of the rights of children. This would result in more problems such as child labour and early marriages especially (with gender differentiation - girls, especially adolescent girls, are much more at risk for child marriage and for forced domestic labour while boys are much more at risk for forced labour such as in agriculture, mining and forced military service).

STRUCTURE OF THE BOOK

The chapters are arranged in four parts. Part I provides the context for the discussion. Part II includes chapters dealing with child poverty, its measurement, and its relationship with monetary poverty and inequality. Part III discusses the evolution of child poverty in the face of crises and emergencies, as well as the impact of social protection to these crises. Part IV explores how social protection could address child poverty, social exclusion, and child protection against abuse.

REFERENCES

ACPF (2014). Outcome Document. Advancing Child Wellbeing in Africa through Social Protection: A Call for Action. Addis Ababa: ACPF.

Bendor-Samuel, J. and R. Hartell, eds. (1989) *Niger-Congo Languages: A Classification and Description of Africa's Largest Language Family* (Lanham, MD: Rowman & Littlefiel).

Boyden, J. A. Hardgrove and C. Knowles (2012) "Continuity and change in poor children's lives: evidence from Young Lives" in A. Minujin and S. Nandy (eds.) *Global child poverty and well-being: Measurement, concepts, policy and action* (Bristol: Policy Press).

Cecchini, S., and Martínez, R. (2011) *Inclusive Social Protection in Latin America: A Comprehensive, Rights-based Approach* (Santiago, Chile: Economic Commission for Latin America and the Caribbean).

Deacon, B. (2013) "Globalisation and social policy in developing countries", in R. Surender and R. Walker (eds.) *Social policy in a developing world* (Cheltenham: Edward Elgar), pp. 217–236.

Dixon, R. and Nussbaum, M. C. (2012) *Children's Rights and a Capabilities Approach: The Question of Special Priority* (Chicago: The Law School, The University of Chicago).

Esping-Andersen, G. (1990) *The Three Worlds of Welfare Capitalism* (Princeton: Princeton University Press).

Evans-Pritchard, E. E. (1940) *The Nuer.* (London: Oxford University Press).

EUROSTAT (2013) *Standard error estimation for the EU–SILC indicators of poverty and social exclusion* (Luxembourg: Publications Office of the European Union).

Gordon, D., S. Nandy, C. Pantazis, S. Pemberton, and P. Townsend (2003) *Child Poverty in the Developing World* The Policy Press (Bristol).

Greenberg, J. (1970) *The Languages of Africa*, 3rd ed. (Bloomington: Indiana University Press).

Hunt, P., Osmani, S. and Nowak, M. (2002), *Draft Guidelines: A Human Rights Approach to Poverty Reduction Strategies* (Geneva: Office of the High Commissioner for Human Rights).

Illife, J. (1987) *The African Poor: A History*. (Cambridge: Cambridge University Press).

ILO (1976) *Employment, Growth and Basic Needs: A One-World Problem* (Geneva: International Labour Organization).

ILO (2008) *Can Low-income Countries Afford Basic Social Security?* Social Security Policy Briefing 3 (Geneva: Social Security Department, International Labour Organization).

ILO (2011) *Social Protection Floor for a Fair and Inclusive Globalization* (Geneva: International Labour Organization).

ILO (2017) *World Social Protection Report, 2017-19* (Geneva: International Labour Organization).

Jones, N., and Sumner, A. (2011). *Child Poverty, Evidence, and Policy: Mainstreaming Children in International Development* (Bristol: Policy Press).

Kidd, S. (2017) "Anti-Social Registries: How have they become so popular?" Pathways' Perspectives on Social Policy in International Development, Issue No 24 (Kent: Development Pathways).

Knox-Vydmanov, Charles (2011) "The Price of Income Security in Older Age: Cost of a universal pension in 50 low- and middle-income countries" Discussion paper, HelpAge International (London: HelpAge International).

Lister, Ruth (2004) *Poverty* (Cambridge: Polity Press).

Lyytikäinen, K., Jones, N., Huttly, S., and Abramsky, T. (2006) "Childhood Poverty, Basic Services and Cumulative Disadvantage: An international comparative analysis" Young lives working paper no. 33. (London: Young Lives and Save the Children Fund UK).

Marshall, Thomas H. (1950) *Citizenship and Social Class and Other Essays* (Cambridge: Cambridge University Press).

Minujin, A., E. Delamonica, A. Davidziuk and E. Gonzalez (2006) "The Definition of Child Poverty: A discussion of concepts and methods", *Environment and Urbanization*, Volume 18, Number 2.

Minujin, A., E. Delamonica, A. Davidzuik, and E. Sweet (2007) "Notes on Social Insurance and Protection Policies for Children, Women and Families" in A. Minujin and E. Delamonica (eds.) *Social Protection Initiatives for Children, Women and Families* (New York: The New School).

Mkandawire T. (2004) "Social Policy in a Development Context: Introduction" in T. Mkandawire (ed.) *Social Policy in a Development Context* (London: Palgrave Macmillan).

Mkandawire, T. (2015) *Africa: Beyond Recovery* (London: Sub-Saharan Publishers).

Morris D. (1978). "A Physical Quality of Life Index" *Urban Ecology*, 3(3), 225–240.

Nébié, G. "Fiscal Space in West and Central Africa", UNICEF WCARO Working Paper Series Number 2/2017 (Dakar: UNICEF West and Central Africa Regional Office).

Nieuwenhuys, O. (1994) *Children's Lifeworlds: Gender, Welfare and Labour in the Developing World* (London: Routledge).

OHCHR (2012) *Guiding Principles on Extreme Poverty and Human Rights* (Geneva: Office of the High Commissioner for Human Rights).

Pearson, L., E. Boyle, R. de Oliveira Campos, C. D. Dillon, W. Guth, A. Lewis, R. E. Marjolin, and S. Okita (1969) *Partners in Development. Report of the Commission on International Development* (London, New York, and Washington: Prager Publishers).

Platteau, Jean-Philippe (1991) "Traditional Systems of Social Security and Hunger Insurance: Past Achievements and Modern Challenges" in *Social Security in Developing Countries,* Ehtisham A, J. Drèze, J. Hills and A. Sen (eds.) (Oxford: Oxford University Press).

Redmond, Gerry (2014) "Poverty and Social Exclusion" in Ben-Arieh, Asher, Ferran Casas, Ivar Frønes, and Jill Korbin (eds.) *Handbook of child well-being* (Dordrecht: Springer).

Sebeok, T. (1971) *Linguistics in Sub-Saharan Africa*, volume 7 of Current Trends in Linguistics (The Hague: Mouton).

Simler, Kenneth R. and Channing Arndt (2011) "Poverty Comparisons with Absolute Poverty Lines Estimated from Survey Data" IFPRI Food Consumption and Nutrition Division Discussion Paper 211 (Washington: International Food Policy Research Institute).

Skocpol, T. (1992) *Protecting Soldiers and Mothers: The Political Origins of Social Policy in United States* (Cambridge: Harvard University Press).

Spicker, P. (2017) "The Relational Elements of Poverty", presented at the International Workshop on The Politics of Inclusion, UNESCO and CROP, Paris.

Streeten, P., Ahmad, E., Drèze, J., Hills, J. and Sen, A. (1981) *First Things First: Meeting Basic Needs in Developing Countries* (New York, Oxford University Press)

Therborn, Göran (1987) "Welfare States and Capitalist Markets" *Acta Sociologica* 237-254.

Trani, J. F. and Biggeri, M. (2013). "The Multidimensionality of Child Poverty: evidence from Afghanistan." *Social Indicators Research* 112 (2), 391-416.

United Nations (2015) *Addis Ababa Action Agenda* (New York: United Nations).

United Nations (2003) *Monterrey Consensus of the International Conference on Financing for Development* (New York: United Nations).

UNICEF (2010) *Child Disciplinary Practices at Home: Evidence from a range of low- and middle-income countries*, UNICEF, New York.

UNICEF (2012) *Integrated Social Protection Systems Enhancing Equity for Children* (New York: UNICEF).

UNICEF (2017), *A Familiar Face: Violence in the lives of children and adolescents*, UNICEF, New York.

Von Braun, Joachim. 1991. "Social Security in Sub-Saharan Africa: Reflections on Policy Challenges" in Ehtisham, J. Drèze, J. Hills and A. Sen. (eds.) *Security in Developing Countries* (Oxford: Oxford University Press).

Wordsworth, D., M. McPeak, and T. Feeny (2005) "Understanding Children's Experience of Poverty: An Introduction to the DEV Framework" Children & Poverty Working Paper 1 (Richmond, Virginia: Christian Children's Fund).

APPENDIX

Child Deprivations, Definitions and Categories Used for Cross-Country Estimates		
Dimension	Severe Deprivation Definition	Unit of Analysis
Shelter	Children living in a dwelling with five or more people per room, a mud floor, or one made out of waste material.	Children 17 and under
Sanitation	Children with no access to a toilet facility of any kind.	Children 17 and under
Water	Children using surface water such as rivers, ponds, streams and dams, or who trek 30 minutes or more (round trip) to collect water.	Children 17 and under
Information	Children with no access to radio, television, or a mobile phone at home.	Children age 3-17
Nutrition/Food	Children who are more than 3 standard deviations below the international reference population for stunting, or wasting, or underweight.	Child under 5
Education	Children who have never been to school or are not currently attending school	Children age 6-17
Health	Children who did not receive immunization against any diseases or who did not receive medical advice or treatment for a recent illness involving diarrhoea, an acute respiratory infection, or malaria.	Children under 5

PART I: CONTEXT

CHAPTER 1

FRAMING SOCIAL PROTECTION WITHIN THE CONTEXT OF GROWING INEQUALITY

Jan Vandemoortele

INTRODUCTION

An estimated one billion children in the world are deprived of at least one necessity, such as food, literacy, health or safe water. Many of them face a daily struggle of survival. Statistics show that children account for nearly half of the extreme poor in developing countries, whilst one in four children in the world's richest countries are considered poor. Everywhere, children are more likely to live in poverty than adults.

Social protection is part and parcel of addressing persistent child poverty. However, less than a third of the poorest children are covered by social protection, posing a formidable challenge for policymakers. Yet, if social protection is seen merely as a technical response to poverty, it is unlikely to yield much impact—no matter how well the programmes are designed. Technical aspects are important and need to be discussed in detail, but this must be done within the right analytical framework. It is of utmost importance to frame social protection within the context of growing inequality.

The main proposition of this chapter is that high inequality has become a major obstacle to reducing child poverty in most countries. As Stiglitz, 2001 Nobel laureate in economics, observes, "we are paying a high price of our inequality – an economic system that is less stable and less efficient, with less growth, and a democracy that has been put into peril" (2012: xii). The weekly magazine The Economist agrees: "Growing inequality is one of the biggest social, economic and political challenges of our time" (2012: 3). The World Economic Forum rates "rising income and wealth disparity as the most important trend in determining global developments over the next 10 years" (2017: 6). Other voices that raise similar concerns about inequality include Wilkinson and Pickett (2009), Galbraith (2012), Piketty (2014), and Atkinson (2015).

Yet, inequality seldom features prominently in the clash of narratives regarding poverty reduction. The dominant narrative is that poverty must be addressed through economic growth, accompanied by interventions such as social protection. Reducing inequality is seen as noble but not as essential for reducing poverty. To many, raising the issue of extreme inequality seems a distraction because the pressing concern is extreme poverty.

This view is exemplified by Lucas, 1995 Nobel laureate in economics, who argues: "the potential for improving the lives of poor people by finding different ways of distributing current production is nothing compared to the apparently limitless potential of increasing production" (2004: 16). Promoting growth, in other words, must be put ahead of combating inequality, based on the belief in trickle-down economics. He observes: "Of the tendencies that are harmful to sound economics, the most seductive, and in my opinion the most poisonous, is to focus on questions of distribution" (2004: 16).

Yet, the fact is that high inequality has become a major impediment to addressing persistent poverty. Shiller, 2013 Nobel laureate in economics, states, "The most important problem we are facing now today, I think, is rising inequality" (quoted in Dorling, 2014: 1). As long as policy makers and development practitioners stick to the belief that poverty reduction is mostly growth-mediated and keep negating that future progress will be either equity-mediated or elusive, the impact of social protection on child poverty will remain marginal at best.

CONCEPTUAL CLARITY

From the outset, it is important to clarify some concepts because the topic of inequality is commonly perceived as having ideological connotations. Whilst reducing poverty or promoting growth are both seen as technical matters, addressing inequality is frequently seen as political. This, of course, is incorrect. All these interventions have political and technical aspects alike, and the focus here is on the technical ones.

Good vs. Bad Inequality

Welch, who espouses the conventional position that inequality ought not to be a major concern, introduces an interesting distinction between two kinds of inequality: good and bad inequality. About bad inequality he writes, "I would argue that inequality is destructive whenever the low-wage citizenry views society as unfair, when it views effort as not worthwhile, when upward mobility is viewed as impossible or as so unlikely that its pursuit is not worthwhile" (1999: 2). Milanovic describes good inequality as that which "is needed to create incentives for people to study, work hard, or start risky entrepreneurial projects"; while bad inequality "provides the means to preserve acquired positions" (2012: 12).

The distinction is important because it underscores the point that inequality is not per se bad. Expressing concerns about high inequality does not imply that one is advocating for a society where everyone would have the same. As Sandel points out,

> If the only advantage of affluence were the ability to buy yachts, sports cars, and fancy vacations, inequalities of income and wealth would not matter very much. But as money comes to buy more and more — political influence, good medical care, a home in a safe neighbourhood rather than in a crime-ridden one, access to elite schools rather than failing ones — the distribution of income and wealth looms larger and larger (2013: 8).

In other words, high inequality undermines the very tenets of meritocracy and democracy. Amongst the pathologies of bad inequality are the rising power of special interest groups and a polarized political context — usually yielding outcomes that are undemocratic and unfair.

Equality vs. Equity

The terms 'equality' and 'equity' are often used interchangeably, although they represent quite distinct concepts. Equality implies that no differences should exist between people. In such a utopian situation, everyone should earn or receive the same. Equity, on the other hand, accepts differences but only when they are earned fairly. Equity allows for differences as long as they are based on a level playing field. As such, it balances the principle of social justice with meritocracy. In essence, equity holds that all citizens should be treated equally, which does not require that they earn the same level of income or possess equal wealth.

Thus, the term 'gender equity' is incorrect because it would imply that some differences in life chances that stem from one's gender would be acceptable. The correct terminology is 'gender equality' because differences due to gender are not tolerated. The same applies for race, where the terms 'racial equity' would imply that certain differences due to race would be acceptable. Therefore, the correct terminology is 'racial equality'.

Concerning human development, the appropriate term is equity because differences will always exist between people. This is so, because people hold different drives, ambition and talents. There is no reason why everyone should earn or receive the same, for people pursue different goals and have different preferences and priorities in life. The vital question is whether the differences are based on fairness and on a level playing field.

EQUITY AND GROWTH: FRIENDS OR FOES?

Recent publications attest that equity and growth are friends, not foes. The editor-in-chief of Finance and Development writes, "A more equal society has a greater likelihood of sustaining longer term growth" (IMF, 2011).

The way the economic pie is cut has a bearing on its size, but not in the manner the conventional narrative has held for so long. High inequality — i.e. which goes beyond the incentive-element — does not make the pie grow faster. The belief that inequality is good for growth is no longer tenable in the face of the emerging evidence.

Based on data from 65 countries, Alesina and Rodrick (1992) document that more equal countries have higher rates of growth; a finding echoed by Corry and Glyn (1994). Persson and Tabellini state, "Both historical panel data and post-war cross sections indicate a significant and large negative relation between inequality and growth" (1994: 600). Temple concludes, "It has become extremely difficult to build a case that inequality is good for growth" (1999: 146).
Ravallion writes,

> On balance, the existing evidence using cross-country growth regressions appears to offer more support for the view that inequality is harmful to growth than the opposite view (2000: 16).

Milanovic argues,

> The pendulum has swung from a rather unambiguous answer that inequality is good for growth to a much more nuanced view that favours the opposite conclusion (2012: 12)

Stiglitz observes,

> Growth has been stronger in periods in which inequality has been lower and in which we have been growing together (2012: 6).

High inequality also affects social mobility. Studies show that the correlation between the income of the parents and their children is stronger in more unequal countries (Blanden, 2009; Wilkinson and Pickett, 2009; Economic Mobility Project, 2009; OECD, 2010). The 'Great Gatsby Curve' depicts a close relationship between high inequality and low social mobility. Corak writes,

> Children are much more likely as adults to end up in the same place on the income and status ladder as their parents in the United States than in most other countries (2012: 1)

Evidence supports the proposition that once inequality gets high, family backgrounds become the dominant factor in determining the individual's outcome, rather than his/her effort, talent or luck.

The conventional narrative frequently refers to the Kuznets hypothesis to dismiss concerns about inequality because inequality will automatically decrease as countries develop. Countless researchers have tried to empirically validate the hypothesis, but none could do so conclusively. Actually, growing inequality in rich countries very much contradicts the hypothesis altogether. Palma concludes,

> There is not much statistical evidence for an 'Inverted-U' path between inequality and income per capita (2011: 95)

Obviously, there is more to inequality than per capita income. Societies are too complex and encompass too many conflicting interests to be subjected to a simple automatic link between income levels and inequality. Kuznets himself emphasizes that the hypothesis is

> Perhaps 5 percent empirical information and 95 percent speculation, some of it possibly by wishful thinking (1955: 24)

He adds that improvements in income distribution will depend on institutions such as the welfare state and trade unions. But these points are conveniently overlooked by the supporters of the conventional view that inequality should not be a concern.

IDEAS VS. EVIDENCE

Since evidence does not always swing public debates, this section reviews some relevant ideas of philosophers and political scientists about the significance of high inequality. It appears that the concern about inequality is as old as the hills. Plutarch, a Roman philosopher (ca. 45–120 CE), argues than an imbalance between rich and poor is 'the oldest and most fatal ailment of all republics.' The Greek philosopher Plato (427–347 BC) reasons that there should exist 'neither extreme poverty nor excessive wealth among citizens, for both are productive of great evil'. He adds that the ideal ratio between the income of the rich and that of the poor in society should be about 4:1. His disciple Aristotle (384–322 BC) accepts a ratio of 5:1.

Those who consider inequality as unimportant or irrelevant frequently point to the work of Adam Smith (1723-90), especially to his book An Inquiry into the Nature and Causes of the Wealth of Nations (1776). In it, he argues that by pursuing one's self-interest in the free market everyone will contribute to collective prosperity. Hence, free competition and laissez-faire should be the concern, not inequality. What they do not mention, however, is Smith's earlier book, the Theory of Moral Sentiments, published in 1759.

In it, Smith exposes the conviction that all human beings underwrite the same moral sentiments of benevolence and sympathy. He calls them 'our benevolent instincts'. He writes: "To feel much for others and little for ourselves; to restrain our selfishness and exercise our benevolent affections, constitute the perfection of human nature" (quoted in Judt, 2010: 63). As an Enlightenment philosopher, Smith retrieves much of the ideas from ancient philosophers, especially Confucius' sentiments of fellow-feeling — called 'Ren'.

Some see in Smith's books evidence that he changed his mind between 1759 and 1776. This is presented as the 'problem of Adam Smith': he emphasizes cooperation and altruism in Moral Sentiments whilst stressing unfettered competition in Wealth of Nations. Indeed, there appears to be a contradiction between his argument about 'our benevolent instincts' in the former and the pursuit of self-interest in the latter. However, there is no 'Adam Smith problem', for he never abandoned the ideas expressed in Moral Sentiments. In 1790, shortly before his death, he issued the sixth and thoroughly revised edition of

Moral Sentiments — making his first book also his last work. He never forsook his views regarding the importance of altruism and cooperation, something his modern acolytes and free market ideologues often claim. The 'problem of Adam Smith' mostly stems from their own selective reading of his opus.

The earlier book is of crucial importance, because Smith's argument about the merits of laissez-faire assumes that actors in the free market will share these moral sentiments, which will temper selfishness and tame greed. He sees moral sentiments as socially beneficial because everyone will be better off if they are widely held in society.

Karl Marx (1818-83) raises a fundamental question regarding Smith's point of view. He asks whether moral sentiments will shape the functioning of the free market, or whether market forces will influence moral sentiments. Will sentiments such as benevolence and empathy determine the functioning of the marketplace — as Smith believes? Or will the free market corrode moral sentiments and lead to selfishness, greed, and ever-growing inequality — as Marx argues? The question is still with us today.

INEQUALITY VS. OPPORTUNITY

Instead of talking about inequality of outcome, the conventional narrative prefers to focus on equality of opportunity. Indeed, the distinction between 'equality of opportunity' and 'equality of outcome' is frequently made in debates about inequality. Most people readily accept that the latter is undesirable because it would undermine the incentives for individual effort and talent development. Outcome-equality, it is argued, would deny the differences that exist among individuals in terms of drives, talents, ambition and choices. Given that equality of outcomes is undesirable and untenable, equality of opportunity is seen as a more sensible aim.

It is quite evident that inequality of opportunity will inevitably lead to more inequality in outcomes. Paes de Barros et al. argue that "in an ideal world, inequality in outcomes should reflect only differences in effort and choices individuals make, as well as luck and talent" (2009: 15). Based on a sample of 19 Latin American countries, they estimate that between "one-half and one-quarter of current inequality of consumption [i.e. a proxy for outcome-inequality] reflects inequality of opportunity, a very sizable share" (2009: 2).

However, the causality also runs in the reverse direction: high inequality in outcomes will thwart equality of opportunity. Although commonly overlooked, it is this causal link that makes high inequality so harmful. The argument that the pursuit of equality of opportunity is sufficient for creating an equitable society assumes that all individuals face opportunities on a level playing field. Yet, that assumption is frequently violated in practice. High inequality in outcomes is not without having an impact on the possibility of achieving equality of opportunity. The two are closely interlinked. Hence, the distinction between equality of opportunity and equality of outcome is of limited value. Palma notes, "It is quite remarkable how mainstream economics assumes that better 'equality of opportunities' in terms of access to education would necessarily lead to a more equal distribution of income" (2011: 108, emphasis in the original). As Chang argues, "equality of opportunity is the starting point for a fair society. But it's not enough" (2011: 210).

INEQUALITY VS. FREEDOM

The conventional narrative prefers to emphasize freedom rather than equality. It argues that if individuals have the freedom to succeed unencumbered by factors beyond their control, inequality should not be a concern. It is with this logic in mind that Welch concludes that "increasing inequality is not necessarily bad" (1999: 16).

Regarding freedom, Fromm (1941) identifies two distinct dimensions to it. The first is freedom from restrictions and interferences by others; the second is the freedom to attain one's full potential. The latter requires the conditions necessary to realize one's choices — i.e. fair rules within a level playing field. The conventional narrative puts the emphasis on 'freedom from' and prefers to ignore the dimension of 'freedom of'. In terms of human rights, it also prioritizes civil and political rights (concerning freedom from) and largely disregards social, economic and cultural rights (covering freedom to). As Fromm argues, however, both are indispensable for achieving genuine freedom, even though they may conflict with each other. Hegel takes a similar view. The Anglo-Saxon view of freedom is limited to the right to be free from interference, the right to be left alone to do as one wishes. Hegel's interpretation of freedom involves also the recognition of one's rightful needs and the ensuing institutional and social arrangements necessary to satisfy these needs. For Hegel, true freedom lies in the nexus of the right not to be interfered with and the support to fulfil legitimate human needs.

Varoufakis reasons that Welch's 'bad inequality' is inevitable since "transactions which, though voluntary, are illiberal because of the systematic imbalance in options of the two sides" (2002: 465). In other words, not all transactions that are agreed to without coercion are necessarily taken freely. The weaker party will not always be in a position to refuse a deal offered by the stronger one — e.g. loans at exorbitant interest rates or jobs with substandard conditions of work. Thus, high inequality pre-empts genuine freedom by forcing the weaker party to accept transactions under duress. This reality is captured by the term illiberal capitalism. Liberty and the free market do not automatically lead to equitable development.

INEQUALITY AND DEMOCRACY

Inequality also influences the political system. Stiglitz observes that "economic inequality inevitably leads to political inequality" (2015: 9). The wealthy and big businesses will seek to manipulate the political system for their own ends. By using their considerable wealth, they subject politics to money so as to shape economic and social policies. This results in 'the capture of the regulators by the regulated', to use an oft-quoted phrase. Jones writes, "Politics has become a closed shop of the privileged" (2015: 68). The distinction between politics, wealth and big business is getting blurred. They are increasingly linked via money and a system of revolving doors whereby special interest groups and lobbyists gain access to political positions, thus transforming affluence into influence.

The revolving doors also involve the media. The wealthy and powerful take control of the media as an investment in shaping public debates and perceptions. Not only news reports get biased; TV programmes such as Downton Abbey impress upon the viewer the notion that nothing is wrong with extreme inequality because the uber-rich are high-minded philanthropists who have everyone's wellbeing at heart. Jones speaks of "mediaocracy" (2015: 85) to expose the closeness between the media, big business and politics. A press that is free from government interventions is not necessarily free from special interests.

The result is a weakening of democratic governance, which is already showing signs of hollowing out in many countries. Membership of political parties is falling; voter turnout is sometimes as low as a third of the electorate, and electoral volatility is on the rise, often leading to sudden surges of populist parties and polarizing candidates. Citizens have a growing sense of disenchantment with the political system; perceiving "government of the 1 percent, by the 1 per cent, and for the 1 percent", as Stiglitz puts it (2012: 99). He observes that "the political system is more akin to "one dollar one vote" than to "one person one vote"" (2012: xix).

INEQUALITY AND PSYCHOLOGY

One of the most important effects of inequality, however, is the bearing it has on the way people relate to each other. When people are primed by money, they invariably become more individualistic and show a reluctance to get involved with others. After conducting a series of experiments, Piff et al. conclude that, "upper-class individuals were more likely to break the law while driving, [...] to exhibit unethical decision-making tendencies, [...] to cheat to increase their chances of winning a prize, and to endorse unethical behaviour at work than lower-class individuals" (2012: 4086). Piff (2013) further demonstrates how privilege and advantage influence people's thoughts and behaviour, often without being aware of it.

In other words, money and power corrode Smith's moral sentiments of empathy and solidarity. In highly unequal countries, people believe more strongly that wealth and virtue are connected. People at the top are convinced that their success is due to personal effort and talent. Loughnan et al. (2011) show that the conviction that one is great is more common in unequal countries as people mimic the self-boosterism of those at the top. They conclude: "Greater self-enhancement was found in societies with more income inequality" (2011: 1254). Dorling writes: "Having a high opinion of yourself — believing you are part of a deserving minority who has got to the top and that there are only a few others like you — is a trait that is much more common in more unequal countries" (2014: 47-8).

The belief is widespread that people's behaviour is mostly driven by self-interest, but evidence does not support this neoliberal thesis. People's behaviour is not only motivated by economic factors that are mostly amoral and self-interested. People also respond to intrinsic ethical and social drives and values. Bowles argues: "people are more generous and civic minded than either economists or evolutionary biologists assumed" (2016: xvi). Most people still subscribe to shared moral sentiments. When asked to indicate what constitutes an ideal level of inequality, most people desire a more egalitarian distribution than the one that prevails in their country. Norton and Ariely observe a surprising level of consensus across the political and income spectrum: "All groups desired a more equal distribution of wealth than the status quo" (2011: 9). Evolutionary psychology and biology confirm that altruism and cooperation — not only competition — help to escape from the Hobbesian state of nature, where life is 'poor, nasty, brutish and short'.

Evidence shows that humans have a deeply rooted instinct for fairness (Henrich et al., 2001; Brosnan and de Waal, 2003). Only a small, narcissistic minority seem deprived of empathy and benevolence, albeit that they increasingly influence society. Ronson (2012) estimates that the proportion of CEOs who suffer from narcissistic personality disorders is four times higher than the prevalence in the general population. Unfortunately, the excessive sense of self-importance of a small minority seems to percolate through society. Dorling warns, "We have a deeply rooted instinct that great inequality is unjust. But not all of us have preserved such instincts, and those perhaps temporarily lacking them are disproportionately found within the 1 per cent" (2014: 60).

Stiglitz observes: "What is remarkable is how few seemed — and still seem — to feel guilty, and how few were the whistle-blowers. Something has happened to our sense of values, when the end of making money justifies the means" (2012: xvii). When Warren Buffett writes that "while most Americans struggle to make ends meet, we mega-rich continue to get our extraordinary tax-breaks" (2011), he expresses Smith's moral sentiment of fairness. Yet, his call on the rich to pay their fair share of taxes — a moral sentiment per Adam Smith — has been dismissed by most of his peers. A report into the business practices at Barclays Bank identifies the "lack of humility and generosity" — basic moral sentiments according to Smith — as causes of the Libor-rigging scandal[1] (Salz, 2013: 82).

It seems, thus, that 'our benevolent instincts' are not as innate as Smith thought. Attitudes towards inequality are not fixed. The John Templeton Foundation (2008) put Marx's question to thirteen contemporary philosophers, scholars and public figures. They were asked: 'Does the free market corrode moral character?' In their essays, four of them respond with a categorical 'no', another four reply with a nuanced 'no', two say 'it depends' and only three out of thirteen answer 'yes'.

CONCLUSION

The significance of high inequality is not to be understood purely in economic terms but also in political ones and particularly in terms of its psycho-social impact. Due to the latter, high inequality undercuts good behaviour. People abstain from acts that are individually beneficial but socially harmful as long as others do so too. Once a certain proportion of the population starts to act selfishly and is perceived to get away with it, good behaviour quickly evaporates. In a context of high inequality, such behaviour easily cascades down the social ladder, undermining the moral sentiments held in society.

High inequality jeopardizes Smith's moral sentiments. Examples abound where the wealthy and special interest groups use lobbyists and spin-doctors to manipulate and distort the public discourse and shape legislation and policies to perpetuate their privileged position — i.e. yielding bad inequality. Many countries seem to be descending into moral deprivation and legislative barbarism. Therefore, it is vital that policymakers accept, from the outset, that extreme inequality has a high price and no redeeming value.

The conclusion is inescapable: the 'inequality question' must be at the centre of any discussion about how to reduce poverty, including through social protection. Policymakers must be thoroughly aware of the

---

[1]   Libor stands for 'London Interbank Offered Rate', the average interest rate major banks across the world charge for borrowing among each other. The scandal involved fraudulent activities at Barclays Bank to manipulate Libor so as to boost profits from trading in derivatives. In 2012, the bank paid multiple fines and settlements for manipulating Libor.

need to curb extreme inequality before they can adequately address the challenge of turning sentiments of fairness and equity into a practical reality – including through social protection. It is crucial to understand and recognize that high inequality is not only economically harmful but also socially corrosive and psychologically toxic. Hence the importance of framing the discussions about social protection in the context of high inequality.

Hirschman writes: "May I urge that changes in values do occur from time to time [...] and that those changes and their effects on behaviour are worth exploring – that, in brief, *de valoribus est disputandum?*" (1984: 90) – the latter being a word play on the saying *de gustibus non est disputandum* (there is no arguing about tastes).

REFERENCES

Alesina, A. and D. Rodrick (1992) 'Distribution, Political Conflict and Economic Growth: A Simple Theory and Some Empirical Evidence', in A. Cuckierman, C. Hercowitz and L. Leiderman (eds.), *Political Economy, Growth and Business Cycles*, Cambridge: MIT Press, pp. 23-50.

Atkinson, A. (2015) *Inequality—What Can Be Done?* Cambridge: Harvard University Press.

Blanden, J. (2009) *How Much Can We Learn from International Comparisons of Intergenerational Mobility?* Discussion Paper No. 111, London: Centre for the Economics of Education.

Bowles S. (2016) *The Moral Economy—Why Good Incentives are no Substitute for Good Citizens*, New Haven and London: Yale University Press.

Brosnan S. and F. de Waal (2003) 'Monkeys reject unequal pay', *Nature*, 425: 297-9.

Buffett, W. (2011) *Stop Coddling the Super-Rich*, The New York Times, Op-Ed contribution, August 14th [Online] Available at: http://www.nytimes.com/2011/08/15/opinion/stop-coddling-the-super-rich.html?_r=1 [Accessed September 2016].

Chang, H-J. (2011) *23 Things They Don't Tell You about Capitalism*, New York: Bloomsbury Press.

Corak, M. (2012) *Inequality from Generation to Generation—The United States in Comparison*, mimeographed, Ottawa: University of Ottawa. [Online] Available at: http://milescorak.files.wordpress.com/2012/01/inequality-from-generation-to-generation-the-united-states-in-comparison-v3.pdf [Accessed October 2016].

Corry, D. and A. Glyn (1994) 'The macroeconomics of equality, stability and growth', in A. Glyn and D. Miliband (eds.), *Paying for Inequality—The Economic Cost of Social Injustice*, London: Rivers Oram Press/IPPR, pp. 205-16.

Dorling, D. (2014) *Inequality and the 1%*, London: Verso.

Economic Mobility Project (2009) *Opinion Poll on Economic Mobility and the American Dream*, Washington D.C.: Pew Charitable Trusts. [Online] Available at: http://www.economicmobility.org/poll2009 [Accessed September 2016].

Fromm, E. (1941) *Escape from Freedom*, New York: Holt & Company (reprinted in 1994).

Galbraith, J. (2012) *Inequality and Instability: A Study of the World Economy Just Before the Great Crisis*, Oxford: Oxford University Press.

Henrich, J, R. Boyd et al. (2001) 'In Search of Homo Economicus: Behavioral Experiments in 15 Small-Scale Societies', *American Economic Review*, 91(2): 73-8.

Hirschman, A. (1984) 'Against Parsimony: Three Easy Ways of Complicating Some Categories of Economic Discourse', *The American Economic Review*, 74(2): 89-96.

IMF (2011) 'All for One: Why inequality throws us off balance', *Finance and Development*, 48(3).

John Templeton Foundation (2008) *Does the free market corrode moral character?* West Conshohocken (PA): John Templeton Foundation. [Online] Available at: www.templeton.org/markets [Accessed October 2016].

Jones, O. (2015) *The Establishment—And how they get away with it*, London: Penguin Books.

Judt, T. (2010) *Ill Fares the Land—A Treatise on Our Present Discontents*, New York: Penguin Books.

Keynes, J. M. (1936) *The General Theory of Employment, Interest and Money*, London: Palgrave Macmillan.

Kuntsche, E. and U. Ravens-Sieberer (2015) 'Monitoring adolescent health behaviours and social determinants cross-nationally over more than a decade: introducing the Health Behaviour in School-aged Children (HBSC) study supplement on trends', *The European Journal of Public Health*, 25(suppl. 2): 1–3.

Kuznets, S. (1955) 'Economic Growth and Income Inequality', *The American Economic Review*, 45(1): 1–28.

Loughnan S., P. Kuppens, et al. 'Economic Inequality is Linked to Biased Self-Perception', *Psychological Science*, 22(10): 1254-8.

Lucas, R. (2004) *The Industrial Revolution: Past and Future*, Essay for the 2003 Annual Report of the Federal Reserve Bank of Minneapolis. [Online] Available at: http://www.minneapolisfed.org/publications_papers/pub_display.cfm?id=3333 [Accessed September 2016].

Milanovic, B. (2012) *The Haves and the Have-Nots—A brief and idiosyncratic history of global inequality*, New York: Basic Books.

Norton, M. and D. Ariely (2011) 'Building a Better America—One Wealth Quintile at a Time', *Perspectives on Psychological Science*, 6(1): 9–12.

OECD (2010) *Economic Policy Reforms—Going for Growth*, Paris: Organization for Economic Co-operation and Development.

Paes de Barros, R., F. Ferreira, J. Molinas Vega and J. Saavedra Chanduri (2009) *Measuring inequality of opportunities in Latin America and the Caribbean*, Latin American Development Forum Series, Washington D.C.: The World Bank.

Palma, J. (2011) 'Homogeneous Middles vs. Heterogeneous Tails, and the End of the 'Inverted-U': It's All About the Share of the Rich', *Development and Change*, 42(1): 87-153.

Persson, T. and G. Tabellini (1994) 'Is Inequality Harmful for Growth?', *The American Economic Review*, 84(3): 600-21.

Piff, P., D. Stancato, S. Cote, R. Mendoza-Denton and D. Keltner (2012) 'Higher social class predicts increased unethical behavior', *Proceedings of the National Academy of Sciences, 109(11): 4086-91.*

Piff, P. (2013) *'Does Money Make You Mean?'* TED Talk. [Online] Available at: https://www.ted.com/talks/paul_piff_does_money_make_you_mean?language=en [Accessed October 2016].

Piketty, T. (2014) *Capital in the Twenty-First Century*, Cambridge: The Belknap Press of Harvard University Press.

Ravallion, M. (2000) *Growth, Inequality and Poverty—Looking Beyond Averages*, Development Research Group, Washington D.C.: The World Bank.

Ronson, J. (2012) *The Psychopath Test: A Journey through the Madness Industry*, London: Riverhead Books.

Salz, A. (2013) *The Salz Review—Independent Review of Barclays' Business Practices*, London: Barclays Bank. [Online] Available at: https://www.salzreview.co.uk/c/document_library/get_file?uuid=557994c9-9c7f-4037-887b-8b5623bed25e&groupId=4705611 [Accessed September 2016].

Sandel, M. (2013) *What Money Can't Buy—The Moral Limits of Markets*, New York: Farrar, Straus and Giroux.

Stiglitz, J. (2012) *The Price of Inequality*, London: Allen Lane.

Stiglitz, J. (2015) *The Great Divide—Unequal Societies and What We Can Do About Them*, New York: W. W. Norton & Co.

Swift, A. (2001) *Political Philosophy—A Beginners' Guide for Students and Politicians*, Cambridge: Polity Press.

The Economist (2012) *For richer, for poorer,* Special Report, October 13th.

Temple, J. (1999) 'The New Growth Evidence', *Journal of Economic Literature*, 37(1): 112-56.

Varoufakis, Y. (2002) 'Against Equality', *Science & Society*, 66:4: 448–72.

Welch, F. 1999. 'In Defense of Inequality', *American Economic Review*, 89(2): 1–17.

Wilkinson, R. and K. Pickett (2009) *The Spirit Level—Why More Equal Societies Almost Always Do Better,* London: Allen Lane.

World Economic Forum (2017) *The Global Risks Report 2017*, Geneva: WEF.

CHAPTER 2

CLUSTERING COUNTRIES IN WEST AND CENTRAL AFRICA FOR IMPROVED POLICY AND TECHNICAL ENGAGEMENT IN SOCIAL PROTECTION[1]

Gustave Nébié

INTRODUCTION

UNICEF West and Central Africa Region (WCAR) comprises 24 countries[2] with very different levels of economic and social development. Within these 24 countries, some are part of the World Bank middle-income countries, while others are low-income countries. Other countries in the region are, however, classified by the World Bank or the Organization for Economic Cooperation and Development (OECD) as fragile countries, or as Least Developed Countries by the United Nations, or as Highly Indebted Poor Countries. Some are rich in natural resources, others are very poor, and an important feature of almost all these countries is weak social indicators, especially those relating to the welfare of children.

It is therefore important to better understand the underlying dynamics of this variegated situation, in order to adapt interventions and recommendations accordingly and for policies to be more efficient and equitable. The main objective of this chapter is to group countries in the region into relatively homogeneous sub-groups, based on the most recently measured key economic and social indicators, and draw operational lessons in terms of strategic planning and priority areas of interventions regarding social protection.

---

[1]   This chapter is a revised version of a paper entitled: "Clustering countries in West and Central Africa for improved UNICEF engagement in the region", which is more general in terms of policy recommendations and in dealing with social and economic policies.

[2]   Benin, Burkina Faso, Cabo Verde, Cameroon, Central African Republic, Chad, Congo, Congo DR, Côte d'Ivoire, Equatorial Guinea, Gabon, Gambia, Ghana, Guinea, Guinea Bissau, Liberia, Mali, Mauritania, Niger, Nigeria, São Tomé e Príncipe, Senegal, Sierra Leone and Togo

EXISTING METHODOLOGIES FOR CLASSIFICATION OF COUNTRIES

There are many organizations that classify countries according to various criteria and for various reasons. We do not pretend to examine in a fully comprehensive way all existing country-classification methodologies but instead, we are just focusing on the most common. The idea is to see how countries in WCAR are positioning themselves vis-a-vis the others according to the different types of classification, and to examine if there is a general pattern that is appearing.

Box 1:   Measuring the size of economies

There are many ways to measure the size and performance of an economy. The relative size of economies can be a useful measure, depending on the specific indicator and the method used to convert local currencies to US dollars. The following are most commonly used:

1. World Bank Atlas method
The World Bank's official estimates of the size of economies are based on GNI converted to current US dollars using the Atlas method. The Atlas method smoothes exchange rate fluctuations by using a three-year moving average, price-adjusted conversion factor.

2. Purchasing Power Parities (PPP)
Purchasing power parity (PPP) conversion factors take into account differences in the relative prices of goods and services — particularly non-tradables — and therefore provide a better overall measure of the real value of output produced by an economy compared to other economies.
PPP GNI is measured in current international dollars which, in principle, have the same purchasing power as a dollar spent in the US economy. Because PPPs provide (in theory) a better measure of the standard of living of residents of an economy, they are often used for inter-country comparisons.

3. Market exchange rates
The total Gross Domestic Product (GDP) data are measured in current US dollars using annual market exchange rates. This means that the values and derived rankings are subject to greater volatility due to variations in exchange rates. Inter-country comparisons based on GDP at market prices should, therefore, be treated with caution.

Source: OECD 2015

Classification according to GNI

The World Bank income per capita is widely used to classify countries. It is based on one indicator, the GNI (Gross National Income) per capita. The classification of countries by the World Bank is for the sake of its own lending procedures, but many other organizations are using it to compare countries and even to determine their own support policy to countries.

Table 1:   Comparing GNI methods

rank[3]	Gross national income per capita 2014, Atlas method and PPP (USD)	Atlas	PPP
1	Equatorial Guinea	13,340	22,480
2	Gabon	9,320	16,500
3	Cabo Verde	3,520	6,320
4	Nigeria	2,950	5,680
5	Congo, Rep.	2,680	5,120
6	Ghana	1,620	3,960
7	São Tomé and Príncipe	1,600	3,030
8	Côte d'Ivoire	1,550	3,350
9	Cameroon	1,350	2,940
10	Mauritania	1,260	3,700
11	Senegal	1,050	2,290
12	Chad	1,010	2,130
13	Benin	810	1,850
14	Sierra Leone	720	1,830
15	Mali	720	1,660
16	Burkina Faso	710	1,660
17	Togo	580	1,310
18	Guinea-Bissau	570	1,430
19	Guinea	480	1,140
20	Gambia, The	450	1,580
21	Niger	430	950
22	Congo, Dem. Rep.	410	700
23	Liberia	400	820
24	Central African Republic	330	610

Source: World Bank

The ranking is the same according to the two methods for the top 6 countries. On average, there is no big differences in the ranking of countries according to the two methods, but the difference in the size of

[3]   The rank is based on the Atlas method ranking

the GNI per capita is huge (almost doubling from the Atlas method to the PPP method). Therefore, one should be very cautious when comparing GNI per capita across countries and make sure the same method is used to compare.

According to the latest classification (2014), WCAR countries are divided as follows:

Table 2:   Classification of WCAR countries (2014)

Low income countries (less than $1046)	Middle income countries		High-income countries (more than $12,736)
	Lower middle-income countries ($1,046 to $4,125)	Upper middle-income countries ($4,126 to $12,735)	
Chad	Cabo Verde	Gabon	Equatorial Guinea
Benin	Nigeria		
Burkina Faso	Congo, Rep.		
Sierra Leone	São Tomé & Príncipe		
Mali	Ghana		
Togo	Côte d'Ivoire		
Guinea-Bissau	Cameroon		
Guinea	Mauritania		
Gambia	Senegal		
Niger			
Congo, Dem. Rep.			
Liberia			
Central African Rep.			

Source: World Bank

When looking carefully at the countries classified according to this indicator (GNI per capita), sometimes there are disturbing facts for children. The graph below (Graph 1) shows the level of GNI as compared to the level of child mortality. As we can see, Equatorial Guinea, the only high-income country in the region[4], has a child mortality level that is among the worst in the region. Low-income countries, such as Togo or the Gambia, are performing much better than Equatorial Guinea in that area.

---

[4]   According to the latest available data at the time of writing from the World Bank in 2016, Equatorial Guinea moved back to the status of upper middle-income country.

We estimate a trend line using a polynomial function of order 2[5], and it seems to have a downward slope for child mortality for countries in the low-income to lower middle-income range (with a few exceptions, for example Nigeria). However, the slope is positive at higher levels of income per capita, (upper middle-income or higher). This is a worrying trend, particularly for richer countries. However, in view of the size of the sample (only one upper middle-income country and one high-income country), and also because of the dispersion around the trend line (e.g. comparing Senegal or Cabo Verde with Nigeria or Gambia with Chad), we should be careful in interpreting these results.

Graph 1:   Level of GNI per capita compared to child mortality

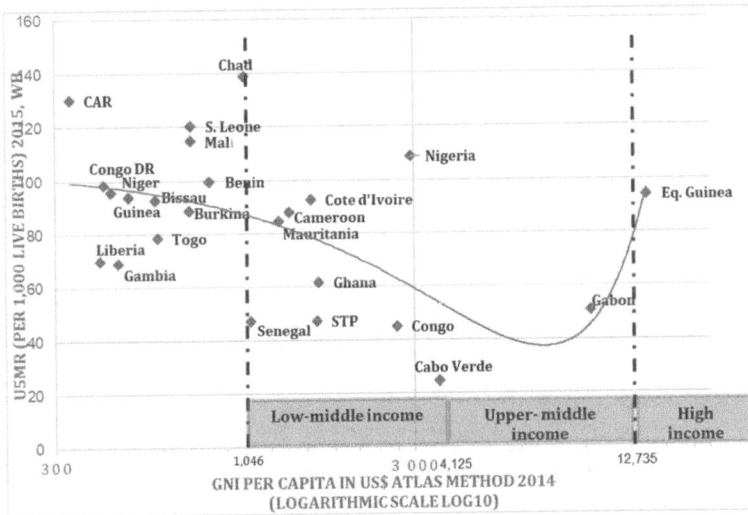

Source: World Bank & UNICEF

---

5   After testing many functions, an order 2 polynomial function seems to best fit the general trend.

Classification according to the level of poverty

a) Monetary Poverty

The national poverty line is the minimum income/consumption level used in a country for determining the proportion of population living in monetary poverty. Those households, whose income/consumption is less than this minimum, are classified as poor households, while households whose income/consumption is equal to or more than this threshold are considered non-poor. Based on this income threshold, a national poverty incidence is determined, which is the percentage of poor in the total population.

Graph 2:   National poverty incidence

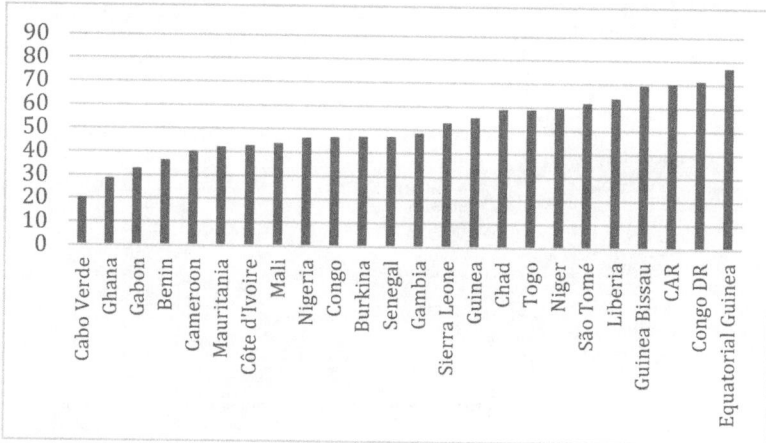

Source: UNDP HDR 2014

b) Multidimensional Poverty

Poverty is not just the absence of income. It is also the multiple consequences of this absence that are simultaneously experienced by people in poverty. Some of these consequences — the non-monetary dimensions of poverty — serve to prolong poverty and can become causes of its perpetuation. This definition of multidimensional poverty embraces a diverse range of characteristics such as material deprivation, social exclusion, lack of basic needs and rights, etc.

The Multidimensional Poverty Index (MPI) identifies multiple deprivations at the household and individual level in health, education and standard of living[6]. It uses micro data from household surveys. Each person in a given household is classified as poor or non-poor depending on the number of deprivations his or her household experiences. This data are then aggregated into the national measure of poverty. The MPI attempts to reflect both the prevalence of multidimensional deprivation, and its intensity – how many deprivations people experience at the same time with a single, dimension-less number. It can be used to create a comprehensive picture of households living in poverty, and permits comparisons both across countries, regions and the world, and within countries by ethnic group, urban or rural location, as well as other key household and community characteristics.

Dimensions included in the MPI are education, health, and living standards. All are equally weighted by one-third each and the scale of the index is from 0 to 1, 0 being no deprivation and 1 meaning maximum deprivation.

Education indicators are a) school attendance for school-age children; and b) school attainment for household members.

Health indicators are: (a) child mortality; and (b) nutrition.

Living Standards indicators include:

- household access to electricity
- household access to improved drinking water sources
- household access to improved sanitation
- household use of solid fuel for cooking and heating
- existence of a finished floor in the house
- existence of other assets that: (1) allow access to information (radio, TV, telephone); (2) support mobility (bike, motorbike, car, truck, animal cart, motorboat); and (3) support livelihood (refrigerator, agricultural land, livestock)

A household is not considered deprived in assets if it has at least one asset from group (1) and at least one asset from groups (2) or (3). A household is considered multidimensionally poor (or MPI poor) if the total of weighted deprivations (deprivation score) is equal to 1/3 or more.

---

[6]   UNDP's Multidimensional Poverty Index: 2014. Specifications Kovacevic and Calderon (2014).

A household is considered severely multidimensionally poor if the deprivation score is 1/2 or more.

A household is considered near-MPI poor if the deprivation score is 1/5 or more but less than 1/3.

A household is considered deprived but not near-MPI poor if the deprivation score is positive but less than 1/5.

If a household is deprived, then all its members are deprived.

Graph 3:   MPI Multidimensional Poverty Incidence

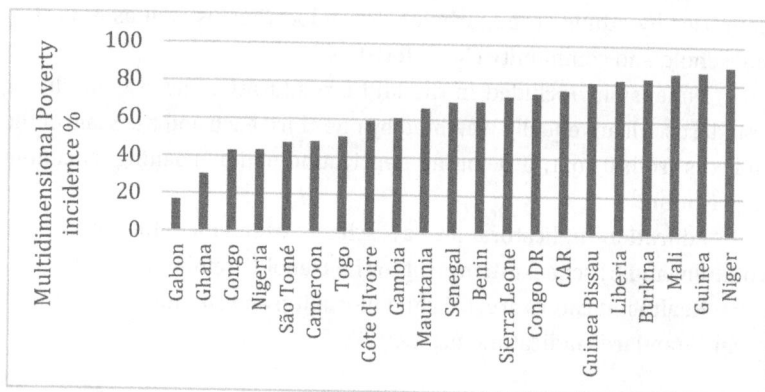

Source: UNDP HDR 2014

For the MPI, three countries in our region do not have data: Cabo Verde, Chad, and Equatorial Guinea, which limits our capacity to compare countries in the region. Furthermore, data used to compare countries vary considerably; for some countries like Benin, data date back to 2006, and for others like Côte d'Ivoire, we have access only to the 2012 data. In general, data are old (2010 in most cases), which for some countries, such as CAR, may have changed considerably in view of the situation of the country today. Considering these limitations, comparing countries using this indicator may not be very appropriate.

Classification according to the level of governance

a) Mo Ibrahim Governance Index

The Ibrahim Index of African Governance (IIAG), produced by the Mo Ibrahim Foundation, measures the quality of governance in every African country. It does this by compiling data from diverse global sources to build an accurate and detailed picture of governance performance in African countries. Published annually, the IIAG provides a comprehensive assessment of governance performance for each of the 54 African countries. The 2015 IIAG consists of 93 indicators which fall into four categories: Safety & Rule of Law; Participation & Human Rights; Sustainable Economic Opportunity; and Human Development. Countries are rated from 0 to 100, with 100 the best possible score.

Cabo Verde is the best performing country in the region, with an index of 74.5, while CAR has the lowest score, 24.9. It appears that there is no relationship between the level of GNI per capita and the quality of governance. For instance, Equatorial Guinea and the Republic of Congo, two countries with the highest per capita income, are among the worst six countries in the region in terms of Governance. On the other end, Benin and Burkina, two low income countries, are among the six best performing countries.

Graph 4:   IIAG score for WCA in 2015

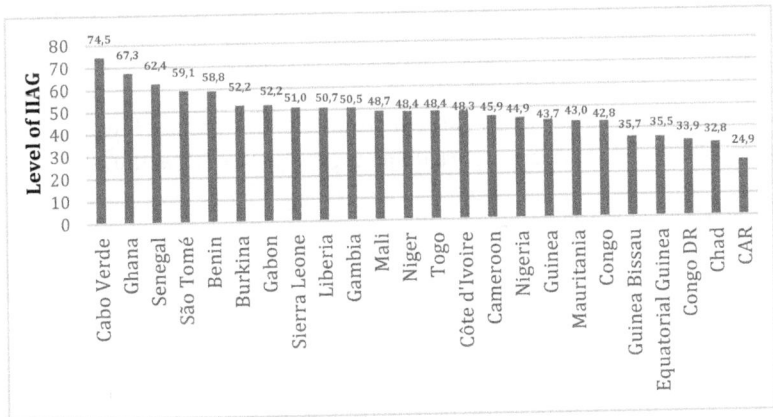

Source: mo.ibrahim.foundation/iiag
Accessed February 2017

b) World Bank CPIA

The World Bank CPIA (Country Policy and Institutional Assessment) exercise is intended to capture the quality of a country's policies and institutional arrangements, focusing on key elements that are within the country's control, rather than on outcomes (such as economic growth rates) that are influenced by events beyond the country's control. More specifically, the CPIA measures the extent to which a country's policy and institutional framework supports sustainable growth and poverty reduction and, consequently, the effective use of development assistance.

The CPIA consists of 16 criteria grouped in four equally weighted clusters: Economic Management; Structural Policies; Policies for Social Inclusion and Equity; and Public Sector Management and Institutions. For each of the 16 criteria, countries are rated on a scale of 1 (low) to 6 (high). The scores depend on the level of performance in a given year assessed against the criteria, rather than on changes in performance compared to the previous year. The ratings depend on actual policies and performance, rather than on promises or intentions. In some cases, measures such as the passage of specific legislation can represent an important action that deserves consideration. However, the manner in which such actions should be factored into the ratings is carefully assessed, because in the end it is the implementation of legislation that determines the extent of its impact.

Unfortunately for this indicator, we do not have data for Gabon and Equatorial Guinea, the two highest ranking countries in term of GNI per capita. The lack of data to rank these two countries may be, by itself, an indication of the governance level in these countries.

Cabo Verde has the highest score, while CAR has the lower, as per the IIAG. Benin and Burkina are doing very well, as per the IIAG index.

Graph 5:   CPIA index

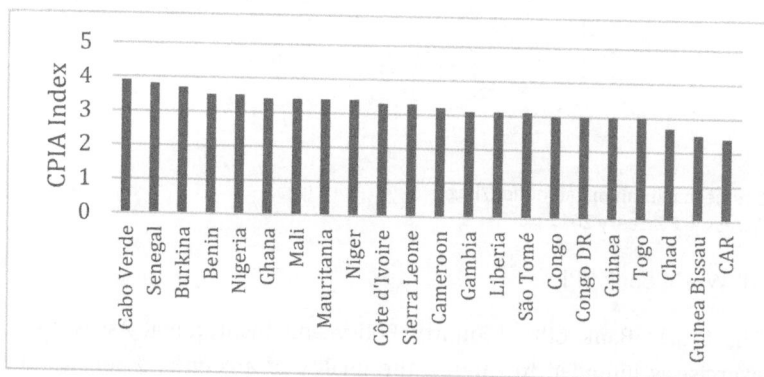

Source: datacatalog.worldbank.org/dataset/country-policy-and-institutional-assessment
Accessed February 2017

c) Transparency International Corruption Index

The Transparency International Corruption Index measures the perceived levels of public sector corruption on a scale of 0 (highly corrupt) to 100 (very clean). It is a composite index — a combination of polls — drawing on corruption-related data collected from a variety of institutions. The index reflects the views of observers from around the world, including experts living and working in the countries.

For Equatorial Guinea, there is no information. Cabo Verde is found to be the least corrupt country and Guinea Bissau the most corrupt, according to this index. One of the weaknesses of this index is that it is based on perception, which is not the same as being based on facts.

Graph 6:   Transparency International Corruption Index 2014

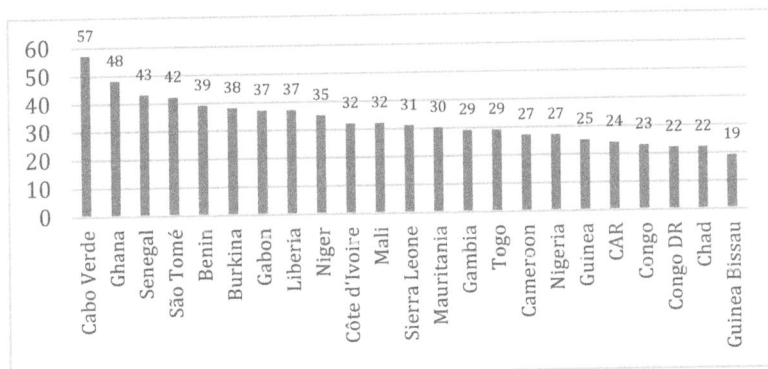

Source: www.transparency.org
Accessed February 2017

Classifications according to fragility

a) OECD Fragile Countries

In order to promote debate and offer a fresh perspective, OECD presents a new tool for analysing fragility based on internationally agreed global priorities for reducing fragility and building resilience. It uses existing data to present five dimensions of fragility that relate directly to the UN's 2015 Sustainable Development Goal. The five dimensions are as follows: 1. Violence: reduction of violence; 2. Justice: access to justice for all; 3. Institutions: effective, accountable and inclusive institutions; 4. Economic foundations: economic foundations, inclusion and stability; 5. Resilience: capacity to prevent and adapt to shocks and disasters.[7]

Fifteen countries in the region are then categorized as "fragile" according to OECD methodology (in alphabetical order): Cameroon, CAR, Chad, Congo, Congo DR, Côte d'Ivoire, Guinea, Guinea Bissau, Liberia, Mali, Mauritania, Niger, Nigeria, Sierra Leone, Togo

b) World Bank Fragile Situations

The World Bank describes Fragile Situations as countries that have either a) a CPIA country rating of 3.2 or less; and/or b) the presence of a UN and/or regional peace keeping or peace building mission during the last three years. Therefore, the World Bank definition of fragile countries is strongly related to the countries' governance score.

Based on that definition, nine countries in the region are defined as fragile by the World Bank:

CAR, Chad, Congo DR, Côte d'Ivoire, Guinea Bissau, Liberia, Mali, Sierra Leone, Togo

This list is much shorter than the OECD one. It is interesting to see that many countries that are categorized by OECD as fragile, are not defined as such according to the World Bank.

c) The Composite Index for Risk Management (InfoRM)

The INFORM initiative began in 2012 as a convergence of interests of UN agencies, donors, NGOs and research institutions to establish a common evidence-base for global humanitarian risk analysis.[8]

---

[7]   OECD (2015)

[8]   Organizations that make part of the INFORM initiative are: ACAPS (The Assessment Capacities Project) - is an initiative of a consortium of three NGOs (HelpAge International, Merlin and Norwegian Refugee Council); DFID (Department for International Development) is a United Kingdom government department; ECHO (Humanitarian Aid and Civil Protection department of the European Commission) - is the European Commission's department for overseas humanitarian aid and civil protection; FAO (Food and Agriculture Organization of United Nations); IASC (The Inter-Agency Standing Committee) is the primary mechanism for inter-agency coordination of humanitarian assistance. It is a unique forum involving the key UN and non-UN humanitarian partners; IOM (International Organization for Migration); OCHA (United Nations Office for the Coordination of Humanitarian Affairs); UNEP (United Nations Environment Programme); UNHCR (United Nations High Commissioner for Refugees); UNICEF (United Nation's Children Fund); UNISDR (The United Nations Office for Disaster Risk Reduction); WFP (World Food Programme); WHO (World Health Organization)

INFORM identifies the countries at a high risk of humanitarian crisis that are more likely to require international assistance. The INFORM model is based on risk concepts published in scientific literature and envisages three dimensions of risk: hazards and exposure, vulnerability and lack of national coping capacity. The INFORM model is split into different levels to provide a quick overview of the underlying factors leading to humanitarian risk.

Table 3:   InfoRM variables

Ranking level	Concept level (dimensions)	Functional level (Categories)	Component level
INFORM	Lack of coping capacity	Infrastructure	Access to Health Systems
			Physical infrastructure
			Communication
		Institutional	Governance
			Disaster Risk Reduction
	Vulnerability	Vulnerable groups	Other vulnerable groups
			Uprooted people
		Socio-economic	Aid Dependency (25%)
			Inequality (25%)
			Development and deprivation (50%)
	Hazard and exposure	Human	Projected Conflict Risk
			Current conflict Intensity
		Natural	Drought
			Tropical Cyclone
			Floods
			Tsunami
			Earthquake

Note: Risk = Hazard and exposure x vulnerability x lack of coping capacity
Source: www.inform-index.org
Accessed February 2017

The INFORM index presents a scale of 0 to 10, 0 being no risk and 10 is maximum risk. INFORM does not distinguish countries between fragile and non-fragile ones. It merely ranks these countries from the least vulnerable to the most vulnerable. It then splits all countries into quartiles according to their level of vulnerability: low, medium, high and very high vulnerability.

Graph 7:   INFORM index (mid 2015)

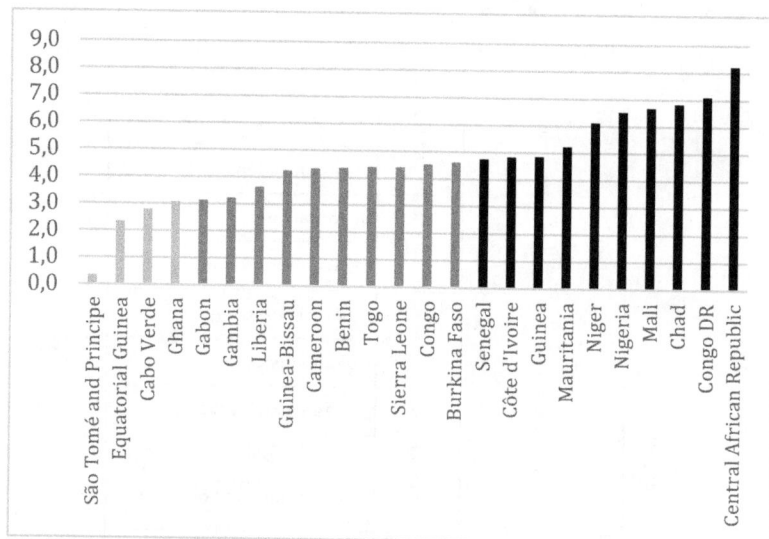

Note: quartiles are shaded darker for higher levels of risk
Source: www.inform-index.org
Accessed February 2017

Countries in the WCA region are ranked according to these global quartiles in Graph 7. No country in the region is in the low vulnerability quartile. In light grey on the left, we have countries that are in the medium vulnerability quartile; then in grey in the middle, countries that are in the high vulnerability quartile. Finally, in black, on the right, countries that are the most at risk, in the very high vulnerability quartile. Curiously, a country like Senegal, which usually performs better in many other rankings, is in the very high-risk quartile globally.

The two main factors affecting countries in this ranking are the drought in the Sahel region, and civil wars in countries such as CAR, DR Congo, Mali, and Nigeria.

Categorization/classification according to composite development indicators

a) The UN Least Developed Countries Classification

The world's most impoverished and vulnerable countries, the least developed countries (LDCs) are a group of countries that have been classified by the UN as "least developed" in terms of their low gross national income (GNI), their weak human assets and their high degree of economic vulnerability. The LDC is made up of the following:

- A low-income criterion based on a three-year average estimate of the gross national income (GNI) per capita
- A human resource weakness criterion involving a composite Human Assets Index (HAI) based on indicators of: (a) nutrition; (b) health; (c) education; and (d) adult literacy
- An economic vulnerability criterion involving a composite Economic Vulnerability Indicator (EVI) based on: indicators of the instability of agricultural production; the instability of exports of goods and services; the economic importance of non-traditional activities (share of manufacturing and modern services in GDP); merchandise export concentration; etc.

Both HAI and EVI are composed of several indicators. The methodology does not rank countries, but just cluster countries in two groups: countries that are least developed and the others that are not. Currently, there are 48 least developed countries in the world, 17 of them being in West and Central Africa. Countries can graduate from the LDCs statute, according to certain thresholds.

WCAR list of LDCs by alphabetic order:

Benin, Burkina, CAR, Chad, Congo DR, Equatorial Guinea, Gambia, Guinea, Guinea Bissau, Liberia, Mali, Mauritania, Niger, São Tomé & Príncipe, Senegal, Sierra Leone, and Togo.

The composition of the LDCs is striking. A country like Equatorial Guinea, the only high-income country of Africa according to the World Bank GNI per capita, is part of the LDCs group, because of the low level of its human resource criterion.[9] Out of the 17 LDCs in WCA, four are middle- or high-income countries according to the World Bank (Equatorial Guinea, Mauritania, São Tomé & Príncipe, Senegal).

LDCs have exclusive access to specific international support in the areas of trade, development assistance, and general support.

b) UNDP Human Development Index

The UNDP HDI is a well-established measure of human development. It is a composite index, comprising income (GNI per capita), health (measured by life expectancy) and education. Countries are ranked on a scale of 1 to 0, 1 being the highest human development, and 0 the lowest. In West and Central Africa, Gabon, Cabo Verde, Ghana, Congo, São Tomé & Príncipe and Equatorial Guinea are the only countries that are classified as having medium human development (in grey in Graph 8 below). The other countries have low human development. Niger, Congo DR and CAR are the weakest, according to the UNDP 2014 Human Development Report. The advantage of this Index is that it includes other dimensions than income to classify countries. Equatorial Guinea, which ranked first according to GNI per capita, was now ranked in the 6th place in the region according to HDI.

Graph 8:   Human Development Index 2014

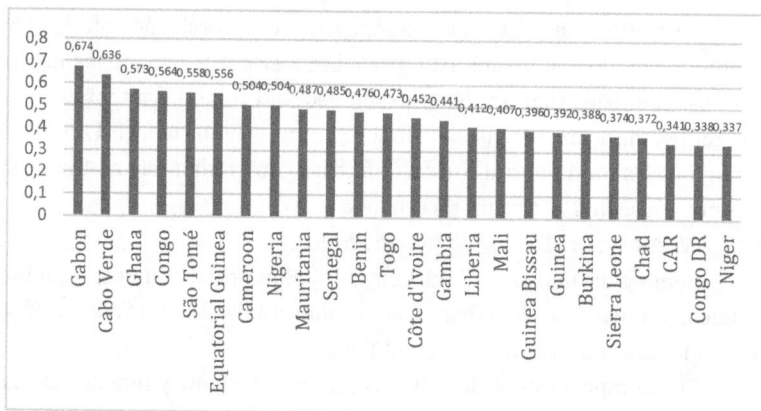

Source: UNDP HDR 2014

---

[9]   Equatorial Guinea graduated from the LDCs in 2017, according to the UN (www.un.org accessed 31 July 2017)

Preliminary conclusion

Based on all the classifications or clustering presented above, we have noticed that depending on the type of indicators used, a country's position can vary significantly from one classification to another. It is therefore difficult to be able to capture all the complexity of a country's situation with a single indicator such as the GNI per capita. Some indicators, such as the Human Development Index, have tried to capture this multidimensionality. They nonetheless use only three dimensions. The HDI is therefore still unable, in our view, to capture the entire picture.

Some countries are among the best in almost all type of classification (Cabo Verde, Gabon and Ghana, for instance), while others are lagging in many areas (such as CAR, Chad and DRC). Therefore, an idea to explore could be to use multiple measures to compare countries, instead of relying on one single multidimensional index. Our position is that a single index is not sufficient to usefully compare countries from a practical policy point of view. For example, two countries can have the same Human Development Index, but be completely different in terms of education outcomes, GDP per capita, or life expectancy. Instead, the methodology we will be proposing in the following pages is designed to cluster countries based on their similarities across various indicators, and therefore to be able to derive common policy options.

PROPOSED CATEGORIZATION

The methodology we are proposing now is not to create a new index and then use it to rank and compare countries. Instead, we have decided to use data analysis techniques to cluster countries in the region in an optimal and homogeneous number of sub-groups, based on a number of indicators. The main reason is then to be able to derive a common engagement strategy for each sub-group.

Choice of indicators

Our classification of countries in WCAR is based on 10 indicators. The selection of these indicators is based on four main criteria:

1. Availability of the indicator for all 24 countries
2. Balanced mix of different type of indicators: economic, social, governance

3. Not too strong a correlation between indicators
4. The measurements indicate something useful about child rights

Based on these criteria, the following 10 indicators have been used:

Economic dependence Indicators
1. Natural resource rents (% of GDP) (World Bank)[10]
2. Official Development Assistance (ODA) in % of national income (World Bank)
3. Workers remittances as a percentage of national income (World Bank)

Income indicators
4. Gross National Income (GNI) per capita (World Bank)
5. National Poverty incidence (World Bank)

Social indicators
6. Education Index[11]
7. Under five mortality (UNICEF)
8. Stunting (UNICEF)

Governance indicators
9. Mo Ibrahim Governance indicator (Mo Ibrahim Foundation)
10. Birth registration (UNICEF)

All data have been standardized (subtracting the mean and dividing by the standard deviation)[12], in order to avoid a scale effect. We then used data analysis software (XLSTAT) to cluster countries in the region using two related techniques: Principal Components Analysis and Hierarchical Agglomerative Clustering.

---

[10] Total natural resources rents are the sum of oil rents, natural gas rents, coal rents (hard and soft), mineral rents, and forest rents. This ratio is an indication of the weight of natural resources in a country economy. It measures the level of dependency on natural resources.

[11] Calculated using Mean Years of Schooling and Expected Years of Schooling

[12] If not standardized, variables measured at different scales do not contribute equally to the analysis. For example, a variable that ranges between 0 and 100 will outweigh a variable that ranges between 0 and 1. Using these variables without standardization in effect gives the variable with the larger range a weight of 100 in the analysis. Transforming the data to comparable scales can prevent this problem. Data standardization procedures equalize the range.

Methodologies for clustering

Principal Component Analysis (PCA) is the general name for a technique which uses mathematical principles to transform a number of possibly correlated variables into a smaller number of variables called principal components. In general terms, PCA uses a vector space transformation to reduce the dimensionality of large data sets. Using mathematical projection, the original data set, which may have involved many variables, can often be interpreted using just a few variables (the principal components). It is therefore often the case that an examination of the reduced dimension data set will allow the user to spot trends, patterns and outliers in the data, far more easily than would have been possible without performing the principal component analysis (Richardson, 2009).

Cluster analysis is a convenient method for identifying homogenous groups of objects called clusters. Objects (countries in our case) in a specific cluster share many characteristics but are very dissimilar to objects not belonging to that cluster. The aim of cluster analysis is to identify groups of objects that are very similar with regards to the variables used and assign them into clusters (Mooi and Sarstedt 2011).

But how do we measure similarity or dissimilarity? Some approaches — most notably hierarchical methods — require us to specify how similar or how different objects are in order to identify clusters. Most software packages calculate a measure of (dis)similarity by estimating the distance between pairs of objects. Objects presenting smaller distances between one another are more similar, whereas objects presenting larger distances are more dissimilar.

In our work, we want to cluster countries based on the 10 variables we mentioned above. Countries that are close according to these variables will be clustered together, while countries that are not similar will be clustered into other groups. The number of clusters can be determined optimally by some software, or pre-determined by the user. On the one hand, we want as few clusters as possible to make them easy to understand and to be able to take action on the results. On the other hand, having many clusters allows us to identify more subtle differences between groups. In an extreme case, we could address each individual country separately with specific recommendations.

In the final step, we need to interpret the solution by defining and labelling the obtained clusters. This can be done by examining the clustering variables' mean values, or by identifying explanatory variables to profile the clusters.

In our work, we use first the PCA to reduce our vector dimension space from ten to two variables, which allows us to plot countries in a two-dimensional graph (Graph 9). This first analysis gives us a hint about countries categorization. We then use hierarchical agglomerative clustering to group countries. The two methods are not interdependent and can be performed independently, but their combination allow us to better analyse and visualise profiles of countries.

Results

a) Principal Component Analysis Results

A visual representation of the results (Graph 9) enables us to think about a possible categorization of countries. The two main Principal Components Axis[13], F1 and F2, represent a total inertia of 64 percent of the original ten variables used. The horizontal axis, F1, is the most representative, with an inertia of 40 percent. The vertical axis has an inertia of 24 percent. The ten variables used for the analysis appear as lines. This is just an indication of how much each Principal Component Axis (F1 and F2) is influenced by the original variables.

For instance, regarding the horizontal axis (F1), when a country is on the left, this means this country has good indicators in governance, birth registration and education, and low level of stunting, under-five-year-old mortality, and poverty. When a country is on the right, then it is the reverse situation, with high poverty rate, high under five mortality, and high level of stunting, as well as low level of governance, birth registration and education.

---

[13]   The two principal components axis are new variables constructed from the dataset

Graph 9:   Principal Component Analysis results

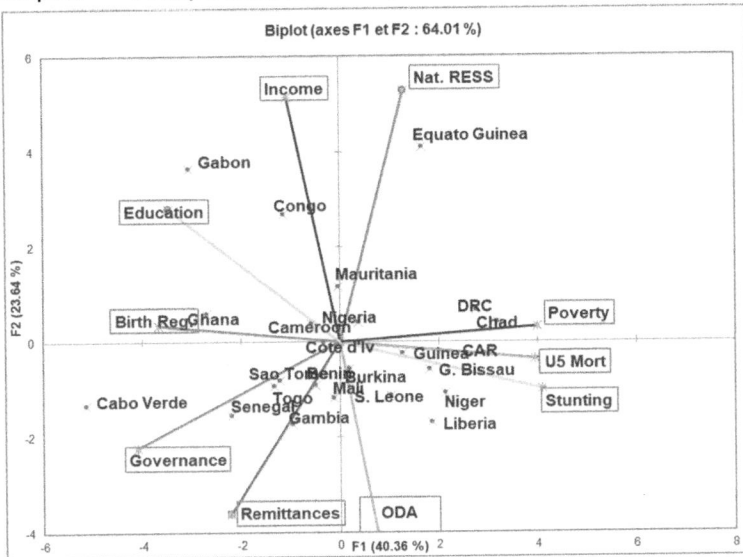

Source: various, as described in the text

Regarding the vertical axis F2, a country with a high income per capita and which relies heavily on natural resources will be on top, while countries with important remittances and ODA will appear at the bottom.

At this stage, we do not have a clustering of countries, but there are clear indications of possible categorization of countries. We have a group of countries located at the top of the graph, even though this group is spread from left to right. Gabon, Congo and Equatorial Guinea are obviously in the same group. We then have a group of countries on the left, with Cabo Verde and Ghana being the clear representatives. We have another group on the right (Chad, DRC, Guinea Bissau, etc.), and finally, we have a group of countries in the middle of the graph (Côte d'Ivoire, Nigeria, Benin, Burkina Faso, etc.).

At this stage, the categorization of countries is based only on the visualization of the graph. We must then use hierarchical agglomerative clustering techniques to confirm the categorizations.

b) Hierarchical Agglomerative Clustering Results

As explained above, two countries are similar if most of their indicators (the ten indicators used here) are close, while two countries are dissimilar if they are at very different levels for the same variables. Let us take a hypothetical example and suppose three countries (A, B and C), with 3 indicators: birth registration, child mortality and stunting. The table below summarized the situation of the 3 countries:

Table 4:   Level of indicators for hypothetical example

Countries	A	B	C
Birth registration (%)	96	85	30
Child mortality (per 1,000 live birth)	20	30	80
Stunting (%)	10	15	30

From the indices presented in Table 4 above, we can estimate the distance between countries based on the three indicators. We can simply compute the difference between the three variables for each pair of countries.

Table 5:   Distance between countries for hypothetical example

	A-B	A-C	B-C
Birth registration (%)	11	66	55
Child mortality (per 1,000 live birth)	10	60	50
Stunting (%)	5	20	15
Total dissimilarity	**26**	**146**	**120**

The distance between A and B (the dissimilarity) is 26, while the distance between A and C is 146 and the distance between B and C is 120. It is therefore obvious that A and B are close (similar) as compared to A and C or B and C. In this simple example, we can cluster A and B together, and distinguish C as a very different country.

The dendrogram below (Graph 10) shows the process of clustering countries when using this method. The vertical axis indicates the dissimilarities. The more we move up along this axis before a country is clustered to another one or to a group of countries, the more dissimilar they are.

For countries clustered in the left of the graph, we can see that in a first step, Guinea (GUI) and Niger (NIG) in one hand, and Guinea Bissau (GBI) and DR Congo (DRC) have been found similar and clustered; then these two groups of countries have been clustered together. Central African Republic (CAR) and Chad (CHD) have been found very similar and clustered also together, and then clustered with the group comprising Niger, Guinea, Guinea Bissau and DRC. And finally, Liberia (LIB) has been clustered with this group of six countries.

Graph 10:   HAC results

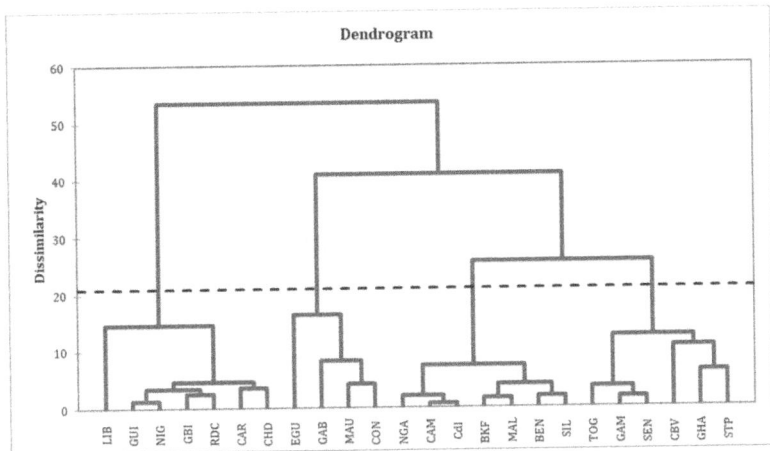

Source: various, as described in the text

The dotted horizontal line indicates at which level the number of clusters has been decided. If this line was up at around 30, for example, then we would have had only three clusters of countries. If this line was down to around the level of 10, then we would have had no less than eight clusters of countries.

The table below (Table 6) shows the countries composing the four groups (this can be seen in the dendrogram also).

- Group 1 (or class 1) comprises 6 countries: Cabo Verde, Gambia, Ghana, São Tomé & Príncipe, Senegal and Togo. These are the best performing countries in the region.

- Group 2 (4 countries): Gabon, Equatorial Guinea, Mauritania and Congo. These are natural resource dependent countries and mixed performing countries.

- Group 3 (7 countries): Guinea, Guinea Bissau, Liberia, Niger, CAR, DRC and Chad. These are low performing countries.

- Group 4 (7 countries): Benin, Burkina Faso, Cameroon, Côte d'Ivoire, Mali and Nigeria. These are average performing countries.

Table 6:   Categorization of countries

Results by class:				
Class	1: Best performing countries	2: Mixed performing countries	3: Low performing countries.	4: Average performing countries
Objects (number of countries)	6	4	7	7
Sum of weights	6	4	7	7
Within-class variance	6.885	9.525	4.992	2.872
Minimum distance to centroid	1.446	1.954	1.260	0.982
Average distance to centroid	2.334	2.614	1.939	1.550
Maximum distance to centroid	3.121	3.493	3.524	1.810
	CBV	GAB	GBI	BEN
	GAM	EGU	GUI	BKF
	GHA	MAU	LIB	CAM
	STP	CON	NIG	CdI
	SEN		CAR	MAL
	TOG		RDC	NGA
			CHD	SIL

Source: various, as described in the text

Based on the Hierarchical Agglomerative Clustering results, we then plot again the same principal component graph (as Graph 9), with more precision regarding groups of countries (Graph 11).

Graph 11:   HAC and PCA combined results

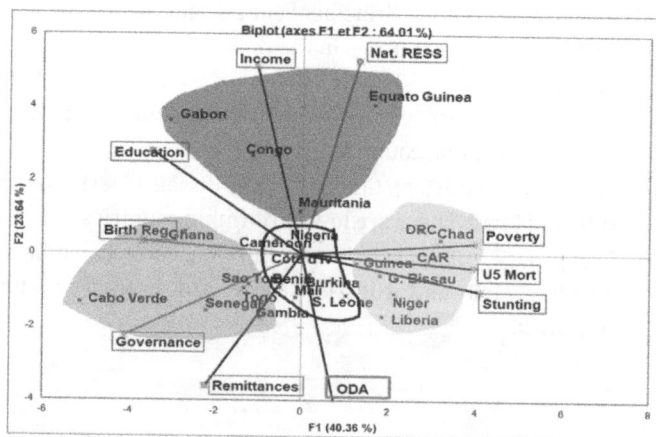

Source: various, as described in the text

From this analysis, we can describe four classes of countries.

Class 1: best performing countries (light grey, on the left)

- Cabo Verde
- Ghana
- São Tomé & Príncipe
- Senegal
- Togo
- Gambia

These countries have the best social indicators in the region. Some have a good governance record (Cabo Verde, Ghana), but others do not (Togo, the Gambia). Most of them are not resource rich (with the exception of Ghana, but even Ghana is not too dependent on natural resources). Most of these countries are dependent on workers' remittances.

Class 2: Natural resource dependent countries and mixed performing countries (dark grey, above)

- Equatorial Guinea
- Gabon
- Congo
- Mauritania

These countries are very dependent on natural resources, especially on extractive industries (oil in particular). These countries have the highest income per capita in the region. But most of them have bad social indicators. If we remove the wealth indices (income per capita and natural resource dependency) from the analysis, Equatorial Guinea will fall into the low performing countries category, while Gabon will be relocated to the best performing countries. Very weak governance indicators are generalizable for this group of countries.

Class 3: Low performing countries (very light grey, on the right)

- Chad
- CAR
- DRC

- Niger
- Liberia
- Guinea
- Guinea Bissau

These countries have the worst social indicators in the region. They have very poor governance indicators in general. There is heightened political instability and/or civil war in many of them. Two out of three of the countries that have recently experienced Ebola are this this group.

Class 4: Average performing countries (white, in the middle)

- Nigeria
- Côte d'Ivoire
- Cameroon
- Burkina Faso
- Benin
- Mali
- Sierra Leone

These countries are in the middle of the spectrum. Some of them are low-income countries with relatively good governance indicators (Benin, Burkina). Others are middle-income countries with weak governance indicators (Cameroon, Nigeria). Some of the group are middle-income countries that are fragile (Côte d'Ivoire). Some are highly dependent on ODA and /or remittances (Mali, Burkina); while others have relatively good natural resources (Nigeria, Côte d'Ivoire, Cameroon).

Outlines of strategies for each group of countries regarding social protection

The purpose of this chapter is to try to derive common strategies for each group as defined above. The strategies are not mutually exclusive, which means that a specific strategy for a group of countries can also apply to another group or a single country in another group. Therefore, even though each group will have a specific strategy, each country could use a mix of strategies from different groups.

a) Class 1: Best Performing Countries

This group of countries is characterised by relatively good social indicators (in comparison to the rest of the region): education, stunting, child mortality, and birth registration are good. In spite of differences and incomplete data, in general these countries have already started to take concrete steps to set up robust and nationwide social protection polices/programmes, and they consequently have the best coverage in the region in term of social protection (for example, Cabo Verde, Ghana and Senegal).

In this group of countries, we have the most advanced countries in the region regarding social protection coverage: Ghana, Cabo Verde and Senegal have a pretty good social protection coverage as compared with the other countries in the region. Therefore, the question is generally not "is the government committed to social protection", but instead, "how to support the government to better extend social protection coverage?"

This analysis suggests that the focus of the international community should be on supporting the government to build a strong and lasting social protection sector, with good policies, institutional setting, support for fiscal space, single registry and so on. Governments in this group of countries are interested in progressively establishing a social protection floor, and financing it in a sustainable manner.

b) Class 2: Natural Resources Dependent and Mix Performing Countries

The main engine of growth for this group of countries is the mineral sector. The economy is an enclave, lacking both backward and forward linkages with the other sectors of the economy. Few jobs are created despite strong economic growth, especially for young people. The informal sector is important, as there are few formal jobs.

The presence of large multinational companies is notable, as they have significant resources, and are a cause for rapid urbanization and migration.

The economy provides important resources for the government, even though there is still low and/or un-transparent revenue mobilisation from the natural resources sector; revenue mobilisation remains low outside the natural resource sector.

There is a low allocation of resources. There remains low efficiency of investments and low levels of implementation of public expenditure particularly in the social sectors. There are low social indicators despite high rates of economic growth. High inequalities persist, but there is a lack of basic statistics, so there remain scant levels of knowledge of the situation of the poor and those suffering various social and economic vulnerabilities.

This group of countries have the resources to finance social protection, at least a basic social protection floor. But this is not the case, which stems mainly from policy choices that demonstrate a poor understanding of social protection. Social protection is often seen as expenditure with no immediate returns. Therefore, in this group of countries, the focus should be evidence-based advocacy for social protection, supported by cost-benefit analysis and high-level advocacy. Training is also important to raise awareness.

Identification of the most vulnerable is important in this group of countries. During this study, we have seen that often, the richer countries (such as Gabon and Equatorial Guinea) lack the basic data on poverty. Therefore, identifying the poor will be crucial for these countries.

In view of the importance of the private sector in these economies, a strategy should be developed to enhance the private sector investment in social protection activities.

Finally, supporting the gradual development of quality and inclusive social protection system is essential.

c) Class 3: Low Performing Countries

This group of countries is extremely fragile. There are current civil wars in CAR, DRC and Chad. Other countries have formerly experienced civil wars and Ebola pandemics (Guinea and Liberia), as well as huge political instability in Guinea Bissau. Niger has experienced drought and rebellion.

The level of social indicators (including social protection) is appalling in this group. Every child-related indicator is of concern: birth registration is less than 16 percent in Chad; child mortality is more than 130/1,000 live births in CAR and Chad; and the level of child stunting is more that 40 percent in Liberia, Niger and CAR.

In this group, social protection should be mainly embedded in a humanitarian context. Social transfers (such as cash, food or vouchers) should be the main tools for social protection. Therefore, support should focus on the implementation of social transfer programmes, from targeting to monitoring and evaluation, with a strong capacity building component.

d) Class 4: Average Performing Countries

It is difficult to have a clear typology of interventions for this group of countries. Countries in this group have different mix of characteristics; a country like Nigeria could use the same recipes as those recommended for natural resource dependent countries (Class 2 countries), but also as fragile countries (as it experiences civil war, high corruption, etc.). In the same way, a country like Mali could be, in many regards, classified with Class 3 countries (fragile).

Therefore, instead of trying to define a set of specific interventions for this group of countries, each of these countries should use a mix of strategies defined for the other groups, depending on their specific situation.

Benin, Burkina Faso, Mali and Sierra Leone in this group are well functioning democracies, but with low level of economic and social indicators, highly dependent on ODA and with low rent on natural resources. But most of these countries are also vulnerable (Mali and Burkina Faso are drought prone countries, Sierra Leone emerged from a long civil war and Ebola crisis). Therefore, this group of countries have some characteristics close to high performing countries (for example, good governance), but also many characteristics of fragile countries. This sub-group of countries should use a balanced mix of strategies coming from best performing and low performing countries, based on their specificities.

Cameroon, Côte d'Ivoire and Nigeria are middle-income countries, with substantial natural resources, but also with bad records regarding governance and social inclusion. Nigeria and Cameroon are classified as fragile countries by OECD, while Côte d'Ivoire is classified as fragile by both OECD and the World Bank. This second sub-group of average performing countries should use a balanced mix of strategies stemming from natural resource rich countries and fragile countries.

CONCLUSION

West and Central Africa comprises a number of countries that are diverse in term of their levels of economic, social, and political development. It is therefore impossible to have a one-size-fits-all policy recommendation regarding economic and social issues in general, and social protection in particular. To circumvent this difficulty, we used clustering methodology to meaningfully group countries in West and Central Africa into four main clusters, based on a number of selected economic, social and governance indicators. This allows us to obtain relatively homogenous and similar groups of countries, to which similar broad policy recommendations regarding social protection can be recommended.

The clustering methodology we use is not perfect, nor are the data. Therefore, we cannot claim that the clusters obtained are a perfect classification. But this exercise is an attempt to group countries in a way that is different from the traditional GDP or GNI per capita classification of countries. We therefore do hope that this will be a starting point for more research in this area and that it will serve as something useful for the international community in order to improve support to countries in the region.

REFERENCES

Kovacevic M. and M. Cecilia Calderon (2014): 'UNDP's Multidimensional Poverty Index: 2014 Specifications', *UNDP Human Development Report Office occasional paper*

Mooi E. and M. Sarstedt (2011), *A Concise Guide to Market Research*, Springer-Verlag Berlin Heidelberg 2011. [online], available at: https://www.scribd.com/doc/71 938809/Cluster-Analysis; accessed 2 November 2015

OECD (2015): *States of the fragility 2015: meeting post-2015 ambitions, revised version, Paris*

Richardson, M. (2009) 'Principal Component Analysis' [online], available at: http://www.dsc.ufcg.edu.br/~hmg/disciplinas/posgraduacao/rn-copin-2014.3/mater ial/SignalProcPCA.pdf [accessed 2 November 2015]

UNDP (2014): *HDR 2014: Sustaining Human Progress: Reducing Vulnerabilities and Building Resilience, New York*

PART II: CHILD POVERTY, INEQUITY, AND INEQUALITY

CHAPTER 3

MEASURING MULTIDIMENSIONAL POVERTY ACCORDING TO NATIONAL DEFINITIONS - OPERATIONALISING TARGET 1.2.2 OF THE SUSTAINABLE DEVELOPMENT GOALS IN BENIN, GABON, GUINEA, LIBERIA, AND MALI

Marco Pomati and Shailen Nandy

INTRODUCTION

The Millennium Development Goals (MDGs) succeeded in focussing and sustaining global attention on the issue of extreme poverty and its correlates in low and middle-income countries (LMICs). The 2015 target date has passed, with UN agencies, governments, and civil society organisations reporting varying degrees of success in meeting set targets; unsurprisingly, not all MDGs were met everywhere. There were differing rates of progress and success. As regards MDG 1, the eradication of extreme poverty and hunger[1], success at a global level was claimed (Pinkovskiy and Sala-i-Martin, 2010; Chandy and Gertz, 2011; United Nations, 2015), not least because of the remarkable rate of poverty reduction in East Asia over the last 30 years. Sceptics, however, have questioned the metrics (Reddy and Pogge, 2002; Vandemoortele, 2002; Townsend et al., 2006) arguing that poverty estimates in many countries are of questionable reliability, given the quality of data on which they are based (Jerven, 2013). In addition to the issue of data quality is the issue of how poverty is measured and defined. Townsend succinctly summed up the link between poverty definition, measurement and the development of policy.

> Any statement of policy to reduce poverty contains an implicit if not explicit explanation of its cause. Any explanation of poverty contains an implicit prescription for policy. Any conceptualisation of poverty contains an implicit explanation of the phenomenon. (1979: 64)

---

[1]   http://www.un.org/millenniumgoals/poverty.shtml, accessed March 4, 2019.

How we define poverty reveals what we think its cause(s) to be and thus, what solutions are needed to tackle it. Narrow definitions of poverty, focusing solely on economic resources or material circumstances, will suggest a very different set of anti-poverty policies than broader definitions, which identify structural processes, power imbalances, and the deprivation of basic material and social needs (Lister, 2004, Alcock, 1993). Townsend's work on poverty and deprivation shaped international and official definitions and agreements on poverty, from the UN to the EU (Townsend, 1993). In arguing that poverty was a relative concept, and defined with reference to time and place, he argued that comparable, reliable, valid and socially realistic measures of poverty could be developed and applied across high, middle and low-income countries (Gordon and Nandy, 2016).

In this chapter we show a practical method to achieve precisely this for child poverty as conceptualised in the rest of the chapters in this book, using data from household surveys in Benin, Gabon, Guinea, Liberia, and Mali.

EVOLVING DEFINITIONS AND MEASURES OF POVERTY

The history of scientific research on poverty, conducted in both rich and poor countries, is long (Booth, 1893; Rowntree, 1901; Naoroji, 1901). While many early studies equated poverty with insufficient resources to maintain minimal or basic levels of subsistence, significant academic work over the past half-century, by sociologists like Townsend (1954, 1970, 1979) and economists like Sen (1987, 1999), have demonstrated that poverty must be measured by much more than simply the ability to feed oneself and one's family. People, wherever they are in the world, value being able to participate in social activities and norms. Recognition of the importance and impact of exclusion from social norms or customary activities (Chase and Walker, 2013) led to the expansion of definitions of poverty in order to incorporate aspects of social participation, which early studies neglected. Concepts and definitions of poverty now routinely acknowledge that it needs to be measured relative to time and place rather than simply using a fixed low income (Anand et al., 2010).

Official European definitions of poverty have long made clear its relativity; in 1975 the European Council defined poverty as "individuals or families whose resources are so small as to exclude them from the minimum acceptable way of life of the Member State in which they live" (Council Decision, 1975). The definition was updated in 1985, with clarification that "resources" which people required were more than solely financial: "the poor shall be taken to mean persons, families and groups of persons whose resources (material, cultural and social) are so limited as to exclude them from the minimal acceptable way of life in the Member state in which they live" (EEC, 1985). Other international definitions of poverty, such as that adopted by 117 governments at the 1995 World Summit on Social Development (WSSD) also reflect the relative nature of poverty, making reference to minimally acceptable standards of living (i.e. going beyond a set basket of goods). The WSSD defined "overall poverty" as:

> ...lack of income and productive resources to ensure sustainable livelihoods; hunger and malnutrition; ill health; limited or lack of access to education and other basic services; increased morbidity and mortality from illness; homelessness and inadequate housing; unsafe environments and social discrimination and exclusion. It is also characterised by a lack of participation in decision-making and in civil, social and cultural life. (United Nations, 1995).

Equally applicable to both high and low-income countries, it provides the theoretical and methodological basis for comparable, relative measures of poverty.

Despite these internationally agreed definitions, most studies and estimates of poverty in low-income countries and regions continue to rely on minimal or absolute measures (Iliffe, 1987; Hall and Midgley, 2004). Official poverty lines traditionally use calorie monetary measures based on 19th century understandings of minimum nutritional needs, and thus fail to reflect important non-material, social or participation dimensions of poverty, or even the need for an adequate and nutritionally balanced diet. Studies often rely on data about economic activity or productivity which, for many countries in Africa, are known to be seriously flawed (Jerven, 2013). Whereas a range of alternative indicators have been developed, such as the UNDP's Human Poverty Index (UNDP, 1997) and its successor, the Multidimensional Poverty Index (Alkire and Santos, 2010), the use of these new scales have been limited, either because of their reliance on aggregate data, and/or because they have been criticised on methodological and conceptual grounds (McGillivray, 1991; Gordon and Nandy, 2012).

In the past decade or so, efforts have been made to expand the definition and measurement of poverty, using relative and non-monetary measures (Statistics South Africa, 2012; INSAE, 2007; Kingdon and Knight, 2006; Klasen, 2000; Sahn and Younger, 2010), but these were limited to a handful of countries, or limited by a reliance on aggregated national level data. Thus, it remains the case that a majority of poverty studies, which adopt a relativist approach, have been conducted in middle and high-income countries; studies of poverty in Africa and Asia continue to use absolute approaches and indicators, with lower thresholds devised by experts in entirely different contexts and times.

Another change in the way poverty is measured has been through the growing use of welfare outcome indicators, which reflect and relate to people's actual living conditions or standards in contexts of poverty (Alkire and Santos, 2010). As such, measures to reflect the quality of peoples' dwellings, levels of overcrowding, access to basic services like water, sanitation, healthcare and education, all of which are central to internationally accepted definitions of poverty, now form the basis of many national and international poverty studies, including ones like UNICEF's recent Global Study of Child Poverty and Disparities (Fajth et al., 2012), which has been conducted across 45 countries. The widening of definitions and measures has meant that poverty, in its different manifestations, can be reflected in a more nuanced manner, so that studies can now use a variety of methods and tools to reflect the different dimensions of poverty. Although the breadth and depth of the indicators used to build these measures vary significantly, what is certain is that academics, researchers and policy makers all acknowledge the value of moving beyond a reliance on out-dated, narrow, solely money-metric measures (World Bank, 2016). The time has come for a change in the way poverty in low income countries is defined and assessed, and for tried and tested methods used successfully in rich countries to be applied in an appropriate manner to improve poverty measurement globally. Extreme poverty for the purposes of the MDGs was narrowly defined, using the World Bank's so-called "dollar a day" indicator; the same narrow indicator has been retained for target 1.1 of the first SDG, which is: "By

2030, eradicate extreme poverty for all people everywhere, currently measured as people living on less than $1.25 a day."[2]

Of interest for poverty researchers is SDG target 1.2, which is: "By 2030, reduce at least by half the proportion of men, women and children of all ages living in poverty in all its dimensions according to national definitions."[3] Two indicators are proposed for this SDG target: 1.2.1 measures "the proportion of population living below the national poverty line, by sex and age" and 1.2.2 looks at "the proportion of men, women and children of all ages living in poverty in all its dimensions according to national definitions".

While much in this is familiar (i.e. a focus on low income, and the use of national poverty lines), target 1.2 nevertheless presents a real opportunity to fundamentally change the way global poverty is conceptualised and assessed. Not only does it call for separate poverty estimates for children and adults, it also determines that the levels of poverty be reflected on more broadly, in all its dimensions, and importantly, according to national definitions. Collecting data to meaningfully monitor target 1.2.2 will be a challenge, given how broadly poverty could be defined "in all its dimensions," across nearly two hundred countries. However, for many years, poverty researchers have developed and been using methods, which can do just this.

THE CONSENSUAL APPROACH TO POVERTY MEASUREMENT

Townsend's seminal work Poverty in the UK (1979), and his theory of poverty as relative deprivation, has formed the basis for many modern studies of poverty, including the 2012 study Poverty and Social Exclusion in the UK.[4] Building on Townsend's work, Mack and Lansley (1985) developed and implemented what is now called the Consensual Approach (CA). Their aim was to seek public consensus about what was an unacceptable standard of living (in the UK), and to discover if anyone fell below that standard. Their contribution, and methodological innovation, was to give the public a voice in the process of defining what poverty was, and in doing so, suggesting how it might be measured. They demonstrated

---

2   http://indicators.report/targets/1-1/, accessed March 4, 2019.
3   http://indicators.report/targets/1-2/, accessed March 4, 2019.
4   www.poverty.ac.uk, accessed March 4, 2019.

that the public were unanimous about the fact that minimum standards of living needed to go beyond basic food and shelter, to include elements such as social activities and cultural/civic participation. Using focus groups of the public to devise a list of items and activities which everyone in the UK was expected to be able to own or do, and not be prevented from owning or doing due to a lack of resources, Mack and Lansley developed a questionnaire which asked a nationally-representative sample of respondents which items and activities they considered "were necessary and which all people should be able to afford, and which they should not have to do without." Respondents were also asked about whether they owned/did the items/activities on the list, and if not, if it was because they did not want them, or because they could not afford them. Respondents unable to afford to own/do items/activities considered "necessary" by most respondents (i.e. 50 percent or more) were considered deprived of social perceived necessities (SPNs). SPNs were produced for both individuals and households.

Mack and Lansley's work made a significant impact, inspiring similar studies around the world. They demonstrated that there was a high degree of consensus about what constituted minimally acceptable standards of living and SPNs across different social and economic groups, and also that a significant proportion of people in Britain lacked these because they could not afford them: 13.8 percent, 7.5 million people, were deprived of three or more necessities (1985). The establishment of SPNs through the Consensual Approach, however, was not without its critics. For example, Walker (1987) argued the set of items respondents are asked to rate are unlikely to be an exhaustive list of every item and activity which people deem essential. Moreover, he argued that surveys are limited in their ability to reflect socially perceived items. This can only truly happen when respondents are given the opportunity to "...listen to the views of others and to discuss "with them" (1987: p. 219) and not through an individually-administered questionnaire. He therefore argued for the use of qualitative techniques to explore the validity of the consensual approach as well as establishing a definition of poverty. More recently McKay (2004) challenged the idea that the Consensual Approach studies show actual consensus about which items people should have. Indeed, "majoritarian" might be a more accurate way of describing this approach; McKay argued that consensus implies that the clear majority of respondents would identify exactly the same set of items as necessary or not necessary, whereas Mack and Lansley's approach has the more modest aim of establishing which individual items are endorsed by the majority. Moreover, as Walker pointed out, input from other methodologies apart from social surveys is indeed important, and social scientists should strive to include in social surveys a wide range of goods and services, which the population can decide to endorse, or not. Despite these potential issues, it is hard to deny that establishing a range of possession, goods and services, which most adults, regardless of education, social and cultural backgrounds, endorse as necessary, can at least contribute to the articulation of a concept of poverty; which is underpinned by the concepts of democracy and citizenship (Veit Wilson, 1987).

To date, the Consensual Approach has been applied successfully in several high-income countries including all 28 European Union countries (EUROSTAT, 2012), as well as in national studies in Belgium (Van den Bosch, 2001), Finland (Halleröd et al., 2006), Sweden (Halleröd, 1994; Halleröd, 1995), Japan (Abe and Pantazis, 2013) and Australia (Saunders, 2011). Researchers have also applied the approach in a series of LMICs including Bangladesh (Mahbub Uddin Ahmed, 2007), Benin (Nandy and Pomati, 2016), Vietnam (Davies and Smith, 1998), Mali (Nteziyaremye and MkNelly, 2001), Tanzania (Kaijage and Tibaijuka, 1996), South Africa (Noble et al., 2004, Wright, 2008) and Zimbabwe (Mtapuri, 2011). More recently (2016/2017), countries as geographically diverse as the Solomon Islands and Tonga in the South Pacific, and Uganda in Africa, have run consensual poverty question modules in national household surveys. Researchers will consequently be able to analyse data on socially perceived necessities alongside information about household income and expenditure, as has been done elsewhere (Halleröd et al., 2006; Pantazis et al., 2006).

While each of the studies run in low-income countries has successfully demonstrated the merits of the Consensual Approach, each is only a single country study; what would be valuable in assessing whether the Consensual Approach would be a useful method for collecting data is to monitor progress towards SDG 1.2 as a cross-national study, which uses the same (or similar) survey instrument across a set of low-income countries. Such data would show whether consensus exists across societies about what people consider to be essential/necessary for a "decent" standard of living, or in the words of the SDGs, what poverty "in all its dimensions" looks like. This could then form the basis of a nationally agreed, democratic definition of multidimensional poverty, which is what SDG target 1.2 requires.

CROSS-NATIONAL, COMPARATIVE DATA ON SOCIALLY PERCEIVED NECESSITIES

The theoretical basis and key assumptions of the Consensual Approach were set out above. We can now show, using data collected by World Bank-funded national surveys, how the Consensual Approach can be used to demonstrate consensus both across and within countries about socially perceived necessities. We have previously detailed (Nandy and Pomati, 2016) how data from the 2006 EMICOV (INSAE, 2007) survey for Benin can be used to develop an index of socially perceived necessities (SPNs), which can then be used to assess the extent and patterning of multidimensional poverty. We subsequently discovered that a similar module of questions on subjective poverty was also distributed in other countries, as part of the Core Welfare Indicator Questionnaire programme (CWIQ) (Ajayi, 2006). These countries included Benin (2006), Gabon (2005), Guinea (2007), Liberia (2007, 2010), and Mali (2006). Data from these surveys was not freely available in the way DHS or MICS data are, and so accessing the data was only made possible through the kind collaboration of staff in the national statistical offices of Liberia and Mali.[5] [6]

The CWIQ surveys investigate peoples' living conditions with regards to the following themes: clothing; food; housing; health care; transport; work and education; and leisure. These are all areas that a meaningful multidimensional measure of poverty would need to reflect. The 2016 report of the Global Commission on Poverty agrees on a similar list of themes that should serve as a starting point, including nutrition,

---

[5]   We would also like to acknowledge the kind support of UNICEF country offices in Mali and Liberia in helping us get access to the data.

[6]   Full details about the CWIQ surveys in each country can be obtained from the International Household Survey Network (IHSN, www.ihsn.org/), where all metadata (questionnaires, sampling details, etc.) and other relevant information about these surveys is deposited.

health status, education, housing, access to work and personal security (World Bank, 2016: p. 158). The CWIQ survey asks respondents two key questions about a list of items:

- Do you feel that the following items are necessary to maintain a minimum standard of living?
- Are you satisfied that your household meets minimum needs such as …?

Responses to these questions can be used to gauge: (i) what people in different countries think is necessary for a minimum standard of living; (ii) whether there is consensus across and within countries about what constitutes a minimum standard of living; and (iii) to what extent people are deprived of a socially-defined minimum standard of living.

The bar charts presented below (Chart 1) show responses from research participants in five West African countries — Benin, Guinea, Gabon, Liberia, and Mali — about whether each item/activity is necessary to maintain a minimum standard of living. Items are grouped according to the themes discussed above. Note that not all countries asked questions for all items, and so there are gaps in the charts.

Chart 1:   **Clothing and household items**

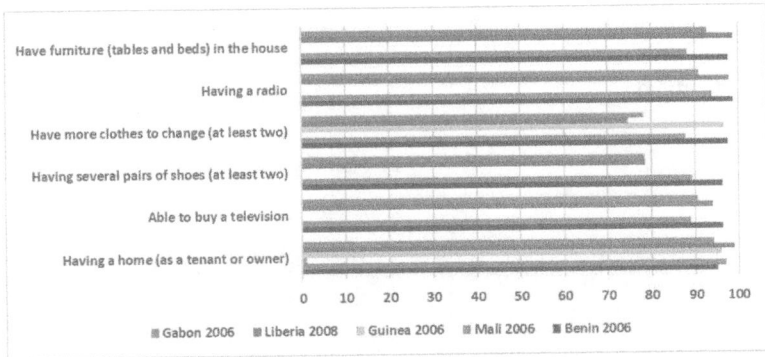

Food-related items and activities

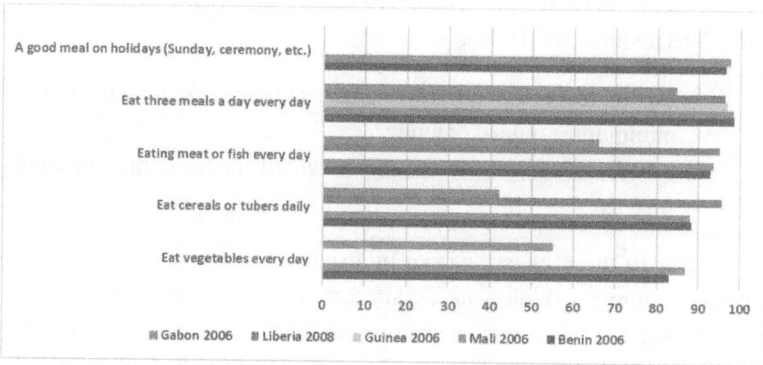

Education and work

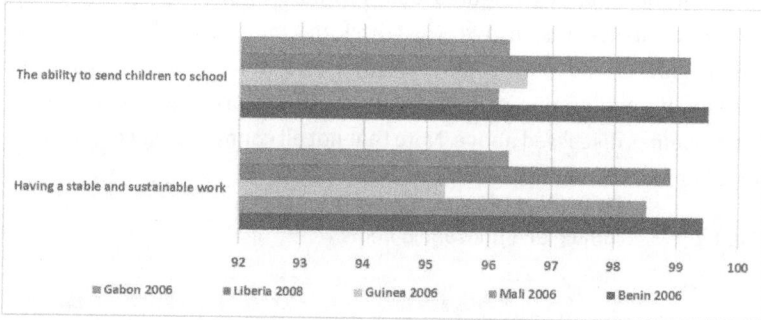

Transportation

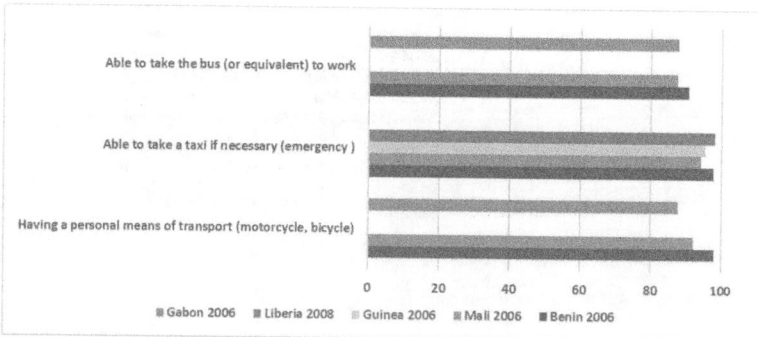

Basic services

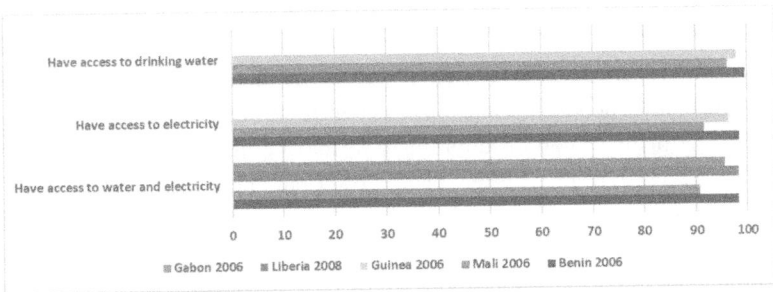

Health and hygiene

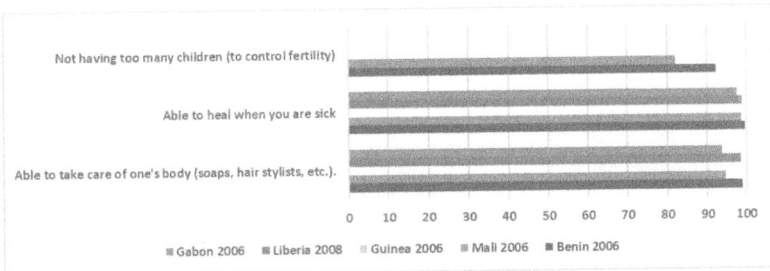

Source: Authors' estimates based on CWIQ surveys

While the items in these particular surveys were not categorised or grouped in terms of the constitutive rights of poverty used in the other chapters in this volume, it would be very simple to design questionnaires that would specifically capture what people[7] actually consider important as a minimum to satisfy those rights. Moreover, what these charts demonstrate is that there is consensus across countries about these items, with near unanimous agreement about what contributes to a minimum standard of living. Over 70 percent of respondents reported that each of these items are necessities. The one exception is Gabon, where less than 50 percent reported that being able to eat cereals/tubers/rice every day was in fact not necessary.

    While international consensus is clearly a target, it is also important that consensus within countries, across different geographic and social groups, be demonstrated. To avoid repetition, we use data from two of

---

[7]   And not just all people in general but children in particular.

these countries — Mali and Benin — to demonstrate how consensus holds across different groups within countries. Chart 2 below demonstrates, in both countries, the proportion of people considering items/activities as necessary, vary according to age, education, region or residence, as well as to whether people live in rural or urban areas.[8] For each of these groups we look at the range of minimum and maximum endorsement of each item as a necessity. The left end of each bar therefore represents the lowest level of endorsement, while the right end represents the highest one. The bars represent the range of responses to the question about individual items being necessary; short bars represent less difference in responses, and long bars represent a greater difference in responses. For example, in Benin the regional endorsement ranges between 94 percent in Alibori to 100 percent in Littoral. In Mali, the regional variation is larger (as shown in the longer bar): it ranges from 69 percent in Gao to 98 percent in Bamako. By omitting the names of the regions and other group categories we can focus more easily on the variation and minimum levels of endorsement.

While some variation is expected, it is minimal, especially when we consider potential differences in outlook and living conditions of adults in different age, education, and rural/urban residence groups. The area of greatest variation is geographic region; the longer bars in Mali suggest greater differences between regions concerning what items are necessary for a minimum standard of living. However, what is most important to note is that in no instance do any bars go below the 50 percent mark. This means that most people in these countries, whether young or old, educated or not, living in a rural or urban setting, think these items are important.

---

[8]   Gender differences in responses were negligible across all items (i.e. less than five percentage points)

Chart 2:   Demonstrating sub-national consensus in Mali and Benin

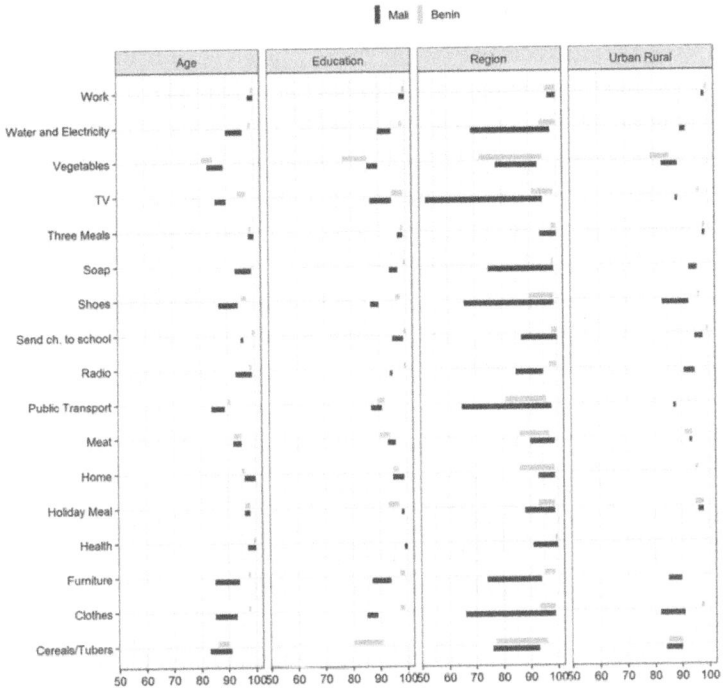

Authors' estimates based on CWIQ surveys

Critics of the Consensual Approach rightly raise the issue of Adaptive Preferences. The theory of Adaptive Preferences posits that poor or deprived people may lower their expectations of what they might otherwise be entitled to (e.g. to receive an education, to gainful employment, to health care when sick and support in times of need); and these lower (or bounded) horizons effectively underplay what they think are the necessities of life for society. As Nussbaum reasonably argues,

> ... people's desires and preferences respond to their beliefs about norms and about their own opportunities. Thus, people usually adjust their desires to reflect the level of their available possibilities... People from groups that have not, persistently, had access to education, or employment outside the home, may be slow to desire these things because they may not know what they are like or what they could possibly mean in lives like theirs. (1999: p. 11)

Thus, the poor are effectively discouraged from demanding radical change or higher norms or standards to meet expert opinions (of peoples' needs), and instead accept their circumstances out of necessity (Sen, 1992). This, it is claimed, is a potential source of bias in that it results in a constrained expression of what social norms really are or should be, rendering them unreliable. Adaptive preferences are important for poverty research and, despite their consideration by academics (Burchardt, 2004; Wright and Noble, 2013; Halleröd, 2006; Nandy and Pomati, 2016) there remains a degree of uncertainty as to whether they operate universally or only in certain contexts.

Chart 3 below provides some evidence about the existence (or lack) of adaptive preferences in Mali and Benin. Using CWIQ data, we plot the relative risk ratios for different groups of poor and non-poor considering individual items as necessities for a minimum standard of living, along with their 95 percent confidence intervals (CIs). Relative risk ratios show the probability, or risk, of one group thinking an item to be essential compared to another group. A relative risk of 2 means that one group is twice as likely to consider the item as necessary compared to the other. Similarly, a relative risk of 0.5 implies the first group is half as likely to consider an item as necessary, etc. Where CIs cross 1, there is no significant difference between poor and non-poor respondents.

Chart 3:   Demonstrating consensus between rich and poor in Benin and Mali

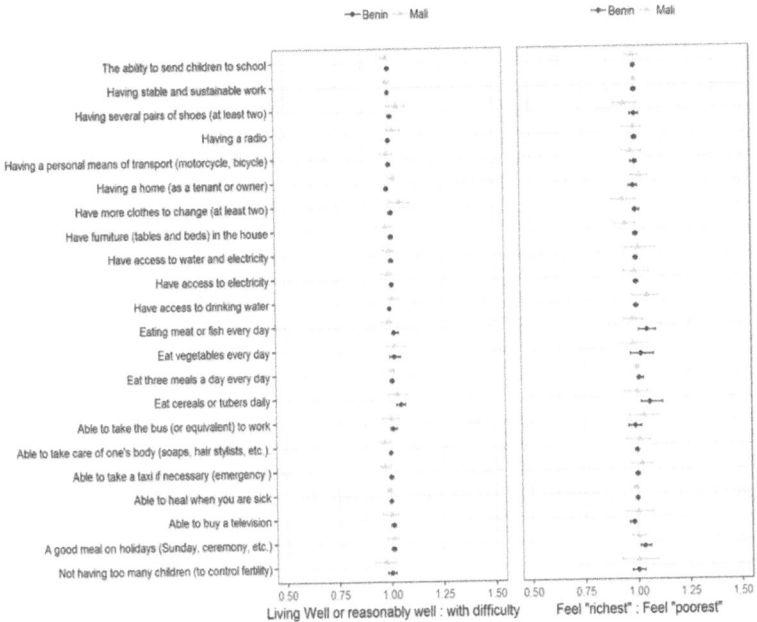

Authors' estimates based on CWIQ surveys

Chart 3 shows that there are few, if any, differences between respondents who reported they were "living well or reasonable well" and those who reported they were living "with difficulty" (a self-reported, subjective evaluation of living conditions); likewise, there was little difference between those who saw themselves as being among the poorest and the richest in their respective communities. Most of the relative risks are very close to 1 and only few are statistically significant. Where they are statistically significant, they are below 1.10 or above 0.90, indicating very small differences in endorsement of items as necessities between respondents with different levels of living standards, whether objective or subjective. We repeated the same analysis comparing respondents who can save money, as compared with those who go into debt; and those with stable incomes as compared with those with unstable ones. We found very similar results. In conjunction with Chart 3, showing sub-national consensus, this data demonstrates a high degree of consensus and agreement about what constitutes a minimum standard of living. The Consensual Approach therefore provides a useful and reliable means for generating data about nationally defined measures of multidimensional poverty, as required by SDG 1.2.

DEPRIVATION OF SOCIALLY PERCEIVED NECESSITIES (SPNs)

The CWIQ surveys also ask if households can meet their minimum needs; those unable to meet these needs can be said to be deprived of SPNs for an acceptable standard of living. Again, using CWIQ data for Benin and Mali, we show differences in the extent to which people are deprived of SPNs. For Benin, there are relative low rates of deprivation for clothing and food items (<15 percent), but higher rates for items like basic services and household items (e.g. electricity, furniture, transport). In Mali, the picture is very similar, but much larger sections of the population are deprived of food-related items, at or around 20 percent (Chart 4).

Chart 4:   Deprivation of socially perceived necessities in Benin and Mali

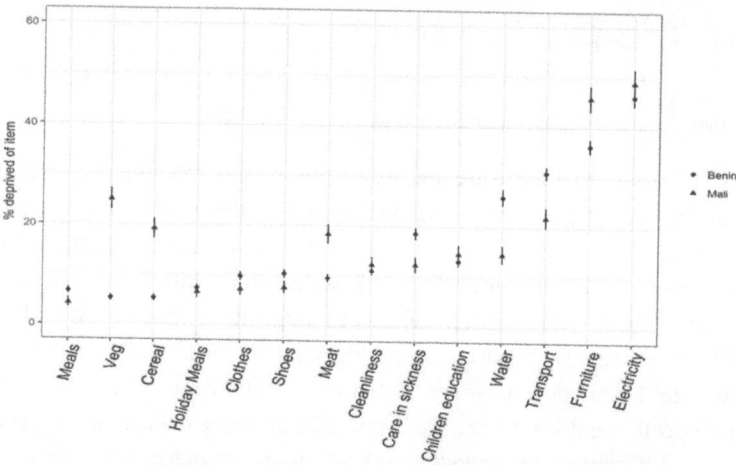

This information could be used to create a comparable index of deprivation of SPNs, and thus to reflect nationally defined measures of multidimensional poverty. Some countries have gone beyond what has been done in CWIQ surveys and are asking questions with regards to the needs of children and adults separately, which, again, is what SDG 1.2 requires. This is now happening in some countries of the South Pacific (e.g. Solomon Islands, Tonga, Tuvalu), and in Uganda, where the 2017 National Household Survey includes a module of questions that use the Consensual Approach.

Well-established research programmes from different academic fields (e.g. the METAGORA (OECD, 2008) and AFROBAROMETER projects[9]) have contributed to our understanding of people's perceptions of democracy and human rights in Africa. We also gain insight into people's (dis)satisfaction with government provision of basic services, and their own economic and political priorities. Other established survey programmes running in most countries in Africa, such as UNICEF's Multiple Indicator Cluster Surveys (MICS[10]) and USAID's Demographic and Health Survey (DHS[11]), collect valuable information about people's living conditions, and are increasingly being used by researchers to study multidimensional poverty (Gordon et al., 2003; Nandy and Gordon, 2009; Alkire and Santos, 2010); the data can also be used to highlight the links between poverty and other issues, such as quality of governance (Halleröd et al., 2013). These survey platforms provide an opportunity to collect cross-national data about multidimensional poverty for the SDGs, thereby coinciding with the inclusion of question modules to national Household Income and Expenditure Surveys (HIES), which has already begun.

CONCLUSIONS

Extreme poverty remains a global challenge, which the SDGs recognise. In calling for the eradication of poverty "in all its dimensions," SDG 1.2 goes beyond the MDGs, requiring governments and international organisations to collect more disaggregated data on poverty, based on national definitions. This chapter has shown how this can be done in a reliable and valid fashion, incorporating people's voices (including children's) to find out what are the thresholds to be used to determine severe, moderate, and mild deprivations along the various dimensions comprising poverty. Moreover, this approach is particularly helpful to

---

9   www.afrobarometer.org
10   www.childinfo.org
11   www.measuredhs.com

estimate multidimensional poverty as it goes beyond lack of affordability to also include lack of access to publicly provided services.

Increasingly, studies are beginning to identify the necessities of life, or minimum standards of living, using consensual approaches. However, to date these have been isolated examples; international comparisons between countries with heterogeneous societies are relatively rare. Our analyses demonstrate it should be possible to develop agreed international standards and norms for items, which reflect a minimally acceptable standard of living, which applies across countries, in order to estimate child poverty based on constitutive rights. Or, to put it another way, to go from measures which show "what is" to "what could be".

REFERENCES

Abe, A. & Pantazis, C. 2013. Comparing Public Perceptions of the Necessities of Life across Two Societies: Japan and the United Kingdom. *Social Policy and Society,* 13, 69-88.

Ajayi, O. O. 2006. Experiences in the Application of the Core Welfare Indicator Questionnaire (CWIQ) Survey Technology in Africa: The Journey So Far. *The African Statistical Journal/Le Journal Statistique Africain,* 3, 189-210.

Alcock, P. 1993. *Understanding poverty,* Basingstoke, The Macmillan Press.

Alkire, S. & Santos, M. E. 2010. Acute Multidimensional Poverty: A New Index for Developing Countries. *OPHI Working Paper Nr. 38.* Oxford, Oxford University.

Anand, S., Segal, P. & Stiglitz, J. E. (eds.) 2010. *Debates on the measurement of global poverty,* Oxford: Oxford University Press.

Booth, C. 1893. Life and Labour of the People in London: First Results of an Enquiry based on the 1891 Census. *Journal of the Royal Statistical Society,* LIV, 600-643.

Burchardt, T. 2004. Are one man's rags another man's riches? Identifying adaptive expectations using panel data. London: Centre for Analysis of Social Exclusion, London School of Economics.

Chandy, L. & Gertz, G. 2011. Poverty in Numbers: The Changing State of Global Poverty from 2005 to 2015. Washington D.C.: The Brookings Institution.

Chase, E. & Walker, R. 2013. The Co-construction of Shame in the Context of Poverty: Beyond a Threat to the Social Bond. *Sociology,* 47, 739-753.

Coucil Decision 1975. 75/458/EEC of 22nd July 1975 - Concerning a programme of pilot schemes and studies to combat poverty *In:* European Commission (ed.) *OLJ 99/3430.7.75.*

Davies, R. & Smith, W. 1998. The Basic Necessities Survey: The Experience of Action Aid in Vietnam. London: Action Aid.

EEC 1985. On specific Community action to combat poverty (Council Decision of 19 December, 1984) 85/8/E.E.C.,. *Official Journal of the European Communities*, 2/24.

Eurostat 2012. Measuring material deprivation in the EU: Indicators for the whole population and child-specific indicators. Luxembourg: European Commission.

Fajth, G., Kurukulasuriya, S. & Engilbertsdottir, S. 2012. A Multidimensional Response to Tackling Child Poverty and Disparities: Reflections from the Global Study on Child Poverty and Disparities. *In:* Minujin, A. & Nandy, S. (eds.) *Global Child Poverty and Well-Being: Measurement, Concepts, Policy and Action*. Bristol: The Policy Press.

Gordon, D. & Nandy, S. 2012. Measuring child poverty and deprivation. *In:* Minujin, A. & Nandy, S. (eds.) *Global Child Poverty and Well-Being: Measurement, Concepts, Policy and Action*. Bristol: The Policy Press.

Gordon, D. & Nandy, S. 2016. Policy-relevant measurement of poverty in low, middle and high income countries. *In:* Braathen, E., May, J., Wrights, G. & Ulriksen, M. (eds.) *Poverty and Inequality in Middle Income Countries: Policy Achievements, Political Obstacles*. London: Zed Books.

Gordon, D., Nandy, S., Pantazis, C., Pemberton, S. & Townsend, P. 2003. *Child Poverty in the Developing World*, Bristol, The Policy Press.

Hall, A. J. & Midgley, J. 2004. *Social Policy for Development*, London, Sage Publications Ltd.

Halleröd, B. 1994. A New Approach to Direct Consensual Measurement of Poverty.: Social Policy Research Centre, University of New South Wales.

Halleröd, B. 1995. The Truly Poor: Indirect and Direct Measurement of Consensual Poverty in Sweden. *Journal of European Social Policy*, 5, 111-129.

Halleröd, B. 2006. Sour Grapes: Relative Deprivation, Adaptive Preferences and the Measurement of Poverty. *Journal of Social Policy*, 35, 371-390.

Halleröd, B., Larsson, D., Gordon, D. & Ritakallio, V. M. 2006. Relative deprivation: a comparative analysis of Britain, Finland and Sweden. *Journal of European Social Policy*, 16, 328-345.

Halleröd, B., Rothstein, B., Adel, D. & Nandy, S. 2013. Bad Governance and Poor Children: A Comparative analysis of government efficiency and severe child deprivation in 68 low- and middle-income countries. *World Development*, 48, 19-31.

Iliffe, J. 1987. *The African Poor: A History*, Cambridge, Cambridge University Press.

Insae 2007. Enquete modulaire integree sur les conditons de vie des menages (EMICov) Benin. Cotonou: Insae.

Jerven, M. 2013. *Poor Numbers: How we are misled by African development statistics and what to do about it*, Ithaca, Cornell University Press.

Kaijage, F. & Tibaijuka, A. 1996. Poverty and Social Exclusion in Tanzania. *Research Series No.109*. Geneva: IILS.

Kingdon, G. & Knight, J. 2006. Subjective well-being poverty vs. income poverty and capabilities poverty? *Journal of Development Studies*, 42, 1199-1224.

Klasen, S. 2000. Measuring poverty and deprivation in South Africa. *Review of Income and Wealth,* 46, 33-58.

Lister, R. 2004. *Poverty,* Cambridge, Polity Press.

Mack, J. & Lansley, S. 1985. *Poor Britain,* London, Allen and Unwin.

Mahbub Uddin Ahmed, A. I. 2007. Consensual poverty in Britain, Sweden and Bangladesh: A Comparative Study. *Bangladesh e-Journal of Sociology,* 4, 56-77.

McGillivray, M. 1991. The Human Development Index: Yet another redundant composite development indicator. *World Development,* 19, 1461-1468.

McKay, S. 2004. Poverty or preference: What do 'consensual deprivation indicators' really measure? *Fiscal Studies,* 25, 201-223.

Mtapuri, O. 2011. Developing and asset threshold using the consensual approach: results from Mashonaland West, Zimbabwe. *Journal of International Development,* 23, 29-41.

Nandy, S. & Gordon, D. 2009. Children Living in Squalor: Shelter, Water and Sanitation Deprivations in Developing Countries. *Children, Youth and Environments,* 19, 202-228.

Nandy, S. & Pomati, M. 2016. Applying the Consensual Method of Estimating Poverty in a Low Income African Setting. *Social Indicators Research,* 124, 693-726.

Naoroji, D. 1901. *Poverty and Un-British Rule in India,* London, Swan Sonnenschein & Co. Ltd.

Noble, M., Ratcliffe, A. & Wright, G. 2004. Conceptualizing, Defining and Measuring Poverty in South Africa: An Argument for a Consensual Approach. Oxford: Centre for the Analysis of South African Social Policy, University of Oxford.

Nteziyaremye, A. & Mknelly, B. 2001. Mali Poverty Outreach Study of the Kafo Jiginew and Nyesigiso Credit and Savings with Education Programs. Davis, CA: Freedom from Hunger.

Nussbaum, M. 1999. *Sex and Social Justice,* New York, Oxford University Press.

OECD 2008. Measuring Human Rights and Democratic Governance: Experiences and Lessons from Metagora *OECD Journal on Development,* 9.

Pantazis, C., Gordon, D. & Levitas, R. 2006. *Poverty and social exclusion in Britain: the Millennium Survey,* Bristol, The Policy Press.

Pinkonvskiy, M. & Sala-i-Martin, X. 2010. African Poverty is Falling .... Much Faster than You think. New York: Columbia University and the National Bureau for Economic Research.

Reddy, S. & Pogge, T. 2002. How not to count the poor. New York: Columbia University.

Rowntree, S. B. 1901. *Poverty: A Study of Town Life,* London, Macmillan.

Sahn, D. & Younger, S. D. 2010. Living Standards in Africa. *In:* Anand, S., Segal, P. & Stiglitz, J. E. (eds.) *Debates on the Measurement of Global Poverty.* Oxford: Oxford University Press.

Saunders, P. 2011. *Down and Out: Poverty and Exclusion in Australia,* Bristol, The Policy Press.

Sen, A. 1987. *The standard of living,* Cambridge, Cambridge University Press.

Sen, A. 1992. *Inequality Re-examined,* Oxford, Clarendon Press.

Sen, A. 1999. *Development as freedom,* Oxford, Oxford University Press.

Statistics South Africa 2012. Subjective Poverty in South Africa: Findings of the Living Conditions Survey 2008/2009. Pretoria: Statistics South Africa.

Townsend, P. 1954. Measuring poverty. *British Journal of Sociology,* 5, 130-137.

Townsend, P. 1970. *The concept of poverty,* London, Heinemann.

Townsend, P. 1979. *Poverty in the United Kingdom,* Harmondsworth, Penguin Books Ltd.

Townsend, P. 1993. *The International Analysis of Poverty,* Milton Keynes, Harvester Wheatsheaf.

Townsend, P., Gordon, D. & Pantazis, C. 2006. The international measurement of 'absolute' and 'overall' poverty: applying the 1995 Copenhagen definitions to Britain. *In:* Pantazis, C., Gordon, D. & Levitas, R. (eds.) *Poverty and Social Exclusion in Britain: The Millennium Survey.* Bristol: The Policy Press.

UNDP 1997. *Human Development Report 1997:Human development to eradicate poverty,* New York, Oxford University Press.

United Nations 1995. The Copenhagen declaration and programme of action: world summit for social development 6-12 March 1995. New York: United Nations.

United Nations 2015. The Millennium Development Goals Report 2015. New York City: United Nations.

Van den Bosch, K. 2001. *Indentifying the poor: Using subjective and consensual measures,* Aldershot, Ashgate.

Vandemoortele, J. 2002. Are we really reducing global poverty? *In:* Townsend, P. & Gordon, D. (eds.) *World Poverty: new policies to defeat an old enemy.* Bristol: The Policy Press.

Veit Wilson, J. 1987. Consensual Approaches to Poverty Lines and Social Security. *Journal of Social Policy,* 16, 183-211.

Walker, R. 1987. Consensual Approaches to the Definition of Poverty: Towards an Alternative Methodology. *Journal of Social Policy,* 16, 213-225.

Watkins, K. 2013. Leaving no-one behind: an equity agenda for the post-2015 goals. *In:* Overseas Development Institute (ed.). London: ODI.

World Bank 2016. Monitoring Global Poverty: Report of the Commission on Global Poverty. Washington D.C.,: World Bank.

Wright, G. 2008. Findings from the Indicators of Poverty and Social Exclusion Project: A Profile of Poverty using the Socially Perceived Necessities Approach: Key Report 7. Pretoria: Department of Social Development, Republic of South Africa.

Wright, G. & Noble, M. 2013. Does Widespread Lack Undermine the Socially Perceived Necessities Approach to Defining Poverty? Evidence from South Africa *Journal of Social Policy,* 42, 147-165.Baiphethi MN and PT Jacobs 2009. "The Contribution of Subsistance Farming to Food Security in South Africa" in *Agrekon,* Vol. 48 (4).

CHAPTER 4

MULTIDIMENSIONAL CHILD POVERTY AND CHILD WELL-BEING IN CAMEROON, CÔTE D'IVOIRE, AND NIGERIA

Ismael Cid-Martinez

INTRODUCTION

This chapter offers three extensions or innovations in the analysis of child poverty. First, it explores the impact on child poverty estimates of adding the right to play dimension, in a way that is consistent with measurement of deprivation in other rights. Second, it introduces a way to show simultaneously all combinations of deprivations as part of the discussion on depth and severity of poverty. And third, the article depicts the correlation between child poverty and other rights violations to assess not just the impact of the level of child poverty, but also of the depth of deprivations (thus, explicitly linking child poverty to equity analysis). This is done with the latest available survey data for Cameroon, Côte d'Ivoire, and Nigeria, which are three of the largest countries in the region, one Anglophone and two Francophone. In addition, time trends and geographic disaggregation of child poverty estimates are provided.

In Part II, the analysis of multidimensional child poverty time trends for Cameroon, Côte d'Ivoire and Nigeria are presented. Changes in the extent of severe deprivation by dimension are also examined as well as the geographic distribution of child poverty. In Part III, a novel way to describe the profile of poverty is introduced. It shows all possible combinations of multiple deprivations, which is a useful tool to analyse where to focus public policies. The correlation, along an equity-based profile of child poverty, with other child rights violations, is also included in this section. In Part IV, a broader definition of child poverty that captures a material deprivation associated with the violation of a child's right to engage in play, as enshrined in Article 31 of the Convention on the Rights of the Child (CRC), is explored. Thresholds for capturing severe, moderate, and mild deprivation in this dimension with available survey data are provided prior to assessing the impact of this additional dimension on the overall level of child poverty (sensitivity analysis). Part V concludes the chapter with some recommendations for further research.

II.   MULTIDIMENSIONAL CHILD POVERTY IN CAMEROON, CÔTE D'IVOIRE AND NIGERIA

Incidence of child poverty since the early 2000s

Gordon et al. (2003) find that by the turn of the 21st century, four out of five children in sub-Saharan Africa suffered from at least one severe deprivation. Nigeria fared no differently. Cameroon and Côte d'Ivoire were only marginally better (see Figure 1). In some dimensions, Côte d'Ivoire and Nigeria performed even worse than the rest of the region. The share of children not vaccinated against any disease, or who did not receive any medical care following a recent illness, were noticeably higher in Nigeria than in the rest of sub-Saharan Africa. The percentage of children not attending school was higher in Côte d'Ivoire than in the rest of the region. However, none of the three countries outpaced others one across all (or the majority) of the indicators.

Figure 1:   Share of children in poverty and suffering from severe deprivation by dimension (circa 2000)

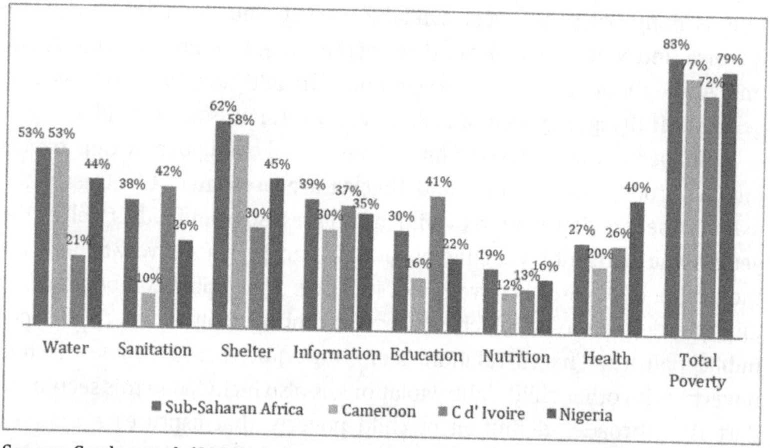

Source: Gordon et al. (2003)

A decade later, none of the three countries have been able to make a major dent on child poverty (Figure 2). Côte d'Ivoire seems to have made the most progress in reducing the overall incidence of child poverty by more than 10 percentage points (and close to 15 percent) since 2000. Despite this progress, well more than half of all children in the country continue to suffer from at least one rights violation. In both Cameroon and Nigeria, more than 7 out of 10 children continue to languish in a state of poverty. Nigeria seems to have made the least progress over the last 10 years. In order to better assess these changes, below we explore the evolution of deprivation in each dimension.

Figure 2:   Time trend of child poverty, 2000-2016

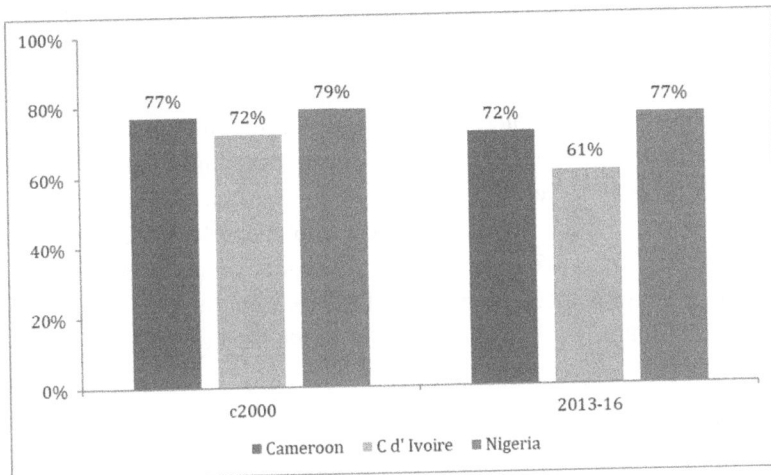

Source: Gordon et al. (2003); author's estimations based on Demographic Health Surveys (DHS, 2013) and Multiple Indicator Cluster Surveys (MICS, 2014 and 2016)

Evolution of severe deprivation by dimension since early 2000s

Access to clean water represents a dimension in which Cameroon has made progress since 2000. More than half of all children were counted as severely deprived in this dimension in the early part of the 2000s (see Figure 3). By 2014, this figure declined to about one-third: nearly 1 in 3 Cameroonian children as of 2014 rely solely on surface water for drinking or need to trek more than 30 minutes to collect water. Access to clean water is better in Côte d'Ivoire (one in five children are deprived). However, there has been no progress since the year 2000 (see Figure 4). In contrast, access to clean water has improved in Nigeria since the early 2000s. More than 40 percent of children were counted as severely deprived in this dimension in the early part of the century (see Figure 5). By 2013, this figure declined to about one-third.

Nigeria has suffered from uneven progress in the sanitation dimension since the early 2000s. A marginally lower share of children was counted as deprived in 2000, when compared to 2013. By 2013, more than 1 in 4 Nigerian children still lacked access to a toilet of any kind in the vicinity of their dwelling. This is particularly concerning given that children are acutely affected by poor sanitation, which is directly linked to diarrhoea and malnutrition. This reality also presents an additional burden for adolescent girls, considering their health and privacy. Even very young children are affected, as the open spaces commonly used for defecation are their main available places for play.

The proportion of Cameroonian children suffering from severe shelter deprivation has remained relatively unchanged since the year 2000. In Côte d'Ivoire, the percentage of children suffering from shelter deprivation is much lower (about a quarter of the children). The share of Nigerian children suffering from severe shelter deprivation has increased five percentage points since the year 2000. About half of Nigerian children live in dwellings with no floor material, or where there are at least five persons sleeping per room.

Figure 3:   Evolution of severe deprivation by dimension (Cameroon, 2000-2014)

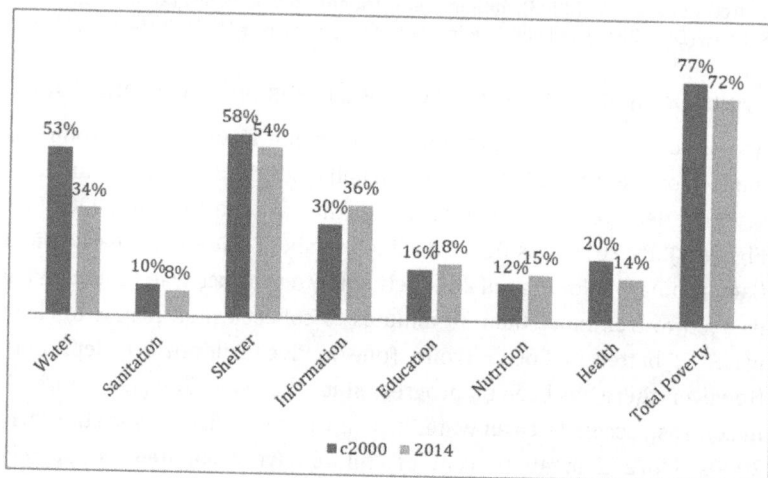

Source: Gordon et al. (2003); author's calculations with MICS (2014)

Figure 4:   Evolution of severe deprivation by dimension (C. d'Ivoire, 2000-2016)

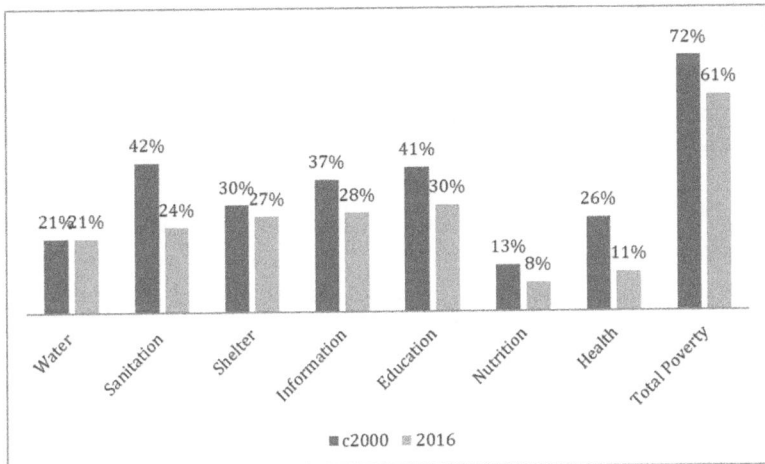

Source: Gordon et al. (2003); author's calculations with MICS (2016)

Figure 5:   Evolution of severe deprivation by dimension (Nigeria, 2000-2012)

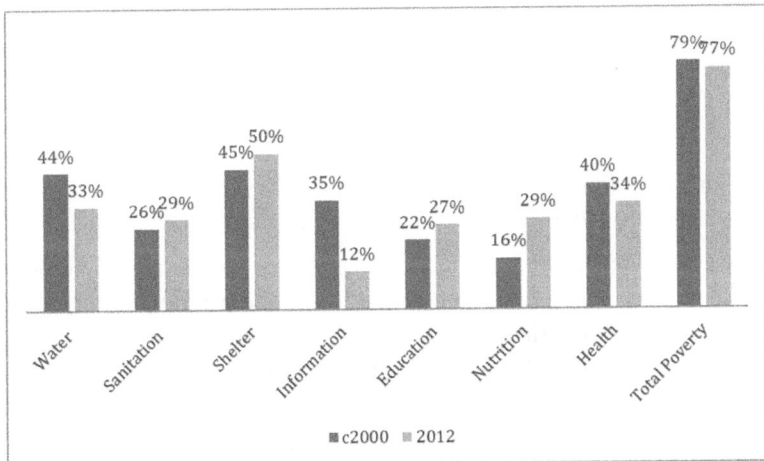

Source: Gordon et al. (2003); author's calculations with DHS (2013)

The information dimension marks a category in which Nigeria has made considerable progress since the turn of the century (with a reduction of about two-thirds by 2013), while it stayed relatively constant in

Cameroon. In Côte d'Ivoire nearly three in ten children lack access to a radio, television, computer, or phone at home.

In addition, while the percentage of children deprived of education in Cameroon stayed constant, the figures clearly illustrate that Côte d'Ivoire and Nigeria parted ways in terms of the right to education; Nigeria worsened, and Côte d'Ivoire improved access to school for their children.

The share of Nigerian children under the age of 5 suffering from severe anthropometric failure has increased substantially (almost doubling from 16 to 29 percent) since the early 2000s. However, it has remained almost constant in Cameroon and Côte d'Ivoire (at around 15 and 8 percent, respectively). Nevertheless, the situation in both Cameroon and Côte d'Ivoire remains dire (as under normal circumstances, only 0.5 per cent of children should be below the international norm for stunting, wasting, or underweight).

Health marks one of the three categories in which Nigeria and Cameroon have made the most progress since the early 2000s. The progress of Côte d'Ivoire is this health dimension is substantial as well; the share of children under 5 who did not receive immunization against any diseases or who did not receive treatment for a recent illness decreased by more than half since the early 2000s (from 26 percent in 2000 to 11 percent in 2016). However, neither Cameroon nor Nigeria reflect improvements in nutrition or education.

Geographic distribution of child poverty in Cameroon, Côte d'Ivoire, and Nigeria

There are similarities and differences in the geographic distribution of child poverty among Cameroon, Côte d'Ivoire, and Nigeria (Maps 1, 2, and 3). In all three countries, the large urban areas (Abidjan, Doula, Yaounde, and Lagos) record the lowest levels of incidence.[1] Also, the Northern areas are generally poorer than the Southern ones.

Comparing the incidence of child poverty in the region or state with the highest and lowest levels, in Côte d'Ivoire the difference is 36 percentage points, but in Nigeria it is almost 50 percentage points. This is

---

[1]   This does not imply that all children are well-off in urban areas. On the contrary, large disparities are found within cities (Minujin et al., 2017)

due to some Nigerian states posting levels of incidence above 90 percent which is not the case in any province in Côte d'Ivoire.[2] In Cameroon, this difference is larger than in the other countries (about 55 percentage points between the regions with the lowest and highest incidence of child poverty) due to the high levels (above 70 percent) in half of the regions.

Map 1:   Geographic distribution of child poverty in Cameroon

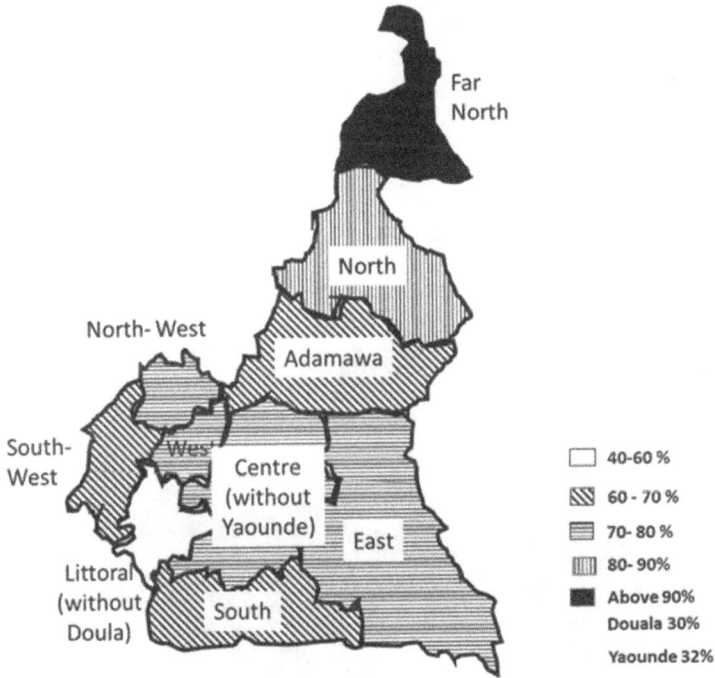

Source: Author's calculation with MICS (2014)

In Nigeria, for example, about 15 states have poverty levels above 80 percent.

Map 2:   Geographic distribution of child poverty in Côte d'Ivoire

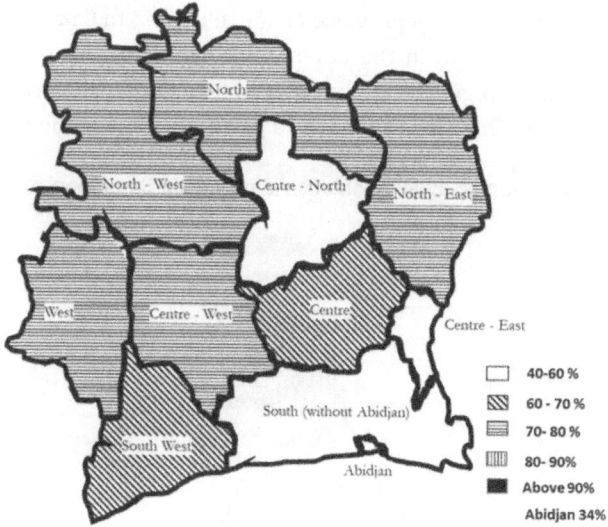

Source: Author's calculation with MICS (2016)

Map 3:   Geographic distribution of child poverty in Nigeria

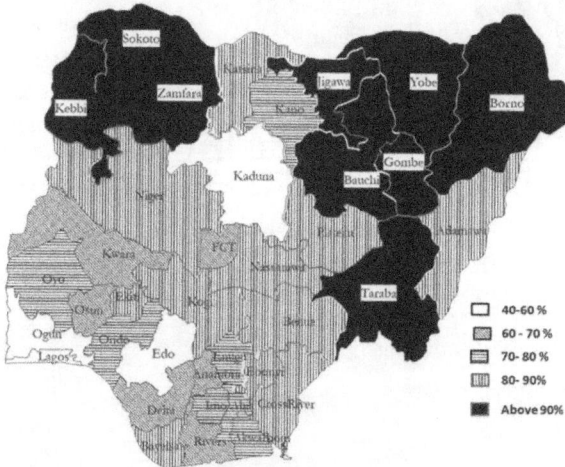

Source: Author's calculation with DHS (2013)

Depth and severity of child poverty

Because the incidence of multidimensional child poverty represents only one aspect of poverty, an assessment of the general wellbeing of children must also account for the depth and severity of child poverty. Thus, beyond the share of children who suffer from a single right deprivation, the average number of deprivations suffered by children can be estimated.

The depth of poverty is highest in Nigeria, when it is compared to Cameroon and Côte d'Ivoire (Figure 6). Nigerian children suffer an average of nearly two severe deprivations. This means that on average, Nigerian children suffer from violations of approximately two of their rights. In both Cameroon and Côte d'Ivoire this figure is much closer to one right violation per child.

The analysis of the depth of poverty also provides insights into the number of deprivations (and which ones) that need to be addressed in order to elevate all children out of poverty (Delamonica and Minujin, 2007). In Cameroon, for instance, the major impact would come from addressing deprivations in shelter, information, and access to clean water. Nigeria, on the other hand, would need to target severe deprivations in health, as well as shelter, and access to clean water. Côte d'Ivoire could make a significant dent on child poverty by addressing deprivations in the areas of information, shelter, and education, where the largest numbers of children are counted as severely deprived. Severe deprivation in the shelter dimension continues to represent a priority for both Cameroon and Nigeria since 2000.

Figure 6:   Depth of multidimensional child poverty in Cameroon, Côte d'Ivoire, and Nigeria (2013-2016)

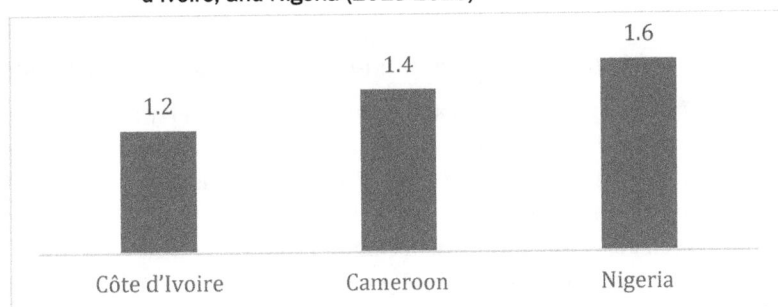

Source: Author's calculation with DHS (2013) and MICS (2014 and 2016)

Figure 7 offers an intuitive view of the severity of child poverty by capturing the share of children who suffer from multiple deprivations. The severity of child poverty is highest in Nigeria, where nearly 1 in 10 children suffer from four or more deprivations. In Cameroon, 1 in 20 children suffer from four or more simultaneous rights violations. The severity of child poverty is about the same in Côte d'Ivoire and Cameroon. This is despite the much lower incidence of child poverty in Côte d'Ivoire. This reality points to the importance of capturing and observing more than just the incidence of poverty. This comparative analysis also enables us to observe that the severity of child poverty is nearly twice as high in Nigeria than in Cameroon and Côte d'Ivoire.

Figure 7:   Share of children suffering multiple (4+) severe deprivations in Cameroon, Côte d'Ivoire, and Nigeria (2013-2016)

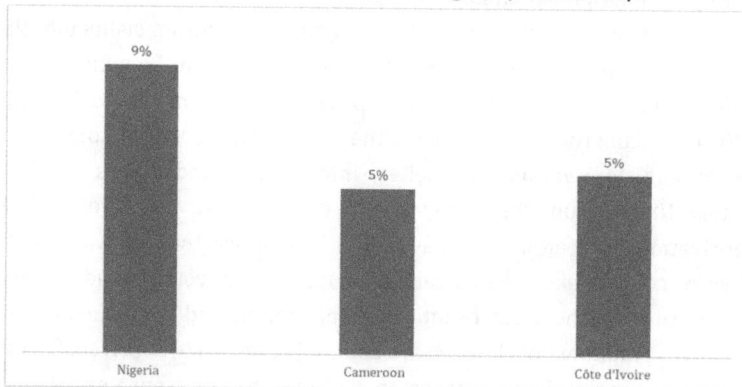

Source: Author's calculation with DHS (2013) and MICS (2014 and 2016)

III.   DEPICTING SIMULTANEOUS DEPRIVATIONS WITHIN A CHILD POVERTY PROFILE

Child poverty profiles and combinations of multiple deprivations

Another way to portray depth and severity of child poverty is by creating a profile of child poverty. This is illustrated in Figure 8, where we capture the share of children suffering from exactly 1 (or exactly 2, or exactly 3, etc.) deprivations across the three countries.

When observing the share of children who suffer a violation of just one of their rights, we see that this figure is about the same in Côte d'Ivoire and Nigeria (28 percent and 29 percent respectively), despite the lower incidence of child poverty in the former. In a similar manner, the same share of children (4 percent) suffer from four simultaneous deprivations in Cameroon and Côte d'Ivoire — despite the higher incidence of child poverty in Cameroon. The share of children suffering from five simultaneous rights violations is also marginally higher in Côte d'Ivoire than in Cameroon. In Nigeria, the incidence of children suffering only four or five deprivations is nearly twice as high as that in the other two countries. In fact, a very small share (less than 1 percent) suffer from six simultaneous rights violations in Nigeria.

Figure 8:   Child poverty profile for Cameroon, Côte d'Ivoire, and Nigeria (2013-2016)

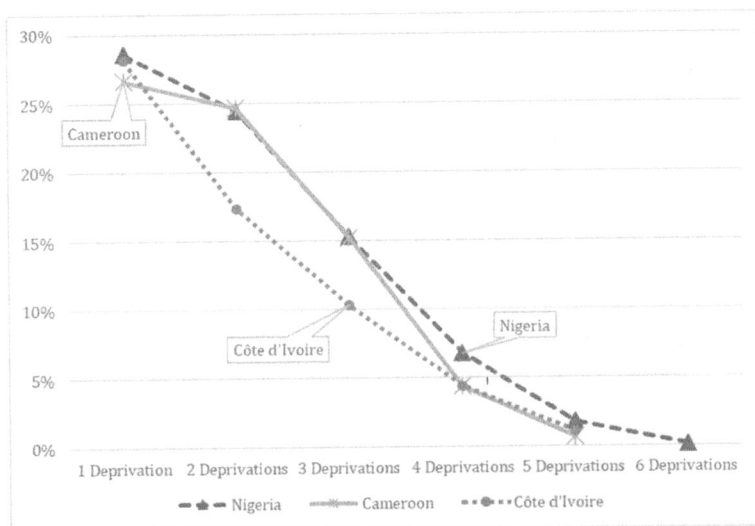

Source: Author's calculation with DHS (2013) and MICS (2014 and 2016)

While this representation allows us to see the quantum of simultaneous deprivations, it does not illustrate which combinations are more common. This is done in Figure 9, which reproduces the values for Nigeria, where the incidence, depth, and severity of child poverty is highest. It can be seen that for Nigerian children the largest single deprivations occur for housing and water (more than 10 percent each of them). The two most common combinations of simultaneous deprivations are: housing and water (almost 5 percent) and housing and sanitation (4 percent). It can also be observed that there are many combinations which, although not very significant, do accumulate to a few percentages points to complete the full mapping of simultaneous deprivations.

Figure 9:   Full mapping of simultaneous deprivations

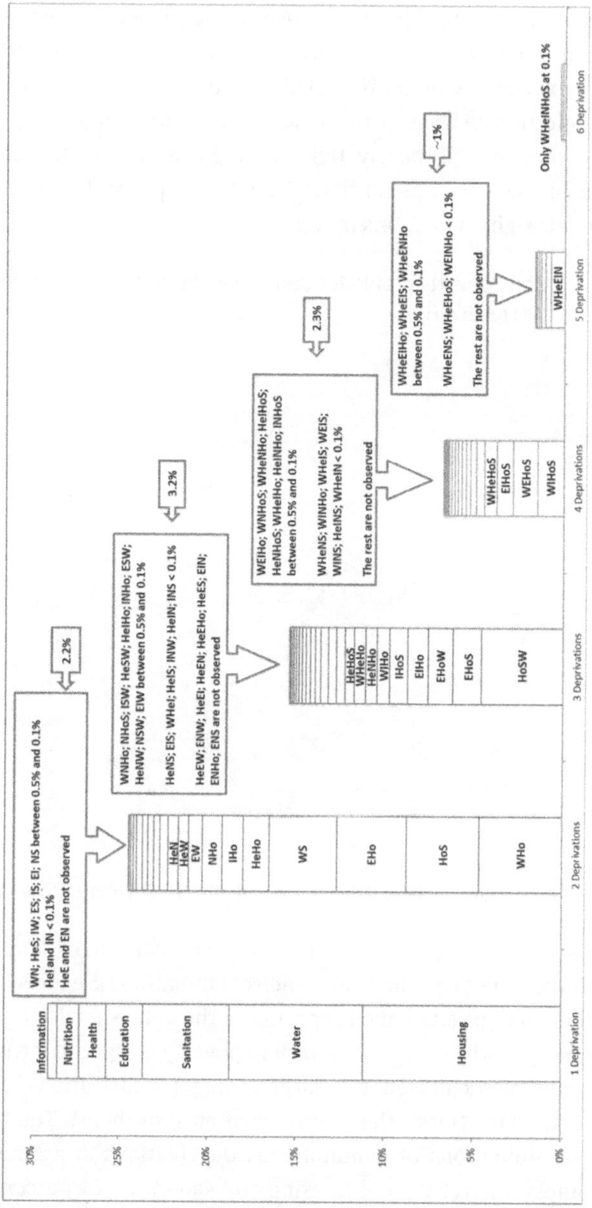

Note: Acronyms should be self-explanatory (e.g. WHo refers to Water and Housing; HeEW, refers to Health, Education, and Water; INHoS, refers to Information, Nutrition, Housing, and Sanitation; etc.). Source: Author's calculation with DHS (2013)

Thus, in Nigeria, for example, the largest share of children are deprived of housing/shelter, water and sanitation. Children deprived of one of these three, and suffering no other deprivations, represent almost a third of all poor children (about 24 percent of the child population). Children suffering from a combination of water and housing deprivation (four percent of the child population), housing and sanitation (three and a half percent), water and sanitation (three percent), and simultaneously all three dimensions of water, housing, and sanitation (about four and half percent) make up about 40 percent of all Nigerian children and more than half of the poor children.

Child poverty profiles and other child rights violations

Child poverty profiles can be combined with an analysis of other child rights violations, which do not constitute poverty (as it is explained in the introduction to this book). Here, it is shown that the impact of each level of depth of poverty on a right violation can be further assessed by quantifying (and concomitantly portraying in a graph) the relative incidence of deprivation for each group of children suffering simultaneous rights violations.

For the case of birth registration, in Côte d'Ivoire (Figure 10) a clear gradient is observed. The percentage of children whose birth is properly registered declines substantially with each additional simultaneous deprivation. In Cameroon (Figure 11) a clear gradient can be observed, where children who are not deprived are much more likely to be registered than poor children. In the first step of the gradient, the drop off for children that suffer only one deprivation is 15 percentage points. Another 15 percentage points are lost for children who suffer exactly two deprivations (compared to those who suffer only one). There is further decline of about 8 percentage points between children suffering two and three deprivations and another 12 percentage points between those suffering three and four deprivations. In both countries, the incidence of birth registration falls below the national average for children who suffer two or more simultaneous rights violations.

Figure 10:   Child poverty profile and birth registration (Côte d'Ivoire, 2016)

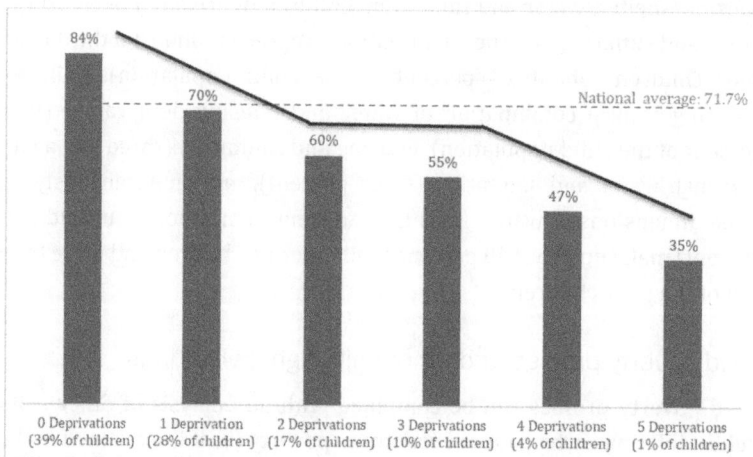

Source: Author's calculation with MICS (2016)

Figure 11:   Child poverty profile and birth registration (Cameroon, 2014)

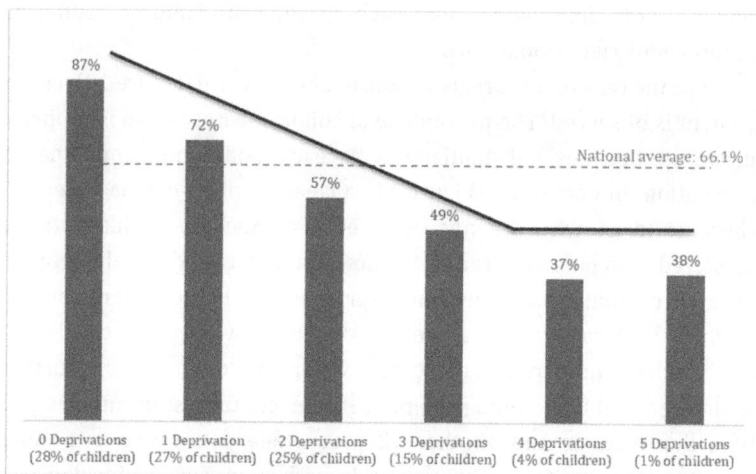

Source: Author's calculation with MICS (2014)

IV. BROADENING THE DEFINITION OF CHILD POVERTY BY ANALYSING DEPRIVATION IN THE RIGHT TO PLAY

Each of the dimensions introduced by Gordon et al. (2003) to capture child poverty is internationally recognized under the Convention of the Rights of the Child (CRC) as child rights (UNHCHR, 2012). For each dimension, and/or indicator, the degree of its satisfaction determines whether a child is classified as enjoying a right directly. Under the information dimension, for example, lack of access to a radio, television, or mobile phone at home constitutes a material deprivation associated with a violation of Article 13 and Article 17 under the CRC — both of which are associated with the right of the child to access information. The CRC recognizes the capacity of access to information to promote the child's "social, spiritual and moral well-being and physical and mental health" (Article 17 of CRC).[3]

In a similar fashion, Article 31 of the CRC recognizes, "the right of the child to rest and leisure, to engage in play and recreational activities appropriate to the age of the child and to participate freely in cultural life and the arts."[4] This right acknowledges that opportunities to play and engage in recreational activities serve a vital role in the early development, and future, of the child. Play, for example, provides children with opportunities to learn independently and build confidence, resilience, and self-esteem (Gleave and Cole-Hamilton, 2012). In highlighting the link between play and future productivity UNICEF (2015) notes:

> Missing out on education in early childhood or living in an environment that provides little stimulation or emotional support can severely restrict a person's productivity as an adult (p. 70).

Yet, it is important to recognize, as does the CRC, that child play need not have an instrumental role. Such an interpretation of child play loses sight of the intrinsic value it provides to the fulfilment of the right of the child to leisure and recreation (Gleave and Cole-Hamilton, 2012; and UNICEF, 2015).

---

[3]   https://www.cypcs.org.uk/rights/uncrcarticles/article-17, accessed July 16, 2019.

[4]   https://www.cypcs.org.uk/rights/uncrcarticles/article-31, accessed July 16, 2019.

The latest round of UNICEF's Multiple Indicator Cluster Surveys (MICS) allows us to capture material deprivations directly associated with violations of a child's right to play (Government of Cameroon and UNICEF, 2017; Roelen and Gassmann, 2012; Universidad de los Andes and UNICEF, 2013). The questionnaire for children under the age of five in MICS, for example, asks mothers and/or caregivers about the things that a child plays with when he/she is at home. Playthings include homemade toys (e.g., dolls and cars, or other toys made in the household), toys that came from a store and household objects (e.g., pots and bowls), or objects and materials found outside the home (e.g., sticks, rocks, animal shells, or leaves). In the latest round of MICS, the percentage of children playing with these different types of toys is presented as an indicator for child development. A "right to play" dimension can be constructed following a similar classification to establish mild, moderate, and severe deprivation.

A "right to play" dimension could define a child (under the age of five) living in a household with no playthings at home as severely deprived. Thus, a child living in a household with at least one type of plaything is counted as not severely deprived. This is irrespective of the type of plaything, or toy, at home.[5] In like manner, children missing two or more playthings are counted as moderately deprived. Mild deprivation in this "right to play" dimension is defined as children missing at least one type of plaything at home. Table 1 provides a summary of these definitions based on the possible eight combinations of types of toys present in the household.[6]

---

[5]   This is done in order to keep the same sample to measure all levels of deprivations; that is, severe, moderate, and mild. Ascribing disparate values to each type of plaything would not enable us to capture the sample of children for all levels of deprivations in this dimension.

[6]   Clearly, if all three types of toys are present in the household, there is no deprivation. This avoids the assumption that only by having manufactured toys bought at a shop the child is not deprived. In other words, this classification is not based on a "western" or a "market-based" view of the toys children should have. However, it does entail that some degree of availability of "material things" is needed to fully realize the right to play. This is based on the premise that poverty is relational, i.e. it is defined socially by the standard considered minimally socially acceptable (Smith, 1776). In most countries across the globe, children are expected to play with toys or objects. If they do not have them, of course they would still be able to play (sing, run, jump, etc.). However, they will be perceived (and they will feel, when they see other children) deprived.

Table 1:   Definition of indicators and thresholds for mild, moderate, and severe deprivation in right to play dimension

Indicators	Mild	Moderate	Severe	Unit of Analysis
Access to: - Households objects/objects found outside (OO) - Homemade toys (HT) - Toys from a shop/ manufactured toys (SM)	Only the combinations OO & HT, or OO & SM, or HT & SM are present in the household.	Only OO or HT or SM present in the household	None present in the household	Children under 5

Source: Author's calculation with MICS (2014 and 2016)

Using the aforementioned definition and thresholds of deprivation to construct the right to play dimension, close to 1 in 5 children under the age of five are counted as severely deprived in Cameroon and Côte d'Ivoire in their latest MICS (Figure 12). These are children with no access to playthings at home. About half of children of the same age are missing 2 or more playthings at home, and thus considered to be moderately deprived of the right to play in both countries. Lastly, about 8 in 10 children under the age of five are counted as missing only one type of plaything at home in Cameroon and Côte d'Ivoire. In both countries, the share of children under the age of five that are severely, moderately, and mildly deprived of playthings (i.e., toys) at home are comparable, yet their impact on the incidence, depth, and severity of child poverty differs.

Figure 12:   Share of children under-5 deprived of access to playthings at home in Cameroon and Côte d'Ivoire, 2014-2016

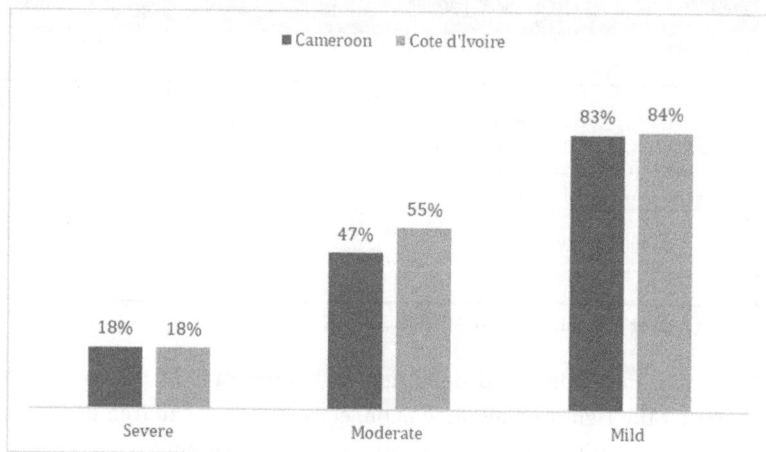

Source: Author's calculations with MICS (2014 and 2016)

Incorporating this dimension into the overall measure of child poverty in both countries, where at least a single severe deprivation constitutes poverty, yields non-trivial results (see Table 2). In Cameroon, for example, the play dimension increases the incidence, depth, and severity of child poverty. While the 1-percentage point increase in the incidence of child poverty is not significant, the rise in the severity of child poverty is indeed. That is, more children suffer from four or more simultaneous rights violations once we incorporate the play dimension. While the average number of deprivations children suffer in Côte d'Ivoire remains unchanged after incorporating child play, we observe an increase in the incidence and severity of child poverty. In this case, the rise in both the incidence and severity of child poverty is statistically significant.

While the relative changes in the incidence and severity of child poverty are statistically significant, they are very small. Thus, they could be considered not substantively significant (McCloskey and Zilliak, 1996). However, it is important to keep in mind the absolute number of children they represent. In both, Cameroon and Côte d'Ivoire well over 100,000 more children would be counted as poor when we consider material deprivations associated with violations of a child's right to play and recreation.

Table 2:   Sensitivity analysis of the incidence, depth, and severity of child poverty in Cameroon and Côte d'Ivoire, 2014-2016

Cameroon (MICS, 2014)			
	Incidence	Depth	Severity (4+ deprivations)
With 7 dimensions	72%	1.4	5%
With 8 dimensions (including access to playthings at home)	73%	1.5	6%*
Côte d' Ivoire (MICS, 2016)			
	Incidence	Depth	Severity (4+ deprivations)
With 7 dimensions	61%	1.2	5%
With 8 dimensions (including access to playthings at home)	63%*	1.2	6%*

Source: Author's calculations with MICS (2014 and 2016); *Change is statistically significant

CONCLUSION AND FURTHER RESEARCH

The last part of this chapter introduced a broader definition of multidimensional child poverty that captures material deprivations associated with violations of a child's right to engage in play and recreation. A methodology for capturing severe, moderate, and mild deprivation in this dimension with available survey data was introduced, as well as a brief sensitivity analysis of the impact of incorporating this 8th dimension in the multidimensional measure of child poverty. This has been done in a way that avoids unduly "marketizing" this right. However, for properly specifying and measuring this right further, cross-cultural analysis is needed — in particular for inter-country comparisons.

The chapter also showed how to prepare a map of all simultaneous deprivations. This exercise is useful to focus policy interventions. It can be expanded by carrying out simulations of the impact on child poverty of interventions in various sectors.

It has been demonstrated, with a practical example and actual evidence that child poverty is correlated with other child rights violations.

For birth registration a clear gradient is observed whereby the percentage of children under five years of age whose births are not registered is higher among the poor; birth registration declines significantly with each additional deprivation (up until four deprivations in Cameroon and all the way to five deprivations in Côte d'Ivoire). Additional analysis along these lines (i.e. correlating child poverty to other non-material child rights violations such as child labour, child marriage, child violence, etc.) should be pursued.

This chapter introduced a consistent analysis of the incidence, depth, and severity of child poverty in Cameroon, Côte d'Ivoire, and Nigeria since 2000. While differences are observed in the progress achieved in reducing the overall incidence of poverty, the analysis of the depth and severity of child poverty enables us to see the challenges that persist in fulfilling all of the rights of the child. This is evidence, as many have argued (including Vandemoortele in this book), of the need to analyse and address both poverty and equity together.

REFERENCES

Delamonica, E., and A. Minujin 2007 "Incidence, Depth and Severity of Children in Poverty" *Social Indicators Research* Vol. 82: 361-374.

Gleave, J. and I. Cole-Hamilton (2012) "A literature review on the effects of a lack of play on children's lives" London: Play England - Making Space for Play.

Gordon, D., S. Nandy, C. Pantazis, S. Pemberton, and P. Townsend (2003) "Child Poverty in the Developing World" *The Policy Press* (Bristol).

Government of Cameroon and UNICEF (2017) *Pauvreté et Privation des Enfants au Cameroun: Une Analyse Multidimensionnelle*, Yaoundé, Cameroon.

McCloskey, D. and Ziliak, T. (1996) 'The Standard Error of Regression', *Journal of Economic Literature*, Vol. 34 (March): 97-114.

Minujin, A, E. Delamonica and P. Ugoagwu (2017) "Children and adolescents in urban settings: Poverty and inequality in Nigerian Cities" presented at the "Putting Children First" Conference, Addis Ababa.

Roelen, K. and Gassmann, F. (2012). Multidimensional Child Poverty in Vietnam. In Minujin, A., and Nandy S. (Eds), *Global Child Poverty and Well-being: Measurement, concepts, policy and* action (307-324). Bristol: Policy Press.

Smith, A. (1776) *An Inquiry into the Nature and Consequences of the Wealth of Nations*, Clarendon, Oxford

UNICEF (2009) "Global Study on Child Poverty and Disparities: National Report Nigeria" UNICEF (Abuja).

UNICEF (United Nations Children's Fund) 2015 "The State of the World's Children 2016: A Fair Chance for Every Child" UNICEF (New York).

Universidad de los Andes and UNICEF (2013) *Análisis de situación de la pobreza infantil en Colombia*, Bogota, Colombia.

DATASETS

DHS (2013) NPC (National Population Commission, Nigeria) and ORC Macro "Nigeria Demographic and Health Survey 2013" (Calverton, MD) National Population Commission and ORC Macro.

Institut National de la Statistique (INS). 2017. Enquête par grappes à indicateurs multiples, 2016, Rapport des Résultats clés. Abidjan, Côte d'Ivoire.

Institut National de la Statistique. 2015. Enquête par grappes à indicateurs multiples (MICS5), 2014, Rapport Final. Yaoundé, Cameroun, Institut National de la Statistique.

CHAPTER 5

CHILD POVERTY AND INEQUALITY IN GHANA: POSITIVE HIGHLIGHTS FROM THE NEW HOUSEHOLD SURVEY

Sarah Hague, Edgar F.A. Cooke, and Andy McKay

INTRODUCTION

Often cited as a good regional example of stable governance, high economic growth and gradual social development, Ghana's development reputation has lost some of its shine in recent years. Increasing levels of inequality and recent economic crises have jeopardised its positive progress in reducing poverty. Having achieved the millennium development goal (MDG) target of halving monetary poverty, more than one in four children continues to be poor, while increasing inequality and stalled progress have significantly reduced the rate of monetary poverty reduction.

Although there have been a few studies on child poverty in Ghana (for instance, Antwi-Asare et al., 2010) there have been no studies based on Ghana's 2013 Living Standards Survey carried out by the Ghana Statistical Service (GSS). We aim to fill this gap in the literature by analysing the extent of monetary poverty among children in the country. To this end we ask whether the reduction in national poverty observed has been greater for children. In other words, have Ghana's poverty reduction efforts been child-friendly?

Using the data from the 2013 Survey, this chapter looks at monetary poverty to explore the possibility that not only are children more likely to be poorer than adults in Ghana, but also that the progress made in reducing their poverty has been slower. In addition, we assess progress in poverty depth.

Regarding inequality, we assess the extent to which inequality of consumption for children has been widening between the richest and the poorest, belying a recent stagnation in the Gini coefficient. We also assess growth incidence and speculate that overall growth has been lower for households where children are concentrated.

CONTEXT

Children are vulnerable to and suffer the most from poverty (Barrientos and DeJong, 2006; UNICEF, 2000). Being a poor child today increases the likelihood that their children will also be poor in the future – thus perpetuating the cycle of poverty (Barrientos and DeJong, 2006; UNICEF, 2000). Child poverty is also associated with lower non-monetary indicators such as missing out on school and low educational attainment (Barrientos and DeJong, 2006). There are longer term impacts of child poverty such as malnutrition and stunting with the potential of malnourished female children more likely to have children with low birth weights in the future (Barrientos and DeJong, 2006). As UNICEF (2000) suggests, poverty reduction must begin with children if the cycle of poverty is to be broken.

Cooke, et al. (2016) explored the trends in Ghana's poverty and inequality data since the 1990s and examined key issues and concerns facing the country's socio-economic transformation. In addition to highlighting the challenge of a country where one in four people remain poor and where inequality has increased steadily since the 1990s, the report also pointed out the higher proportion of children, as compared to adults, that live in poverty. Given the specific vulnerabilities of children and the intergenerational impacts that child poverty causes, it is important to further explore this issue of child poverty in greater detail.

This chapter looks specifically at consumption poverty for children, otherwise referred to as monetary poverty. This means that we do not look at deprivation in specific wellbeing indicators in this analysis – such as health and education – rather, we take consumption standards as a proxy. This approach has been extensively debated in the literature for being narrowly focused. For instance, UNICEF (2000) suggests that a multidimensional approach is better suited in analysing poverty since it goes beyond an analysis of income. A key limitation is the assumption that children living in poor households are always poor and children in wealthier households are not poor, whereas evidence in the very few intra-household surveys that exist show that this generalisation is not always the case. We do not seek to challenge this thinking, but rather present our analysis as a holistic complement to the extensive research on non-monetary wellbeing in the country. In addition, we take a brief look at the overlap between monetary and multidimensional child poverty.

Non-monetary indicators in Ghana present an overall improving picture for children's wellbeing. Child mortality has shown important progress since 2003, and literacy levels have continued to gradually rise, especially for women, although education quality is a major concern in the country. Additional progress has been made in the expansion of access to utilities such as electricity and water, although water quality remains a concern. There has also been a considerable increase in mobile phone coverage. Thus non-monetary poverty indicators have also been improving in Ghana in recent years. However, inequalities in such indicators have not improved and have worsened in many cases — a monetary poor child is now almost three times more likely to be stunted than a better-off child, and a poor pregnant woman is half as likely as a well-off woman to have a skilled attendant at her delivery.

Table 1: Trends in selected non-monetary indicators in Ghana

	1998	2003	2008	2013/14
Infant mortality rate (per 1,000 live births)	57	64	50	41
Under-5 mortality rate (per 1,000 live births)	108	111	80	60
Stunting (%)	30.3	35.0	26.8	18.8
Wasting (%)	9.9	8.4	8.7	4.7
Literacy: Male	-	72.9	76.8	81.2
Literacy: Female	-	55.0	62.9	67.1
Has electricity: Yes	42.6	48.3	60.5	70.6
% with adequate drinking water source	73.7	79.7	80.0	87.7
% with improved and not shared toilet	-	-	-	15
% having received all vaccinations	62.0	69.4	79.0	63.6

Source: Adapted from McKay, et al. (2015: 14), table 7 and Demographic and Health Survey (DHS) 2014.

METHODOLOGY AND DATA

Monetary poverty analysis

We present results for monetary poverty based on the Foster, Greer and Thorbecke (FGT) poverty indices. The poverty headcount (incidence) and the poverty gap (depth) are the main FGT indices reported in this chapter. The headcount provides the percentage of individuals living below the poverty line, while the poverty gap multiplies the incidence of poverty by the average distance of the poor population's income from the poverty line. The sample weights reported in the survey are used to provide results that are representative of the entire population of the country.

Our welfare indicator is the adult equivalence scale for consumption as used by GSS in the national surveys. This allows our work to be comparable to estimates of poverty based on the Ghana living standards survey datasets. Banks et al. (1991) defines an adult equivalence scale as, "the proportionate increase in income per adult necessary to maintain a certain level of household living standard given some change in demographic circumstances (typically, the introduction of children)" (Banks, et al., 1991: 16). The scale therefore takes into account the differing needs of household members while also accounting for the fact that younger children consume fewer calories than adults; consumption is adjusted for the various members of the households based on their gender and age.

As is standard in Ghana, we report our poverty results based on two poverty lines issued by the GSS. An upper (food and non-food) poverty line of GHS 1314 (approximately 687 USD at the time) per year and a lower (food) poverty line of GHS 792.05. Households living below the upper poverty line are simply referred to as living in poverty in this chapter. Those living below the food poverty line are referred to as living in extreme poverty. Our analysis is disaggregated by urban/rural, regions, gender of the household head, number of children and gender of children. Children are judged as being poor if they are living in a poor household.

Inequality analysis

For examining inequality between rich and poor children in Ghana, we do not analyse the standard inequality measures such as the Gini coefficient and the various generalised entropy (GE) measures in any detail. Instead, based on previous research, we find it more illustrative to consider consumption inequality, specifically: (a) the consumption levels of the bottom 10 percent, median and top 10 percent, (b) the decile ratios (90th/10th and 90th/50th), (c) the Palma index and (d) growth incidence curves to show the growth occurring in consumption between 2006 and 2013.

The Palma index, a measure of inequality that has gained prominence in recent years, provides the ratio of the share of consumption of the top 10 percent compared to the share of the bottom 40 percent of the population[1]. Cobham, et al. (2016) suggest that inequality is best explained by comparing changes in income in the top decile and the bottom four deciles. The Gini rather considers distribution over the entire income range and therefore puts more emphasis on the median population.

Therefore, by focusing more on individual deciles/percentiles at the top and bottom of the distribution, we are able to better understand what is truly happening to inequality in a country.

Data

We use household data obtained from the Ghana Statistical Service. The last two Ghana living standards surveys, carried out in 2006 (GLSS5) and 2013 (GLSS6) are principally used in the current analysis. One issue in our choice of the two surveys is that the poverty analysis conducted on those two surveys is not directly comparable to that done on the 1992 and 1998 surveys. This is largely due to the fact that the consumption basket underlying the poverty line was updated in two main ways. First, some of the components and weights of the poverty line basket were updated to reflect the changing consumption patterns. For instance, spending on mobile phones has become more important to households. Second, the GSS updated the consumer price index (CPI) used to estimate the prices of goods purchased with new price deflators (cf. Cooke, et al., 2016). As a result, our comparison focusses on 2006 and 2013 which are more directly comparable after updating the 2006 survey with the new price deflators obtained from the 2013 poverty line.

The 2013 GLSS surveyed 16,772 households, representing a population of approximately 6,601,484 households or 26.4 million individuals. Further detailed information about the surveys can be found in GSS (2008, 2014).

---

[1]   The Palma index is based on work by José G. Palma (see Palma, 2006; 2011; 2014). For a critique of the Palma ratio see Hazledine (2014). Palma (2014) provides a response to Hazledine's critique. Cobham and Sumner (2014) favour the Palma index over other inequality measures because of its simplicity and the ease with which policy makers and citizens can understand and track the Palma index to see what is happening to inequality in the country.

RESULTS

Ghana's child population

Reflecting population distribution, there is considerable regional variation in the distribution of children across the country (Figure 1). The Ashanti region remains the region with the largest concentration of children (approximately 2.4 million in 2013). Upper West continues to be the region with the lowest population of children (approximately 369,000 in 2013). Some changes in the population distribution can be observed. Notably, the child population of Greater Accra surges forth between 2006 and 2013 from 1.2 million to 1.7 million.

Figure 1:   Distribution of the Child Population across Regions, Urban/Rural and Male/Female Categories

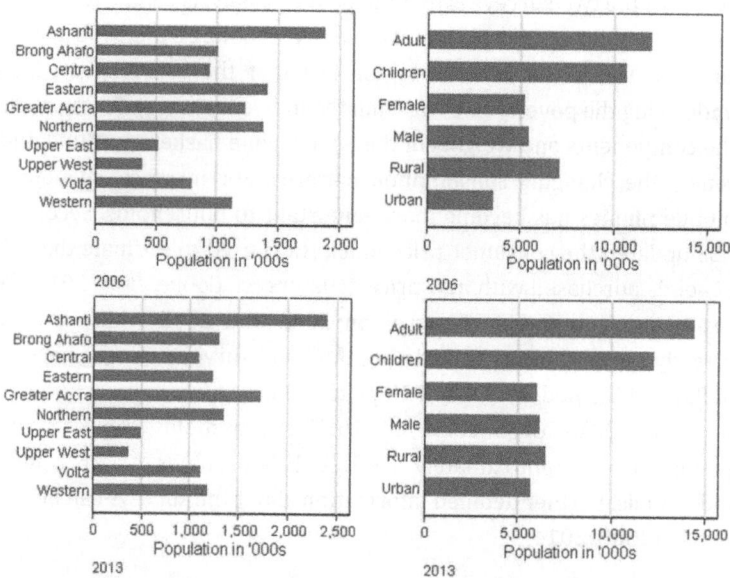

Notes: Apart from the Adult bars all the remaining disaggregation is based on only the population of children. Data for 2006 is shown in the top row and 2013 shown in the bottom row.
Source: Authors' elaboration of GLSS5 and 6

Also notable in Figure 1 is that the gap between the population of rural and urban children has reduced substantially over this period. In 2006 there were 3.6 million more children in rural areas than urban zones, the gap reducing to around 781,000 more children in 2013. This change reflects two main factors. First of all, it reflects general rural-urban migration that continues to occur in Ghana (which became a predominantly urban country in 2013). Secondly, it reflects that some previously rural areas have grown in size to now be classified as urban. And thirdly, we cannot discount increases in fertility in urban areas compared to rural areas (McKay, et al. 2015).

Regarding the numbers of monetary poor children (see Table 2), we note in particular that the number of children living in poverty has declined from approximately 3.9 million to 3.5 million in 2013. This is a percentage decline of 10.6 percent, which contrasts with a much larger decline in the proportion of children living in poverty of 22.3 percent. This is a striking fact, as it means that poverty reduction is not keeping pace with population growth. Indeed, similar to many Sub-Saharan countries in recent years, Ghana's reductions in its fertility rate have stalled since the late 1990s when it stood at 4.4 in the 1998 Demography and Health Survey (DHS) and remained at 4.2 in the 2014 DHS.

Table 2:   Child population and number of poor, 2006-2013

	Distribution of the Poor		Distribution of the Poor (%)			Distribution of Population (%)		
	2006	2013	2006	2013	Change	2006	2013	Change
Urban	501,767	745,442	13.0	21.5	8.5	33.4	46.8	13.5
Rural	3,377,879	2,723,433	87.0	78.5	-8.5	66.6	53.2	-13.5
Total	3,879,646	3,468,875	100	100	0	100	100	0

Note: The distribution of the poor is the share of the urban (or rural) poor child population out of the total poor child population. The distribution of the population is the total urban (or rural) child population divided by the population of children in the country. Source: Authors' elaboration of GLSS5 and 6

Consumption levels

We turn now to examining consumption levels according to the number of children in a household (Figure 2). The majority of Ghana's households are comprised of between 0 and 10 children (only around 1 percent of households have more than 10 children). The results show that households with more children have lower adult equivalent consumption compared to those with fewer or no children. Furthermore, households with 10 children saw almost no improvement in their consumption levels between 2006 and 2013, despite smaller households making better progress.

Figure 2:   Mean consumption per adult according to the number of children in a household (GHS)

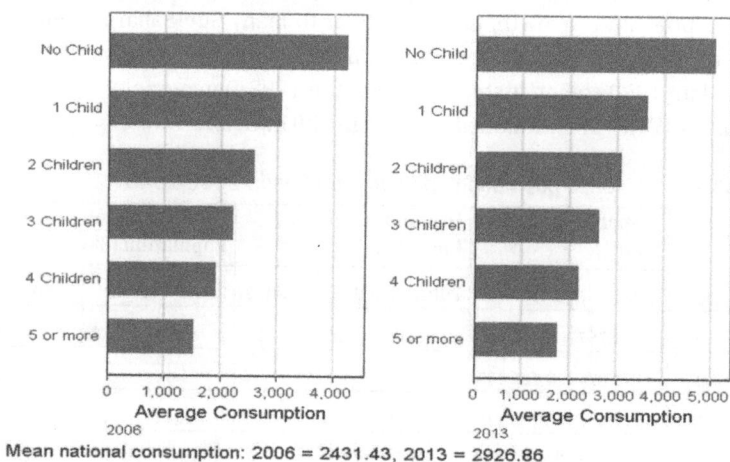

Mean national consumption: 2006 = 2431.43, 2013 = 2926.86

Note: Average adult equivalent consumption in GHS currency reported is based on the number of children living within a household. Data for 2006 is shown on the left, 2013 on the right. Source: Authors' elaboration of GLSS5 and 6

Child poverty

When turning to trends in the incidence of monetary child poverty, we first look at national poverty levels for the entire population to provide context. Figure 3 shows the trend in poverty from 1992 to 2013. The pattern emerging is one of declining national monetary poverty incidence and depth. Over the entire period national poverty incidence has declined from 56.5 percent in 1992 to 24.2 percent in 2013. This indicates that

Ghana successfully met the millennium development goal of halving poverty, and in advance of the 2015 deadline. Similarly, the index capturing the depth of poverty has fallen from 20.9 percent to 7.8 percent between 1992 and 2013. The pattern observed for extreme poverty is even more impressive. The incidence of extreme poverty has fallen significantly faster from 33.2 percent to 8.4 percent in the past 20 years.

However, we note that the rate of reduction of overall poverty has slowed significantly in recent years, from a rate of 1.8 percentage points per year in the 1990s to 1.1 percentage point since 2006. In comparison, we see that child poverty has fallen by an average of 1.07 percentage points per year since 2006. This means that we cannot say that child poverty has been reduced faster than overall poverty.

Figure 3:   National poverty rates, 1992-2013 (2013 prices)

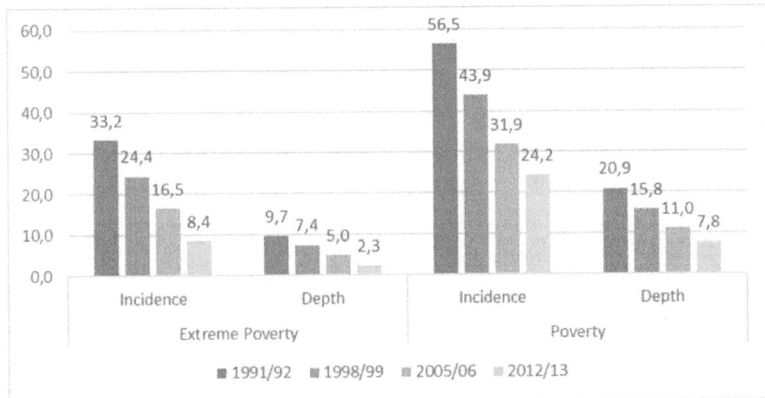

Source: Author's calculations based on GLSS3 – GLSS6

Regarding children, Table 3 shows the incidence of poverty among the population in Ghana according to the number of children in the household. We break this down in three ways. We show poverty according to the number of children in a household and adults versus children.

In line with the results on consumption levels above, a clear pattern emerges — the more children living in the household the higher the level of poverty. Households with five or more children have a poverty incidence of 55.2 percent, compared to an incidence of 24.2 percent amongst households with just two children. The relative contribution to national poverty of households with five or more children is almost 40 percent whereas households with two children comprise just 14 percent of the nation's poverty. Essentially, the representation of large households in the poor population is larger than that of the smaller households.

Regarding the incidence of child poverty, it declined overall from 36.4 percent to 28.3 percent over the 2006–2013 period and declined across all categories between 2006 and 2013. This represents a percentage decline since 2006 of 22.3 percent. In contrast, as noted above, the percentage decline in overall national poverty levels was almost 24.1 percent in the same period, showing that child poverty is being reduced at a slower rate than overall poverty levels.

The poverty incidence among children is 1.4 times larger than that of adults. Around 28.3 percent of children are poor compared to 20.6 percent of adults in 2013. The result is consistent with the earlier finding that poorer households contain more children. The gap has worsened substantially since the 1990s when children were just 1.15 times more likely to be poor than adults.

Although not traditionally thought of as a country with a problem of child-headed households, it is interesting to note that our analysis shows that the number of child-headed households increased from approximately 5,700 households in 2006 to 8,000 households in 2013. The age of the children heading these households ranges between 15 and 17 years. The ability of child-headed households to cope with shocks is clearly very limited compared to other households. However, given the small sample we cannot estimate any meaningful poverty measures for this subgroup of households.

Table 3:   National poverty incidence 2006-2013

	2006			
	Headcount	Population share	Absolute contribution	Relative contribution
No Child	0.092	0.118	0.011	0.034
	0.005	0.002	0.001	0.002
1 Child	0.161	0.134	0.022	0.068
	0.005	0.002	0.001	0.002
2 Children	0.242	0.178	0.043	0.136
	0.006	0.002	0.001	0.003
3 Children	0.308	0.192	0.059	0.187
	0.006	0.002	0.001	0.004
4 Children	0.377	0.151	0.057	0.180
	0.007	0.002	0.001	0.004
5 or more	0.552	0.227	0.125	0.395
	0.006	0.002	0.002	0.005
Adult	0.275	0.528	0.145	0.458
	0.003	0.003	0.002	0.005
Children	0.364	0.472	0.172	0.542
	0.004	0.003	0.002	0.005
Population	0.317	1.000	0.317	1.000
	0.003	0.000	0.003	0.000
	2013			
No Child	0.073	0.130	0.010	0.039
	0.003	0.002	0.000	0.002
1 Child	0.122	0.144	0.018	0.073
	0.004	0.002	0.001	0.002
2 Children	0.164	0.187	0.031	0.127
	0.004	0.002	0.001	0.003
3 Children	0.231	0.186	0.043	0.177
	0.004	0.002	0.001	0.003
4 Children	0.319	0.142	0.045	0.187
	0.005	0.002	0.001	0.003
5 or more	0.455	0.210	0.096	0.396
	0.005	0.002	0.001	0.004
Adult	0.206	0.540	0.111	0.461
	0.002	0.002	0.001	0.004
Children	0.283	0.460	0.130	0.539
	0.003	0.002	0.001	0.004
Population	0.242	1.000	0.242	1.000
	0.002	0.000	0.002	0.000

Note: Standard errors reported in italics, all estimates are significant. The population share in the total population is reported. Poverty results based on the household. Results have been weighted using household weights (individual weights x household size). Source: Authors' calculation based on GLSS5 and 6

Table 4 presents disaggregated results for child poverty. The results are separated out by urban and rural zones, Ghana's regions and gender (of both the children and the household head). In considering urban versus rural poverty, although both zones have seen a decline in child poverty, the decline in rural areas has been slightly faster over this recent period. The rural area has a greater share of children — although the share declined from 66.6 percent to 53.2 percent between the two survey years. While rural child poverty makes up 78.5 percent of child poverty overall, urban poverty accounts for the remaining fifth.

Considering changes in child poverty by region, six regions experienced reasonable reductions since 2006. Three regions experienced relatively impressive reductions — Greater Accra (54 percent reduction, from 16 to 7 percent), Ashanti (40 percent), and Upper East (36 percent). While the Eastern region experienced an increase in child poverty from 20.8 percent in 2006 to 26.2 percent in 2013, despite the fact that the share of children in the Eastern region fell. Despite the decline in child poverty in the three Northern regions — Upper East, Upper West and Northern regions — they still exhibit high levels of child poverty (48 percent, 74.1 percent and 54.3 percent in 2013 respectively). The results are not qualitatively different from the national picture whereby the three Northern regions are the regions with the highest poverty levels. Greater Accra remains the region with the lowest incidence of child poverty at 7.3 percent in 2013 even with the modest increase in the region's share of the total population of children. The country's biggest concern is the northern region, which with a high and stagnating poverty rate and a large population, contains the largest amount of poor people.

In terms of gender, both the male children and male-headed households experience a higher incidence of poverty compared to their female counterparts. Boys record an incidence of poverty of 29.8 percent whilst that of girls stands at 26.8 percent in 2013[2]. Female-headed households register a 22.9 percent poverty rate compared to 30.1 percent for

---

[2]   A t-test (assuming unequal variances) indicates that the difference between male children and female children is significant at the 1 percent level of significance. The larger households have more male children compared to female children.

male-headed households in 2013. The latter point might be due to the fact that households recorded as female-headed are often receiving remittances from outside the household.

Table 4:   Poverty incidence among children, 2006-2013

	2006				2013			
	Head-count	Popu-lation share	Absolute contri-bution	Relative contri-bution	Head-count	Popu-lation share	Absolute contri-bution	Relative contri-bution
Urban	0.141	0.334	0.047	0.130	0.130	0.468	0.061	0.215
	0.005	0.004	0.002	0.005	0.004	0.004	0.002	0.006
Rural	0.475	0.666	0.317	0.870	0.418	0.532	0.222	0.785
	0.005	0.004	0.004	0.005	0.004	0.004	0.003	0.006
Western	0.274	0.106	0.029	0.080	0.250	0.097	0.024	0.085
	0.012	0.003	0.001	0.004	0.010	0.002	0.001	0.004
Central	0.273	0.088	0.024	0.066	0.218	0.089	0.019	0.068
	0.014	0.002	0.001	0.004	0.009	0.002	0.001	0.003
Greater Accra	0.158	0.115	0.018	0.050	0.073	0.141	0.010	0.036
	0.009	0.003	0.001	0.003	0.005	0.003	0.001	0.003
Volta	0.417	0.076	0.032	0.087	0.384	0.091	0.035	0.123
	0.014	0.002	0.001	0.004	0.009	0.002	0.001	0.004
Eastern	0.208	0.132	0.027	0.075	0.262	0.101	0.027	0.094
	0.010	0.003	0.001	0.004	0.008	0.002	0.001	0.003
Ashanti	0.286	0.176	0.050	0.138	0.172	0.196	0.034	0.119
	0.008	0.003	0.002	0.004	0.007	0.003	0.002	0.005
Brong Ahafo	0.393	0.094	0.037	0.102	0.313	0.106	0.033	0.117
	0.013	0.002	0.001	0.004	0.009	0.002	0.001	0.004
Northern	0.593	0.129	0.077	0.210	0.543	0.110	0.060	0.211
	0.011	0.003	0.002	0.006	0.008	0.002	0.001	0.004
Upper east	0.752	0.049	0.037	0.101	0.480	0.040	0.019	0.068
	0.012	0.001	0.001	0.003	0.011	0.001	0.001	0.002
Upper west	0.915	0.037	0.034	0.092	0.741	0.030	0.022	0.079
	0.007	0.001	0.001	0.003	0.008	0.001	0.000	0.002
Male children	0.382	0.507	0.194	0.532	0.298	0.507	0.151	0.533
	0.006	0.004	0.003	0.006	0.004	0.004	0.002	0.006
Female children	0.346	0.493	0.170	0.468	0.268	0.493	0.132	0.467
	0.005	0.004	0.003	0.006	0.004	0.004	0.002	0.006
Male – headed households	0.399	0.761	0.304	0.835	0.301	0.752	0.227	0.800
	0.005	0.004	0.004	0.005	0.003	0.003	0.003	0.005
Female – headed households	0.252	0.239	0.060	0.165	0.229	0.248	0.057	0.200
	0.007	0.004	0.002	0.005	0.006	0.003	0.001	0.005
Population	0.364	1.000	0.364	1.000	0.283	1.000	0.283	1.000
	0.004	0.000	0.004	0.000	0.003	0.000	0.003	0.000

Note: Standard errors reported in italics. The population share in the total population is reported. Poverty calculated at the individual level by keeping children below the age of 18 and weighted by the individual sample weights provided by the GSS.
Source: Authors' calculation based on GLSS5 and 6

Table 5 shows the estimates of the average child poverty gap index. Noticeable improvements in the average poverty gap occur for households with or without children. As with poverty incidence, children have a higher average poverty gap than adults, meaning that not only are they more likely to be poor than adults, but that when poor they are more likely to live deeper in poverty than adults. And again, the improvement in the poverty gap has been slower for children than adults.

We find that the average poverty gap has deteriorated for children living in the Eastern, Volta and Western regions since 2006. The largest improvement of 18.2 percentage points occurs in the Upper East region. Upper West also shows considerable improvement in the average poverty gap measure (17.3 percentage point decline). The three Northern regions remain the poorest regions in terms of poverty depth — with poor children in the Upper West region still living on average a third below the poverty line. Considering urban versus rural zones, we find that children in urban areas have a substantially lower average poverty gap compared to those in rural areas, with rural poor children living almost five times deeper in poverty than their urban counterparts.

In per capita terms, the annual cost of closing the monetary poverty gap in Northern, Upper East and Upper West regions is 327.19 GHS, 488.81 GHS and 696.42 GHS respectively[3]. Male children and male-headed households remain further below the poverty line compared to female children and female-headed households respectively. The poverty gap makes it possible to estimate the theoretical resources required to close the gap in incomes between households below the poverty line and the minimum level of consumption represented by the poverty line. On average, each poor household (with a child) needs an extra income of GHS 120 per year which amounts to 1.1 percent of GDP or 416.3 million GHS[4].

---

[3]   Obtained by multiplying the poverty gap index by the poverty line (for example, Northern region is 0.249 x 1314 = 327.19)

[4]   The estimate is based on multiplying the child poverty gap estimate by the poverty line of 1314 GHS. We then multiply the average income gap (120GHS) by the population of poor households with children (3.5 million) to obtain 416.3 million GHS.

Table 5:   Poverty gap among children 2006-2013

	2006				2013			
	Average poverty gap	Population share	Absolute contribution	Relative contribution	Average poverty gap	Population share	Absolute contribution	Relative contribution
Urban	0.043	0.334	0.014	0.113	0.030	0.468	0.014	0.154
	0.002	*0.004*	*0.001*	*0.005*	*0.001*	*0.004*	*0.000*	*0.005*
Rural	0.167	0.666	0.111	0.887	0.145	0.532	0.077	0.846
	0.002	*0.004*	*0.002*	*0.005*	*0.002*	*0.004*	*0.001*	*0.005*
Western	0.067	0.106	0.007	0.056	0.069	0.097	0.007	0.073
	0.004	*0.003*	*0.000*	*0.004*	*0.003*	*0.002*	*0.000*	*0.003*
Central	0.066	0.088	0.006	0.046	0.064	0.089	0.006	0.062
	0.004	*0.002*	*0.000*	*0.003*	*0.003*	*0.002*	*0.000*	*0.003*
Greater Accra	0.044	0.115	0.005	0.040	0.023	0.141	0.003	0.036
	0.003	*0.003*	*0.000*	*0.003*	*0.002*	*0.003*	*0.000*	*0.003*
Volta	0.104	0.076	0.008	0.063	0.114	0.091	0.010	0.113
	0.004	*0.002*	*0.000*	*0.003*	*0.003*	*0.002*	*0.000*	*0.004*
Eastern	0.047	0.132	0.006	0.050	0.070	0.101	0.007	0.078
	0.003	*0.003*	*0.000*	*0.003*	*0.003*	*0.002*	*0.000*	*0.003*
Ashanti	0.078	0.176	0.014	0.109	0.039	0.196	0.008	0.084
	0.003	*0.003*	*0.001*	*0.004*	*0.002*	*0.003*	*0.000*	*0.004*
Brong ahafo	0.110	0.094	0.010	0.083	0.084	0.106	0.009	0.097
	0.005	*0.002*	*0.001*	*0.004*	*0.003*	*0.002*	*0.000*	*0.003*
Northern	0.249	0.129	0.032	0.256	0.212	0.110	0.023	0.255
	0.006	*0.003*	*0.001*	*0.007*	*0.004*	*0.002*	*0.001*	*0.005*
Upper east	0.372	0.049	0.018	0.144	0.190	0.040	0.008	0.084
	0.008	*0.001*	*0.001*	*0.005*	*0.005*	*0.001*	*0.000*	*0.003*
Upper west	0.530	0.037	0.019	0.155	0.357	0.030	0.011	0.118
	0.007	*0.001*	*0.001*	*0.004*	*0.005*	*0.001*	*0.000*	*0.003*
Male children	0.133	0.507	0.067	0.537	0.097	0.507	0.049	0.539
	0.002	*0.004*	*0.001*	*0.007*	*0.002*	*0.004*	*0.001*	*0.006*
Female children	0.118	0.493	0.058	0.463	0.085	0.493	0.042	0.461
	0.002	*0.004*	*0.001*	*0.007*	*0.001*	*0.004*	*0.001*	*0.006*
Male-headed household	0.142	0.761	0.108	0.862	0.099	0.752	0.074	0.812
	0.002	*0.004*	*0.002*	*0.005*	*0.001*	*0.003*	*0.001*	*0.005*
Female-headed household	0.073	0.239	0.017	0.138	0.069	0.248	0.017	0.188
	0.003	*0.004*	*0.001*	*0.005*	*0.002*	*0.003*	*0.001*	*0.005*
Adult	0.095	0.528	0.05	0.457	0.065	0.540	0.035	0.457
	0.001	*0.003*	*0.001*	*0.005*	*0.001*	*0.002*	*0.000*	*0.005*
Children	0.126	0.472	0.059	0.543	0.091	0.460	0.042	0.543
	0.002	*0.003*	*0.001*	*0.005*	*0.001*	*0.002*	*0.001*	*0.005*
Population	0.126	1.000	0.126	1.000	0.099	1.000	0.099	1.000
	0.002	*0.000*	*0.002*	*0.000*	*0.002*	*0.000*	*0.002*	*0.000*

Note: Standard errors reported in italics. The population share in the total population is reported. Poverty calculated at the individual level by keeping children below the age of 18 and weighted by the individual sample weights provided by the GSS.
Source: Authors' elaboration of GLSS5 and 6

In terms of extreme poverty, a reduction in incidence is observed for almost all categories listed in Figure 4. The absolute reduction in extreme poverty incidence is larger in bigger households. A reduction of 1.3 percentage points occurs for households with no children whereas households with five or more children saw the largest reduction of 15.9 percentage points. Children experienced a larger decline in extreme poverty (9.1 percentage points) compared to adults (7 percentage points).

Figure 4:   Extreme poverty incidence among children 2006-2013

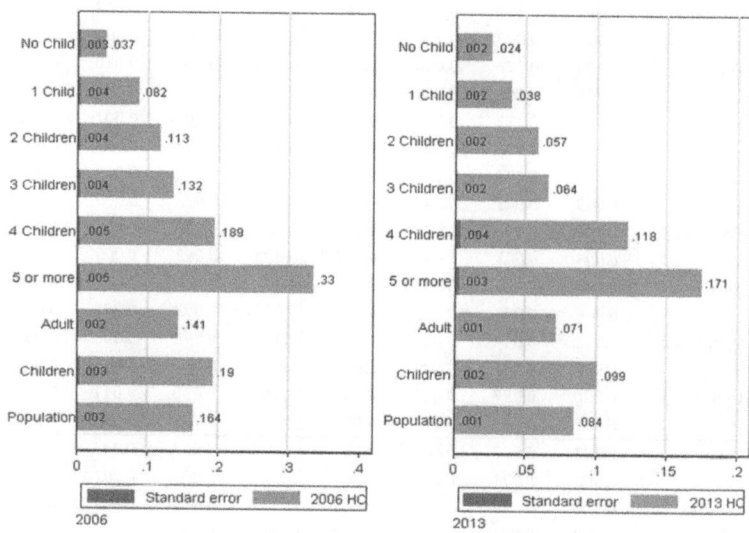

Note: HC is the headcount index. The values within the bars represent the standard error while the values outside the bar represent the headcount index. The chart on the left is for 2006 and 2013 is on the right. Source: Authors' elaboration of GLSS5 and 6

In Figure 5, we briefly note that there has been remarkable progress in reducing the incidence of extreme poverty in the three Northern regions. Northern, Upper West and Upper East experience a 14.2, 29.3 and 35.5 percentage point decline in incidence between 2006 and 2013. Yet, the incidence of extreme poverty in these three regions remains high compared to the other regions of Ghana. The level of extreme poverty in Upper West is astronomically high at almost 50 percent.

The progress made in extreme poverty for children in rural areas has been impressive — a decline of 8.8 percentage points compared to a decline among children in the urban zones of 3.7 percentage points. In spite of the rapid decline in extreme poverty incidence, children in the rural areas continue to have a higher incidence compared to children in urban zones. Male-headed households and male children have a higher incidence of extreme poverty compared to female-headed and female children respectively. However, there has been stronger progress made by male-headed households compared to female-headed households.

Figure 5:   Extreme poverty incidence among children by region, 2006-2013

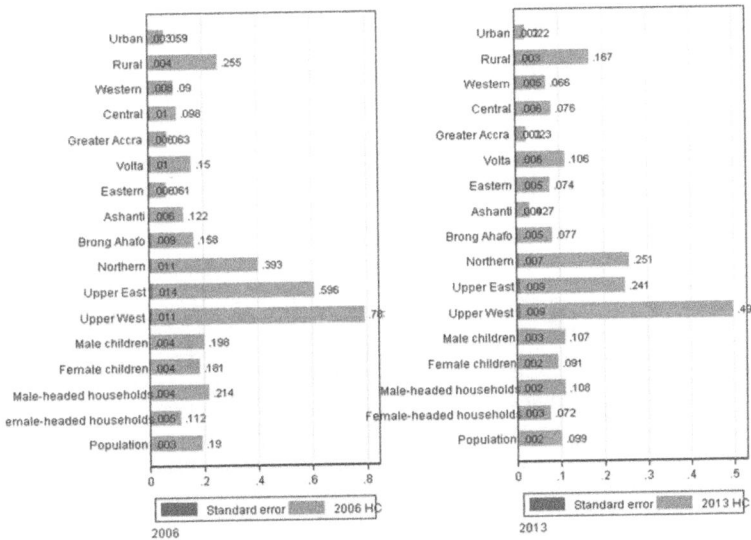

Note: HC is the headcount index. The values within the bars represent the standard error while the values outside the bar represent the headcount index. The chart on the left is for 2006 and 2013 is on the right. Source: Authors' elaboration of GLSS5 and 6

Comparing monetary poverty against multidimensional poverty

As stated above, this chapter focuses on monetary poverty as a proxy indicator for poverty. However, it is noted that it is useful to consider how monetary child poverty relates to multi-dimensional child poverty and to what extent the two overlap. We use the results of a recent analysis of the same GLSS data as presented by staff from the Ghana Statistical Service at the Child Poverty Measurement Workshop in Calabar, Nigeria, in October 2016. The analysis looked at whether children suffered deprivations in six different areas, including health, education, water, sanitation, shelter, and access to information. The results of this analysis showed that overall 70 percent of children experience at least one type of deprivation, clearly a significantly higher proportion than the 28 percent found by this analysis to live in monetary poverty. They found that just over one-third of children (35.2 percent) suffer from one deprivation, a quarter (23.5 percent) suffer from two deprivations, and the remaining one in ten (11.4 percent) suffer from three of more deprivations.

The results shown in Figure 6 illustrate that where children are poor in monetary terms, they are also very likely (almost 90 percent) to be poor in multidimensional terms. However, what stands out is that the analysis showed that around 60 percent of children who are not poor in monetary terms are actually suffering from at least one deprivation.

Figure 6:   Monetary poverty status compared to multidimensional poverty
             status

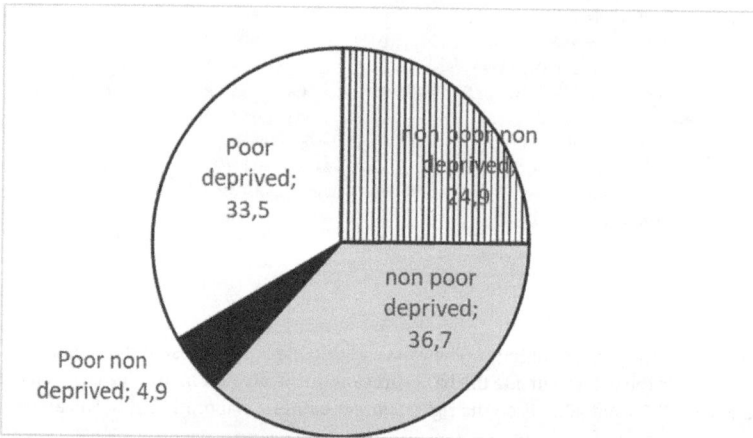

Note: Comparison of poor and non-poor according to monetary poverty as measured in the GLSS, compared to being deprived and non-deprived according to multidimensional poverty as described above. Source: GSS staff analysis and presentation 2016.

Inequality

Inequality has increased in Ghana since the 1990s (Cooke, et al., 2016). The reported Gini coefficient increased from 37 to 41 since 1992, although this increase stalled between 2006 and 2013 as it barely changed from 40.6 to 40.9. However, the Gini coefficient places more weight on changes occurring in the middle of the distribution than in its tails, whereas decile measures focus by definition on the top and bottom of the distribution. The Palma index is also more sensitive to changes occurring at the tails of the distribution (Cobham, et al., 2016; Hoy, 2015). When examining inequality, we are arguably more concerned about the relative contrast between the poorest groups and the wealthiest.

In this section therefore, in order to look more closely at inequality between rich and poor, we examine consumption for the various deciles of the distribution for the child population as well as the Palma index. Table 6 shows the consumption of the poorest, median and richest 10 percent of the population of households with children and for all households overall.

Table 6:   Adult equivalent consumption, urban versus rural households, 2006-2013

	Households with Children				
	Consumption p.a.			Ratios	
	p10	p50	p90	p90/p10	p90/p50
2006					
Urban	1121.92	2506.47	5452.93	4.9	2.2
Rural	585.46	1381.00	3003.67	5.1	2.2
Total	679.34	1706.06	3972.78	5.8	2.3
2013					
Urban	1212.55	2687.72	6325.84	5.2	2.4
Rural	637.00	1531.76	3531.24	5.5	2.3
Total	818.42	2018.99	5061.25	6.2	2.5
	All Households				
	Consumption p.a.			Ratios	
	p10	p50	p90	p90/p10	p90/p50
2006					
Urban	1183.65	2730.25	6197.84	5.2	2.3
Rural	604.14	1446.57	3276.98	5.4	2.3
Total	714.77	1846.16	4543.38	6.4	2.5
2013					
Urban	1282.69	2918.12	7243.74	5.6	2.5
Rural	655.55	1610.53	3914.04	6.0	2.4
Total	849.79	2166.74	5788.83	6.8	2.7

Note: The values shown in the table are computed based on the value of consumption at the stated percentile. The percentile ratios, for instance the p90/p50 is calculated by dividing the value of adult equivalent consumption at the 90th percentile by the value at the 50th percentile.
Source: Authors' calculations based on GLSS5 and 6

Again, we note that households with children have lower median per adult consumption levels (2019 GHS per year at the median) compared to the national median (2166 GHS). Considering consumption inequality, we see that the disparity between rich and poor has actually increased significantly since 2006. The 90th percentile of households with children consumed 5.8 times what the tenth percentile consumed in 2006, rising to 6.2 times in 2013. This disparity is actually slightly lower than for all households overall. This shows that growth in consumption levels for households with children has been skewed toward the wealthier households. The tenth percentile saw their consumption rise by 20 percent over the seven-year period, whereas the 90th percentile saw their consumption increase by 27 percent. Similar patterns are seen comparing the 1st and 99th percentiles.

Despite these analyses and the increasing gaps between rich and poor, it is important to note that these changes are likely to be significant underestimations given difficulties of measurement at the extreme top and bottom of the distribution.

Table 7:   Palma index 2006-2013

	2006	2013
All Households		
National	2.24	2.31
Urban	1.76	1.76
Rural	1.85	2.19
Households with children		
National	1.88	1.86
Urban	1.49	1.41
Rural	1.51	1.78
Households without children		
National	1.73	1.95
Urban	1.59	1.63
Rural	1.41	1.99

Note: The Palma index is the ratio of the share of adult equivalent consumption held by the top 10 percent of the population to the share of adult equivalent consumption held by the bottom 40 percent. The fact that the national Palma index values are higher than those in both the urban and rural areas is accounted for by the significant increase between 2006 and 2013 in the proportion of the sample coming from the wealthier urban areas and corresponding reduction in poorer rural areas.
Source: Authors' calculation based on GLSS5 and 6

The Palma index reported in Table 7 shows that the richest 10 percent consume more than twice as much as the bottom 40 percent of the population put together[5]. The index has increased between 2006 and

---

[5]   Cobham and Sumner (2013) note that a Palma index of 2 is consistent with a reported Gini coefficient of 41percent. The Palma index of 2.24 and 2.36 reported in the text are consistent with the Gini coefficients of 40.6 percent and 40.9 percent observed in 2006 and 2013. Given that our data is not directly comparable to other countries we avoid a direct comparison in this chapter.

2013 for all households in Ghana. While the increase has been larger in rural areas, urban areas have experienced a stagnation in the index (the index remained at 1.76 for both periods). When we consider households with children, one notices a marginal decline of less than 0.1 percentage points nationally and in urban areas. The increase in the index between 2006 and 2013 for rural areas is worrying. It is an indication that while poverty has fallen in rural areas and income has risen in the country, it has not been enough to slow down the increase in inequality in rural areas.

Households without children have seen an increase in the Palma index nationally, in urban and in rural areas. The increase in the index for households without children is 0.2 percentage points. Urban households without children experience a marginal increase of 0.03 percentage points while rural households experience an increase of 0.58 percentage points. Again, the rural households experience a larger increase compared to urban households.

The rise in the Palma index is consistent with the increase in the consumption gap between the richest 10 percent and the bottom 40 percent. The mean adult equivalent consumption for the top 10 percent in 2013 is 10,651 GHS while that of the bottom 40 percent is 1154 (the corresponding values for 2006 is 9,532 GHS and 1,062 GHS). The difference between the two values gives us what Hoy (2015) calls the "absolute Palma." The "absolute Palma" increased from 8,470 GHS to 9,497 GHS between 2006 and 2013 — implying an increase in the gap in mean adult equivalent consumption between the richest 10 percent and the poorest 40 percent.

Growth rates and incidence

In this section we develop the inequality analysis by looking at growth rates experienced by Ghana's child population at different percentiles. We provide the consumption growth at each decile point for the child population and for the total population alongside.

Table 8:   Annual consumption growth rates at each decile 2006-2013

Deciles	2006-2013 annual growth – for children	2006-2013 annual growth – nation-wide
National	2.8	3.1
10	3.1	2.9
20	2.7	2.8
30	2.7	2.8
40	2.5	2.8
50	2.6	2.7
60	2.5	2.9
70	2.9	3.1
80	2.7	3.6
90	3.8	4.1

Source: Authors' calculation based on GLSS5 and 6

First, consistent with the inequality analysis, we note that growth rates are lower for households with children than for the population as a whole in 9 out of 10 deciles. Furthermore, 6 decile groups of children record lower growth than the national average, a result shown again in the growth incidence curves presented below. To analyse this further we consider the incidence of growth across the percentiles of the population in the same period, 2006 to 2013, comparing households with children and those without. Overall, the growth incidence curves presented in this section indicate that in the majority of cases greater growth has occurred among the top percentiles of the population compared to the lower percentiles. Additionally, all the growth incidence curves lie above zero, indicating that all groups of people have experienced at least some growth (i.e. no groups have seen declines in consumption).

In Figure 7 we compare the growth incidence curves for all individuals in Ghana with all children. As in Table 8, we note that the growth occurring has been lower for the child population compared to the entire population. On average, growth rates are also lower for poorer people in both groups. The results are consistent with the increasing inequality and the higher level of poverty exhibited among the child population in the country. However, the very poorest have seen relatively high growth rates and those in households with children are even higher. It is presumably this growth that has therefore contributed in large part to the impressive reductions in extreme poverty in the country.

Figure 7:   Growth incidence curves, 2006-2013 (all individuals versus children)

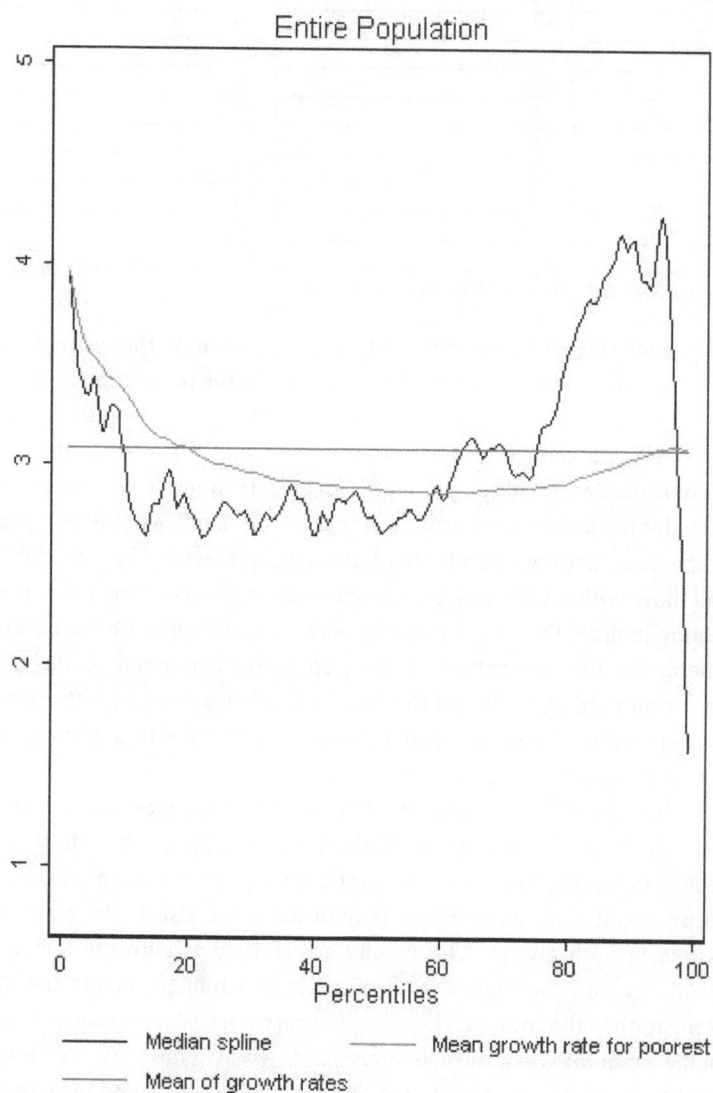

Entire Population

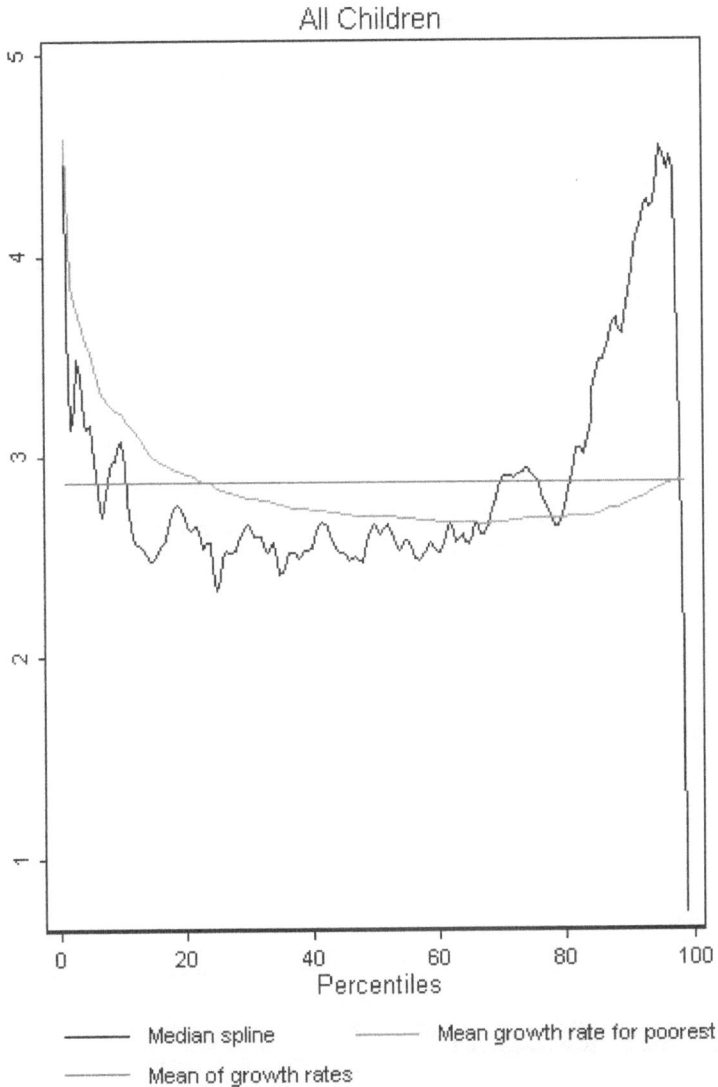

Source: Authors' elaboration of GLSS5 and 6

In Figure 8, we plot the growth incidence curve for urban households with children and rural households with children. Rural households with children show much higher growth across all percentiles compared to the

168   Hague et al.

urban households in the 2006 – 2013 period. The rural growth incidence curve is above 2 percent for almost all percentiles while a greater portion of urban households show a growth incidence curve below 2 percent. In particular, the figure presents two important points. First of all, some of Ghana's most impressive growth has been in urban ultra-poor households — where the bottom percentile was experiencing growth of well over 5 percent per year, compared to the average of just 1.04 percent. How has such growth been created, and can it be extended to slightly better-off groups? And given the substantial urbanisation that is still occurring, how long can such high growth rates for this group be maintained? Secondly, we notice another urban story — that a large chunk, perhaps most closely resembling a low-middle class, have experienced the lowest growth rates for the country. This urban low middle class, located approximately between the 15th and 50th percentile in urban areas, has experienced growth of under 1 percent. This may reflect the reality of rapid urbanisation and rising prices in urban areas in recent years.

This implies that government should learn from the positive growth experience of the ultra-poor in urban areas but also need to turn greater attention to the low growth of the rest of the poor and the bottom middle class in urban zones. While rural households tend to be poorer than urban counterparts in relative terms, there is a rapidly growing number of urban poor who are being left behind by their wealthier counterparts.

Figure 8:   Growth incidence curves, 2006-2013 (urban and rural households with children)

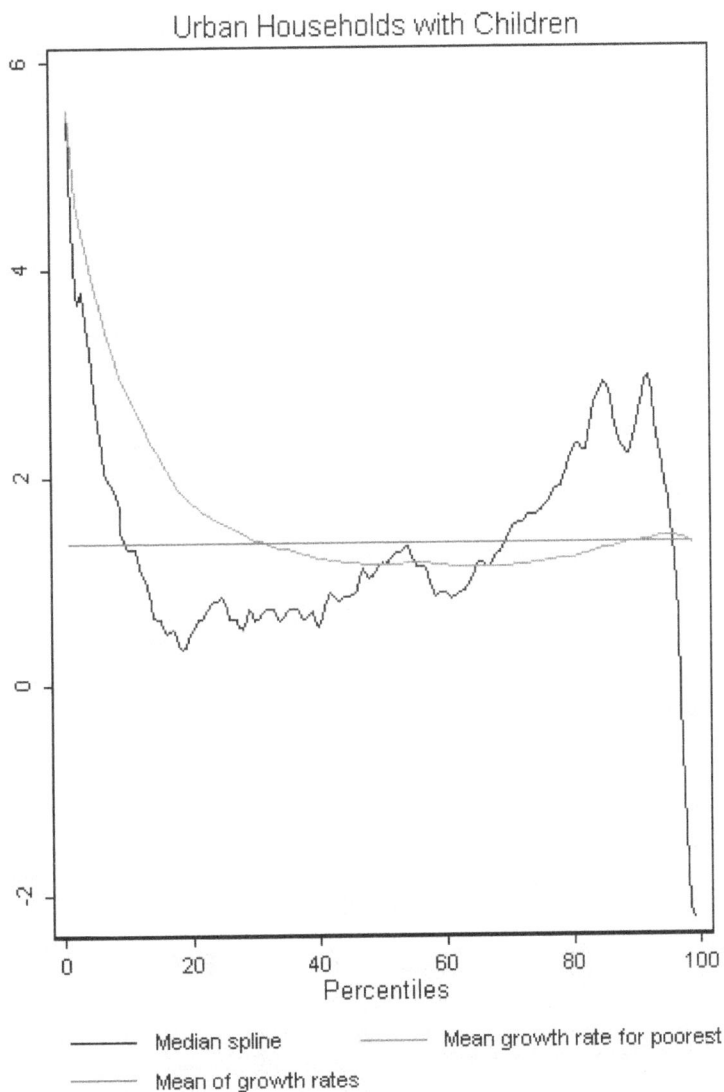

Urban Households with Children

Median spline	Mean growth rate for poorest
Mean of growth rates	

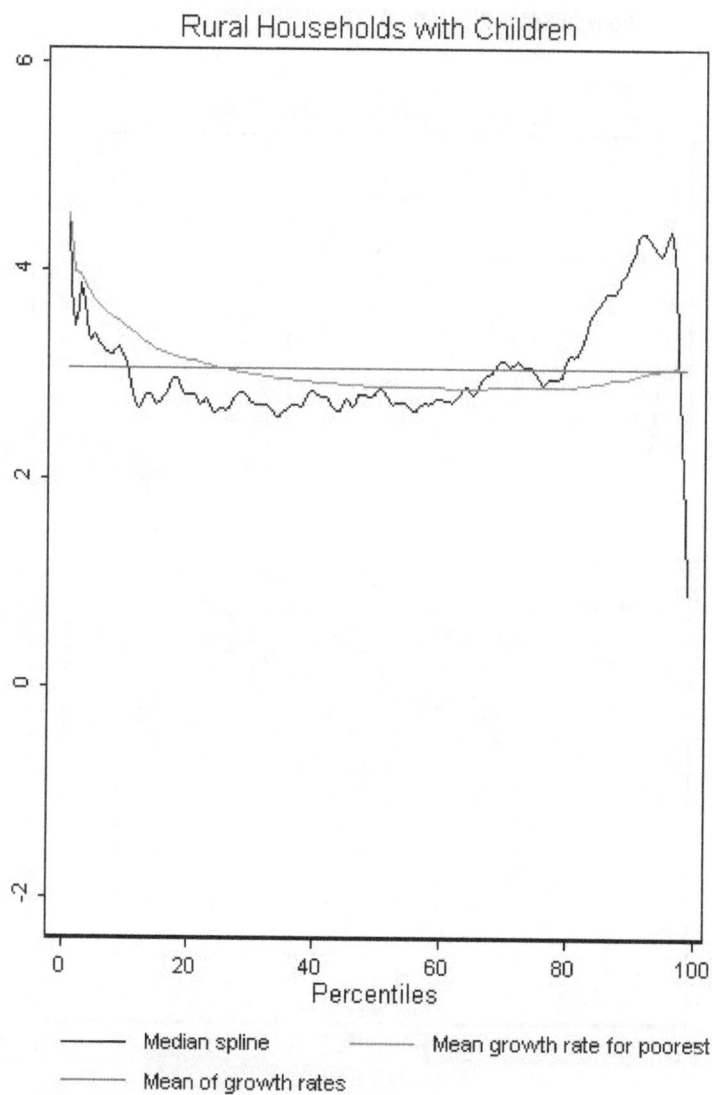

Rural Households with Children

Legend:
Median spline ——— Mean growth rate for poorest
——— Mean of growth rates

Source: Authors' elaboration of GLSS5 and 6

CONCLUSION

Given the specific vulnerabilities of children and the intergenerational impacts that child poverty causes, it is important to explore the issue of child poverty in greater detail. Furthermore, with almost 45 percent of the population being younger than 18 years of age in Ghana, not capturing what is happening with child poverty may lead to over-confidence about progress to eliminate poverty. In this chapter, we looked specifically at consumption poverty (i.e. monetary poverty) for children between the last two household surveys of 2006 and 2013 as a complement to the extensive research on non-monetary wellbeing in the country.

Despite Ghana's impressive achievement of meeting the MDG target of halving poverty, its progress in cutting the numbers of poor children has been much slower. In addition, as larger households are poorer, we find that child poverty is 40 percent higher than adult poverty, and that it is not being cut any faster than adult poverty. In addition to the fact that the country's poverty reduction performance is slowing and that we find that poor children live deeper in poverty on average than poor adults, this means that Ghana's policy-makers need to assess how children will benefit from the new strategies being discussed to promote inclusive development in the country.

In terms of inequality in the country, we find that inequality has continued to rise in Ghana, belying the stagnation in the Gini coefficient. For households with children, consumption is lower than the national average, and growth in that consumption is also lower than average. While we find that growth incidence has been generally higher for wealthier groups, we also find that growth rates are lower for households with children than the population as a whole in 9 out of 10 decile groups. However, it is interesting to see higher growth rates for the ultra-poor especially in urban areas, which, although hard to accurately capture, is encouraging and needs further exploration.

Although children are more vulnerable to monetary poverty than adults, child poverty is more common, more severe and is reduced more slowly than that of the population as a whole. There are some positive lessons to learn from our research; however, it is clear that while the country's population continues to grow rapidly, Ghana's development trajectory will need to consciously become more inclusive. This will ultimately make Ghana's development trajectory more sustainable by engaging the poorest while accelerating the expansion of protection to children living in poverty.

172   Hague et al.

REFERENCES

Antwi-Asare, T., J. Cockburn, E.F.A. Cooke, I. Fofana, L. Tiberti, and D.K. Twerefou (2010) 'Simulating the Impact of the Global Economic Crisis and Policy Responses on Children in Ghana', *UNICEF Innocenti Working Paper*, IWP-2010-05, UNICEF Regional Office for West and Central Africa.

Banks, J., R. Blundell, and I. Preston (1991) 'Adult Equivalence Scales: A Life-Cycle Perspective', *Fiscal Studies* 12, 16–29. doi:10.1111/j.1475-5890.1991.tb00159.x

Barrientos, A. and J. DeJong (2006) 'Reducing Child Poverty with Cash Transfers: A Sure Thing?', *Development Policy Review* 24, 537–552. doi:10.1111/j.1467-7679.2006.00346.x

Barrientos, A. and J. DeJong (2004) 'Child poverty and cash transfers', *CHIP Report* No. 4. London: Childhood Poverty Research and Policy Centre.

Blackorby, C., D. Donaldson, and M. Auersperg (1981) 'A New Procedure for the Measurement of Inequality within and among Population Subgroups', *The Canadian Journal of Economics / Revue canadienne d'Economique* 14, 665–685. doi:10.2307/134822.

Burniaux, J.-M., T.-T. Dang, D. Fore, M. Förster, M. M. d'Ercole and H. Oxley (1998) 'Income Distribution and Poverty in Selected OECD Countries', Economics Department Working Papers No. 189. Paris: OECD. Available at: http://www.oecd.org/eco/eco.

Claro, R.M., R.B. Levy, D.H. Bandoni, and L. Mondini (2010) 'Per capita versus adult-equivalent estimates of calorie availability in household budget surveys', *Cadernos de Saúde Pública* 26, 2188–2195. doi:10.1590/S0102-311X2010001100020

Cobham, A. and A. Sumner (2013) 'Is It All About the Tails? The Palma Measure of Income Inequality', CGD Working Paper 343. Washington, DC: Center for Global Development. Available at: http://www.cgdev.org/publication/it-all-about-tails-palma-measure-income-inequality, accessed March 10, 2019.

Cobham, A. and A. Sumner (2014) 'Is inequality all about the tails? The Palma measure of income inequality', Significance 11, 10–13. doi:10.1111/j.1740-9713.2014.00718.x

Cobham, A., L. Schlögl, and A. Sumner (2016) 'Inequality and the Tails: the Palma Proposition and Ratio', *Global Policy* 7, 25–36. doi:10.1111/1758-5899.12320

Cooke, E.F.A., S. Hague and A. McKay (2016) *The Ghana Inequality and Poverty Report: Using the 6th Ghana Living Standards Survey*, Accra: UNICEF

Ghana Statistical Service [GSS] (2000), Poverty Trends in Ghana in the 1990s, Accra: Ghana Statistical Service.

Ghana Statistical Service [GSS] (2008) *Ghana Living Standards Survey Report of the Fifth Round (GLSS5)*, Accra: Ghana Statistical Service.

Ghana Statistical Service [GSS] (2014) *Ghana Living Standards Survey Round 6 (GLSS6): Main Report*, Accra: Ghana Statistical Service.

Hazledine, T. (2014) 'Does the Centre Hold? Testing Palma's Proposition (A Comment)', *Development and Change* 45, 1409–1415. doi:10.1111/dech.12105

Hoy C. (2015) 'Leaving no one behind: The Impact of Pro-Poor Growth', ODI report. London: Overseas Development Institute. Available at: https://www.odi.org/sites/odi.org.uk/files/odi-assets/publications-opinion-files/9996.pdf

McKay, A., J. Pirttilä, and F. Tarp (2015) 'Ghana: Poverty reduction over thirty years', *UNU-WIDER Working Paper* 2015(052) Helsinki: UNU-WIDER.

Muellbauer, J. (1979) 'McClements on equivalence scales for children', *Journal of Public Economics* 12, 221–231. doi:10.1016/0047-2727(79)90015-X

Palma, J.G. (2006) 'Globalizing Inequality: 'Centrifugal' and 'Centripetal' Forces at Work', UN DESA Working Paper 35. New York, NY: UN DESA.

Palma, J.G. (2011) 'Homogeneous Middles vs. Heterogeneous Tails, and the End of the "Inverted-U": It's All About the Share of the Rich', *Development and Change* 42, 87–153. doi:10.1111/j.1467-7660.2011.01694.x

Palma, J.G. (2014) 'Has the Income Share of the Middle and Upper-middle Been Stable around the "50/50 Rule", or Has it Converged towards that Level? The "Palma Ratio" Revisited', *Development and Change* 45, 1416–1448. doi:10.1111/dech.12133

OECD (2011) *Divided We Stand*, Paris: Organisation for Economic Co-operation and Development.

OECD (2015) *In It Together: Why Less Inequality Benefits All*, Paris: Organisation for Economic Co-operation and Development.

UNICEF (2000) *Poverty Reduction Begins with Children*, New York: UNICEF. Available at: http://www.unicef.org/publications/index_5616.html

APPENDIX

Table A1:   Summary statistics

2006

	count	mean	p50	min	max
Urban					
Number of children	13056	2.36	2	0	5
Children and adults	13056	0.42	0	0	1
Gender	13056	0.52	1	0	1
Region	13056	4.42	4	1	10
Gender of household head	13056	0.29	0	0	1
rural					
Number of children	24072	3.08	3	0	5
Children and adults	24072	0.50	1	0	1
Gender	24072	0.51	1	0	1
Region	24072	5.45	6	1	10
Gender of household head	24072	0.20	0	0	1
Total					
Number of children	37128	2.81	3	0	5
Children and adults	37128	0.47	0	0	1
Gender	37128	0.52	1	0	1
Region	37128	5.06	5	1	10
Gender of household head	37128	0.23	0	0	1

2013					
	count	mean	p50	min	max
Urban					
Number of children	27478	2.38	2	0	5
Children and adults	27478	0.43	0	0	1
Sex of individual	27478	1.53	2	1	2
Region	27478	4.51	4	1	10
Sex of household head	27478	1.30	1	1	2
Rural					
Number of children	44894	3.01	3	0	5
Children and adults	44894	0.49	0	0	1
Sex of individual	44894	1.51	2	1	2
Region	44894	5.40	6	1	10
Sex of household head	44894	1.20	1	1	2
Total					
Number of children	72372	2.69	3	0	5
Children and adults	72372	0.46	0	0	1
Sex of individual	72372	1.52	2	1	2
Region	72372	4.95	5	1	10
Sex of household head	72372	1.25	1	1	2

Note: Summary statistics shown in the table are based on all individuals in the dataset. The mean values have been weighted with sample weights reported in the dataset. Source: Authors' elaboration of GLSS5 and 6

Figure A1:   Child- and adult-headed households

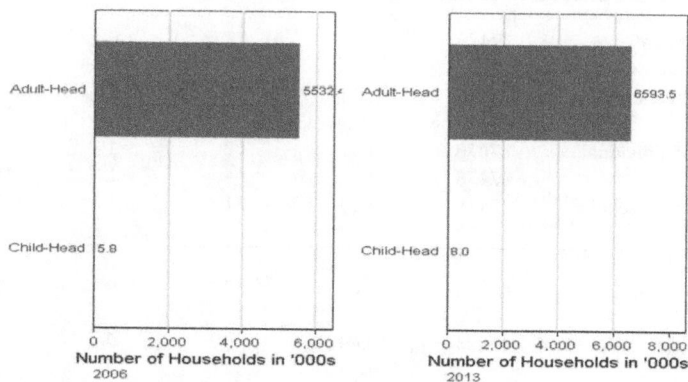

Note: Weighted results using sample weights from the GLSS. We only report the presence of a few child-headed households. The sample of child-headed households is too small for any meaningful analysis of their level of poverty.
Source: Authors' calculation

PART III: CHILD POVERTY, HUMANITARIAN CRISES, AND SOCIAL PROTECTION

CHAPTER 6

CHILD POVERTY AND DISASTER RISK IN MAURITANIA

Daniela Gregr[1]

INTRODUCTION

Over the last decade, the link between disaster risk reduction (DRR)[2] and sustainable development has been given increased attention. Recent high-level development summits and their respective outcome documents are a testimony to that evolution, bringing forth the scale and importance of the challenge and the different dimensions of this converging agenda. Research and academic literature have been discussing and documenting these important linkages for even longer (e.g. Bankoff et al. 2003; Gaillard 2010; Pelling et al. 2004; Schipper and Pelling 2006; Wisner et al. 2004) and have benefited from the increased prominence of the issue at the international level to impact the global policy agenda.

At the same time, it has been widely recognised — based on abundant and irrefutable evidence — that the poor and in particular poor women, children, the elderly and people living with disabilities, are disproportionally affected by disasters. This is through the pernicious combination of exposure, socio-economic vulnerability and reduced capacities to recover from shocks.[3] Children, in particular under two

---

[1] The author would like to acknowledge the contribution of Mr Isselmou Mohamed, who worked tirelessly on the data analysis and accommodated our many methodological requests. The author would also like to acknowledge the assistance provided by the National Statistics Institute (www.oms.mr), in particular by Mr Elyas Didi, Director of Demographic and Social Statistics, and Mr Pierre Klissou, Chief Technical Advisor on the National Census (UNFPA). This analysis was carried out chiefly for internal programming purposes and all shortcomings are the author's alone.

[2] Disaster risk reduction aims at preventing new and reducing existing disaster risk and managing residual risk (i.e. risk that remains in unmanaged form, even when effective disaster risk reduction measures are in place, and for which emergency response and recovery capacities must be maintained) (UN 2016b: 10, 22).

[3] The definition of disaster and disaster risk used in this chapter is: "The potential loss of life, injury, or destroyed or damaged assets which could occur to a system, society or a community in a specific period of time, determined probabilistically as

years of age, are often impacted irreversibly (e.g. Alderman et al. 2006; Ampaabeng and Tan 2013), contributing to the long-term and intergenerational impoverishing effects of disasters. Yet, unfortunately, multidimensional child poverty has not been systematically included in disaster risk analysis, despite its potential to capture essential dimensions of vulnerability to shocks of girls and boys in different age groups as well as household responses and their adaptive capacities. This chapter intends to contribute to filling this gap in the literature by establishing this vital conceptual link and by presenting and discussing the results of a child poverty and vulnerability analysis for Mauritania (UNICEF Mauritania 2016a, 2016b).

SUSTAINABLE DEVELOPMENT AND CHILD POVERTY

A risk-informed post-2015 agenda

In September 2015, the much-anticipated Sustainable Development Summit led to the adoption of the new global agenda for development and set the tone for a "risk-informed and resilient post-2015 agenda"[4] by introducing DRR-related targets under several of the 17 Sustainable Development Goals (SDGs).[5] The resulting document also clearly committed signatory Heads of State and Government to holistic disaster risk management (DRM).[6] This commitment was fully in line with the March 2015 World Conference on Disaster Risk Reduction, at which

---

a *function of hazard, exposure, vulnerability and capacity* [emphasis added]" (UN 2016b: 14).

[4]   Statement by Margareta Wahlström, Special Representative of the UN Secretary-General for Disaster Risk Reduction at the Third International Conference on Financing for Development, 13-16 July 2015, Addis Ababa, Ethiopia

[5]   These are in particular: Targets 1.5 (resilience of poor and vulnerable populations, reducing exposure to shocks); 2.4 (resilient agricultural practices); 3.d (early warning and risk reduction in terms of health risks); 9.1 (resilient infrastructure); 11.1 (safe housing, slum upgrading); 11.5 (reduction of disaster related deaths); 11.b (urban policies and plans for resilience to disasters). However, all goals and targets related to preserving natural resources and eco-systems to fight climate change (e.g. Goals 12 to 15), as well as those aiming at promoting peaceful societies (e.g. Goal 16) or those targeting "vulnerable" population groups (e.g. Target 6.2 — sanitation and hygiene needs for women and girls in vulnerable situations) could reasonably also be cited here. See: https://sustainabledevelopment.un.org/

[6]   Disaster risk management is the application of disaster risk reduction policies and strategies (UN 2016b: 15). Accordingly, DRM can be prospective, corrective or compensatory.

States had reiterated their pledge to building resilience to disasters in the context of sustainable development (UN 2015a: 9).[7]

The means of implementation of the new agenda were agreed at the Third International Conference on Financing for Development held in Addis Ababa in July of the same year. The Addis Ababa Action Agenda – considered an "integral part of the 2030 Agenda for Sustainable Development" (UN 2015c: 28) – recognises that "development finance can contribute to reducing social, environmental and economic vulnerabilities and enable countries to prevent or combat situations of chronic crisis related to conflicts or natural disasters" (UN 2015b: 30). The need for "coherence of developmental and humanitarian finance to ensure more timely, comprehensive, appropriate and cost-effective approaches to the management and mitigation of natural disasters and complex emergencies" was also underscored (Ibid. 32). The fact that "humanitarian assistance alone can neither adequately address nor sustainably reduce the needs of over 130 million of the world's most vulnerable people" (UNSG 2015: 2), and that humanitarian, development and peacebuilding efforts need to be decisively and deliberately brought together (UN 2016a: 2) would subsequently be reiterated at the first World Humanitarian Summit in May 2016.

Last, but not least, as DRR can no longer be dissociated from the need for climate change adaptation (CCA), the contribution of the Paris COP21, the 2015 United Nations Conference of Parties on Climate Change, must be duly acknowledged. The Paris Agreement (UNFCC 2015) aims to strengthen the global response to the threat of climate change, in the context of sustainable development and poverty eradication (Article 2). Parties recognized the importance of averting, minimizing and addressing loss and damage associated with the adverse effects of climate change, including extreme weather, events and slow onset events, and the role of sustainable development in reducing the risk of loss and damage (Article 8).

---

[7]   At the regional level, climate resillience and natural disasters preparedness have been among the priority areas of the African Union's 2063 Agenda, since its adoption in 2013. See: https://au.int/agenda2063/goals (Accessed 25 June 2019).

Leaving no one behind?

This increasing momentum of the DRR/sustainable development nexus has been fuelled by convincing evidence that climate change is likely to increase the frequency and severity of extreme weather events as well as slow onset meteorological phenomena such as droughts. Climate change thus has the potential to reverse hard-gained development results and further divert already scarce development funding towards disaster response.

It is in fact low-income countries and Small Island Developing States that bear the brunt of disasters, incurring disproportionately large damage relative to their assets (e.g. Rentschler 2013), including a significant erosion of essential development resources, such as schools, health facilities, roads and local infrastructure. Expressed as a proportion of social expenditure, expected annual losses in low-income countries are five times higher than in high-income countries (UNISDR 2015: v). This is still likely to be an underestimation as it is extensive risks (minor but recurrent disaster risks) that are responsible for most disaster morbidity and displacement in low and middle-income countries. The cost of extensive risk is not visible and tends to be underestimated because it is usually absorbed by low-income households, communities and small businesses (Ibid: iv).

In fact, the equity dimension of disaster risk becomes even more acutely visible at the household level. It is low-income households and communities that suffer a disproportionate share of disaster losses (e.g. DFID 2004; Rentschler 2013; UNDP 2014; UNISDR 2009, 2015; Wisner et al. 2003). Disaster risk is shaped not only by income poverty, but also by a range of social and economic factors, including access to services, socio-economic status and political participation, all of which determine capabilities and susceptibility to shocks (e.g. Shepherd et al. 2013). Key factors in underprivileged areas include low quality and insecure housing; limited access to basic services such as health care, public transport and communications; limited access to infrastructure such as water, sanitation, drainage and roads; a low asset base; and the absence of a safety net (Ibid.). In other words, individuals and households who are subject to multi-dimensional poverty are more likely to live in hazard-exposed areas and are less able to invest in risk-reducing measures (UNISDR 2015: 186).

The missing link

Socio-economic factors and the non-income dimensions of poverty thus make children, alongside women, the disabled and the elderly, highly susceptible to shocks (e.g. Lovell and Le Masson 2014). Not only does children's physiology make them more susceptible than adults to malnutrition and certain health impacts of disasters,[8] they also rely on caregivers, who may be unprepared or overwhelmed or children may become separated from them, increasing vulnerability further. Moreover, children are often perceived as "victims" rather than agents and hence not systematically included in DRR decision-making, which not only limits their contribution, but also heightens their vulnerability (Ibid.: 9).

Disasters affect children quite differently than it affects adults; this is particularly in terms of potential long-term and sometimes irreversible effects, depending on the age of the child at which he or she is affected,[9] including any indirect effects of disasters.[10] Disasters can disrupt or damage educational and health-care facilities, reducing or interrupting the availability of essential services. A child may be too sick — be it due to contaminated water sources, malnutrition or pneumonia related to overcrowding and exposure to smoke from cooking fires in overcrowded shelters – to attend school. Households may lose income (due to destruction of assets and/or illness or death of income-earning household

---

[8] Kousky explains, for example, that children breathe more air per pound of body weight than adults do, and their bodies contain less fluid, making them more susceptible to dehydration. Children may also have greater trouble processing emotional trauma (Kousky 2016: 76).

[9] The first two years of life are usually considered the critical period for child development, although there is some discussion on the criticality of specific windows within that period in response to shocks. For example, Glewwe and King (2001) as well as Maccini and Young (2009) find that malnutrition is particularly determining during the second year of life (post-weaning). Mendez and Adair (1999), on the other hand, find that malnutrition in the first six months of the life of a child is critical largely because it increases risk of severe stunting which in turn is linked to irretrievable loss of stature and cognitive deficits. UNICEF and other international organizations simply refer to the "first 1000 days of life", including also the period from conception until birth, as the window of opportunity for every child.

[10] The distinction between 'direct' and 'indirect' impacts of disasters is taken from Baez et al. 2010. The former refers to the physical destruction of infrastructure, loss of human life, etc., while the latter can be observed at either macro-economic (e.g. fiscal constraints) or micro-economic levels (e.g. loss of income and household coping strategies).

members) and/or face expenditures for disaster repairs. This in turn can cause these households to reduce expenditures on medical care, food, or school supplies or to send children into the labour force — all negative, potentially long-term effects not only for the children themselves, but also to future generations (e.g. Baez et al. 2010; Maccini and Young 2009; Maluccio et al. 2009; Victora et al. 2008).

Today, over half a billion children live in extremely high flood occurrence zones; nearly 160 million live in high or extremely high drought severity zones (UNICEF 2015). Overall, children typically make up 50 percent of those affected by disasters (Save the Children 2008). It is therefore unfortunate that no systematic and explicit linkages have been established between child poverty/deprivation analysis and assessments in the framework of DRM. This is despite the fact that many countries regularly conduct child poverty type analysis on the one hand,[11] while DRR analytical and programming tools are being developed and perfected on the other.[12]

Child poverty analysis covers some of the most essential dimensions of children's capacity and — conversely — vulnerability to hazard impact such as health and education status, access to water and sanitation, housing and access to information, especially if combined with socio-economic data on the households in which deprived children live. Child deprivation analysis thus has the potential to make a non-negligible contribution to effective DRR. It is multidimensional in nature and bears the potential to disaggregate by sex, age group and region, thus making a sub-group of the general population particularly prone to long-term, irreversible effects of disasters — children — and their differential needs visible to decision-makers. In preparedness,[13] child deprivation analysis ought to be part of vulnerability assessments and mapping to influence preparedness plans, including sector preparedness plans. In the recovery phase, it could be fitted into post-disaster needs assessments and reconstruction programmes.[14]

---

[11]   See e.g. UNICEF 2016 and 2017 and https://www.unicef-irc.org/research/258/ (Accessed 21 December 2017)

[12]   See www.unisdr.org for an overview

[13]   DRM is often viewed as having five focal areas: prevention, mitigation, preparedness, response and recovery (OPM 2015: 7).

[14]   Child poverty analysis could, for example, draw attention to the fact that shock responsive social protection need not be restricted to one specific instrument,

Vulnerability, as defined by UNICEF's social protection framework (UNICEF 2012: 4), captures the interaction between exposure to risk and the capacity to respond and cope. While no causality can be implied, given that a disaster's effects are mediated by the individual characteristics of children, families and communities (Kousky 2016: 76), it is safe to assume that the higher the depth of deprivation/poverty of children in hazard exposed areas, the higher their vulnerability to further stresses.[15] Combining child deprivation analysis with natural hazard exposure mapping also reveals how many children that are currently not deprived or moderately deprived, could potentially fall (further) into poverty. Last, but not least, child poverty analysis can yield interesting insights into capacities: areas exposed to frequent hazards, but with limited child deprivations, potentially point to robust household resilience mechanisms, which would merit much closer attention. More specifically, the absence of child deprivation in terms of access to education and information can reveal a potential for prevention and preparedness.

The following section presents child poverty and vulnerability analysis for Mauritania to illustrate the preceding arguments. The analysis combines child deprivation data with risk exposure to both rapid onset and slow onset disasters and extensive risk, with different degrees of deprivation representing different degrees of susceptibility to hazard impact or, conversely, capacity to anticipate, cope with, resist and recover from hazard impacts (DFID 2004: 2). The objective is not to unravel causality linkages, as this would require much more in-depth and region-specific investigations, but rather to call for methodological and interdisciplinary linkages. At the core of the analysis also lies a compelling policy argument: measures aimed at reducing child poverty contribute to disaster risk reduction by boosting children's capacity to cope with hazard impacts. Conversely, DRR efforts can promote (child) poverty reduction by helping to avoid the impoverishing effects of disasters, including their intergenerational effects.

---

such as cash transfers, but could also include education-specific instruments such as school feeding or health-specific interventions such as community-based health insurance schemes (OPM 2015: 3).

[15] More research is needed on the impact on children not just of disasters themselves, but of living in areas where disaster risk is high (Kousky 2016: 77).

186   Gregr

CHILD POVERTY AND VULNERABILITY ANALYSIS FOR MAURITANIA: METHODOLOGICAL CHOICES

The analysis of child poverty in Mauritania (UNICEF 2016) is multidimensional and uses national census data (ONS 2015a) as the main source. The exposure of children to natural hazards is examined with the help of food insecurity data as well as the geographic distribution of flood-prone areas, droughts and floods being the most frequently occurring natural hazards for Mauritania.[16] Food security data is used as proxy for drought given that food insecurity in Mauritania, whose rural population relies heavily on rain-fed agriculture, is most frequently triggered by drought. Moreover, food security data is collected regularly and reliably through the Food Security Monitoring System (FSMS), while drought as slow onset and high frequency disaster is often not recorded as such in international databases.

Child deprivation analysis

Gordon et al. 2003 have developed the first operational measure of absolute poverty for children. The approach chosen by Gordon and his team, after thorough review of alternative and prevailing methods of poverty measurement, is one based on deprivations, as defined by Townsend (1987)[17] and direct indicators of living standards (in contrast to consumption, an indirect indicator). Gordon's definition of absolute poverty and the different categories of deprivation for children are derived from the Convention of the Rights of the Child (CRC), but more specifically from the definition of the 1995 Copenhagen Summit for Social Development. The summit defined absolute poverty as "a condition characterised by severe deprivation of basic human needs, including food, safe drinking water, sanitation facilities, health, shelter, education and information" (UN 1995 as cited in Gordon et al. 2003: 5).

---

[16] See for example the Mauritania Country profile on the GAR website: http://www.preventionweb.net/english/hyogo/gar/2015/en/home/data.php?iso=MRT (Accessed 21 December 2017)
[17] "Deprivation may be defined as a state of observable and demonstrable disadvantage relative to the local community or the wider society or nation to which an individual, family or group belongs" (Townsend 1987 as cited in Gordon et al. 2003: 6).

Based on this definition, Gordon et al. set out to define threshold measures of severe deprivation for these domains, based on data availability for a large number of children and in line with internationally agreed standards and conventions. They defined "severe deprivation of basic human need" as those circumstances that are highly likely to have serious adverse consequences for the health, well-being and development of children (Gordon et al. 2003: 7). They intentionally defined the thresholds in very severe terms to ensure "that few would question that these living conditions were unacceptable" (Ibid: 9).

The analysis for Mauritania follows Gordon et al.'s approach based on child deprivations, adopting the same definition of absolute poverty (children suffering from at least two severe deprivations) and the same thresholds for severe deprivation, within the limits imposed by the decision to use census data (see below). The thresholds proposed by Gordon et al. were deemed appropriate as they are based on internationally agreed standards; moreover, a national adaptation would have been overly ambitious for the intended scope of the analysis. The study also follows Gordon et al.'s decision to consider only severe deprivations for the analysis, defined by rather unforgiving thresholds. Just as Gordon's measurements of the extent and depth of child poverty in the developing world, the analysis of child vulnerabilities and disparities for Mauritania may thus also be considered to under-estimate child deprivations, due to the severity of measures used (Ibid: 31).

Data sources

As indicated, the main source of data for the analysis of child vulnerabilities and disparities in Mauritania is the national 2013 census (*Recensement général de la population et de l'habitat, RGPH*). In their analysis, Gordon et al. found that "the most appropriate available data which could be used to operationalise the measurement of child poverty in developing countries were the DHS [Demographic and Health Surveys]" (Ibid.: 7). However, in an earlier reflection on possible data sources, Gordon et al. did in fact include census data. They cited ECOSOC to highlight census data as "one of the primary sources of data needed for effective development planning and the monitoring of population issues and socio-economic and environmental trends, policies and programmes aimed at the improvement of living standards" (Gordon et al. 2001: 17).

For the child vulnerability analysis for Mauritania, the choice of the national census data was one born out of necessity, since the analysis was carried out in 2015 and up-to-date Multiple Indicator Cluster Survey (MICS) data was not yet available.[18] At the same time, in a national context where disaggregated data is scarce and a more fine-grained geographic targeting of development interventions challenging, the analysis sought maximum disaggregation while avoiding major data manipulation. With the census, the main unit of disaggregation was the commune level, rather than the regional (Wilaya) or district (Moughataa) levels at which all other household surveys were set. The choice to use census data was further encouraged by the fact that the 2013 census for Mauritania has not only been fully aligned with international standards and guidelines, but has also previously collected GPS data of dwellings, localities as well as basic services (such as health centres, schools, water points, etc.); thus offering a plethora of additional analytical options.

Yet, the decision to use census rather than MICS data has inevitably imposed some limitations on fully applying Gordon et al.'s approach to child poverty. In fact, the census did not provide information on severe nutrition deprivations[19] or severe health deprivations[20] as defined by Gordon et al. (2003:7). For the severe safe drinking water deprivation, only the data on the usage of surface water could be used, as the 2013 census did not collect data on the distance to the nearest water source at the household level. The deprivation in terms of access to basic social services had to be left out for the same reasons.[21]

---

[18]   The National Statistics Office implemented the MICS5 survey in 2015 and data became available in November 2016. The previous MICS survey for Mauritania dated back to 2011; see: http://mics.unicef.org/surveys (Accessed 21 December 2017).

[19]   Children whose heights and weights for their age are more than –3 standard deviations below the median of the reference population.

[20]   Children not vaccinated against any disease or young children who had a recent illness involving diarrhoea and had not received any medical advice or treatment.

[21]   GPS data collected on all community infrastructures (by locality) in the census could potentially allow crossing data on households with children with GPS data by locality to calculate distance.

This table summarises Gordon's taxonomy and thresholds for child deprivations and how they were replicated for Mauritania's child vulnerability analysis:

Basic human need	Severe deprivation (Gordon et al.)	Severe deprivation (Mauritania)
Nutrition	Malnutrition (severe anthropometric failure)	Data not available in census; deprivation analysis and mapping supplemented by SMART[22] survey data
Safe drinking water	Long walk to water source (more than 200 meters or 15 minutes) or unsafe drinking water (surface water)	Use of surface water adopted as definition of severe deprivation
Sanitation facilities	No access to sanitation of any kind in or near dwelling	Data available in census; same definition of severe deprivation used
Health	No immunisation against any diseases	Data not available in census; this deprivation has not been covered in the analysis
Shelter	More than five people per room (severe overcrowding) or with no flooring material	Data available in census; same definition of severe deprivation used
Education	School age children who have never been to school and who are currently not attending school	Data available in census; same definition of severe deprivation used
Information	Children aged between 3 and 18 with no access to radio, television, telephone or newspapers at home	Data available in census; same definition of severe deprivation used
Basic social services	Children living 20km or more from any type of school or 50km or more from any medical facility with doctors	Data not available in census; this deprivation has not been covered in the analysis

To compensate for the lack of census data for the food/nutrition deprivation, the analysis used SMART survey data (the severe acute malnutrition (SAM) rates) of July 2013 (Ministère de la Santé 2013), which was disaggregated at Moughataa (district) level[23] (see section on mapping below).

---

[22]   Standardized Monitoring and Assessment of Relief and Transitions
[23]   SMART surveys for Mauritania are usually disaggregated at regional (Wilaya) level; the July 2013 survey was an exception together with the June 2015 edition.

Further methodological choices

Apart from the limitations imposed by the use of census data as the main source for the deprivation analysis, the analytical framework differs from Gordon et al.'s in a couple other aspects, including the addition of data informing of hazard exposure.[24]

Falling short from the more ambitious goal of elaborating a deprivation index and for easier visual representation of the most extreme combined deprivations, which require urgent and multi-sectoral intervention (depth of child poverty), the analysis has proposed a further grouping of severe deprivations by number:

Not poor	Poor	Absolute poor	Very poor	Extreme poor
No severe deprivation	One severe deprivation	Two severe deprivations	Three severe deprivations	Four severe deprivations or more

Secondly, taking full advantage of the census data as a main source for the analysis, the socio-demographic characteristics of households where deprived children live have been analysed. The objective here was to highlight, among other aspects, the sex and level of education of the head of household, household size and the language spoken by the head of household (as proxy for the ethnic affiliation of the household).

Last, but not least, another addition to the multi-dimensional methodology is the combination of child deprivation measurements with exposure. The analysis uses 2013 national food security data, sourced from the FSMS, produced bi-annually by the Food Security Commission (Commissariat à la Securité Alimentaire) and the World Food Programme (WFP). Data on flooding risk was taken from the Emergency Events Database (EM-DAT)[25] which is maintained since 1988 by the Centre for Research on the Epidemiology of Disasters (CRED)[26] at Louvain

---

[24]   Hazard and exposure are defined here respectively as a "process, phenomenon or human activity that may cause loss of life, injury or other health impacts, property damage, social and economic disruption or environmental degradation" and the "situation of people, infrastructure, housing, production capacities and other tangible human assets located in hazard-prone areas" (UN b 2016: 18).

[25]   http://emdat.be/ (Accessed 30 April 2016)

[26]   http://www.cred.be/ (Accessed 30 April 2016)

University as well as national sources as compiled by the National Flood Contingency Plan (2014).

Maps constituted the main output of the analysis. As Bedi et al. explain:

> Maps [are] a powerful communication tool because the maps summarize poverty estimates […] on a single page and in a visual format that is readily understandable by a wide audience. The presentation as a map not only summarizes a large volume of data concisely, but it also enhances the interpretation of that data by preserving the spatial relationships among different areas, something that simply is not possible in a tabular data format. (2007: 3)

Maps, to some extent, also facilitated — at least visually — the combination of different data sets at different levels of disaggregation. The census-based child deprivations analysis and the data on flooding risk were set at the commune level; the district level (Moughataa) was used for examining nutritional data, standing in for the absence of anthropometric indicators in the census; and food security data was set at the regional level (Wilaya).

Based on the different levels of disaggregation and the main steps in the analysis — analysis of child deprivations based on census data and the combination of the results with data on hazard exposure — two categories of maps were produced:

- Single indicator maps displaying the incidence of child vulnerabilities, as classified by number of severe deprivations experienced by children in different communes; and
- Multiple indicator/combined maps, merging information of the child deprivation analysis with exposure to the hazards of food insecurity (drought) and flooding.

SELECTED RESULTS

This section presents some of the key results of the analysis of child poverty and vulnerability in Mauritania. After a quick demographic overview, this section will introduce the deprivation analysis, both by individual deprivation and multi-dimensionally. This will be followed by the combined deprivation and hazard exposure analysis as well as some of the findings on the socio-demographic profile of households where deprived children live. Due to space and format restrictions, only a limited number of maps will be included as examples. Some of the more complex maps, combining all vulnerability and risk factors, could not be included in this chapter due to readability concerns. The full analysis as well as the high-resolution maps can be consulted in the background paper (UNICEF Mauritania 2016a) as well as the cartographic summary (UNICEF Mauritania 2016b).

Demographic overview

The total population of Mauritania as of the 2013 census is 3,537,000.[27] The total number of children (0-18 years) is 1,786,000, i.e. 50.5 percent of the total population, of which 901,000 girls (50 percent) and 885,000 boys (50 percent). 54 percent of children live in rural areas and 44 percent in urban areas while 2 percent are nomadic.[28]

Children under 5 years of age represent 17 percent of the population (615,000 children). Children between 6 and 14 years of age – the compulsory schooling age – represent 23 percent (817,000 children), and the 15 to 17 age group represents 6 percent (222,000 children). The communes that have the highest concentration of children are located in the capital Nouakchott (nine communes), as well as the other main urban centres. Nouakchott itself is home to one-third of Mauritania's children.

---

[27] All numbers (except those included in tables) are rounded up to the nearest 1.000.
[28] The present analysis does not include the 2 percent of nomadic children in Mauritania. In fact, the child poverty indictors used in the analysis would need to be adapted to that specific subgroup. This point would merit a study of its own. Subsequent numbers therefore refer to the total number of children, excluding nomad children, i.e. 1,753,000.

Map 1:   Number of children per commune

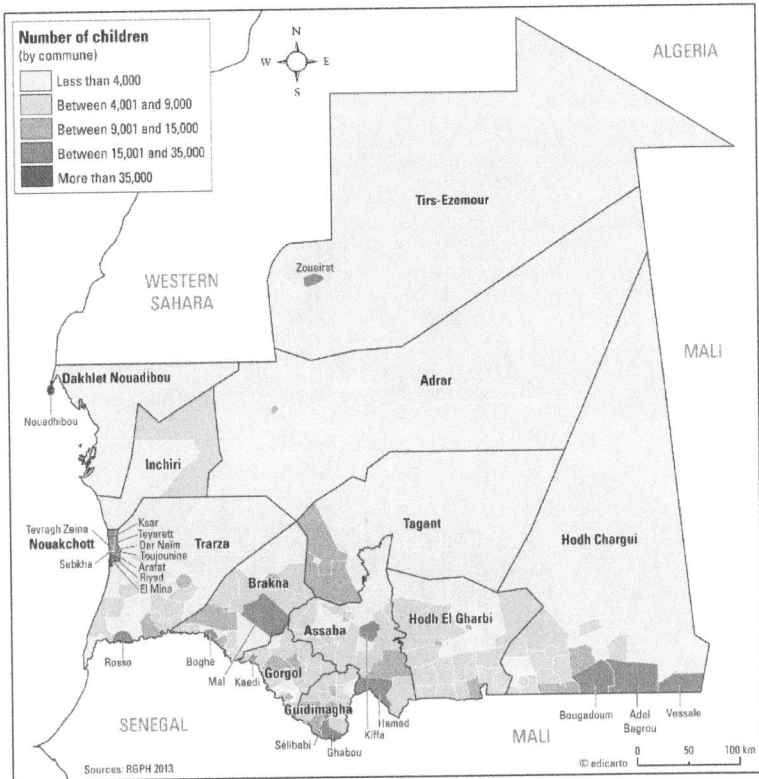

Sources: RGPH 2013

Analysis by depth of poverty

978,000 Mauritanian children live with at least one severe deprivation
(56 percent of children). 472,000 children suffer from at least two severe
deprivations, which means that about 27 percent of Mauritanian children
live in absolute poverty as defined by Gordon et al. Sixteen communes
account each for more than 5,000 children in absolute poverty,
representing 24 percent of absolute poor children in Mauritania.

Map 2:   Number of children living in absolute poverty

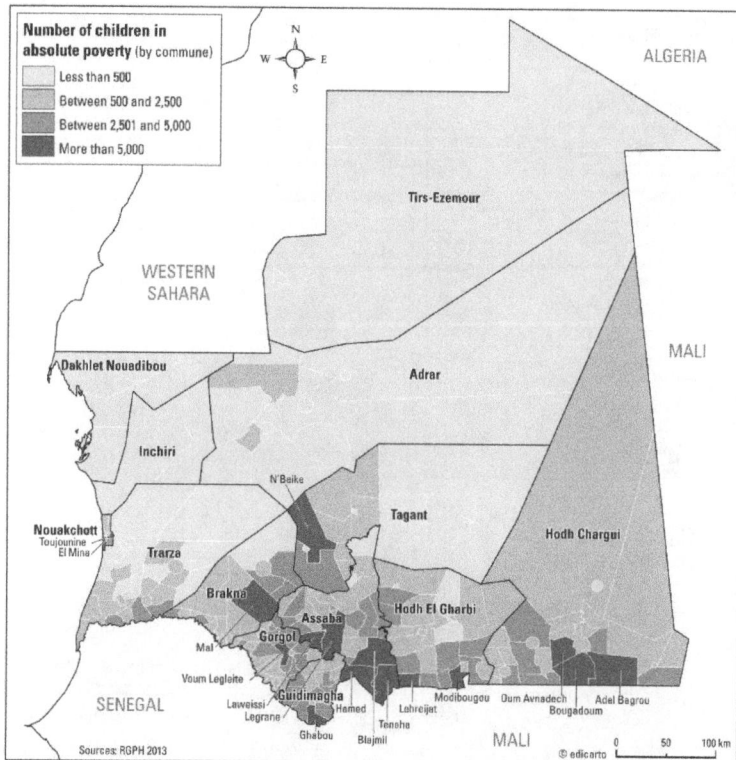

Number of children in absolute poverty (by commune)

- Less than 500
- Between 500 and 2,500
- Between 2,501 and 5,000
- More than 5,000

ALGERIA

Tirs-Ezemour

WESTERN SAHARA

Dakhlet Nouadibou

MALI

Adrar

Inchiri

N'Beike

Tagant

Nouakchott
Toujounine
El Mina

Trarza

Hodh Chargui

Brakna

Assaba

Hodh El Gharbi

Gorgol

Mal

Voum Legleite

SENEGAL

Guidimagha

Laweissi-Legrane

Hamed

Lahreijat

Modibougou   Oum Avnadech   Adel Bagrou
Bougadoum

Tenaha

Ghabou   Blajmil

MALI

Sources: RGPH 2013

© edicarto

0   50   100 km

Map 3:   Proportion of children living in absolute poverty

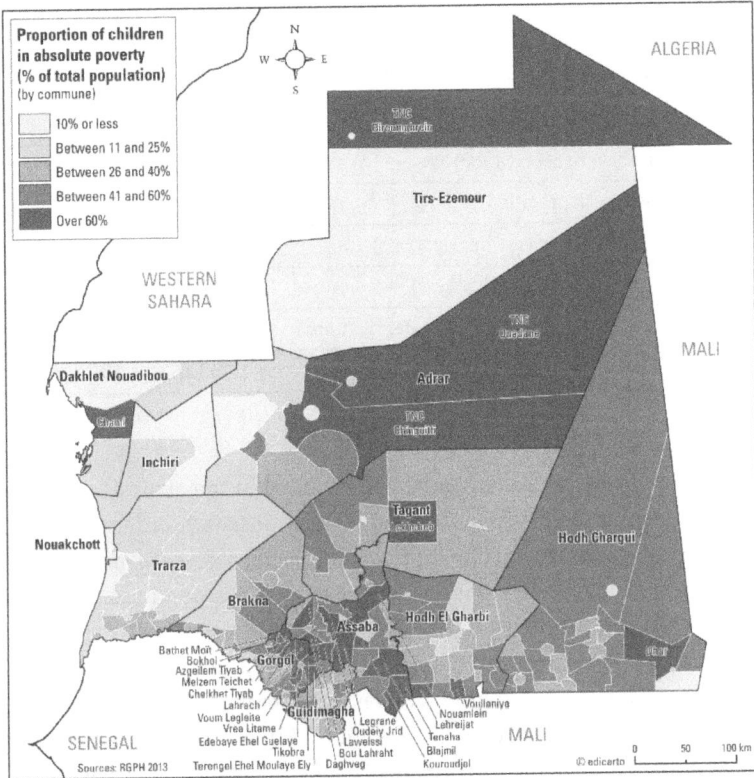

The communes with the largest numbers of children living in absolute poverty are located in the southern regions of the country (Brakna, Gorgol, Assaba, Guidimakha, Hodh Gharbi, Hodh Chargui). However, equity considerations call for an analysis based on the proportion of deprived children, which shows a different picture as sparsely population northern regions are added to the fold, showing large percentages of children in absolute poverty.

Over 160,000 Mauritanian children live with three severe deprivations (6 percent of Mauritanian children) and over 19,000 live in extreme deprivation (four severe deprivations or more, 1 percent of children). Gorgol, Hodh Chargui and Assaba are the regions with the largest number of very poor children (three or more deprivations). In the

Nouakchott region, 76 percent of children live without any severe deprivation; only 1 percent live with three or more severe deprivations.

Number and proportion of children per number of severe deprivations

Number of severe deprivations	Number	%
Not poor (no severe deprivation)	774,870	44%
Poor (one severe deprivation)	506,100	29%
Absolutely poor (two severe deprivations)	346,282	20%
Very poor (three severe deprivations)	106,624	6%
Extremely poor (four or more severe deprivations)	18,370	1%
Total	1,753,153	100%

Analysis by category of deprivation

Two main deprivations, among those included in the analysis stand out for children in Mauritania: sanitation and decent housing. Some 42 percent of Mauritanian children do not have access to any type of sanitation in their home and in the immediate surroundings. About 82 percent of these children live in rural areas compared to 18 percent in urban areas. 27 percent of Mauritanian children do not have access to decent housing (more than 5 persons per room and with no flooring material). This is the case for 37 percent of children in rural areas and 15 percent of children in urban areas. Map 4 below illustrates severe deprivations in terms of access to sanitation.

Other severe deprivations are less prevalent, even if not negligible:

- In terms of access to safe drinking water, 42,000 children (over 2 percent) use only surface water. 98 percent of those children live in rural areas.
- 8 percent of children are deprived of any access to information – 4 percent in urban areas and 16 percent in rural areas.
- About 200,000 children of school age do not currently go to school. This represents roughly 10 percent of Mauritanian children, made up of 2 percent in urban areas and 8 percent in rural areas.

Map 4:   Number of children who do not have access to toilets by commune

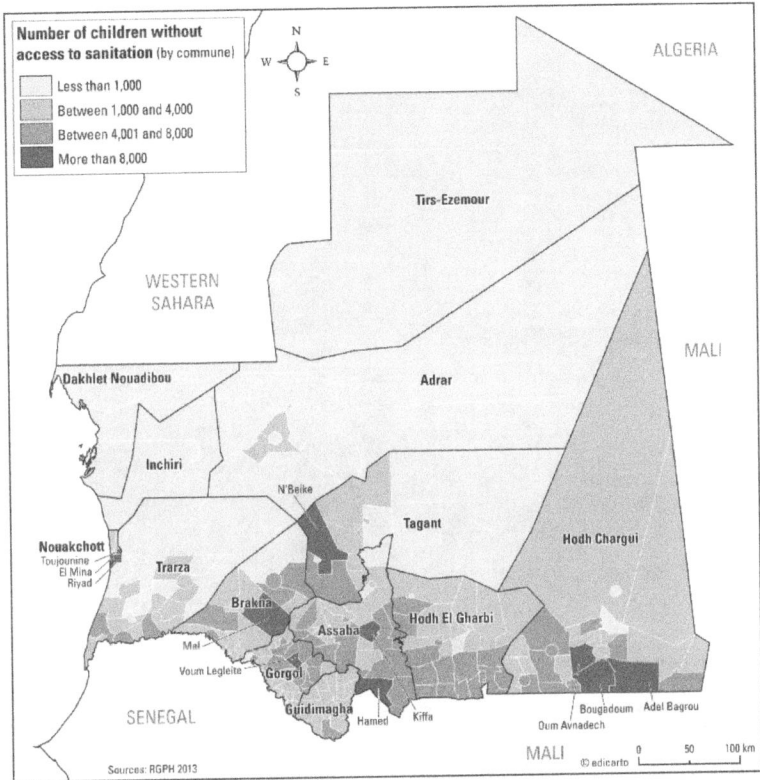

Overlapping deprivations with exposure to hazards

Overlaying 2013 food insecurity data – the proxy indicator for drought – with absolute child poverty (two severe deprivations or more) as based on the 2013 census, the overlap is particularly strong in the southern Assaba, Gorgol and Guimakha regions. The Tagant region, situated north of the aforementioned regions, shows severe food insecurity during the 2013 lean season, but is more sparsely populated with children living in absolute poverty.

Map 5:   Absolute child poverty and food insecurity

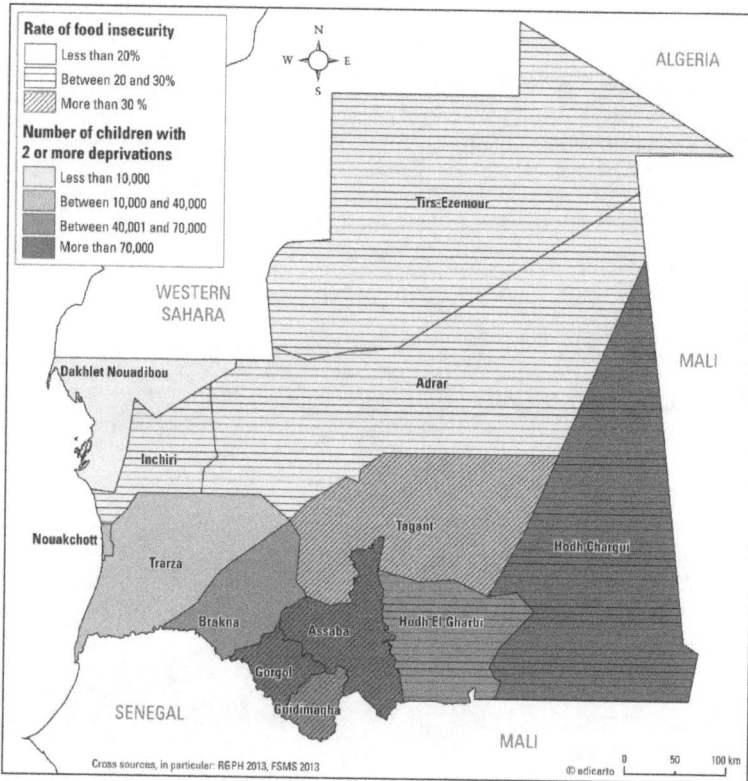

Rate of food insecurity
Less than 20%
Between 20 and 30%
More than 30 %

Number of children with
2 or more deprivations
Less than 10,000
Between 10,000 and 40,000
Between 40,001 and 70,000
More than 70,000

WESTERN
SAHARA

ALGERIA

Tirs-Ezemour

MALI

Dakhlet Nouadibou

Adrar

Inchiri

Tagant

Nouakchott

Hodh Chargui

Trarza

Brakna

Assaba

Hodh El Gharbi

Gorgol

Guidimgaha

SENEGAL

MALI

Cross sources, in particular: RGPH 2013, FSMS 2013

© edicarto

0   50   100 km

Mauritania, known as an arid territory, is also, paradoxically, a country exposed to high risk of flooding. The floods are mainly located in the watershed of the Senegal River and the frequency of disasters has been on the increase since the 2000s. Nouakchott, where more than a quarter of the Mauritanian population lives (and one third of Mauritanian children), is particularly at risk of flooding by the Senegal River as well as coastal flooding, aggravated by high population growth and the near absence of sanitation.

Many of the communes where children live, including those in absolute poverty, are at risk of flooding. The communes most at risk and with the highest number of children in absolute poverty are N'Beika, Mal, Tekane, Laweissi, Voum Legleite, Legrane, Tenaha, Lehreijat, Hamed, Blajmil, Ghabou, Modibougou, Oum Avnadech, and others located in the south of the country, close to the border with Senegal and Mali.

Map 6:   Children in absolute poverty in communes exposed to flooding

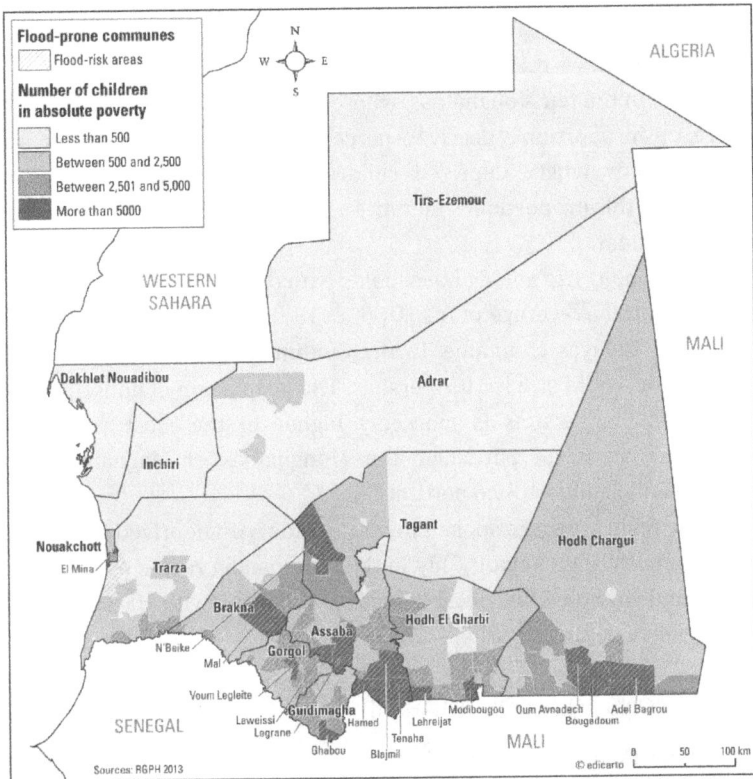

Socio-demographic analysis of households where deprived children live

The demographic characteristics of households where deprived children live reveal that the majority of those households are headed by men (64 percent); only 36 percent of households where deprived children live, are headed by women. However, in some regions (Wilaya), this proportion is inverted: for example, nearly 52 percent of households with children in absolute poverty are headed by women in the Trarza region. Moreover, a more refined analysis at district level (Moughataa) shows that in the 10 districts with the highest proportion of very poor children (three or four deprivations), up to 60 percent of households with deprived children are headed by women. These are also the districts with the highest prevalence of child marriage (between 9-16 percent depending on the Moughataa)[29] and child labour.[30]

Some 97 percent of the heads of households where deprived children live have reached primary school level or do not have any education. In the ten Moughataas, where child deprivations are the most severe, this proportion is nearly 99 percent. Slightly over half of the heads of households where deprived children live (53 percent) have an occupation; this proportion is merely 43 percent in the above-mentioned ten Moughataas.

Household size among households with deprived children is higher than the national average of 6.2 (ONS, 2015d: 5), especially in the most vulnerable Wilayas commune. In the Guidimakha region, for example, average household size is 10.7 persons. The proportion of households of more than six persons is markedly higher in the most vulnerable geographic areas, in particular the Moughataas of Maghama (91.2 percent) and Selibaby (89.6 percent).

The main language spoken in households with deprived children is predominantly Hassaniya.[31] Only in the Guidimakha region as well as in Gorgol and Brakna, other local languages are used, with Hassaniya still being spoken by the majority.

CONCLUSIONS AND LOOKING AHEAD

The vulnerability and disparities analysis for children in Mauritania follows a multi-dimensional approach and uses national census data together with available data sets on severe acute malnutrition, food insecurity and flooding hazards. Vulnerability maps, depicting either single or combined deprivations as well as exposure to shocks, are the main output of the analysis.

---

[29] The census refers to "early marriage" defined as marriage of children under the age of 18, the legal age for marriage. The distinction is made between very young children (10-14 years) and older children (15-19 years). See ONS 2015c: 24.

[30] The census looks at the activity and employment of children between 10 and 18 years of age, noting that the data collected on employment, including for children, by the census do not allow for a comprehensive analysis (e.g. the number of hours worked, labour conditions, child labour under the age of 10, etc.). See ONS 2015b: 46.

[31] The official language in Mauritania is Arabic. Hassaniya is the form of Arabic predominantly spoken in the country. Other languages spoken in Mauritania include French, Pulaar, Soninke and Wolof.

The objective of the analysis was not to unravel causality, but to firmly establish the policy argument that DRR and measures to reduce child poverty are mutually reinforcing. Another objective was to call for methodological and interdisciplinary linkages. In fact, child poverty analysis covers some of the most essential dimensions of children's capacity and — conversely — vulnerability to hazard impact. Through its multidimensional nature as well as the potential to disaggregate by sex, age group and region, and by making the differential needs of children in the face of disaster visible, child deprivation analysis has the potential to make a non-negligible contribution to effective DRR.

Establishing the link between child poverty and disaster risk opens up a whole field of investigation, most notably about the transmission mechanisms between disaster impact and different types and degrees of child deprivation, as mediated through households and community capacities and coping strategies. More research is also needed on how children are impacted when they live in areas where disaster risk is high, independently of the impact of a disaster event.

REFERENCES

Alderman, H. et al. (2006), "Long term consequences of early childhood malnutrition", *Oxford Economic Papers*, No. 58, pp. 450-474

Ampaabeng, S.K. and C.M. Tan (2013), "The long-term cognitive consequences of early childhood malnutrition: The case of famine in Ghana", *Journal of Health Economics*, Vol. 32, pp.1013-1027

Baez, J. et al. (2010), "Do Natural Disasters Affect Human Capital? An Assessment Based on Existing Empirical Evidence", *IZA Discussion Paper*, No. 5164, September 2010

Bankoff, G. et al. (2003), *Mapping Vulnerability: Disasters, Development, and People* (Earthscan Publishers: London)

Bedi, T. et al. (2007), "Poverty Maps for Policy Making: Beyond the Obvious Targeting Applications", in Bedi T. et al. (eds.), *More than a Pretty Picture: Using Poverty Maps to Design Better Policies and Interventions* (Washington DC: World Bank), pp.3-22

Commissariat à la Sécurité Alimentaire (CSA) [Food Security Commission] and WFP (2013), *Enquête de suivi de la sécurité alimentaire* [Food Security Monitoring System Survey], July 2013

Datar, A. et al. (2013), "The impact of natural disasters on child health and investments in rural India", *Social Science & Medicine*, Vol. 76, January 2013, pp. 83–91

DFID (2004), *Disaster risk reduction: a development concern. A scoping study on links between disaster risk reduction, poverty and development*, Overseas Development Group, December 2004

Gaillard, J.C. (2010), "Vulnerability, capacity and resilience: Perspectives for climate and development policy", *Journal of International Development*, Vol. 22, Issue 2, March 2010, pp.218–232

Glewwe, P. and E. King (2001), "The impact of early childhood nutritional status on cognitive development: Does timing of malnutrition matter?", *World Bank Economic Review*, Vol. 15, No. 1, pp.81-113

Gordon D. et al. (2003), *Child poverty in the developing world* (University of Bristol: The Policy Press)

Gordon D. et al. (2001), *Child Rights and Child Poverty in Developing Countries - Summary Report to UNICEF* (Centre for International Poverty Research: Bristol)

Kousky, C. (2016), "Impacts of Natural Disasters on Children", *The Future of Children*, Vol. 26, No. 1, Children and Climate Change (Spring 2016), pp. 73-92

Lovell, E. and V. Le Masson (2014), *Equity and Inclusion in Disaster Risk Reduction: Building Resilience for All*, ODI Working Paper, November 2014

Maccini, S. and D. Young (2009), "Under the Weather: Health, Schooling, and Economic Consequences of Early-Life Rainfall", *American Economic Review*, Vol. 99, No. 3, pp.1006-1026

Maluccio, J.A. et al. (2009), "The Impact of Improving Nutrition during Early Childhood on Education among Guatemalan Adults", *The Economic Journal*, Vol. 119, No. 537, pp.734-763

Mendez, M.A. and L.S. Adair (1999), "Severity and Timing of Stunting in the First Two Years of Life Affect Performance on Cognitive Tests in Late Childhood", *The Journal of Nutrition*, Vol. 129, No. 8, pp.1555-1565

Ministère de la Santé [Ministry of Health] (2013), *Enquête nutritionnelle nationale* [National Nutrition Survey] (July 2013)

Office National de la Statistique (ONS) [National Statistics Institute] (2016), *Profil de la Pauvreté en Mauritanie* [Mauritania Poverty Profile] (Nouakchott: ONS)

Office National de la Statistique (ONS) [National Statistics Institute] (2015a), *Synthèse des Résultats définitifs du RGPH 2013* [Summary of Final Results of the 2013 National Population and Housing Census] (Nouakchott: ONS)

Office National de la Statistique (ONS) [National Statistics Institute] (2015b), *Recensement Général de la Population et de l'Habitat (RGPH) 2013: Volume 5 - Caractéristiques des groupes spécifiques* [2013 National Population and Housing Census: Volume 5 - Characteristics of specific groups]

Office National de la Statistique (ONS) [National Statistics Institute] (2015c), *Recensement Général de la Population et de l'Habitat (RGPH) 2013 - Chapitre 3: Etat matrimonial et nuptialité* [2013 National Population and Housing Census: Chapter 3 - Marital Status and Nuptiality]

Office National de la Statistique (ONS) [National Statistics Institute] (2015d), *Recensement Général de la Population et de l'Habitat (RGPH) 2013* – Chapitre 10: Caractéristiques des ménages et des Chefs de Ménages [2013 National Population and Housing Census – Chapter 10: Characteristics of Households and Heads of Household]

Oxford Policy Management (2015), *Shock-responsive Social Protection Systems: Working Paper 1 – Conceptualising Shock Responsive Social Protection* (October 2015)

Pelling, M. et al. (2004), *Reducing Disaster Risk: A Challenge for Development* (New York: United Nations, 2004)

Penrose, A. and M. Takaki (2006), "Children's Rights in Emergencies and Disasters", *The Lancet*, Vol. 367, Issue 9511, pp.698-699

Rentschler, J. E. (2013), "Why Resilience Matters: The Poverty Impacts of Disasters", Policy Research Working Paper 6699, November 2013 (Washington, D.C.: The World Bank)

Save the Children (2008), *In the Face of Disaster: Children and Climate Change* (London: International Save the Children Alliance)

Save the Children (2007), *Legacy of Disasters: The Impact of Climate Change on Children* (London: International Save the Children Alliance)

Schipper, L. and M. Pelling (2006), "Disaster risk, climate change and international development: scope for, and challenges to integration", *Disasters*, Vol. 30, Issue 1, March 2006, pp.19-38

Shepherd, A. et al. (2013), *The geography of poverty, disasters and climate extremes in 2030* (London: Overseas Development Institute, October 2013)

Townsend, P. (1987), "Deprivation", *Journal of Social Policy*, Vol. 16, No. 2, pp. 125-46

UNDP (2014), *Human Development Report, Sustaining Human Progress: Reducing Vulnerabilities and Building Resilience* (New York: UNDP)

UNFCC (2015), The Paris Agreement

UNICEF (2017), Knowledge for Children in Africa: 2017 Publications Catalogue

UNICEF (2016), Knowledge for Children in Africa: 2016 Publications Catalogue

UNICEF (2015), *Unless We Act Now: The Impact of Climate Change on Children* (New York: UNICEF, Division of Data, Research and Policy)

UNICEF (2012), *Integrated Social Protection Systems Enhancing Equity for Children: UNICEF Social Protection Strategic Framework* (New York: UNICEF)

UNICEF Mauritania (2016a), *Etude sur la cartographie des vulnérabilités et des disparités chez les enfants de Mauritanie* [Study on the Mapping of Vulnerabilities and Inequalities of Children in Mauritania]

UNICEF Mauritania (2016b), *Etude sur la cartographie des vulnérabilités et des disparités chez les enfants de Mauritanie: Cartographie* [Study on the Mapping of Vulnerabilities and Inequalities of Children in Mauritania: Maps]

UNISDR (2015), *Making Development Sustainable: The Future of Disaster Risk Management. Global Assessment Report on Disaster Risk Reduction* (Geneva, Switzerland: United Nations Office for Disaster Risk Reduction)

UNISDR (2009), *Global Assessment Report on Disaster Risk Reduction: Risk and Poverty in a Changing Climate* (Geneva, Switzerland: United Nations Office for Disaster Risk Reduction)

United Nations (2016a), Outcome of the World Humanitarian Summit: Report of the Secretary-General, General Assembly document 71/353 of 23 August 2016

United Nations (2016b), Report of the open-ended intergovernmental expert working group on indicators and terminology relating to disaster risk reduction, General Assembly document 71/644 of 1 December 2016

United Nations (2015a), Sendai Framework for Disaster Risk Reduction 2015-2030 (endorsed by General Assembly resolution 69/283 of 3 June 2015)

United Nations (2015b), Addis Ababa Action Agenda of the Third International Conference on Financing for Development (Addis Ababa Action Agenda) (endorsed by General Assembly resolution 69/313 of 27 July 2015)

United Nations (2015c), Transforming our World: The 2030 Agenda for Sustainable Development (endorsed by General Assembly resolution 70/1 of 25 September 2015)

United Nations (1995), The Copenhagen Declaration and Programme of Action, World Summit for Social Development, New York 6-12 March 1995

United Nations Secretary General (2015), Chair's Summary by the United Nations Secretary-General, "Standing up for Humanity: Committing to Action", World Humanitarian Summit, 23-24 May 2016

Vandermoortele, J. (2012), "Equity Begins with Children", in Minujin A., Nandy S. (eds.) (2012), Global child poverty and well-being: Measurement, concepts, policy and action (University of Bristol: The Policy Press), pp.39-53

Vásquez, W. F. and Alok K. Bohara (2010), "Household shocks, child labor, and child schooling: Evidence from Guatemala", *Latin American Research Review*, Vol. 45, No. 3 (2010), pp. 165-186

Victora, C.G. et al. (2008), "Maternal and child undernutrition: consequences for adult health and human capital", *The Lancet*, Vol. 371, pp.340-57

Wisner, B. et al. (2004), *At Risk: Natural Hazards, People's vulnerability and disasters* (2nd Edition) (London: Routledge)

CHAPTER 7

THE IMPACT OF SOCIAL PROTECTION PROGRAMMES ON THE EBOLA SCOURGE IN SIERRA LEONE: LESSONS AND RECOMMENDATIONS

Maryam Abdu

INTRODUCTION AND STRUCTURE

Sierra Leone is a country which has had many trials since independence in 1961. It came out of a war in 2000 to try to meet the Millennium Development Goals (MDGs). The country's leaders struggled to handle challenges in human resources, systems and structures, caused by the years of war. Just when things were improving, however, the Ebola outbreak daunted the possibility of seeing a sustainable light at the end of the tunnel. Since May 2014, when the first case was recorded, the country encountered increasing difficulties. At the beginning, efforts were channelled towards curbing the spread with minimal success. It was not until community engagement took prominence that the country began to see some success. By the end of 2015 the country was coming out of Ebola. Yet, individual cases kept sprouting up even after the country had been declared outbreak-free, leaving questions to be answered, just when the country was supposed to be tackling the new Sustainable Development Goals (SDGs).

The country within the space of less than one year suffered the loss of close to 4,000 persons from Ebola (out of 137,000 affected persons). In addition, there were 14,000 more than usual teenage pregnant girls during the nine months extended stay-at-home period. There was also a general decreased utilisation of health facilities due to fears from Ebola and increased maternal and child deaths. Many of the most severe consequences of these developments would only be apparent at a later stage. In the short term, at the macroeconomic level, the increased foreign reserves inflows to combat the Ebola outbreak enabled banks and financial institutions to stay afloat. However, since the end of 2015 when most of the donors left, after the country was declared Ebola-free, there was left a gap leading to increased inflation and economic uncertainty.

During the Ebola crisis, the government (with the support of other stakeholders) extended the incipient social safety net programme to cover households with people affected by or survivors of Ebola. Selection of beneficiaries of the Rapid Ebola Social Safety Net (RESSN) programme were based on a light means-testing methodology, trying to reach families affected by Ebola (with or without survivors). This has also raised some concerns as the crisis has increased the number of orphans from families which have lost both parents. This further put pressure on the already weak social protection and welfare system. Nevertheless, the emergency social protection intervention did manage to soften the blow of the crisis.

This chapter, therefore, addresses the key question of how social protection during an emergency like Ebola might impact child poverty and children's needs, thus potentially reducing children's engagement in harmful practices that can damage their opportunities for a better future. Field reports, assessments by international institutions, and surveys carried out on the impact of Ebola on households and the analysis of the cost of Ebola provided data for the analysis of the possible impact of the cash transfer programme. This chapter first outlines the recent trends in child poverty and briefly reviews the existing social protection programmes prior to the Ebola outbreak. This is followed by a summary of the direct impact of Ebola on children, and the economic effect of the emergency. The response to the epidemic and the impact of social protection are discussed before the concluding comments.

BACKGROUND

Child deprivation in Sierra Leone 2010

Multidimensional Child Poverty and Deprivation

Child poverty estimates based on the Multiple Indicator Cluster Survey (MICS) of 2010 stood at 77.4 percent, meaning eight out of every ten Sierra Leonean children are deprived of one or more rights constituting child poverty. These deprivations are shelter, sanitation, education, health, water, information and nutrition.

The measurement of trends in child poverty in Sierra Leone was carried out using the MICS of 2010 and the Demographic and Health survey (DHS) of 2013, just prior to the Ebola crisis, providing baselines to monitor the indicator of child poverty for the SDGs. A comparison of the estimates of child poverty in Sierra Leone between 2010 and 2013 is presented below (Table 1).[1] It is worth noting that although the two surveys use different methodologies and calculate indicators differently they can still be used to check for trends within a country (Hanciouglu and Arnold, 2013).

Table 1: Child poverty, 2010 and 2013 compared (% deprived)

Dimension	MICS 2010	DHS 2013	Statistically different?
Nutrition	27.19	33.3	Yes
Water	39.5	53.4	Yes
Sanitation	28.79	20.3	Yes
Health	5.83	15.3	Yes
Shelter	62	64.3	No
Education	24.16	25.4	No
Information	42.26	26.1	Yes
Child poverty estimate	77.4	85.2	Yes

Source: Estimates of child poverty on the basis of author's calculations using data from MICS and DHS

The water, sanitation and housing dimensions are measured for all children irrespective of their age. Household-level data are used to assess deprivation on each of these dimensions. Data on the other dimensions, with the exception of the information dimension[2], are individual-level data.

The housing dimension is, by a large margin, the dimension in which the largest proportion of children are found to be deprived. Just over 62 percent of children either live in a dwelling with five or more people per room, or in a dwelling where the floor is made of mud, sand or dung.

More than 30 percent of children in the respective age groups are deprived in the health, information and water dimensions. Some 37 percent of children aged 0-4 years old have either not received a full course of basic vaccinations or have had a case of diarrhoea that was not treated. 34 percent of children aged 3-17 have no access to television, radio or a phone. 33 percent of children live in households that either only

---

[1] For these estimates, the same definitions and criteria as in the introduction and other chapters in this book have been used.

[2] As it will be seen below, besides being a constitutive right of poverty, it also played a very important instrumental role in the response to the Ebola Crisis.

have access to surface water or is more than a 15-minute walk from the nearest water source.

Levels of deprivation in the sanitation and nutrition dimensions are slightly lower, but still well above 20 percent. About 29 percent of children are sanitation deprived, living without access to any toilet facilities whatsoever. 27 percent of children aged 0-4 years old are nutrition deprived, being either severely stunted, underweight or wasted.

The education dimension is the one in which the smallest proportion of children are deprived. Some 17 percent of children aged 7-17 are deprived of education, meaning that they have never attended school.

The proportion of children deprived of at least one dimension is shown in Figure 1 (with confidence intervals). It can be seen that child poverty is highest in the South and lowest in the West.

Figure 1:   Child poverty incidence by district with confidence intervals

DISTRICT	MEAN	CONFIDENCE INTERVAL	
		UPPER	LOWER
EAST			
Kailahun	77.6	79.4	75.9
Kenema	76.6	78.4	74.9
Kono*	80.3	82.1	78.5
NORTH			
Bombali*	70.6	72.5	68.7
Kambia	87.3	88.5	86.1
Koinadugu	87.4	88.9	86.0
Port Loko*	83.6	85.0	82.2
Tonkolili	86.6	88.1	85.2
SOUTH			
Bo*	75.9	77.6	74.2
Bonthe	91.2	92.4	90.0
Moyamba	88.3	89.8	86.8
Pujehun	93.0	94.2	91.8
WEST			
Western Rur*	52.4	54.8	50.0
Western Urb*	45.8	47.5	44.1

Note: * denotes that results are statistically significantly different from districts in the same region

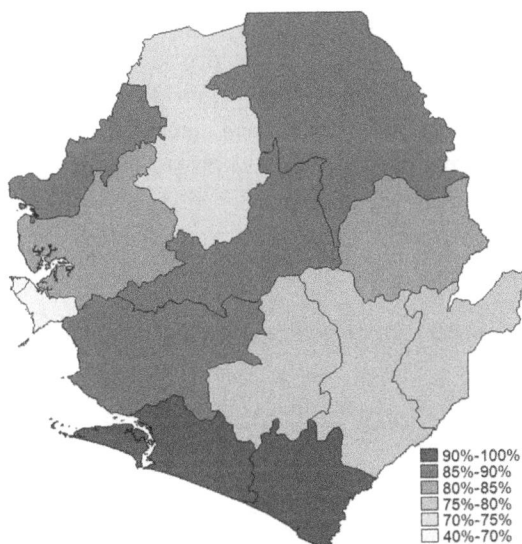

90%-100%
85%-90%
80%-85%
75%-80%
70%-75%
40%-70%

The Depth, Severity, and Gender Disaggregation of Child Poverty

Incidence is only one aspect of poverty. It is also important to analyse its depth (Delamonica and Minujin 2007). The average number of deprivations suffered by children in poverty can be used to assess the depth of poverty. Table 2 shows the average number of deprivations suffered by children in Sierra Leone nationally and by region.

Table 2:   Average number of deprivations by region

REGION	AVERAGE NO. OF DEPRIVATIONS
National	2.2
East	2.0
North	2.3
South	2.5
West	1.3

At the national level, poor children suffer an average of 2.2 deprivations. Mirroring the pattern found for the incidence of child poverty, the South is the region where poverty is the deepest. Poor children in the South suffer an average of 2.5 deprivations compared to an average number of deprivations of 2.3 in the North and 2.0 in the East. Child poverty is the least deep in the West, where the average number of deprivations suffered by poor children is 1.3.

As with any average, however, these figures hide a significant amount of detail. Two very different distributions of deprivation can produce very similar figures for both the incidence and depth of poverty. Figure 2, which shows the number and percentage of children suffering from specific numbers of deprivations (none, one, two, etc.), provides a more detailed picture of the severity of child poverty in Sierra Leone. It can be seen that one in ten children in Sierra Leone suffer from at least four deprivations.

Figure 2:   Number and percentage of children by number of deprivations

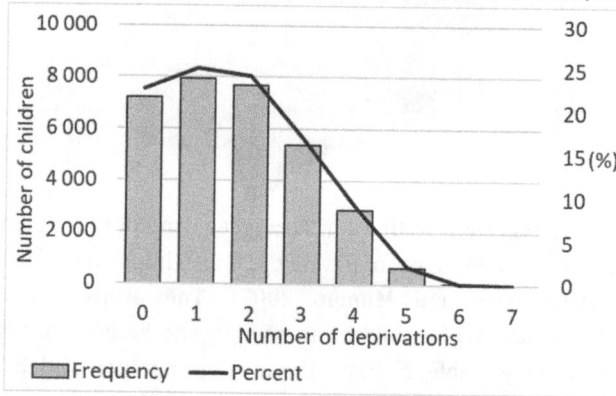

Number*	% of children
1+	77.4
2+	52.3
3+	28.1
4+	11.2
5+	2.2
6+	0.1
7	0

*number of deprivations

Results can also be broken down by sex. These are only meaningful, however, where information on children is available. Differences by sex in the nutrition, health and education dimensions are shown below in Figure 3.

Figure 3:   Nutritional, health and educational deprivations by gender

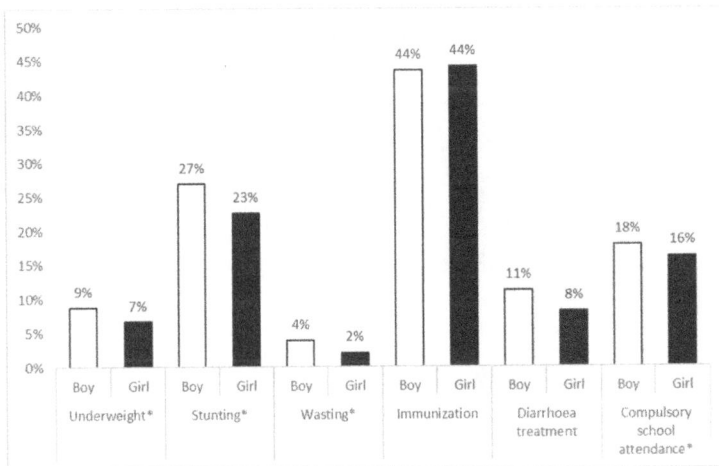

Note: * denotes that there is a statistically significant difference between the means

Although there is no direct correlation between the incidence of child poverty and Ebola confirmed cases per district (Figure 4), some of the worst hit districts have high incidence of child poverty except for Western areas. The spread of Ebola in the West is probably due to the high population size and crowdedness. Another factor influencing the high number of cases is the proximity to the borders with Liberia and Guinea.

Figure 4:   Geographic spread of Ebola cases

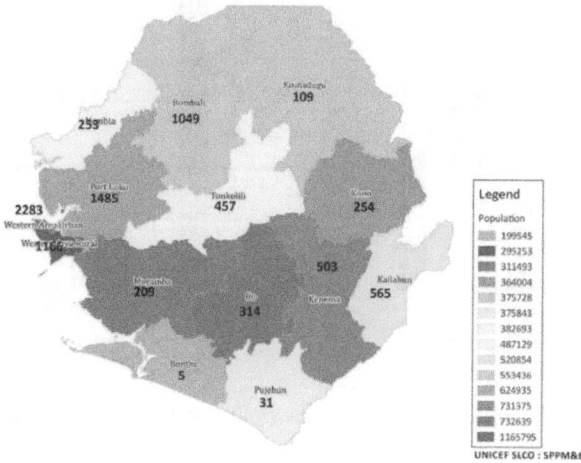

Cumulative confirmed cases of EVD in Districts (23/05/14 TO 20/08/15)

Legend	
Population	
	199545
	295253
	311493
	364004
	375728
	375843
	382693
	487129
	520854
	553436
	624935
	731375
	732639
	1165795

UNICEF SLCO : SPPM&E

Social protection interventions

The Government of Sierra Leone had started to develop a National Social Protection Policy in 2011 and was in the process of developing a national strategy when Ebola struck. Social protection initiatives, though minimalist in coverage in the country, targeted the Popoliopos (who are the extreme poor and make up about 14 percent of the poor). The aim of the cash transfer programme was to smoothen consumption for the extreme poor, enabling them to meet their basic needs while putting in place other programmes to enhance their skills and capacity to take on new jobs and livelihoods opportunities. With donor support, the government established the school feeding programme for public and government supported schools. Though this programme has not lived up to the expectations of the communities, there is a large number of communities still requesting the continuation of the programme. They believe that this would help improve the quality of learning in education especially for the children. No evaluation has been carried out to determine the efficiency and effectiveness of the programme. However, anecdotal evidence showed that though the programme did not meet expectations. Some community people have also prescribed a more inclusive programme for future school feeding interventions.

EBOLA: DIRECT IMPACTS

In March 2014, the UN Secretary General, Ban Ki-Moon had referred to Sierra Leone as "one of the world's most successful cases of post-conflict recovery, peacekeeping and peacebuilding".[3] Although the systems were improving, they were still weak. The government, after several years of consolidating peace, stability and democratic governance, commenced the implementation of the Agenda for Prosperity and other developmental projects, which were on course to gain positive momentum. Before the Ebola crisis, the government's health infrastructure reforms, education, water and sanitation services had started to bear fruit. For example, the implementation of the Free Health Care (FHC) initiatives, targeting both curative and preventive services, led to remarkable improvements in child and maternal healthcare indicators.

According to the Sierra Leone Demographic and Health Surveys (SLDHS, 2008 and 2013) an improvement in vaccination coverage and the under-five mortality rate was registered. The vaccination coverage during the first year of life among children aged 12 – 23 months almost doubled from 31 percent in 2008 to 58 percent in 2013. In the same year, under-five mortality rate of 156 deaths per 1,000 live births was reported showing a decline compared to 227 deaths per 1,000 lives birth observed in 2005. Documented results also show that by 2013 over 59 percent of pregnant women had delivered under the care of a skilled health personnel.

However, the outbreak of EVD greatly impacted the health sector and the economy as a whole, eroding the country's achievements. The Ebola situation in the country overwhelmed the existing health infrastructure. High mortality of heath sector personnel and infected patients were registered.

The purpose of this section is to provide a consolidated analysis of the short-term social and demographic impact of the EVD on children and women in Sierra Leone. It is focused on these key issues:

- Impact on child mortality
- Increased numbers of orphans
- Strains on the existing health services and infrastructure
- Unexpected nutrition outcomes
- Stagnation of progress in education

---

[3]   www.un.org/sg/en/content/sg/speeches/2014-03-05/opening-remarks-press-conference-president-sierra-leone, accessed July 30, 2017.

Child mortality

Infant and child mortality rates generally reflect the level of socio-economic development and overall quality of life in a country. Understanding the patterns of childhood mortality assists the health sector to identify population groups that are at risk. The government of Sierra Leone is implementing the Free Health Care Initiative (FHCI), which was launched in 2010. One of the aims of this initiative is to reduce childhood mortality.

Figure 5 below suggests that there has been a decline in Infant and Under-5 mortality rates (IMR and U5MR) in Sierra Leone over time. There was a reduction in IMR between 2010 and 2013, by roughly 30 percent. A rapid analysis in 2015 called the EVDI (Ebola Virus Disease Impact Assessment Survey) found that there was no improvement between 2013 and 2015, so essentially Ebola reversed the progress.[4] The situation and pattern for U5MR are the same.

Figure 5:   Trend in infant and under-five mortality rates, Sierra Leone 2010-2015

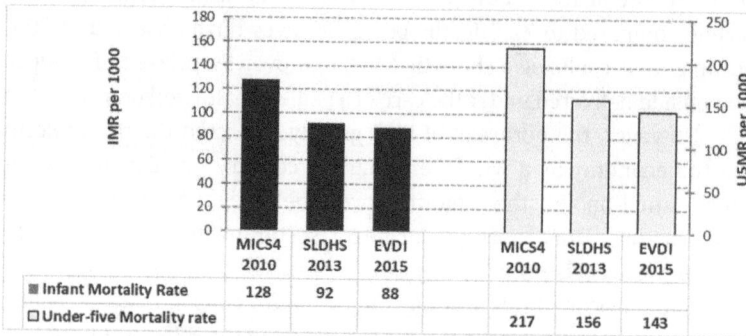

	MICS4 2010	SLDHS 2013	EVDI 2015	MICS4 2010	SLDHS 2013	EVDI 2015
■ Infant Mortality Rate	128	92	88			
☐ Under-five Mortality rate				217	156	143

Long-term trend in under-five mortality rate

Figure 6 shows the series of U5MR estimates over time as calculated using data between 1955 and 2015. These estimates are based on responses of women from different age groups and refer to various points in time. The data can thus be used to show the estimated trend in U5MR in Sierra Leone over the past 60 years. Similar data are included from the DHS

---

4   A Rapid Assessment Survey carried out to measure some of the impact of the Ebola Crisis.

2008, DHS 2013, MICS1, MICS2, MICS3 and MICS4 surveys[5]. Taken together, the data suggests that the U5MR decline in Sierra Leone stagnated until the late 1990s (coinciding with the height of the internal conflict) and has gradually declined (improved) since then, up until a stalling in 2014/2015 due to the Ebola crisis.

Figure 6:   Trends in under-five mortality rates in Sierra Leone 2015

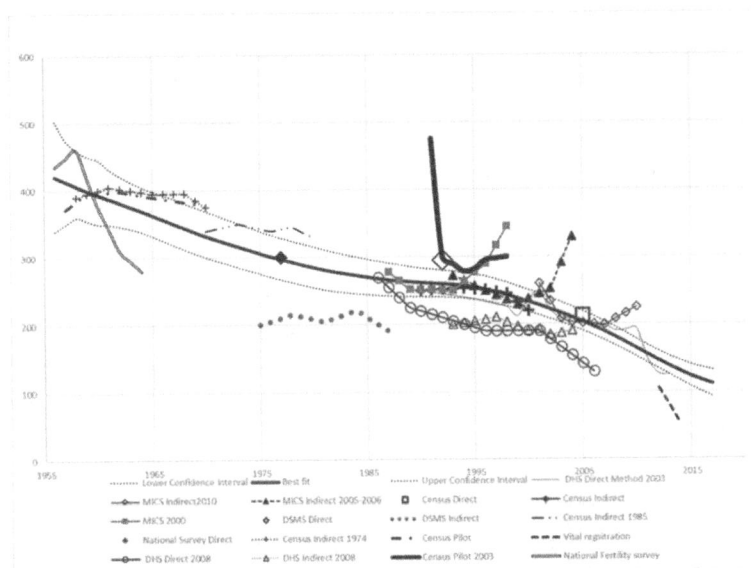

Source: UNIGME. http://data.unicef.org/child-mortality/under-five

Ebola deaths and orphans

Between May 2014 and September 2015, the outbreak of the Ebola in Sierra Leone directly affected about 13,700 persons. Out of them, 8,700 were confirmed cases of Ebola and more than 3,500 deaths were recorded. Figure 7 indicates that, out of the close to 13,700 affected individuals, 64 percent were confirmed cases of Ebola, 34 percent were suspected cases and only 2 percent were classified as probable cases. Of the confirmed cases, 80 percent were adults (women and men), 17 percent were children under the age of 18 years, while health workers

---

5   It should be noted that the DHS calculates mortality estimates using direct estimation techniques (through the completion of a birth history for each respondent), unlike the MICS surveys.

constituted 3 percent. Confirmed deaths due to Ebola were 3,587 people reflecting a case fatality ratio (CFR) of 41.2 percent.

About 1,500 children were infected and 8,600 orphans have been registered as a result of Ebola.

Figure 7:   Number of confirmed, probable and suspected EVD cases in Sierra Leone (May 2014-September 2015)

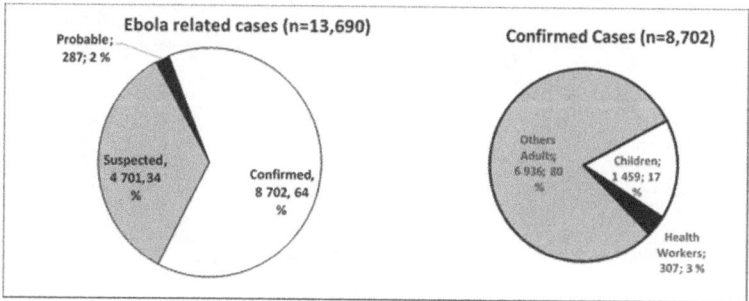

The burden of Ebola, in terms of accumulated Ebola related cases and deaths by district, is shown in Table 3. The volume of infected persons and CFRs differed across districts, for example, the Western Urban, Western Rural, Port Loko, and Bombali districts were the most affected districts, with over 1,000 confirmed cases and high number of deaths recorded. Despite the fact that the CFR in Bonthe (100) and Pujehun (51.6) districts were high because of the few cases that occurred, these two districts were least affected by the Ebola epidemic.

Table 3:   Number of cumulative Ebola relate cases and deaths by district

Name of District	Cumulative cases			Cumulative Deaths			CFR
	Sus-pected	Prob-able	Con-firmed	Sus-pected	Prob-able	Con-firmed	
Bo	341	44	314	8	43	114	36.3
Bombali	231	25	1,049	22	19	390	37.2
Bonthe	97	1	5	1	1	5	100.0
Kailahun	52	67	565	4	35	228	40.4
Kambia	198	9	258	6	9	159	61.6
Kenema	364	0	503	5	0	265	52.7
Koinadugu	60	64	109	0	32	57	52.3
Kono	415	20	254	2	19	186	73.2
Moyamba	268	21	209	9	20	78	37.3
Port Loko	650	2	1,485	74	1	586	39.5
Pujehun	77	2	31	3	2	16	51.6
Tonkolili	160	25	457	4	21	161	35.2
Western Rural	495	2	1,166	12	2	528	45.3
Western Urban	1,278	5	2,283	8	4	813	35.6
Missing		0	14	0	0	1	7.1
Sierra Leone	4,701	287	8,702	158	208	3,587	41.2

Vaccinations

By 2015, approximately 94 percent of children aged 12-23 months received a BCG vaccination against tuberculosis by the age of 12 months and the first dose of Diphtheria-Pertussis-Tetanus (DPT) was given to 77 percent. The percentage declined for subsequent doses of DPT to 66 percent for the second dose, and 46 percent for the third dose (Table 4). Similarly, 85 percent of children received Polio 1 by the age of 12 months, but this declined to 56 percent by the third dose. Some 78 percent of children received measles and yellow fever vaccine by the age of 12 months.

Table 4: Percentage of children age 12-23 months currently vaccinated against childhood disease, Sierra Leone, EVDI 2015

	BCG	Polio at birth	OPV 1	OPV 2	OPV 3	DPT 1	DPT 2	DPT 3	Measles	Yellow fever	None	Percentage with vaccination card seen
Sex												
Male	94.0	85.7	80.6	62.8	50.3	73.5	65.2	39.7	80.5	80.7	2.5	49.4
Female	94.1	82.4	88.4	71.5	61.0	81.8	66.7	52.5	75.8	74.8	4.8	58.4
Area												
Urban	93.5	86.2	89.6	76.1	61.0	86.4	76.6	62.7	74.4	74.2	5.5	56.6
Rural	94.1	83.8	83.0	64.6	54.2	74.7	63.1	40.5	79.1	78.7	3.3	53.3
Province												
East	95.7	81.5	88.9	80.5	69.4	83.1	63.9	79.5	78.4	77.7	3.5	67.3
North	94.8	74.7	84.5	72.6	61.9	74.0	52.7	71.8	74.7	73.7	2.4	61.4
South	92.4	90.2	80.3	53.4	39.7	74.3	72.1	14.9	83.7	84.3	4.4	37.8
West	92.7	88.2	88.2	66.1	61.1	88.7	76.5	53.7	70.1	69.6	6.1	55.0
District												
Kailahun	100.0	92.3	98.3	91.1	79.1	100.0	94.7	67.4	82.8	82.8	0	78.3
Kenema	89.9	63.5	88.5	85.3	74.5	71.9	71.9	92.4	74.3	72.4	8.1	67.8
Kono	98.4	88.3	78.7	63.3	51.2	81.6	41.1	79.6	78.7	78.7	1.6	54.4
Bombali	98.0	90.0	91.6	74.4	62.2	77.2	63.5	61.4	76.2	74.0	0	63.0
Kambia	95.5	79.9	79.1	73.4	49.9	100.0	76.5	72.8	80.3	76.8	4.5	42.6
Koinadugu	100.0	100.0	98.2	84.0	75.9	65.9	43.0	34.7	75.2	70.0	0	80.6
Port Loko	89.7	67.3	78.3	61.4	55.2	71.6	44.3	65.6	68.0	67.2	6.6	53.3
Tonkolili	94.2	62.5	79.7	74.6	64.5	65.4	45.0	96.0	77.4	79.2	1.4	63.6
Bo	98.8	92.7	96.9	81.9	75.0	92.7	87.7	40.8	88.2	89.1	0	74.0
Bonthe	76.6	100.0	84.4	67.1	52.6	100.0	100.0	43.9	58.2	56.4	14.9	40.3
Moyamba	93.8	89.3	70.4	33.5	15.6	71.2	69.2	8.3	86.0	86.1	2.7	15.8
Pujehun	79.9	100.0	96.5	96.5	94.1	40.5	40.5	100.0	75.6	79.9	17.3	75.1
Western Rural	95.3	90.0	80.4	62.3	57.0	76.5	63.5	67.7	58.5	59.0	3.8	53.0
Western Urban	92.3	87.9	89.3	66.6	61.7	90.6	78.6	51.8	71.7	71.1	6.4	55.2
Total	93.9	84.3	84.5	67.2	55.7	77.0	65.8	45.5	78.1	77.7	3.7	54.0

The vaccination coverage estimates among children 12-23 months observed from the EVDI survey slightly declined but this decline was not significantly different from vaccination coverage in the previous five years, when compared to MICS 2010 report estimates (Figure 8).

Figure 8: EVDI 2015 and MICS 2010 comparison of the vaccination coverage for recommended vaccines

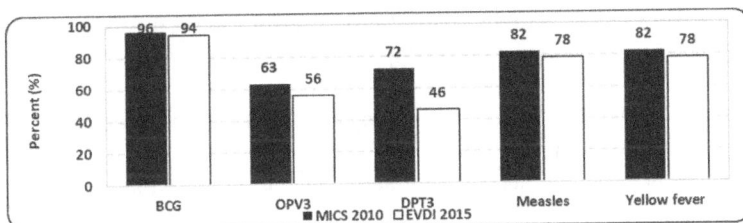

Nevertheless, an outbreak of measles (in 2018 in the Northern part of the country) may be accrued to the lack of vaccinations during the Ebola crisis as many families kept away from the hospitals; also the no-touch policy prevented the vaccination of children.

Impact of Ebola on health systems and their personnel

It is important to note that the Ebola epidemic took a heavy toll on the health workforce in Sierra Leone and overwhelmed the already weak health system. With higher risks of exposure in caring for others, health workers were disproportionately impacted and traumatized by Ebola. Their risk of infection was worsened by the lack of adequate information about the disease, both by the health workers and the general population, which made it difficult to immediately determine the extent to which the disease had spread. The absence of infection prevention and control standards at health facilities, the lack of occupational health and safety expertise, and the lack of trained staff at the onset of the epidemic, also exacerbated the infection among health workers. This could partly be blamed on the weak health system in Sierra Leone that is characterised by poor infrastructure, supply shortages, attrition, and hazardous working conditions. These factors stalled the response to EVD as the lack of knowledge of the disease made hospitals to refer patients to other districts instead of restricting their movement. This resulted in accelerating the spread of the disease across the country. Furthermore, realization of the risks involved in the caring of the Ebola infected patients without training and protective gear created fear among health workers who deserted their duty stations, thus increasing the spread of the disease and death.

Among health workers reported and confirmed to have been infected by Ebola, three-quarters have died. The case-fatality ratio among infected health workers by category was not significantly different across groups. However, due to the doctor/nurse ratio, the majority of those who died were nurses and support staff (Table 5).

Table 5:   Number of confirmed cases of Ebola among health workers by category

Category of Health Workers	Confirmed Cases	Dead	CFR (percent)
Medical Officers/Doctors	10	7	70
Nurses	172	123	72
Midwifes	11	8	73
Laboratory personnel	25	18	72
Pharmacy personnel	7	5	71
Community health workers	21	15	71
Ambulance	9	7	78
Support staff	52	38	73
Total	**307**	**221**	**72**

Source: WHO/EVD/SDS/REPORT 2015.1, MoHS

Nutrition

Children's nutritional status is a reflection of their overall health (and also it feedbacks as a driver of their health status), parents' education and income, and hygienic living conditions. When children have access to an adequate, available and affordable food supply, they are not exposed to repeated illness, and are well cared for, they reach their growth potential and are considered to be well-nourished.

Malnutrition is a leading cause of child deaths worldwide. Undernourished children are more likely to die from common childhood ailments and — among those who survive — to suffer from recurring illnesses and faltering growth. Three-quarters of the children who die from causes related to malnutrition are only mildly or moderately malnourished and show no outward sign of their vulnerability.

Low birth weight

Overall, 48 percent of births were weighed at birth and approximately 9.2 percent of infants were estimated to weigh less than 2,500 grams at birth (Table 6). These findings are not significantly different from what other surveys such as SLDHS 2013 and MICS 2010 have reported. According to the SLDHS 2013 and MICS 2010 surveys, the births that were weighed at birth was 40 percent and 48 percent respectively, while infants weighing less than 2,500 grams at birth was 10 percent for SLDHS 2013 survey and 7 percent for MICS 2010 survey.

Table 6:   Percentage of live births in two years preceding the survey weighing below 2,500 grams at birth, and percent weighed at birth

	Low-birth weight infants (<2,500 grams)	weighed at birth	Number of last live births in the two years preceding the survey
Area			
Urban	11.3	47.6	739
Rural	8.7	48.2	1444
Province			
East	8.3	47.2	374
North	9.0	39.5	940
South	9.6	58.4	348
West	10.1	46.5	521
Total	**9.2**	**48.0**	**2183**

Anthropometric measures

Table 7 shows that by 2015 one in eight children under the age of five in Sierra Leone are moderately underweight (13.1 percent) and 3.2 percent are classified as severely underweight. About one-third of children (29.8 percent) are moderately stunted or too short for their age and 5.2 percent are moderately wasted or too thin for their height.

Table 7: Percentage of children under age 5 by nutrition status according to three anthropometric indices: weight for age, height for age, and weight for height, Sierra Leone, 2015

	Underweight				Stunting				Wasting			
	Weight for age				Height for age				Weight for height			
	% <2 sd	% <3 sd	Mean Z-Score	Number of children	% <2 sd	% <3 sd	Mean Z-Score	Number of children	% <2 sd	% <3 sd	Mean Z-Score	Number of children
Sex												
Female	10.4	2.1	6.3	1,649	27.5	9.5	18.5	1,666	4.2	1.7	3.0	1888
Area												
Urban	11.6	3.0	7.3	1,020	23.9	8.3	16.1	1,033	6.9	2.7	4.8	1019
Rural	13.8	3.3	8.6	2,229	32.5	12.9	22.7	2,251	4.5	1.7	3.1	2229
Region												
East	13.9	3.7	8.8	619	31.7	10.2	21.0	628	5.2	2.3	3.8	619
North	12.8	2.9	7.9	1,362	30.9	11.8	21.4	1,371	4.3	1.5	2.9	1362
South	14.4	2.7	8.6	603	33.8	16.8	25.3	610	3.8	1.5	2.7	603
West	11.9	3.9	7.9	665	22.1	7.7	14.9	675	8.4	3.5	6.0	664
District												
Kailahun	16.2	4.6	10.4	216	36.5	14.9	25.7	222	4.2	2.3	3.3	216
Kenema	15.0	4.2	9.6	214	31.9	9.3	20.6	216	8.9	3.7	6.3	214
Kono	10.4	2.1	6.3	193	25.8	6.2	16.0	194	2.1	0.5	1.3	193
Bombali	12.7	3.8	8.3	369	28.5	12.2	20.4	369	6.2	1.4	3.8	369
Kambia	9.9	3.3	6.6	91	20.9	5.5	13.2	91	4.4	2.2	3.3	91
Koinadugu	13.7	1.2	7.5	161	32.3	12.2	22.3	164	3.1	0.0	1.6	161
Port Loko	12.8	3.3	8.1	454	29.7	10.8	20.3	454	3.5	2.0	2.8	454
Tonkolili	13.1	1.8	7.5	283	38.4	14.5	26.5	289	3.9	1.4	2.7	283
Bo	12.7	2.9	7.8	204	37.2	21.7	29.5	207	2.0	0.5	1.3	204
Bonthe	14.8	0.0	7.4	108	27.9	10.8	19.4	111	5.6	1.9	3.8	108
Moyamba	18.5	3.5	11.0	173	33.9	14.9	24.4	174	5.2	1.7	3.5	173
Pujehun	11.0	3.4	7.2	118	33.1	12.7	22.9	118	3.4	2.5	3.0	118
Western Rural	10.6	3.9	7.3	282	20.2	5.2	12.7	282	7.1	4.3	5.7	282
Western Urban	12.8	3.9	8.4	383	23.5	9.5	16.5	383	9.4	2.9	6.2	382
Total	**13.1**	**3.2**	**8.2**	**3,249**	**29.8**	**11.4**	**20.6**	**3,284**	**5.2**	**2.0**	**3.6**	**3,248**

From Table 7 it can be observed that boys under the age of five in Sierra Leone were more likely to be underweight than girls of the same age. The same applies to stunting or wasting.

The underweight and stunted prevalence among the under-5s are observed to be higher in the rural areas than in urban areas. However, the prevalence for children who are too thin for their height is slightly higher in urban than in rural areas (Table 7). On average, malnutrition rates based on the anthropometric indices slightly varies across districts with more children in Western urban and Western rural districts likely to be more wasted than others.

It is important to compare underweight, stunting and wasting prevalence estimates from MICS 2010 with those obtained from EVDI 2015 analysis. Figure 9 below reveals that there has been a decline in malnutrition prevalence in all anthropometric measures, suggesting an improvement in the nutrition status of children in Sierra Leone. These findings may however not directly reflect the current nutrition status of children that might have deteriorated as a result of Ebola crisis in the country. The improvement could be attributed to interventions put in places by government and partners prior to the Ebola outbreak in May 2014, or to the interventions put in pace to counter the impact of Ebola.

Figure 9:   Anthropometric indices

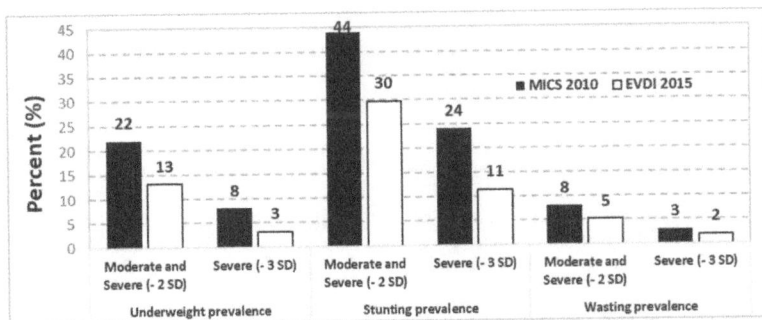

Literacy and education

Literacy among young women

During the EDVI survey literacy was assessed on the ability of the respondent to read a short simple statement or based on school attendance. Table 8 indicates that slightly above half of women in Sierra Leone are literate and that literacy status varies by area. Of the women interviewed, about 58.5 percent had either completed secondary or higher-level learning, and those with a primary level qualification were actually able to read the statement shown to them. Some 41.5 percent of the women were not literate. More literate women were found in the urban areas than in the rural regions and districts.

About half (50.7 percent) of the women in the rural areas were literate, whereas over 75 percent in the urban areas were literate. Compared with other regions, literacy rates in the North were lower (47.5 percent) and much lower than two-fifth in the districts of Kambia (34.4 percent) and Koinadugu (39.7 percent).

Table 8:   Literacy among young women: Percentage of women aged 15-
24 years who are literate (i.e. who have completed secondary
education or who can read a short simple statement)

| | Percentage who are: | | Number of women aged |
	Literate	Not – Literate	15-24 years
Area			
Urban	75.6	24.4	1,409
Rural	50.7	49.3	1,544
Region			
East	57.3	42.7	457
North	47.5	52.5	1,062
South	58.1	41.9	456
West	79.2	20.8	978
District			
Kailahun	50.8	49.2	185
Kenema	60.0	40.0	171
Kono	59.5	40.5	108
Bombali	53.0	47.0	351
Kambia	34.4	65.6	127
Koinadugu	39.7	60.3	95
Port Loko	43.1	56.9	355
Tonkolili	56.8	43.2	127
Bo	60.1	39.9	165
Bonthe	46.1	53.9	85
Moyamba	49.9	50.1	86
Pujehun	72.8	27.2	120
Western Rural	75.9	24.1	362
Western Urban	79.9	20.1	616
Total	**58.5**	**41.5**	**2,953**

THE MACROECONOMIC IMPACT OF EBOLA

During the Ebola disease outbreak borders were closed, trade in goods
came to a halt, and some businesses were folded for fear of infection.
Some of the elite class relocated to Europe and America, thus creating a
shortage of skilled professionals in the country (World Bank, 2015).

Though in the latter part of the crisis a few of the international
carriers and businesses returned, as of the time of writing (2018) the
country is yet to recover fully. The mining sector was worst hit, with most
of the companies closing and laying off staff, which had implication for the
livelihoods of the individuals and the community.

As mentioned above, there were extra 14,000 teenage pregnant girls (compared to past trends) in the nine months of government-ordered extended stay-at-home period. Many of the most severe consequences of these developments will only be felt at a later stage. These girls would lose nine months' wages in the future as a result of late entrance into the labour market, even assuming a best-case scenario where all these girls went back to school and work after delivery. This has grave implications for the country and the individual. This can cost as high as an average of about seven percentage points of the GDP loss if the girls do not return to school, or a loss of about three percentage points if they do (EPRI-UNICEF, 2016).

Figure 10:   Cost of Ebola to education discounting for the future gains or loss

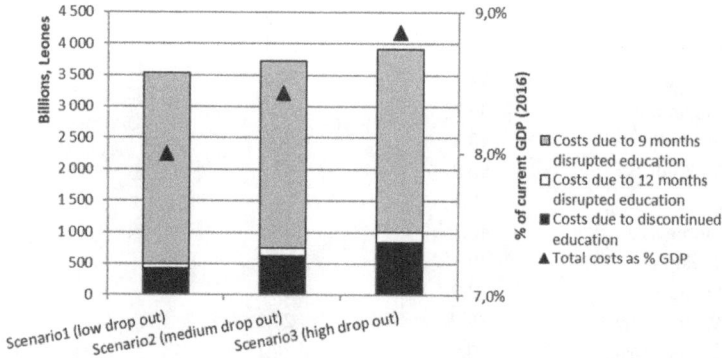

In the short term, at the macroeconomic level the increased foreign reserves inflows to combat the Ebola outbreak enabled banks and financial institutions to stay afloat. However, since the end of 2015, when most of the donors scaled down on funding after the country was declared Ebola-free, there was still a gap leading to increased inflation and economic instability.

In the health sector, as it was overstretched, many other diseases were ignored during the Ebola outbreak. This included malaria, HIV/AIDS and, to a lesser extent, measles. Nevertheless, it can be estimated than in the future, as years go by, the long-term economic impact of Ebola will become minimal, while the other diseases will have increasing impact. Unless addressed, this could cause a significant delay in the recovery trajectory of the country on the agenda for prosperity, and for achieving the SDGs. This is visible in Figure 11.

Figure 11:   The road to recovery with and without health effects

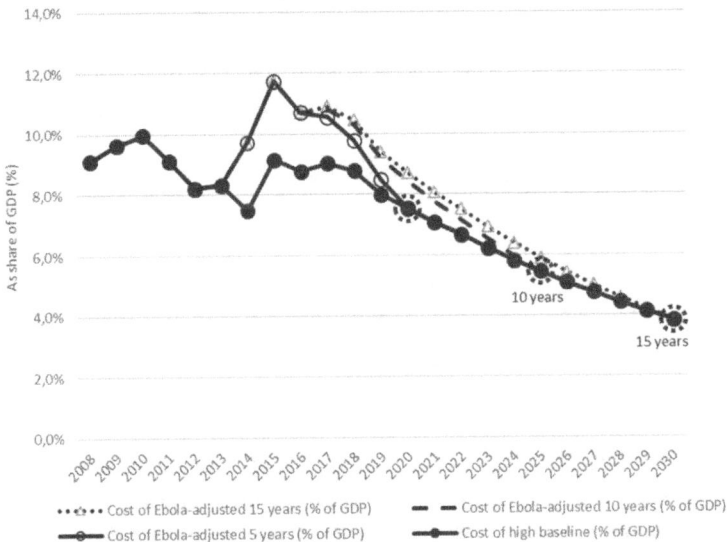

CUSHIONING THE IMPACT OF EVD THROUGH SOCIAL PROTECTION

Rapid Ebola Social Safety Net (RESSN) Programme

Saidu Conton Sesay, Chief of Staff in the Office of the President, said the following during the launch of Social Safety Net/RESSN programme:

> This new Social Safety Net program builds on the country's Agenda for Prosperity whose core objective is to achieve middle-income status by 2035 by reducing the number of Sierra Leoneans below the poverty line. It will strengthen coordination and implementation of social protection programs that improve nutrition and health services, and access to education, in order to break the inter-generational cycle of poverty (Sesay 2015).

During the Ebola crisis, the government (with the support of other stakeholders) extended the social safety net programme to cover households with people affected by, or survivors from, Ebola. The ravaging crisis within a year cost the country the loss of over 3,500 persons (including the already limited medical professionals and other professions) and over 8,000 children orphaned by the loss of one or both parents.

Thus, the launch of a programme by government to cushion the impact of the emergency on households and families was timely and needed. The programme – the Rapid Ebola Social Safety Net (RESSN) was implemented in Kailahun, Kenema, Bo, Tonkolili, Port Loko and Western Urban Area (Figure 12). Selection of beneficiaries of the RESSN programme was based on a light means-testing methodology and trying to reach families most affected by the Ebola outbreak (with or without survivors).

These districts were worst hit in terms of number of infected cases and deaths during the emergency. About 9,000 households affected by EVD benefited from a monthly benefit level equivalent to about 30 US dollars. The objective of the project was to smoothen consumption and to soften the impact of the loss of one member of the family (and concomitant income loss). The project was implemented for one year, at the end of which the programme reassessed the situation of beneficiary households to know which would still require support. Those found still to be in high need were migrated to the normal Safety Net programme. Reports from a World Bank mission in 2015 showed that the RESSN programme helped to support families to send their children back to school, increased health seeking behaviours, and some beneficiaries invested in petty trading as a form of future resilience strategy.

From anecdotal evidence from mission reports and reviews, it seems that the situation of children in terms of school attendance, feeding and health seeking behaviours by parents in selected districts have improved. There are, however, some persistent deprivations that are beyond the power of the family, such as sanitation, water and health. The situation of these sectors seems to have been badly affected by the crisis, and more interventions are required to complement the SSN/RESSN, in order to be able to make meaningful changes in the lives of children in Sierra Leone.

A major concern to address is the increase in the number of orphans within a short time frame. Some of the affected homes were found to be headed by children who had lost both parents. This further put more strain on the already weak social protection and welfare system. It is estimated that children under the age of 18 represent 17 percent of EVD cases. As the crisis escalated, they suffered multiple violations of their basic rights to survival, development and protection. The loss of many social services professionals in the early stages of the epidemic in 2014, especially in the health sector, will definitely have a long-term impact on the health of children. There is not just the cost of training and eventually replacing lost staff, there is also the loss of experience which cannot be recovered. The loss to education through stay-at-home of pupils for nine months and the loss of professional teachers also has grave consequences for the future of children in the country. On a more positive note, the targeted social protection strategy during Ebola emergency contributed to the improvement of addressing children's psychosocial needs, thus potentially reducing children's engagement in harmful practices that can damage their chances for a better future.

Other social protection (SP) initiatives included cash for work programmes for the youth, and a one-off social transfer to survivors of Ebola disease. Survivors after being quarantined were provided packages, which included basic home necessities and cash of about the equivalent to 70 US dollars.

Figure 12:   Distribution of RESSN and SSN targeted communities

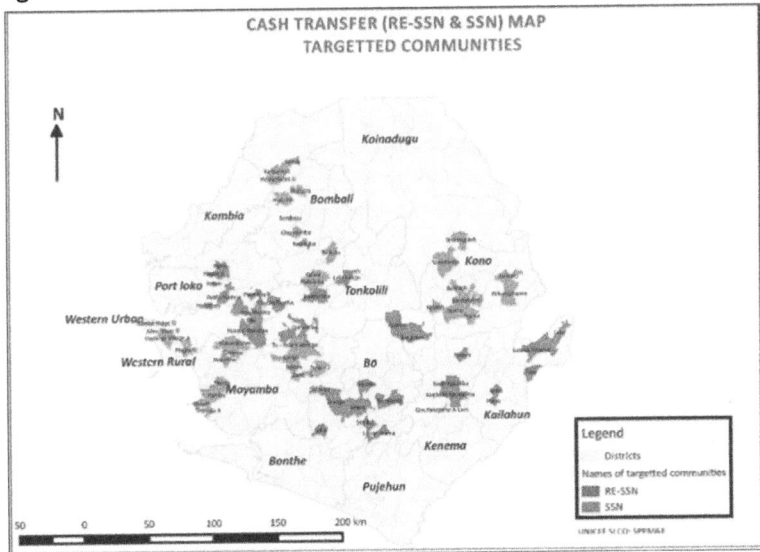

Emergency Radio Programme listenership

During the EVDI survey children and youth aged 5 – 24 where assessed to establish whether they listened to the Emergency Radio Programme (ERP) which was setup by UNICEF to bridge the education gap created during the shutdown of schools due to Ebola crisis. They were also asked whether they reported back to school when schools reopened in April 2015. Overall (Table 9) only 26 percent of the children targeted by the ERP listened to the radio program. The vast majority of those who listened to the radio program (about 99 percent) indicated they have listened to the programme at least twice a week or daily. Listening was higher in the Western region than in other regions. At district level, Koinadugu registered the lowest levels of listening to the ERP (6 percent) compared to other districts. Followed by Kono and Pujehun districts with a listening rate of 11 percent.

In addition, more than 80 percent of the children reported back to school when schools reopened in April 2015. At Bonthe district, where listening was among the lowest in the country, less than 70 percent of children reported back to school compared to other districts.

Table 9:   Emergency Radio Programme listening among children and youth age 5-24 years

	Percentage of children 4-24 who listened to the emergency radio programme			Percentage of children 4-24 years who reported back to school when schools reopens in April 2015			
	Listened	Did not listen	Number	Reported back to school	Did not report back to school	Missing	Number
Region							
East	21.3	78.7	1,781	84.8	10.2	4.9	535
North	26.8	73.2	4,146	86.2	6.3	7.5	1,121
South	14.3	85.7	1,620	84.0	11.9	4.1	451
West	54.7	45.3	3,530	90.8	8.1	1.1	2,167
District							
Kailahun	34.7	65.3	621	83.2	13.2	3.6	258
Kenema	22.3	77.7	622	92.1	7.9	0.0	196
Kono	11.5	88.5	564	72.6	7.7	19.7	98
Bombali	30.4	69.6	1,260	93.4	3.5	3.0	230
Kambia	43.5	56.5	507	84.0	6.9	9.1	261
Koinadugu	6.3	93.7	388	75.4	5.5	19.1	53
Port Loko	29.0	71.0	1,313	90.7	9.3	0.0	379
Tonkolili	20.4	79.6	652	79.4	5.3	15.3	181
Bo	15.0	85.0	549	91.4	7.3	1.3	106
Bonthe	19.9	80.1	227	64.4	15.5	20	127
Moyamba	14.4	85.6	395	85.7	14.3	0.0	158
Pujehun	11.7	88.3	449	94.1	5.9	0.0	60
Western Rural	52.2	47.8	1,327	86.4	11.6	1.9	773
Western Urban	55.0	45.0	2,203	91.3	7.6	1.0	1,394
Area							
Urban	43.4	56.6	5,086	89.0	8.0	3.0	2,667
Rural	17.7	82.3	5,991	84.7	9.8	5.5	1,607
Total	**26.4**	**73.6**	**11,077**	**87.0**	**8.9**	**4.2**	**4,274**
Frequency of listening to the ERP by children and youth aged 5-24 years							
Never	56.7	43.3	531	87.2	12.3	0.5	246
Once	98.3	1.7	1,338	92.8	6.9	0.3	1,300
Twice	99.4	0.6	935	91.7	7.3	0.9	909
Daily	99.8	0.2	1,236	95.0	5.0	0.0	1,202
Do not know	77.1	22.9	59	55.1	44.9	0.0	73
Missing	0.0	100.0	13	1.3	4.4	94.3	139
Total	**91.4**	**8.6**	**4,112**	**87.7**	**7.8**	**4.4**	**3,869**

Though much effort was made by development partners including UNICEF to set up alternative learning measures for children during the compulsory nine months stay-at-home period, many of the children and youth did not make use of the opportunities. Overall, only about a quarter of the students between the ages of 4–24 listened to the radio programme.

Kono, Pujehun and Koinadugu, all border towns to Guinea and Liberia, recorded very few students who listened to the radio. This could be attributed to the distance between the districts, and the coverage of the Radio programme and the fact that many of the children are generally deprived of their right to information.

Nevertheless, those districts closer to Freetown seemed to record higher number of children who listened to the radio programme. As with other indicators, and child poverty measurements, the rural/urban divide was obvious: percentage number of students listening who listened to the emergency radio in the urban areas were double that number in rural areas.

SOCIAL PROTECTION AND ITS IMPACT ON CHILD POVERTY IN THE TIME OF EBOLA

Social protection not only cushioned the effect of the Ebola crisis, but also addressed some of the determinants of child poverty. The efficacy of the Sierra Leone social protection system was put to test during the Ebola crisis. Based on qualitative evidence, many of the families who benefited from the RESSN testified that it enabled them to send their children to school, to increase food intake, and to practice better health seeking behaviour. Although no evaluation has been carried out since the end of the outbreak, a micro simulation of the possible cost of Ebola to the different sectors such as education and health showed that the stay-at-home period (nine months) resulted in a possible loss of per capita income of about 3 – 7%. However, cash transfers administered to the worst hit communities and households contributed to the return of children to school, and thus reduced the loss to the economy.

Another possible impact on child poverty is the increased social transfers to family through food for adults. This intervention improved nutrition for breastfeeding infants and children under 1 year of age.

CONCLUSIONS, LESSONS AND RECOMMENDATIONS

It is clear that the Ebola crisis affected children dramatically, and that social protection interventions instituted during the crisis had an impact on child poverty. Nevertheless, no evaluation has been carried out to ascertain the actual impact of the interventions in quantifiable terms. However, qualitative evidence showed that households with cash transfers did spend more on food and sending their children to school, as well as improving health seeking behaviour. The link between the transfers and the success or failure of children to return to school have not been assessed; particularly for pregnant teenage girls, it would be worth reviewing to see if the RESSN contributed to their return to school.

Lesson 1: It is possible to quickly set up social protection interventions in an emergency, even in low income countries.

It is however clear that for the country to return back to the growth trajectory as planned, more resources have to be committed to health and education amongst other sectors. If investment is made in improving health for children and mothers, especially in the early stage of the child's life — in diseases like measles prevention, malaria and HIV/AIDS prevention, spread and treatment — the country may be able to return to its pre-Ebola trajectory. On the other hand, in order to re-gain the time missed in education, additional investments are required to fast-track return of children to school and provide programmes to enable them catch up with their studies.

Lesson 2: In spite of relatively successful emergency social protection interventions, there are still future costs and risks needing a bridge to, and coordination with, standard social protection.

These findings and analyses beg for the instituting of a social protection policy that, along with the Social Protection Floor guidelines, ensures free education is made available for all children. This would require, among other interventions, that all the necessary accessories, such as uniforms, school feeding, adequate water and sanitary facilities and educational materials are provided free of cost, including for children with disabilities.

Lesson 3: Social protection needs to be complemented with investments in basic social services, both in the short- and long-term.

A closer focus on an inclusive social protection system that considers the needs of all the country's citizens would be welcomed. This also calls for the review of the National Social Protection policy which was approved in 2011. A review would be timely as it would incorporate the concerns of survivors, as well as present measures for any emergency situation, whether that is related to an epidemic, or another human-caused or natural disaster. This would ensure that the country navigates properly and surely in the achievement of the SDGs so its citizenry can thrive and succeed.

REFERENCES

Delamonica, E. and A. Minujin. 2007. Incidence, Depth and Severity of Children in Poverty. *Social Indicators Research* 82: 361-374.

EPRI-UNICEF 2016 *The long-term cost of the impact of Ebola in Sierra Leone*

Hanciouglu, A. and F. Arnold. 2013. "Measuring coverage in MNCH: Tracking Progress in Health for Women and Children using DHS and MCIS Household Surveys", *PLOS Medicine* 10(5): 1-8.

Sesay, Saidu Conton, Chief of Staff in the Office of the President during the launch of SSN/RESSN programme in May 2015

UNIGME. http://data.unicef.org/child-mortality/under-five, accessed August 1, 2019.

World Bank Report on the social and economic cost of Ebola 2015

CHAPTER 8

CHILD POVERTY AND ECONOMIC SHOCKS IN TOGO: POLICIES MATTER

Aristide Kielem

BACKGROUND

In 2008-2009 the world experienced a financial crisis coupled with food and fuel price volatility that impacted almost all countries in their economic, social and financial sectors. Developing countries have suffered as their progress toward the Millennium Development Goals (MDGs) were challenged and in some cases even stopped or reversed. In many developing countries, including Togo, this crisis resulted in a drastic increase of the basic consumption basket cost. This led to a decrease in purchasing power, especially for the urban poor (Kielem, Diagne, Agbodji and Bouare, 2013). In addition, food security and children's welfare have been impacted as food prices increased drastically following the increase in the price of fuel in the global market (figure 1).

Figure 1: Oil prices and inflation

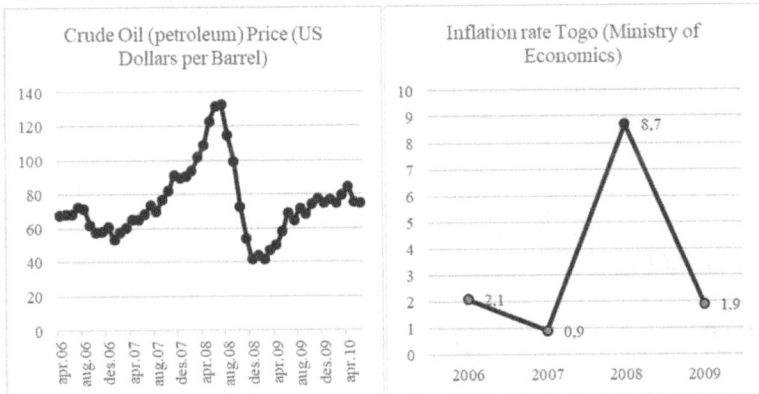

Mendoza (2009) found that in some countries (especially in Asia), the rising food prices may have impacted differently net producers and net consumers, but monetary poverty increased in almost all countries.

However, in most of the countries he analyzed, monetary poverty rates were below 40 percent.

Before the crisis, Togo was characterized by a precarious nutritional situation and generalized monetary poverty (62 percent in 2006) that had been exacerbated by the 2005 post-electoral war and the 2007 flood. This was amplified by the structural weaknesses of the Togolese economy, especially the agricultural sector that was still largely archaic with weak access to markets for many farmers. To cope with the effects of the reduced income and the increase in commodities prices, households adjusted by reducing spending on education, health and food quantity and/or quality. Children were the most affected by these regressive coping mechanisms.

To face the crisis and its effects, the Togolese government implemented a set of measures, especially aimed at the rural population, to restore and improve the agricultural sector outcomes. Those measures have also had an impact on poverty and on children. The impact of the crisis and policy responses on poverty and child poverty dimensions have been explored, but there has, as of yet, been no analysis of how the crisis may have impacted child multidimensional poverty as a whole. Ever since the study led by Cornia et al. (1988) on "adjustment with a human face," an interest on post-crisis adjustment packages has arisen. In fact, Cornia et al. (1988) proposed that the post 1980 and 1985 IMF adjustment policies could have been designed in a way that simultaneously protected poor groups while restoring economic growth. This has been the goal of most of developing countries' governments, including Togo during the 2008–2009 economic and financial crisis.

The purpose of this chapter is to explore what has been the child poverty trends before, during, and after the crisis, and how policies implemented by the government have impacted households and children welfare in Togo.

CHILD POVERTY LONG-TERM PROFILE IN TOGO

Child poverty is a complex notion that has been explored by many authors. One of the most common indicators used for defining poverty is based on income or spending. According to this indicator, children are considered poor if they live in households whose spending/income is below the poverty line. However, children experience poverty differently as the intra-household distribution of income may affect their rights. In this context, the approach to child poverty is based on deprivations. Households and their children are then considered as living in poverty depending on insufficient access to drinking water, sanitation, nutrition, health, shelter, education, or information (Gordon et al. 2003; Delamonica and Minujin 2006).

The dimensions, indicators and thresholds used in this paper are the following:

Table 1:   Dimensions and thresholds of child poverty estimates

Dimensions	Indicators	Thresholds
Water	Access to drinking water	Drinking water from natural sources (rivers, streams)
		More than 15 minutes to go to main drinking water point
Sanitation	Sanitation sewer connection (waste disposal)	Do not have access to improved drinking water source
Dwelling	Ratio of persons per room	Overcrowding: 4 persons per room
	Flooring material	No flooring material or mud flooring
Education	Never been to school	Aged between 6 and 18 who had never been to school
	Drop out	Aged between 6 and 18 who have been to school but are not currently attending school
Health	Medical care	Fever or vomiting with no medical care
	Immunization	Have not received all mandatory vaccinations
Information	Access to information	Children aged between 3 and 18 with no access to radio, television, telephone (mobile or landline) at home.

To estimate child poverty in Togo, data from the 2006, 2010, and 2013 Multiple Indicators Cluster Surveys (MICS) and Demographic and Health Surveys (DHS) have been used. The estimates show that child poverty decreased from 2006 to 2010 from 78.9 percent to 78.1 percent (Figure 2). This decrease has been greater from 2010 to 2013, after the crisis. In fact, contrary to Mendoza's findings on Asian countries, child poverty decreased in Togo about four percentage points when it reached 75.6 percent in 2013. While the decrease from 2006 to 2010 is not statistically significant, the drop in poverty from 2010 to 2013 is. The decrease after 2010 may be the result of the countercyclical policy measures implemented by the government to cope with the crisis that reduced the impact on the food price increase and fast-tracked the recovery while increasing household's welfare (Kielem et al. 2013).

Figure 2:   Child poverty trend (2006-2013)

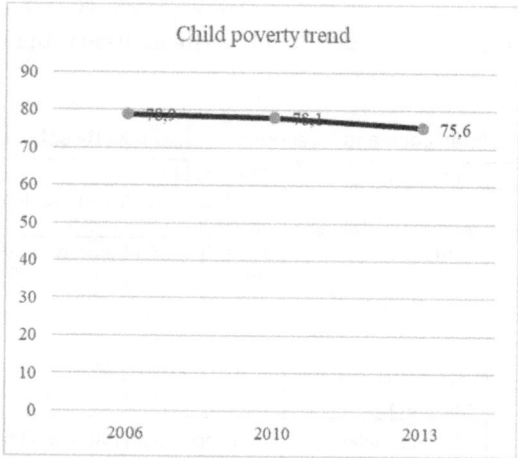

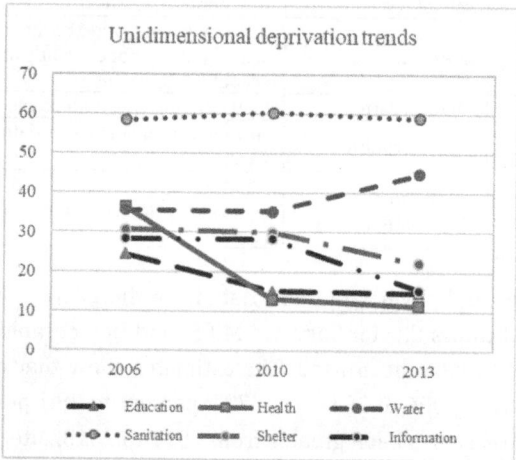

Data from Togo also show that sanitation is the dimension in which children are the most deprived. In addition, progress in this dimension has been weak over time. This is due to the lack of sanitation infrastructure for most of the households, and also due to traditional behaviour which reduce the impact of public interventions to improve access to sanitation facilities. The water dimension also shows a negative trend, as more children are facing a severe water deprivation in 2013 compared to 2010 and 2006. The issue in Togo is not the lack of water but the availability of safe drinking water, especially in rural areas. The municipal water connection system is only in place for urban areas, and water points may be hardly reachable for the rural population; this is particularly the case in the hilly Plateaux and central regions as well as in the dry Savanes Region.

In Togo, poverty depth has also improved since 2006 from 1.7 average deprivation per child to 1.5 in 2013.

Disaggregating child poverty in Togo

Child poverty has declined between 2006 and 2013 in both urban and rural areas. However, it appears clearly that children living in rural areas are more deprived of their rights and have experienced less progress in their welfare over time (Figure 3). This coincides with the findings on monetary poverty showing that poverty is much more rural than urban in Togo.

Figure 3:   Child poverty rates per region (2006-2013)

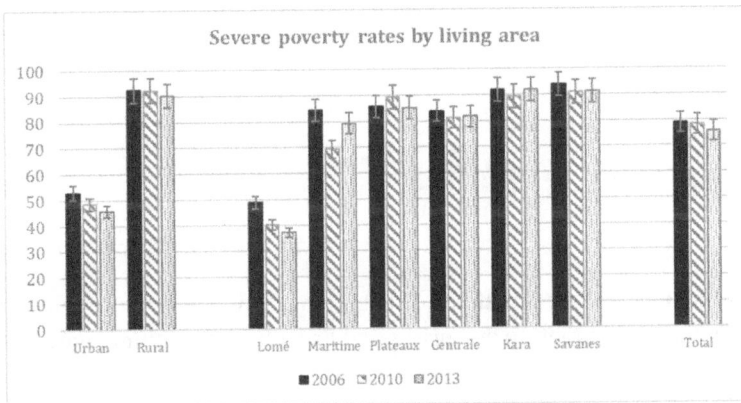

Poverty in the capital city (Lomé) has dropped since 2006 but this decrease has not been enough to significantly reduce poverty at the national level. Lomé also appears to be the wealthiest region. At the national level, poverty has declined but this decline has not been statistically significant from 2006 to 2013. This slight decrease (and also the fact that child poverty did not increase) is probably due to the longer-term effects of policies implemented to respond to the 2008-2009 financial crisis that were mostly maintained after the crisis. Poverty in the regions outside of Lomé is not significantly different. Kara and Savanes regions are among the poorest in the monetary dimension, and they also record the highest child poverty rates.

Data also show that child poverty remained unchanged for those in the poorest welfare quintile and that most of the changes occurred in the two richest quintiles (figure 4). This means that most of the changes occurred for the households that are above the monetary poverty line (as poverty is around 60 percent and the richest quintiles concern the 40 percent better-off households). This implies that the poorest households did not improve their children's situation at all.

Figure 4:   Child poverty rates per welfare quintile (2006-2013)

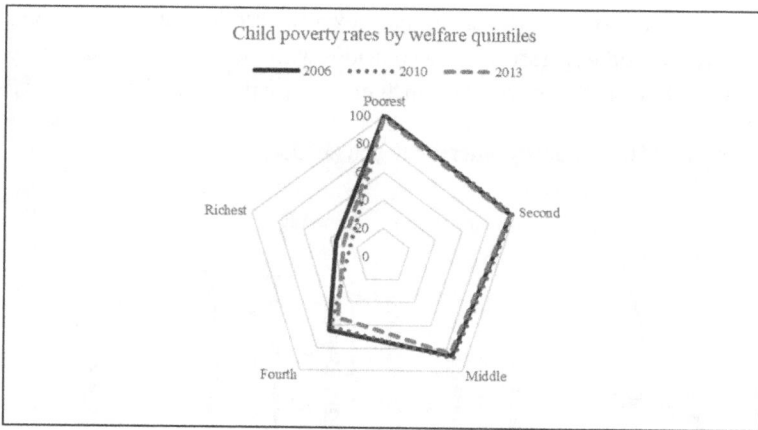

This finding is coherent with the distribution of government core subsidy policy that was targeting fuel prices and henceforth benefiting more the richest households.

THE 2008-2009 CRISIS: POLICY RESPONSES AND THEIR IMPACT ON POVERTY

GDP growth was mainly driven by the primary/agricultural sector in Togo during the crisis. Because 95 percent of the crop production is domestic, the rising food prices have been the main channel though which the economic crisis impacted the economy and individuals. Between the first and second half of 2007, the price of millet, cowpea and local rice increased by 48 percent, 41 percent and 30 percent, respectively. For all products, rising commodity prices continued to reach a critical point in the first half of 2009. The price of maize grain has experienced the most drastic increase at 105 percent.

Impact on monetary poverty

The assessment of the impact of the crisis on monetary poverty is done using the Questionnaire des Indicateurs de Base du Bien-être (QUIBB, or, in English, CWIQ – Core Welfare Indicators Survey). Using micro simulation technics derived from Deaton (1989), we simulate the impact of the crisis on households' consumption and welfare (consumption per equivalent adult). This allows us to build a pseudo panel, enabling us to estimate the change due to the price increases.

The first estimate demonstrates the impact of the rising food prices on consumption, while the second considers both consumption and production. In fact, the crisis has resulted in price increases on the market but also on an increase in the price paid to producers. However, all producers may not have benefited from all the price increases, as intermediaries capture part of the surplus.

In Togo 66.3 percent of households are net consumers (51.3 percent living in rural areas) and 33.7 percent are net producers (93 percent in rural areas).

The simulations using the first scenario (impact on consumption only, assuming that farmers do not take advantage of the price increases) show that the food price variations have resulted in an increase of 4.1 points for monetary poverty (from 61.7 percent to 65.8 percent). This increase in poverty would have been higher for rural households that would experience an increase of 4.5 points (from 74.3 percent to 78.8 percent), while urban households would have seen their poverty rate rise from 36.8 percent to 40.3 percent.

Table 2:   Change in monetary poverty due to food price variation
              (Hypothesis 1: impact on consumption)

Impact on consumption ONLY

	share	Initial (2006)	Simulation	Variation	t-student*
National	**100%**	**61.7**	**65.8**	**4.1**	**16.4**
Agricultural HH	62.42%	78.8	82.7	3.9	10.7
AREA					
Urban	31.09%	36.8	40.3	3.5	8.6
Rural	68.91%	74.3	78.8	4.5	13.9
HH HEAD GENDER					
Male	49.87%	64.3	68.0	3.7	**1.6**
Female	50.13%	50.0	56.5	6.5	9.5
REGIONS					
Lomé	18.54%	24.5	26.5	2.0	4.8
Maritime	16.54%	69.4	74.7	5.3	8.4
Plateaux	17.86%	56.2	63.1	6.9	9.1
Centrale	13.49%	77.7	81	3.3	6.2
Kara	15.45%	75	79.1	4.1	6.9
Savanes	18.11%	90.5	92.2	1.7	4.5

Source: QUIBB 2006
* = significant at 1%

Considering that the food price increases affected both consumption and
expenditures, the Deaton semi-equilibrium model estimates shows that
poverty decreased from 61.7 percent to 59.9 percent. This decrease is
counterintuitive but is easily understood when considering that most of
the workforce is in agriculture and farmers are selling part of their
production, earning more when prices go up. They also suffer less from
the food prices increases than their urban counter parts, as they consume
part of their production and buy less on markets. In fact, net producers
mostly living in rural areas have seen their welfare increase, while net
consumers, mostly from urban areas, have seen their welfare decrease,
meaning that with the same spending level, they had a lower
consumption.

As a result, poverty decreased by 3.7 percent in rural areas and
increased by 1.9 percent in urban areas. The decrease in rural areas is
mainly due to the drastic drop of 6 points in poverty among agricultural
workers' households.

Table 3:   Change in poverty due to food price variation (Hypothesis 2:
            impact on consumption and production)

Impact on consumption and production					
	share	initial (2006)	simulation	Variation	t-student
National	100%	61.7	59.9	-1.8	-3.96
Agriculture	62.42%	78.8	72.8	-6	-9.36
Milieu de residence					
Urban	31.09%	36.8	38.7	1.9	3.57
Rural	68.91%	74.3	70.6	-3.7	-5.98
Genre du chef de ménage					
Male	49.87%	64.3	61.5	-2.8	-5.81
Female	50.13%	50	52.9	2.9	3.54
Regions					
Lomé	18.54%	24.5	26.6	2.1	4.86
Maritime	16.54%	69.4	67.9	-1.5	-1.56
Plateaux	17.86%	56.2	52.2	-4	-2.84
Centrale	13.49%	77.7	72.4	-5.3	-4.92
Kara	15.45%	75	74.1	-0.9	-7.82
Savanes	18.11%	90.5	88.3	-2.2	-2.73

Source: QUIBB 2006
* = significant at 1%

The commodities price increases can be seen as a taxation (Figure 5) on food items. Analysing the distributive impact of this tax using a Lorenz curve shows that poor households are less affected.

Figure 5:   Progressivity analysis (Lorenz curve)

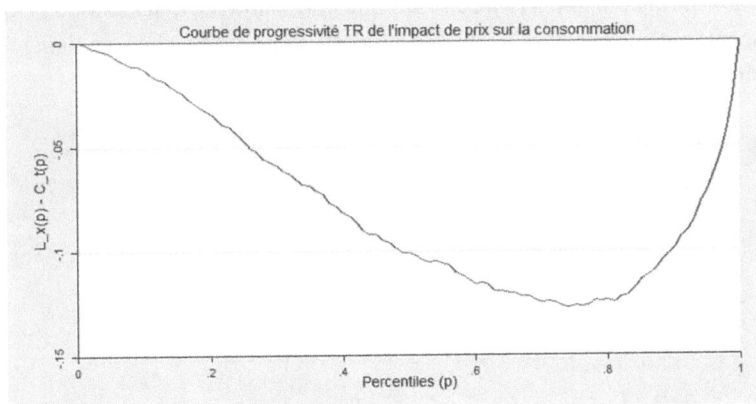

Courbe de progressivité TR de l'impact de prix sur la consommation

This is due to the fact that the poverty profile in Togo has shown that poor households are mainly coming from rural and agricultural households.

THE IMPACT OF THE CRISIS ON CHILD POVERTY

The crisis has had an impact on child poverty dimensions. To analyse how the crisis has impacted child poverty we explore the trends in food poverty and education.

Child monetary (food) poverty has increased

When households experience a decline in their income, they take coping measures that may affect negatively children and their wellbeing. To analyse this impact, we assessed the impact of the rising food prices on monetary poverty. We assumed that a child is poor if she or he lives in a household whose consumption per equivalent adult is below the food poverty line. Food poverty is preferred as this has a direct impact on children nutrition and survival. To analyse this, we used data from QUIBB 2006 and applied the methodology developed by Deaton (1989).

The results of the simulations in the table below show that monetary child poverty has increased dramatically when considering the impact of the rising food prices on consumption only. The results are mitigated for the simulation on both production and consumption, especially for the children who are 0-5 years old.

Despite the drop in monetary poverty, when considering the impact of the increase in food prices on both production and consumption, the 1.3 percentage point change in child poverty is not significant. However, the potential increase of 10.2 percent in child poverty is significant, when considering the impact on consumption only, showing that the food price increases has negatively affected children. In any case, children living in urban areas have seen their welfare level decrease drastically.

Table 4:   Variation in poverty rate among children

	Simulation 1: Effect on production and consumption				Simulation 2: Effect on consumption only			
	All	0 - 5	6 - 10	11 – 14	All	0 - 5	6 - 10	11 – 14
National	-1.3	-0.8	-2	-1.1	10.2	10	10.5	11.1
Area								
Urban	7.3	6.8	7.3	8	9.5	8.4	9.7	11.2
Rural	-4.6	-3.8	-5.1	-5.3	10.8	10.6	10.8	11.2
Region								
Lomé	8.6	8.1	8.7	9.6	9.4	8.5	9.3	11.4
Maritime	0.5	2.2	0.3	-2.3	14.4	13.7	14.7	15
Plateaux	-2.2	-1.4	-3	-2.3	11.3	9.7	11.7	13.6
Centrale	-10.5	-11.3	-9.1	-11.5	7.4	7.4	8.2	5.9
Kara	-0.3	0.2	-2.5	2.8	10.3	11	8.7	12.4
Savanes	-7.4	-7.3	-8.3	-5.9	7.6	8.2	7.4	6.8

Source: QUIBB 2006

However, when comparing rural and urban areas, it is clear that while farmers can take advantage of the price increases on the market, and their rural children experience a drop in their poverty; urban children nonetheless become poorer.

Whatever hypothesis is retained, the crisis has potentially increased the proportion of children living in poor households in the capital city Lomé by at least 8 percent. This means that the decline observed in Lomé in multidimensional child poverty may have been caused by the policies implemented rather than a change in households welfare.

The impact of the crisis on education

Several researches (Filmer and Pritchett 1998; Skyt 2001; Handa 2002; Diagne 2005; Handa and Simler 2005; Glick and Sahn 2006) have shown that the level of parents' income, as well as their education, affect children's schooling. As a result, a decline in household's purchasing power may result in a decline in household's investment in their children's education.

The results of the probit model used for our estimates shows that there is a positive relation between schooling and consumption level in Togo.

Simulating the impact of the financial crisis on school attendance shows that the food price increase has not significantly affected the probability for children to go to school. This result can be analysed in the

Togolese context with regard to the local vision and practices in education. In fact, households tend to prioritize children's education. A large proportion of schools in rural Togo are built and managed by communities, with volunteer teachers being paid by these communities. Education may decline in the long term if/when household welfare levels deteriorate, but households tend to cut education investment only as a last resort.

Table 5:   Probit estimation result

	Schooling	
	Coef.	P>|z|
Ln (consumption per capita)	5.54	0.078
Age (Child)	-0.18	0.000
Household size	0.67	0.064
Area (urban=1)	-1.14	0.000
Gender (child)	0.21	0.014
HH head gender (male = 1)	-0.07	0.337
HH head education (Yes=1)	0.22	0.000
Maritime Region	1.92	0.031
Plateaux Region	0.98	0.050
Centrale Region	2.79	0.041
Kara Region	2.80	0.041
Savanes Region	2.94	0.072
Constant	-69.53	0.091

Number of observations = 7149
Wald chi2 (14) = 1338.24
Prob> chi2 = 0.0000
Log likelihood = -5118.25

POLICIES MATTER: THE IMPACT OF SOCIAL PROTECTION POLICIES ON POVERTY

The crisis has taught lessons concerning the impact of policies on poverty and child wellbeing. As a response to the rising prices, the government implemented different policies. The most important one was intended to increase rural income and control food prices by stimulating crops production through seeds and fertilizers subsidies. We analyse the impact of this policy on poverty as well as the impact of a hypothetical cash transfer programme targeting children. This programme is not entirely hypothetical, however, as its parameters were under discussion in the government-led social protection working group. The evaluation was then done in relation to a new cash transfer programme that was being designed to respond to the impact of the crisis on child poverty.

The impact of the progressive agriculture subsidies

To ensure that food prices did not increase to the extent seen in other developing countries, the Togolese government chose to subsidize seeds and fertilizers, and to facilitate loans for agriculture.

The empirical methodology used to analyse the impact of this measure is based on usual impact evaluation techniques. Using panel data, we consider the subsidy as a treatment and use a double difference strategy to isolate the impact of the programme on beneficiary households. We try to isolate the impact on poverty and nutrition. As the assignment to the programme was not randomized, there is likely to be a bias in the Ordinary Least Squares estimates. This difference in the poverty trends of beneficiaries and non-beneficiaries show that the potential impact of the programme is a drop of 23.4 points in poverty rate for the beneficiary households compared to the non-beneficiaries (Figure 6).

Figure 6:   Monetary poverty trend between beneficiary and non-beneficiary households

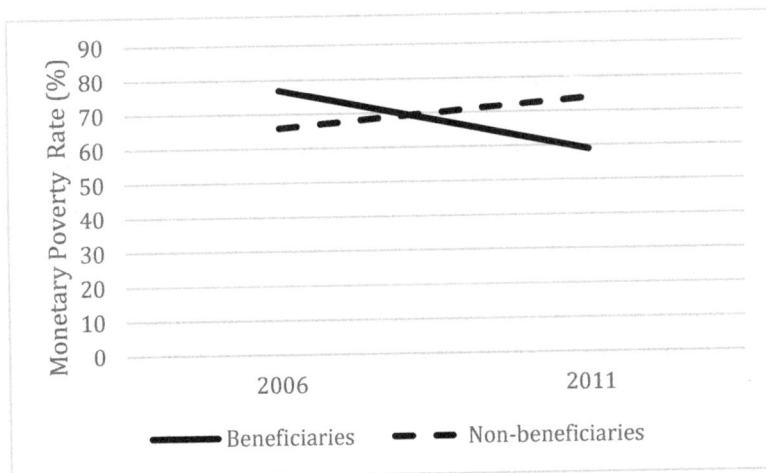

Source: QUIBB 2006. PSIA 2011

The agricultural subsidies seem to have helped reduce the impact of the crisis on the beneficiaries. However, this drastic difference in poverty change between beneficiaries and non-beneficiary households may be the result of the design of the policy itself. In fact, this programme targeted poor agricultural households that may have also benefited from the increases in crop prices. They may then have experienced an increase in their production due to increased availability of subsidized agricultural inputs (resulting in lower production cost and higher production), and at the same time benefited from the higher producer prices gained during the crisis.

Cash transfers can reduce monetary poverty in the short term

Cash transfer programmes are becoming more and more common in Africa and Latin America. It has become one of the most used poverty alleviation tools, helping households to cope with shocks and to ensure children's rights. The Togolese government has undertaken reflections to select the best social protection programmes, including cash transfers. No study to date has proven the potential success of such programmes in the country. To fill this analytical gap, we estimate the potential impact of three cash transfer designs on monetary poverty and nutrition:

- Design 1: Giving the equivalent to the poverty gap (5000 CFA Francs monthly) to all poor households
- Design 2: Target households with children living in the two poorest regions with a transfer amount of 5000 CFA Franc monthly (poverty gap equivalent).
- Design 3: The joint UNICEF/World Bank programme that targets all undernourished children aged 6 to 24 months in the northern regions (Savanes and Kara) with a transfer amount of 5000 CFA Francs to the household.

The results of the simulations show that the implementation of these programmes have a positive short-term impact on households' monetary poverty.

Table 6:   Potential poverty reduction impact of cash transfer programmes

Target population	yearly transfer (CFA)	Impact (Beneficiaries)	Impact (Total Population)	Total cost (%GDP)
Design 1	60 000	-36.04%	-21.73%	14.0%
Design 2	60 000	-10.41%	-6.23%	2.2%
Design 3	60 000	-13.53%	-1.56%	1.6%

While Design 1 has a higher impact, it costs 14% of the GDP yearly and seems to be unsustainable for the Government. The two other designs have to be analysed for policy decision. While the second design has a higher impact on beneficiaries and costs less (1.6 percent of GDP), this option would not be the most cost effective as the third design could allow a bigger drop in poverty (3 points below Design 2) at a lower cost (an economy of 0.6 percent of the GDP compared to Design 2).

CONCLUSION

Whereas child poverty is not only related to household income, poor families do tend to host more poor children. Analysing child poverty as a multidimensional issue helps to focus on child rights and the negative factors that can harm children in their future lives.

When shocks arise, households tend to adopt coping strategies that can be harmful to children in the short and long run. In addition, programmes and policies implemented by governments have both direct and indirect impacts on children.

The 2008-2009 crisis has provided a natural experiment of a covariate shock. The increase in prices has affected negatively households and children welfare. Policies implemented by the government such as cash transfer programmes have been instrumental in helping reduce the impact of the shock, and bringing back households to a more acceptable welfare level; at this level governments are more capable of influencing the environment in which children are living, and consequently, of reducing child poverty levels.

Building on these findings, social policy work should focus on influencing government policies and programmes to reduce child poverty and build a child-friendlier future.

REFERENCES

Atkinson. A. B. (1987). "On the Measurement of Poverty". *Econometrica.* 55(4). pp.749-764.

Aksoy M.A. and A. Isik-Dikmelik (2008). "Are Low Food Prices Pro-Poor? Net Food Buyers and Sellers in Low-Income Countries?". *World Bank Policy Research Working Paper* 4642. World Bank: Washington DC.

Alderman H. J. Hoddinott et B. Kinsey (2006). "Long Term Consequences of Early Childhood Malnutrition". *Oxford Economic Papers.* 58(3). pp. 450–474.

Bibi. Sami. John Cockburn. Massa Coulibaly et Luca Tiberti (2009). « L'impact de la hausse des prix des produits alimentaires sur la pauvreté des enfants et les réponses politiques au Mali ». *Innocenti Working Paper*. no. 2009-02. Florence. UNICEF Innocenti Research Centre.

Cornia G.A., Jolly R., and Stewart F. (1988) *"Adjustment with a Human Face"*. Volume 2, Ten Country Case Studies, Clarendon Press.

Cornia. G.A. and L. Deotti (2008) "Millet Prices. Public Policy and Child Malnutrition: The Case of Niger in 2005". *Innocenti Working Paper* No. 2008-04. Florence. UNICEF Innocenti Research Centre.

CWIQ 2006. Core Welfare Indicators Questionnaire (CWIQ)/ Questionnaire des Indicateurs de Base du Bien-être (QUIBB). Direction Générale de la Statistique et de la Comptabilité Nationale. République Togolaise 2006.

Datt. G. et M. Ravallion (1992). "Growth and Redistribution Components of Changes in Poverty Measures: A decomposition with applications to Brazil and India in 1980s". *Journal of Development Economics*. 38. pp. 275-295.

Deaton, A. (1989). "Rice Prices and Income Distribution in Thailand: A Non-Parametric Analysis". *The Economic Journal*. 99(395). pp. 1-37.

Diagne A. (2005). "Une modélisation des déterminants des décisions de scolarisation primaire des ménages au Sénégal". *African Development Bank Review*. 17(2). pp. 244-273.

Duclos. J.Y. and Araar. A. (2006). *Poverty and Equity: Measurement. Policy and Estimation with DAD*. Springer/CRDI.

Filmer. D. and L. Pritchet (1998). 'Educational Enrollment and Attainment in India: Household Wealth. Gender. Village. and State Effects' Working Paper. World Bank.

Glick P. and D. Sahn (2006). "The demand for primary schooling in Madagascar: Price. quality and the choice between public and private providers". *Journal of Development Economics*. 79. pp. 118-145.

Handa. S. (2002). 'Raising Primary School Enrollment in Developing Countries: The Relative Importance of Supply and Demand'. *Journal of Development Economics*. 69. pp. 103–28.

Handa. S. and K. R. Simler (2005). 'Quality or Quantity? The Supply Side Determinants of Primary Schooling in a Poor Rural Economy'. *Journal of African Economies*. 23. pp. 59-90.

Ichoku et Leibbrandt (2003). "Demand for Healthcare Services in Nigeria: A Multivariate Nested Logit Model". *African Development Bank Review*. 15(2-3). pp. 396-424.

IFPRI (2008a) *Global Food Crisis: monitoring and Assessing Impact to Inform Policy Responses*. IFPRI Food Policy Report. IFPRI: Washington DC.

Jensen. R.T. et N.H. Miller (2008) "The Impact of the World Food Price Crisis on Nutrition in China". *Faculty Research Working Papers Series*. Harvard Kennedy School.

Kakwani. N.. S. Khandker et H.H. Son (2004). "Pro-Poor Growth: Concepts and Measurement with Country Case Studies". Washington. Working Paper 1. International Poverty Center. United Nations Development Program.

Lachaud. J-P. (2007). "Scolarisation et travail des enfants : Un modèle économétrique à Régimes endogènes appliqué à Madagascar-2001-2005". Centre d'économie du développement Université Montesquieu Bordeaux IV. DT/134/2007.

Mendoza. Ronald U. 2009. "Aggregate shocks, poor households and children: Transmission channels and policy responses." UNICEF mimeo

Mwabu. G. (2009). "The Production of Child Health in Kenya: A Structural Model of Birth Weight." *Journal of African Economies.* 18(2). pp. 212-260.

Pongou R.. J.A. Salomon and M. Ezzati (2005) "Economic Crisis and Declining Child Nutrition in Cameroon During the 1990s: The Mediating Role of Household Effects". Working Paper Series. 15(2). Harvard Center for Population and Development Studies.

Skyt Nielsen. H. (2001). "How Sensitive is the Demand for Primary Education to Changes in Economic Factors?". *Journal of African Economies.* 10. pp. 191-218.

Wodon. Q. and H. Zaman (2008) "Rising Food Prices in Sub-Saharan Africa: Poverty Impact and Policy Responses". World Bank Policy Research Working Paper 4738. World Bank. Washington DC.

World Bank (2007). Profil de la pauvreté et de la vulnérabilité au Togo. 2007

World Bank (2008). "Rising Food and Fuel Prices: Addressing the Risks to Future Generations". World Bank.

PART IV: SOCIAL PROTECTION, SOCIAL EXCLUSION, AND CHILD PROTECTION

CHAPTER 9

A DIFFERENT PERSPECTIVE ON SOCIAL PROTECTION: THE IMPORTANCE OF CONSIDERING CHILD POVERTY IN THE CONTEXT OF EXTENDED FAMILIES AND COMMUNITIES IN BURKINA FASO, THE CENTRAL AFRICAN REPUBLIC, AND THE DEMOCRATIC REPUBLIC OF THE CONGO

Diana Skelton and Jacqueline Plaisir

INTRODUCTION

Rapid changes in society have strained families in new ways. In some cases, this leads children to leave home and live in the streets. Social protection and welfare services in Europe and North American countries have on many occasions contributed to separating children from their families, all too often due to a bias in child protection services against parents in poverty, particularly those facing severe and multiple disadvantages. Because such practices cause harm, it is important that mistakes made in Northern countries not be reproduced in Africa.

There are also good practices in reuniting and keeping children in their families and communities. Positive outcomes for children living in poverty can be created in three ways:

- by making it possible for extended families to renew relationships with children who have left home, as demonstrated in a pilot project in Burkina Faso
- by reinforcing the efforts of young people in low-income communities who feel a natural responsibility to protect all young children, as shown in the Central African Republic
- by following the lead of children who can play an active role in strengthening their communities and all the families there, as in the Democratic Republic of the Congo (DRC).

This chapter reflects the methodology of ATD Fourth World. Its long-term relationships with people living in poverty make it possible for them to pool their knowledge together with others. International collaboration can help people in poverty draw inspiration from one another. It broadens their understanding of the realities of their lives in the context of global factors. This approach has developed projects that strengthen families and communities despite the harsh realities of poverty. ATD Fourth World has been present since 1981 in Burkina Faso, since 1984 in the Central African Republic, and since 1997 in the DRC. In addition, ATD Fourth World has worked for decades with people in poverty in Western Europe and North America. Their experiences with, and analysis of, the Northern social protection model has become an important reference point for many people in Africa.

A critical look at Northern social protection and welfare services models is needed

In countries where social protection includes providing low-income families with financial support, this protection is linked to a high degree of scrutiny. While this scrutiny can provide life-saving child protection in crisis,[1] the most common reason for removing children from parental custody is "neglect"—which can simply mean having too few resources to provide for all the needs of one's family. In the United States, "child neglect cases [that should be] treated as matters for counselling and assistance were being treated as crimes. Poor mothers were led away in handcuffs because they left a child unattended while trying to buy milk at a grocery store, or because a child wandered away during a family eviction." (Bernstein, 2001: 438)

Discrimination—whether racial or poverty-based—has long been a factor in the removal of children from their homes (despite this contravening article 9 of the Convention on the Rights of the Child[2]). In the 1980s in the UK, children from low-income families were 700 times more likely than children from other backgrounds to be removed from parental custody (Bebbington and Miles, 1989). The legal system of child protection has increasingly failed to account for the impact of poverty on family life, instead interpreting difficulties to cope in terms of neglect and

---

[1]   For example, in families of any economic background, if a parent is physically incapacitated, incarcerated, or abusive, social services may need to take custody of the child.

[2]   A similar article (number 19) is present in the African Charter on the Rights and Welfare of the Child.

abuse. This leads authorities to permanently end parental custody when parents are not able to evidence change against highly prescriptive criteria and pressurised judicial timescales. Families most severely affected by persistent poverty are many times more likely to be subject to social service investigations, subsequent care proceedings and Care Orders; yet the strong link between poverty, care and child protection issues has not been adequately studied (Bywaters et al., 2016).

In the US, where 72 percent of the population is white,[3] only 42 percent of children in foster care are non-Hispanic white. The majority of children removed are black, Hispanic, multiracial, or of "other races" (Child Welfare Information Gateway, 2016). In Switzerland, in 2012, the government made a formal apology to people who were victimised by unilateral decisions to remove them from parental custody "without their own or their parents' consent, and ... because they were poor, born out of wedlock, living in difficult family circumstances, or considered to be 'difficult,' unruly, or uncooperative'" (Skelton et al., 2016: 123).

In many cases, the premature removal of children from their home is actually what harms them (Arsham, 2001). Children may struggle with a sense of loss and guilt, like a man in France who recalls, "When I was 12, a social worker put me in a group home. I could actually see my family's house from the upstairs window. My brothers and sisters were still there with our parents. I spent so much time wondering, 'Why me? Am I the bad one?'" (Skelton, 2014). After children grow up, the lifelong sorrow of having been removed from their parents can be compounded by the view of many social workers that people removed from their parents' care as children are likely to become negligent parents. One British mother described her childhood history in foster care as a "life sentence," discussed anew every time she requested help. A father noticed an attitude change in social service workers when they realised that he had been in care as a child. He said, "I went from being a parent with problems to being a 'problem parent'" (Skelton and Brunner, 2004: 140). There has been a shift away from any kind of preventative family support, causing parents in poverty to fear requesting help, and dooming certain families to generations of broken relationships.

---

[3]   US Census, 2010

Part of ATD Fourth World's approach is to offer people living in poverty the opportunity to meet and think with people who are also living in poverty in other countries and continents. At one such conference, on hearing low-income children and parents in Europe speak about these experiences, an adult living in poverty in West Africa asked, "How is it possible that a continent with such impressive architecture and engineering does not even know enough to help families stay together?"

Northern models influence the global South

Economic and social realities vary widely from North to South. However, when people who live in poverty in Africa and in Europe meet one another, they identify a common element. On both continents, society distrusts the parenting skills of people in poverty. Children observe: "people treat my parents like children." They often see parents disrespected by teachers or other authority figures.

Top-down international development aid worsens this disrespect. Not only are parents in poverty distrusted by their own compatriots in every country; there are also Northern aid workers who strongly distrust parenting abilities in the global South. This leads them to design orphanages that separate children from the community and fail to draw on community strengths. These institutions leave many children disoriented. Cut off from their communities, institutionalised children can grow up without important lasting relationships.

The prevailing development narrative—that countries with economic wealth have more to offer children in poverty than do developing countries—encourages many parents in poverty to believe they have nothing to offer their own children. In this context, some parents even approach foreign tourists, saying, "You take my child, there's nothing here for him." This desperation reflects economic despair and belief that life is better elsewhere. These parents are particularly vulnerable to the pitfalls in international adoption: corruption, fraud, and vast misunderstandings (Joyce, 2013). For instance, relatives of siblings in the DRC awaiting international adoption "were hoping that the children would be taken to America, get educated and eventually send cash home or sponsor other family members to emigrate" (Eckholm, 2013). The Congolese relatives imagined a lasting connection between their two families. However, the American adoptive parents thought the children should leave behind their African past. When The New York Times published this article by Eckholm about international adoption, comments on their website defended international adoption as the best response to the ravages of poverty, illness, and warfare. That is also the view of the Southern Baptist Convention, an American network of churches with sixteen million members, which is "creating an adoption culture;" it calls on its churches to "provide financial and other resources to those called to adopt" (Southern Baptist Convention, 2009). The harm that can be done by this approach includes Western families "adopting three, four, five or more children without the appropriate tools to help the children—many of whom have faced early trauma and deprivation— thrive. Convinced that love is all these kids need, the families struggle, the adopted children are unhappy (and in some cases, abused because of their behaviour), and the adoptions disrupt. Even more egregious are children procured by 'finders' who promise still-extant birth families an overseas education for their children, not adoption.[...] In these cases, some organisations are wilfully lying to families, essentially stealing their children, [...] merely as pawns for Christians intent on expanding God's kingdom" (Mock, 2013).

BURKINA FASO: CHILDREN REBUILD RELATIONSHIPS AFTER LIVING ON THE STREETS

Societal change leads children to leave home

Cultural tradition invests a teenage boy's first departure from home with meaning. Leaving in the context designed by the community marks the fulfilment of his education. In Burkina Faso, during the dry season, parents will bless the boy's journey to a city. Finding work there is a rite of passage in the eyes of the boy and his community. If he succeeds, his return home will mark increased well-being in the community. The boy will be respected for having made his own success the success of everyone. Thanks to this milestone, the whole community will support his future steps, such as marrying, or opening a shop.

Over the past few decades, however, both girls and boys have been leaving home at younger ages, and without community preparation or recognition of their maturity. A child who leaves home without guidance is not urged to come home if life goes awry. This child becomes more likely to spend years sleeping under market stalls. Most children living in the streets of the capital (Ouagadougou) left their villages hoping to earn money for their families—and are embarrassed to return empty-handed. One child says:

> My family is poor, and I did not succeed either. For me, the streets are just a dead-end. I can't go forward, and I can't go back either (Charvon, 2012: 4).

A generation ago, extended families were prepared to support their members through crises. Today, urbanisation, globalisation, economic insecurity, and other rapid changes in society have frayed extended families and led girls as well as boys to leave home. In addition, the nuclearisation of joint-family households weakens parents' support networks. There are fewer adults who have a role of authority over a child. While better-off families adapt to this situation, families in extreme poverty grow increasingly isolated. The adult's authority role in the eyes of the child can be damaged by economic weakness. Some parents say, "Children won't listen to you if you're poor." When parents live in poverty, their work, their culture, and their identity are undervalued. Some children say, "My father does nothing." This is false but the words reflect a feeling of worthlessness. Sometimes struggling parents decide to entrust their child to a relative or a religious teacher. But if the child's new living conditions prove harsh, either materially, or because affection is lacking, the child knows that returning home would overrule his parents' decision. Instead, the child may run away to the city (Charvon, 2012: 4).

Changes in society make families more vulnerable to abuse. Girls are sometimes convinced to leave home with older men, seeing them as protectors, despite the fact that this can lead to abuse or underage pregnancies. Rural children may also leave home for the fascination of urban life. Living on the streets endangers children's health, well-being, and survival, but many children also see freedom in this lifestyle. Some say, "By doing odd jobs here, I earn enough to eat 500 CFA Francs-worth of rice every day. I couldn't go back to living the way my parents do" (Charvon, 2012: 5).

The proliferation of institutional homes for children living in the streets has unintended consequences, inciting some children to leave home hoping for a better life in an institution. One child left home specifically because he wanted to join a training program in a centre for "street children" and saw no other way to access education. His mother lamented, "a centre like that might have a good teacher, but they are not your family, and anything could happen there." Despite the sincere efforts of institutional staff, many children's lives do not stabilise with these programmes. Children keep hoping that a "perfect centre" will exist one day. Each time a new centre opens, they rush to move there, quitting projects they have begun in other centres. This infatuation wears off, but it can be too late for them to return to the previous incomplete project. New private initiatives crop up continually, with no common public standards to measure their competence and effectiveness. Children are buffeted from one experience to another, often failing, and thus growing disillusioned.

Rebuilding family relationships

Since 1984, ATD Fourth World's full-time Volunteer Corps members have worked in Burkina Faso with children living in the streets. Their work is reintegrating these children into the lives of their extended families. This reintegration requires extensive preparation. Children who chose to leave home feel humiliated if they have not succeeded. Children may also fear being distrusted on their return home. Some children in the streets are interviewed by journalists who offer a meal in exchange for a life story. A child in that context wants to show gratitude and please their host. Their narrative may be untrue or embellished. True or not, they may later regret words they think dishonoured their family. Their shame can become another obstacle to returning home.

In Ouagadougou, children living in the streets often first encounter volunteers at the "Streetlight Library," a mobile cultural activity run by ATD Fourth World. At dusk, when the markets where children do odd jobs are closing, volunteers read storybooks to children under the roadside streetlight. Volunteers also run a Courtyard of a Hundred Trades. Local craftspeople and artists each freely offer their skills to teach a trade to children living in the streets. Each child has the chance to design something that she or he can be proud of. The volunteers' focus is to seek out in particular children who have grown discouraged with formal structures and who feel resigned to living in the streets. Their pedagogy of non-abandonment is founded on the belief that all people can succeed, and that when the children who have been the most damaged by life succeed, this gives hope to all those around them.

Children gradually gain in self-confidence by succeeding in the Courtyard workshops. This prepares them to invite volunteers to visit their extended family in their native villages. Over time, these visits build relationships with relatives who can begin preparing for their children's possible return. Parents whose child left years ago need time to rediscover that child. The child is now more mature than when she or he left. A new age-appropriate role should be prepared for the child to play in returning to the community. This could involve taking on specific responsibility to care for certain livestock or practicing a trade they learned in Ouagadougou.

Ambiguity can surface when a child's future is discussed. Relatives wonder what the children have been through and what they have done to survive. People who are joyful to see their child return may then say to the adult who brought the child home, "My child may stay with you if he wants." It is very difficult for a low-income family to imagine that they could offer more to their child than an organisation could.

To rebuild relationships, it is crucial to focus on hidden strengths in the family and the community. In a global context that undervalues rural communities in general, and particularly people in poverty, families are often unaware of how much their children have to gain from their love, and the wisdom of their unique life experience.

Case Study 1: A father's perspective

At age 7, Malik left home. For eight years, his father, Seydou Kabre, found no trace of him. When Malik was 15, volunteers were able to reunite them. In February 2016, when Malik was 23, his father looked back on this experience:

> I had lost my child. People said I must have sold him to buy medicine. But everyone could see that I had nothing at all. I made efforts to send Malik to school. He started primary school and the teacher liked him. But then during an arts festival, strangers came here to buy crafts the children made. Malik got a taste of earning cash. And that's when he became what people call a 'street child.'...
>
> One day two ATD volunteers visited me: Guillaume Charvon and Elie Dikoudgo. They asked whether I had a son named Malik. I am grateful. My village is 100 km from the capital. They travelled all this way. They went even further to my

parents' village so that we could all prepare for Malik to return home. They came to meet us without judging us. Their goal was for Malik to find his footing here in a village he left so long ago.

All that I wanted was for Malik to return home. But it was not easy. When Malik first came home, he saw that we did not have what he was used to finding in the streets of the capital, so he left again. Guillaume found him and offered him a toolbox so that even in our village he could do the wood-working that he had begun learning at the Courtyard of a Hundred Trades. Malik really did want to work as a carpenter. So I paid an artisan to explain the trade to him and to buy Malik more tools. But Malik was still not sure that he really wanted to set up a trade in front of my home. He thought it might be better to work at the marketplace. But Guillaume and I insisted that it is important for him to be connected to our family, instead of on his own, or with a boss who would not give him half of the money he brings in. And to this day, Malik has continued running his business right in front of the house.

Our separation is still with us and my son is still fragile. But now he benefits from two families: we support him here at home, and he also now has an ATD family that is rooting for him over the long term.

Case Study 2: Children's efforts to remain reconnected

One young man in Burkina left his village as a child and spent six years living in the streets. Today, the capital remains the only place where Sawadogo[4] is able to earn money by doing odd jobs. However, once able to re-connect with his family, he decided that he would never again sleep in the street. He now returns to his native village every night—although it takes him three hours to walk there because he cannot afford the bus ride. He and other young people who grew up participating in the Courtyard of a Hundred Trades are still coping with challenges. But they also say it strengthens them to be connected to all the others in the Courtyard. Because of this, they make a point of supporting younger teenagers there. Now Sawadogo tells younger children not to leave home, saying "I crossed the desert, so now I can recognise that my family is an oasis".

THE CENTRAL AFRICAN REPUBLIC: YOUNG PEOPLE SUPPORTING CHILDREN

As in many countries, young people in poverty feel a natural responsibility to protect all children—their brothers and sisters, neighbours, and children in other communities as well. Young people

---

[4]   This is a pseudonym to protect his privacy.

whose lives have been hard and who grew up benefiting from Street Libraries (mobile cultural activities like the "Streetlight Library" in Ouagadougou) are often the first to volunteer their time to facilitate these activities for younger children. Their own experience has honed their understanding of the challenges faced by other children and families in poverty. Supporting the efforts of these young people by offering them training and encouragement helps boost their efforts. In addition, ATD Fourth World regularly brings together young people who facilitate activities with children from across Central and West Africa for international workshops. During these opportunities, they all share ideas and help one another overcome challenges.

Case Study 3: Wartime street libraries

When civil war erupted in the Central African Republic in December 2012, despite the dangers forcing families to stay indoors as much as possible, the young facilitators of the Street Libraries remained highly motivated to continue bringing books and games to children, sparking their curiosity and dreams. Facilitators shifted the venue of these activities to emergency camps where families were displaced. They emphasised the importance of all activities taking place where the whole community can see what is going on, and in such a way that any child can join in.

When schools closed down for eleven months, beginning in March 2013, Street Libraries were one of the rare places that fostered joy, provided education, and offered a chance to build a small haven of peace. In early 2013, the Street Library project was based on a comic strip that children had designed in drawing workshops over the previous months: Tolis and the children of Tapori Village. One volunteer, whom we call Y. to protect his identity, wrote:

> Today G. and Y. returned from the Street Library, drenched to the bone despite the sheet of plastic they held over their heads. They were singing at the top of their lungs: "We'll go to the end of the world! The Street Library will not fail!" They told us they surprised a taxi driver by telling him, "We're building peace!" They showed us messages from children who hope for peace so they can go back to school. Grinning as they remembered joyful moments of storytelling and colouring with the children, they had come in from the downpour as though returning from war, with all the strength that comes from knowing themselves still alive, and from having passed men carrying automatic weapons, while they were carrying only their drawing case... But the following Thursday, they arrived looking tense. Their first words were about armed men

who interrupted their activity. The children had been panicking—but several young people asked them not to give in to fear, saying, "You're messengers of peace; your joy must show. A few gunshots can't replace your joy." So the children continued drawing. Seeing the confusion of the armed men, the young people explained what they were doing. They showed them the comic strip, and when the armed men asked, gave them two copies of it. (Skelton and Brand, 2016)

Even though the war made Y. sick at heart, he did not remain shut in at home. Several times he insisted, "We have to do something for peace." Another young person said, "Talking about the past only sows seeds of hatred." All the young facilitators were aware that their time running the Street Library allowed children to believe in peace and "not to keep evil in them."

Case Study 4: Protecting children from violence

Some of the facilitators approached militia members to defend individual children and their families. This happened when 11-year-old Pierre was injured. His family had taken refuge in a large camp at the airport of Bangui, where he regularly took part in the Street Library. One day he went back to his home neighbourhood to look for wood for heating and to run errands for his family. On his way back to the camp that evening, Pierre realised he had forgotten one errand, so he turned around. By the time he finished it was late and the sun had set. As he was hurrying back to the airport, a young man attacked him with a whip and left him at the roadside with a broken foot, bleeding badly. Eventually a passer-by heard Pierre crying and carried him to the camp.

Daniel, a Street Library facilitator, said, "In the camp, everyone knows that when a child is lost, you should go to ATD. If your child needs the hospital, you bring him to ATD because people at the hospital know us." Pierre was brought to young people who volunteer with ATD. They asked Pierre where his family slept, but he was too weak to respond. Daniel took him to the camp infirmary. By morning, a cast was put on Pierre's foot and he had recovered enough to say where his family was, so they could be reunited.

The next day, Daniel was talking with the anti-balaka militia group. Because he knew some of its members, he spoke with them often, encouraging them to pursue peace. It was risky work, but he felt that since they knew each other well, he would be safe. He told them what happened to Pierre, saying, "This kind of thing is dangerous. Hurting children will bring about so much hatred." The anti-balaka said they would investigate to find out whether it was one of them who had attacked Pierre. Soon, they found the perpetrator, Vianney. According to Vianney, when he and Pierre lived in the same neighbourhood before the war, Pierre had insulted him unforgettably; so when he saw Pierre on the streets that night he beat him up.

Daniel suggested that Vianney ask forgiveness of Pierre's family "so that this hatred does not continue." They went to Pierre's family together. Vianney spoke to Pierre's in simple words, telling his story and asking forgiveness. Pierre's grandmother said, "I wanted revenge for the blood of my grandchild. But since you have come and spoken with me, I will not do anything now." Pierre's family says that Vianney's apology made it possible for them to let go of their anger. Hatred had begun with Pierre's hurtful words, causing him to get beaten, and then leading to his family's desire for revenge. No military force can end this damaging cycle. Breaking that cycle required the daring of young people like Daniel and Vianney and the generosity of people like Pierre's family (Skelton and Brand, 2016).

THE DRC: CHILDREN STRENGTHEN COMMUNITIES

Case Study 5: The Tapori Children's Movement[5] in Bukavu

In the eastern Kivu region of DRC, two decades of armed conflict, violence, and insecurity have destroyed many community initiatives. Teachers, civil servants, police and military officers can go for years on end without salaries. People do what they can to survive. The poorest families live in the hills five to ten kilometres outside Bukavu city. Most parents leave home in the early hours to walk into the city where they hope to sell fruit or a few cigarettes. Some will try their luck at jobs loading trucks. They usually do not get home until late. Their children are often left home alone. Many cannot afford school registration fees. However, it is these very children who build hope for their community.

Young people who grew up here understand how worried parents are for their children. In 1997, one of these young people heard about the

---

[5]   http://tapori.org/, accessed July 30, 2019.

Tapori Children's Movement. Faustin Ndrabu was friends with a Congolese priest who had travelled to Europe and wrote to him about a network that was reaching out to bullied or stigmatised children, building a movement of friendship that included all children. This inspired Faustin and others to begin making home visits to children in Bukavu who were on their own all day. They began corresponding with the international Tapori secretariat in Switzerland, which regularly sent them encouraging messages from children and young people in different parts of the world. Faustin recalls:

> I ended up spending all day with the children. At first, parents thought someone must be paying me to do it, because they knew I was being housed by the parish priests at the time. So they didn't believe me when I said I had no money. But little by little they saw that, aside from a place to sleep, I had nothing. I was like them. My own family had fled into the forest, and I had no more news from them.

> When I told parents that Tapori is a movement for overcoming poverty, starting with children, they didn't believe me because Tapori wasn't distributing anything. What Tapori does is help children in their efforts to support their own families. Some do housework and take care of younger children. They haul well water, hunt for firewood, and scrub laundry. So we all helped each other, for example, to carry sugar cane, or to find something to feed goats, rabbits, or guinea pigs. The children are very aware of their family responsibilities. Some of them walk out to meet their parents coming home in the evening because they know there is a load they can help carry. Others are in charge of selling matches, candy, or petrol. Once these chores are finished, we play and sing with the children. Those who are able to go to school learned poems they teach the others who are not in school. So parents thanked us, saying: "Now, we know that our children are not alone anymore."

> Little by little, the children in Bukavu discovered how children were living around the world, through the Tapori mini-books, which tell true stories of children's courage. In stories from Guatemala, the United States, and Senegal, they discovered how other children help their parents. Gradually, they agreed to help other people too. For example, there is a communal faucet on the hillside. When it needed to be reinforced by a mason, the children went to the bottom of the hillside to fetch sand he could use for the cement. They also helped to fix the mud wall of an old lady's home.

> I always try to teach them new things. For example, how to raise livestock properly. Or how to read. Now everyone here knows us very well. Our group has grown to include about a hundred children. We are encouraged when parents say, "Since my son joined Tapori, he has taken responsibility for our rabbit hutch." Or, "Now my children have stopped just hanging around in the street. Instead, they play football, and they have more self-respect." (Hamel and Hamel, 2005)

Parents say Tapori gives them hope that, despite violence and poverty, their children are growing up as good people. When Tapori children play football, parents are struck that they do not need a referee to avoid arguments. The parents are also touched by their children's initiatives to help the weakest members of the community, including children who are barred from school. The children's determination encourages their parents to follow suit by daring to speak to people from different ethnic groups, and to overcome the distrust that harms communities.

As each generation of Tapori children grows up, several choose to volunteer their time to facilitate the group's activities as Faustin did. As those who are involved move to different communities around Bukavu, new groups have spread to Burhiba, Kadutu, and Muhungu. There are now thirty facilitators, aged 14 to 18, running these three Tapori groups. Their goals are preparing Tapori activities for children; ensuring that no child will ever feel left out; regularly thinking with each other and with adults about their lives; and organising community solidarity projects. René Muhindo was part of the Tapori group when he was a child. He says, "If you ask teenagers why they want to help children, some cannot put it into words. But you have only to watch them to see how they thirst to deliver life itself to those around them" (ATD Fourth World, 2012). Muhindo also says:

> Here, we all treat each other with respect, whether a person has been able to wash or not, and whether a person has sandals or is barefoot. When a Tapori child passes someone poor who may smell strange, the child will have the courage to greet that person. Tapori children are not afraid to greet everyone because they know that every person has the right to exist. It is with the children that I learn tolerance and forgiveness. (Hamel and Hamel, 2005)

Case Study 6: Tapori community projects

Since 2008, the Tapori group in Bukavu has run a weekly radio broadcast on a community-owned station. Different subjects include:

- What does it mean to be "poor"?
- Young people and television
- Why is there hunger? What are its consequences for children?
- When life no longer inspires hope, is a person necessarily ready to commit violence?
- Even as a child, is it important to have a dream for the world?
- Does listening help us build peace? Is it important to learn to listen to others?

Every Sunday, the children speak about what they do during the week, giving listeners concrete examples of what they mean by "the right to friendship for all." With the support of their parents and facilitators, their community projects show that they refuse to accept poverty or exclusion. They act according to the saying, "The fire will burn brightly if each person brings one twig." So during their broadcasts, the children invite others to join them in helping to make a difference.

One of these projects, in April 2014, was to repair a local road that had become impassable because of potholes. Through this activity, Tapori members raised community awareness about disease caused by stagnant water in potholes, and spoke to local authorities, police, and school administrators. Seeing the children's actions, many neighbours and the police joined in. One mother brought stones for plugging holes. A father crushed the stones into gravel. Another person donated broken bricks. Others contributed ideas and encouragement. The road was successfully repaired.

Other community projects over the years have included a birth registration campaign and traveling north to support victims of a volcanic eruption. Once, the children saw that a drainage canal was clogged. They began cleaning part of it—and were soon joined by their parents who realised that a bigger effort was needed to prevent flooding.

During an international Tapori campaign about water, called Many Drops Make a River, the Bukavu radio broadcast focused on the high cost of water. The children met with public authorities and non-governmental organisations, requesting a wartime reduction of water bills for poor families. Civil society took up the children's request, lobbied parliament for it, and this became the policy in one city.

The Tapori group has urged public authorities to strive for peace, and to support stable farming as a bulwark against malnutrition. The facilitators have composed songs about the children's experiences, calling for human respect of every person, sharing, friendship for all, and peace. They have organised concerts as a way to meet new people.

Case Study 7: Reaching out to people in difficult situation

Eric, aged 8, works at Lake Kivu port. He attended only one year of school because his family could not afford the fees. At the port, he and other children look for fallen pieces of cassava, corn, or sorghum to sell. Speaking to a child from the Tapori group, he said:

I am glad about the way you treat us. Other people shoo us away. They compare us to stray dogs hunting through rubbish to find a bone. We're poor, but we would like to have friends. If we try to greet some people, they don't even answer because they think we're going to beg. When people like you come to greet us, we feel good.

One of the priorities for the Tapori group is to ensure that children like Eric, who are likely to be left out, can become comfortable participating fully in the group. Rosine is a Tapori facilitator who remembers that when she was a child, "My facilitators taught me never to make fun of anyone. That's why I became a facilitator: to show children what I learned. We teach them not to fight or to make fun of someone who trips. This is how they will become good people." Another facilitator, Nathalie, says, "I make a point of considering all the children equal and making sure that everyone who would like to speak can do so. I don't pay extra attention to the ones who go to school and can read and write. If a child cannot write, but has an idea, I write it down myself to make sure that we are paying attention to him as well" (ATD Fourth World, 2012).

Over the years, the Bukavu Tapori group has visited the local prison and the hospital. In particular they have made a point of visiting patients with malnutrition, in the "indigent" ward, or who are stigmatised because of AIDS. A hospital staffer said, "The Tapori movement has taught me to spend time with the poor who have no visitors. I sit and talk with them. I listen to them and tell others what they said so that their situation will no longer be miserable" (Hamel and Hamel, 2005).

Once, a Tapori child asked the facilitators if they could visit a centre for demobilised child soldiers. Before making the visit, the Tapori group prepared dances, poems, and songs about what it means to them to be a "Tapori kid." They spoke about the importance of peace and laying down weapons. Following their visit, the child soldiers decided to stay in touch with the Tapori group.

In 2015, to mark the International Day of the Rights of the Child, the Tapori group in Bukavu visited a school for children who are visually impaired or hearing impaired. The Heri Kwetu School is the only one in the city that teaches children with disabilities, and its students rarely meet children without disabilities. When the Tapori group arrived, a visually impaired girl made a welcome speech. A Tapori 8-year-old was very surprised, asking, "How can she do that without being able to see her paper? Did she have to memorise the whole speech?" In fact, the girl was reading her speech in braille. It was a discovery for the 8-year-old that someone who cannot see could read as well as he could. The children spent the day together singing, dancing, doing theatre, and sharing poetry. As one of the Tapori children said, "We've done things that any child can do, no matter what, to smile, to share their talent and ideas, and to cooperate on a project together."

When the Tapori group realised that some children are excluded because their parents were accused of witchcraft, they did not hesitate to make friends with them. One of the Tapori children said, "We have nothing to fear because they are children like us—they must be too young to do anyone any harm." However, it was more daunting for them to see schoolteachers exclude certain children. Teachers had made a separation in the classroom isolating the children of people accused of being enemies in the armed conflict. The Tapori children enrolled in school felt determined to change this—but unsure of how to confront adult educators. So they made a plan. Outside of school, they made friends with the children being excluded. Then, together, they prepared jokes to tell at school demonstrating that all children like to laugh together. At the same time, Tapori facilitators met with the teachers outside of school. The combination of these efforts succeeded in changing the teachers' approach.

Case Study 8: The teenage Tapori facilitators

Facilitators point out that they benefit from Tapori too. Nadine feels that she learns from the children, saying "they teach me the value of friendship. When grown-ups fight, they split apart. But children make up after a fight." Laurent says, "I like that we advise each other as facilitators on how to act in our neighbourhoods. We can never set a bad example, because the children see us wherever we go." Not all young people who took part in Tapori as children want to become facilitators. But Julien is one who was determined to come back to Tapori, saying, "Tapori is like my left lung."

The Tapori group's founders continue training and encouraging new facilitators. In the context of their country's unrelenting conflict, violence, and fear, these teenagers see peers "make bad choices." They have many questions about the meaning of their lives, and how they should behave. Saleh says, "It's very important to be able to talk with other teens, and also to be able to talk to the adults. They can answer our questions, for example, about AIDS, or about how to carry oneself in life" (ATD Fourth World, 2012).

For the 20th anniversary of the Convention on the Rights of the Child in 2009, children in the DRC exchanged messages with other children in Benin, Burkina Faso, Cameroon, the Central African Republic, Côte d'Ivoire, Mali, and Senegal. They wrote an "Appeal from the hearts of the children of Africa," proclaiming:

> To grow up properly, we learn a lot of things from our family. ...Among ourselves, we help each other out. Friendship is stronger than hunger. What stops us from growing up properly is when our parents feel humiliated by their poverty. Sometimes children are made fun of because their shoes are falling apart, or they are badly dressed. ... Those of us who live on the street don't even enjoy the respect of their little brothers.

> ...We live in the hope that if we have a job, we will manage to look after our parents. ...To succeed in life means keeping a good name and being someone who wants to do things for others. To our parents, we say, "Don't lose trust in us." To those who stand before us, we say, "If you get involved in this struggle, many things will change. Help our parents to take care of us and help us to grow up properly. This is your duty. In that way, there will be no more separations to destroy or bewilder us." Let those who are lucky enough to have something share it with others. We want peace to roam from house to house and to enter the hearts of all people.

CONCLUSION

Children and adults living in poverty in Europe and North America urge the international community not to repeat mistakes made in the North, where poverty-based discrimination can splinter families apart. In Western and Central Africa, while poverty, urbanisation, and armed conflict all put increased stress on extended families and communities, it is in their own families and communities that children can find the solace and support they need to thrive.

In Western and Central Africa, the basic building blocks of social and child protection work should be discovering and supporting parents' hidden resources of resilience, strength, and intelligence. Leaders in society should be aware of the damage that can be done when rural children receive the message that the future is somewhere in an urban office—which implies that they have nothing to learn or gain in their own villages. They also need to know that children intuit very quickly when their parents are not respected. A child who feels that her or his parents are not respected at school can feel that succeeding in school may actually constitute a betrayal of the family.

In every community, children, teenagers, and young people can become leaders to strengthen communities, as long as there are adults who believe in their potential and who guide them in making sure that no one is left out.

ACKNOWLEDGEMENTS

With thanks to the following colleagues and peers who supported this research: Florent Bambara, Joan Burke, Fabienne Carbonnel, Guillaume Charvon, Tom Croft, Philippe Hamel, Mahamadou Kone, Patricia Lanigan, Sylvain Lestien, Sophie Marechal, Dave Meyer, Jacques Ogier, Sophie Razanakoto, Alban Soussango, and Jean Venard.

REFERENCES

ATD Fourth World (2012) "After Growing Up with Tapori, Young People Ensure that Other Children Do Too" [Online] Available at: <http://www.atd-fourth world.org/growing-tapori-young-people-ensure-children/> [Accessed 21 January 2019].

ATD Fourth World (2016) "'Welcome Babies': Early Childhood Development Thanks to Parental Involvement," [Online] Available at: <http://www.atd-fourth world.org/welcome-babies-early-childhood-development-thanks-to-parent al-involvement/> [Accessed 21 January 2019].

Arsham, M. (28 June 2001) "The Child Welfare Organising Project," Oral statement during a United Nations panel discussion, New York: NGO Committee on Families.

Bebbington, A. and J. Miles (1989) "The Background of Children Who Enter Local Authority Care," *British Journal of Social Work*, 19, Oxford: Oxford University Press.

Bernstein, N. (2001) *The Lost Children of Wilder: The Epic Struggle to Change Foster Care*, New York: Pantheon Books.

Bywaters, Paul et al. (2016) *The Relationship Between Poverty, Child Abuse and Neglect: an evidence review*, Joseph Rowntree Foundation.

Charvon, G. (2012) "Présentation du projet dans le cadre des accords de coöperation ONG/UNICEF," report submitted by ATD Fourth World to UNICEF.

Child Welfare Information Gateway (2016) "Foster care statistics 2014" (Washington, DC: U.S. Department of Health and Human Services, Children's Bureau). [Online] Available at: https://www.childwelfare.gov/pubPDFs/foster.pdf#> [Accessed 21 January 2019].

Eckholm, E. (31 May 2013) "Eager to Adopt, Evangelicals Find Perils Abroad", *The New York Times*. [Online] Available at: http://www.nytimes.com/2013/06/01 /us/moved-to-adopt-evangelicals-find-children-and-pitfalls-abroad.html?> [Accessed 21 January 2019].

Hamel, P. and E. Hamel (May 2005) "Des enfants semeurs de paix dans la communauté," *Revue Quart Monde* n°195, Baillet-en-France: ATD Quart Monde. [Online] Available at: <https://www.revue-quartmonde.org/548> [Accessed 21 January 2019].

Joyce, K. (2013) *The Child Catchers: Rescue, Trafficking, and the New Gospel of Adoption,* New York: Public Affairs, Perseus Books Group.

Mock, Melanie Springer (17 May 2013) "Why Christians Like Me Should Listen to Critiques of Evangelical Adoption," *The Nation*. [Online] Available at <https://www.thenation.com/article/why-christians-me-should-listen-critiques-evangelical-adoption/> [Accessed 21 January 2019].

Skelton, D. and V. Brunner (2004) *How Poverty Separates Parents and Children: A Challenge to Human Rights,* Mery-sur-Oise, France: Fourth World Publications. [Online] Available at: <http://www.atd-fourthworld.org/how-poverty-separates-parents-and/> [Accessed 21 January 2019].

Skelton, D. (April 2014) "'Why Me?' When a Bird's Nest Is Broken," *Together In Dignity: Reflections on a World Without Poverty*, Mery-sur-Oise, France: ATD Fourth World. [Online] Available at: https://medium.com/together-in-dignity/why-me-when-a-birds-nest-is-broken-86176294b2d2 [Accessed 21 January 2019].

Skelton, D., Brand, E., Carbonnel, F., Meyer, D., and Venard, J. (2016) *Artisans of Peace Overcoming Poverty, Volume 3: Understanding the Violence of Poverty,* Pierrelaye, France: ATD Fourth World.

Skelton, Diana 2015 "The Central African Republic," Ed. Mehmet Odekon, *SAGE Encyclopedia of World Poverty*, Second Edition, (Thousand Oaks, CA: SAGE Publications).

Southern Baptist Convention, (2009) "On Adoption and Orphan Care," Resolution No. 2 (Louisville, Kentucky, US) [Online] Available at: <http://www.sbc.net/ resolutions/1194> [Accessed 21 January 2019].

US Census Bureau (2010) "2010 Census Shows America's Diversity" (Washington DC) [Online] Available at: <https://www.census.gov/newsroom/releases/ archives/2010_census/cb11-cn125.html> [Accessed 21 January 2019].

CHAPTER 10

CHILD DOMESTIC SERVITUDE IN GHANA: EXPLORING THE CONTOURS OF CHILD POVERTY, CHILD PROTECTION, AND SOCIAL PROTECTION

C. Nana Derby, Samuel Okposin, Shelley Okposin, and Christiana O. Adetunde

INTRODUCTION

Social protection (SP) is a right entrenched in several international and domestic treaties (Pino and Confalonieri, 2014). According to the International Labour Organization (ILO):

> Social protection floors are nationally defined sets of basic social security guarantees that should ensure, as a minimum that, over the life cycle, all in need have access to essential health care and to basic income security which together secure effective access to goods and services defined as necessary at the national level.[1]

Consequently, social is protection is about safety net (Standing, 2007), risk coping, and "having security in the face of vulnerabilities and contingencies...it is having access to health care... and it is about working in safety" (Abebrese, quoting Garcia and Gruat, 2003). Social protection thus comprises "the public actions taken in response to levels of vulnerability, risk and deprivation... which are deemed socially unacceptable within a given polity or society" (Norton, Conway, and Foster, 2001: 7). Programmes of social protection encompass all support systems and strategies of survival that promote security in the areas of health, education, nutrition, and shelter. Social protection works even in times of acute vulnerabilities such as extreme poverty and deprivation, the denial of formal education, escalated risks of trafficking, and child labour exploitation. The programmes must perform dual social and economic functions that promote "social equity and economic growth" (Berhane et al., 2014; Pino and Confalonieri, 2014: 128). Thus, effective

---

[1] https://www.ilo.org/secsoc/areas-of-work/policy-development-and-applied-research/social-protection-floor/lang--en/index.htm, accessed June 28, 2019.

social protection programmes consist in measures capable of mitigating social and economic risks and providing the necessary support for households that are poor and vulnerable to deprivations, or unable to cope with economic and social risks (Kabeer, 2008; Bailey, 2010). Programmes that revolve around this framework must address vulnerabilities that erode health, work, and general coping strategies.

This article focuses on child labour exploitation within the household and argues that social protection programmes could address vulnerabilities that increase the risk of domestic servitude and jeopardize children's safety. We recognize the intersection between human rights and SP and argue that successful social protection programmes must be designed, implemented, monitored, and evaluated on grounds of human rights, both in terms of the outcomes and the processes of the programmes (Sepulveda and Nyst, 2012). Kaplan and Jones (2013) further postulate that for purposes of child sensitive social protection, targeted programmes must help children to grow healthily and provide a foundation to thrive.

Both exogenous and endogenous factors interact to intensify exclusion from formal education and from access to quality healthcare. They may also generate heightened risks of labour exploitation and trafficking — primarily of impoverished populations and their children. Exogenous factors include socio-structural and cultural factors, which households are incapable of influencing, whereas the endogenous factors include attributes and choices within their control. A resultant condition of the interplay of such factors is poverty, which is an influential factor in the exploitation of children's labour. Social protection programmes could address these and, as Long (2012) suggests, they must be long-term because households fall in and out of poverty if appropriate strategies of social protection are not implemented. Therefore, social protection programmes are effective only if they are long-term and provide increased chances of survival, opportunities of choice, and independence among otherwise impoverished and excluded households, i.e. "transformative social protection" as described by Mkandawire (2004). Based on this perspective, social protection programmes may be deemed ineffective if consequent to their implementation, no significant impact is made in the lives of the impoverished. Such failures are observable in the unchanged vulnerabilities and limited opportunities for growth and improvement.

There are formal and informal (or traditional) social protection programmes (Norton, Conway, and Foster, 2001). Traditional forms of social protection characteristically precede government programmes. However, in instances where the two co-exist, the traditional programmes seemingly address vacuums emergent from government-sponsored programmes. They are community-based, primarily independent of the government, and may be undertaken by individuals or groups of individuals and are not guided by formal regulations of social protection (Oduro, 2010). Informal social protection may take any of several forms, such as contributions made to support community members after a disaster, or reconstruction of dilapidated school buildings in an effort to increase formal education for children. Formal programmes of social protection may be categorized into social assistance, social insurance, and labour market interventions. Formal programmes of social protection must enhance the effectiveness and functionality of traditional programmes rather than inhibiting them (Harvey et al., 2007).

Social assistance programmes comprise cash transfers, social pensions, in-kind transfers, and public works programmes (Browne, 2015). These programmes have often been located in World Bank recommendations (Conway et al., 2000). The interplay of economic crises in the 1970s through the 1990s, ineffective adjustment programmes (Phukon, 2008), and leadership vacuums and the attendant problems of economic mismanagement and corruption that persistently heightened vulnerabilities in many African and Latin American nations (Barrientos, 2010; Holzman and Hinz; 2005; Kaplan, 2013) have culminated in several internationally monitored and sponsored projects whereby countries implement social protection programmes which impact on children. Examples are school feeding and cash transfer programmes that have typically attempted to pursue the promotion of health, education, and nutrition.

Child sensitive social protection programmes, as Kaplan and Jones (2013) postulate based on frameworks by Devereux and Sabate-Wheeler (2004), Jones and Holmes (2010), and Mkandawire (2004) should be transformational as well as protective, preventive, and promotional.

Protective programmes should effectively secure household incomes and adequate consumption levels towards the preservation of children's basic wellbeing. Preventive programmes should be geared towards the provision of alternative coping strategies that would eliminate any conditions that might increase risks. Promotional programmes should support active investments in child development, such as healthcare and education. Transformative social protection programmes address structural conditions that create and sustain exclusion and inequalities while simultaneously empower families and children (Kaplan and Jones, 2013).

The Government of Ghana has been implementing various social protection interventions along protective, preventive, and promotional lines. There is the cash transfer programmes, known as the livelihood empowerment against poverty (LEAP), which came into effect in 2008. Ghana's Government implemented this scheme with the expectation that the funds would increase local consumption, energize local businesses, and subsequently decrease the impacts of deprivation, such as school dropouts (Debrah, 2013). In 2008 when LEAP was launched, poor households in only three (out of nine) regions received cash transfers. (Mochia et al., 2014). According to Mochia et al., households with one eligible member received approximately 8 cedis (or $5.70). Two-member households received a total of 10 cedis (or $7.10), and three-member households 12 cedis (or $8:50). Households with at least four eligible members were paid 15 cedis (or $10.70).[2]

The literature evaluating the effects of LEAP on Ghanaian households fails to conclude that these cash transfers have been completely positive. In interviews with researchers, some households lauded the government for LEAP because the funds enhanced their farming, petty trading, labour supply, and debt repayment (Davis and Daidone, 2014; Handa et al., 2013). In a 2013 publication on Ghana's LEAP, Handa et al. noted that school enrolment increased by about 7 percent and reduced absenteeism by about 10 percent. While these are positive outcomes that deserve to be celebrated, as we emphasized above, the funds were made available in only three regions. Due to rural-urban migration and the attendant overpopulation in urban centres, some cities

---

[2]   These dollar amounts were derived using 2013 exchange rates.

in the excluded regions could be home to some of the country's most deprived households. In addition, a majority of the beneficiaries interviewed assessed the impact of LEAP in negative terms. Concerns were raised about the amount of cash paid out and the frequency. In 2011, for instance, cash transfers were delayed for about eight months. The implication of this is with high inflation, the real value of the money depreciated once it arrived. Handa et al. (2013) argued that prior to 2013 when Ghana's cumulative inflation hovered around 19 percent, the real value of the transfers to households covered only 7 percent of household consumption. Later, when the cash amount increased coupled with lower rates of inflation, the cash transfers could cover about 21 percent of basic consumption (Handa et al., 2013).

Ghana's school feeding programme, an in-kind social protection intervention, sought to augment access to formal education. The first phase of Ghana's School Feeding Program originally commenced in 2007 and drew to a close in 2011 (Ghana School Feeding Program, 2011; Pino and Confalonieri, 2014). They aimed at increasing school enrolment and the economic well-being of the communities in which they operated, through a policy of spending approximately 80 percent of the budget on local produce and resources (Ghana School Feeding Program, 2011).

In 2003, Ghana implemented a national health insurance programme that sought to provide easy access to healthcare throughout the nation. As part of the scheme, pregnant women could attend antenatal care at no charge. Free healthcare services were also provided to the aged. The very poor among Ghanaians were not required to pay any premium. However, Ghanaians face challenges with the insurance scheme due to its administration. From the middle of 2012, the scheme has been unable to pay hospital bills, the premiums or the 2.75 percent levies. Insured cardholders were turned down at both government and private hospitals, and the cards are now perceived to be unusable.

LEGAL BACKGROUND: GHANA'S CONFORMITY WITH INTERNATIONAL CONVENTIONS ON CHILD PROTECTION

Ghana's position as the first nation to ratify the Convention on the Rights of the Child signalled the extent of their commitment to the fight against any abuses of children's rights and the protection of children from exploitation of all kinds. The Government's commitment to children's protection was further demonstrated with the promulgation of the Children's Act of 1998. According to the Act, children are to be protected from all forms of discrimination including those emanating from gender, disability, and religion, or whether they originate from rural or urban regions. Particularly relevant to this article is the stipulation in Section 5 that "No person shall deny a child the right to live with his parents and family and grow up in a caring and peaceful environment...." Furthermore, through specific stipulations on children's work, the Act explicitly protects children against exploitative labour and other hazardous work. It defined exploitative labour as those that deprived children of health, education, and development. Hazardous work was categorized as that which engaged children at sea, in mining or quarrying, in porterage of heavy loads, the manufacturing of chemicals, workplaces where heavy machines are used, or in hotels, bars, and entertainment places where they could be exposed to immoral behaviour.

Ghana also ratified the ILO Convention against the Worst Forms of Child Labour (Convention 182) on June 13, 2000. This Convention requires member states that ratified it to, as a matter of urgency, implement programmes that would immediately and effectively prohibit and eliminate worst forms of child labour. The promulgation of the Children's Act partly satisfied the requirements stipulated in Convention 182. On August 21, 2012, Ghana acceded the Protocol to Prevent, Suppress and Punish Trafficking in Persons Especially Women and Children, supplementing the United Nations Convention against Transnational Organized Crime and subsequently promulgated the Human Trafficking Act of 2005. Following the ratification of the Palermo Accord on anti-human trafficking as a transnational crime, relevant institutions were created to implement and adhere to the stipulations of these laws. Among them were the Ministry of Gender, Children and Social Protection and the Anti Human Trafficking Unit of the Ghana Police. There were other governmental agencies, such as the Women and Juvenile Unit of the Ghana police (WAJU), which is now known as the Domestic Violence and Victim Support Unit (DOVVSU).

EMPIRICAL EVIDENCE: RESEARCHING DOMESTIC SERVITUDE IN GHANA

This chapter is part of a larger action research funded by the Office to Monitor and Combat Trafficking in Persons at the United States of America's Department of State. This was a three-year project that sought to rescue children from servitude, reunite them with their parents, and either enrol them in elementary schools or apprentice training. Child participants were mostly identified in Accra or other relatively urban communities. The project reunited 359 beneficiaries with their parents in 20 communities in the Central and Eastern Regions. Fourteen beneficiaries were located in the Volta Region while 15 young women and adolescents who had been trafficked to Nigeria were reunited with their families in the Northern Region. The action-oriented nature of this project required the pre-implementation of situational assessment to determine the nature and extent of child trafficking and child domestic servitude in the Greater Accra Region. Then, participant selection strategies were mapped out, in order to ensure their reintegration back into their respective communities. Collaborative strategies were identified to work with other governmental and non-governmental organisations (NGOs) that pursued children's welfare and protection against child labour exploitation, human trafficking, and contemporary slavery. Throughout the project, we worked with the Department of Social Welfare, the Anti-Human Trafficking Unit of the Ghana Police, several public schools, volunteer teachers, staff from the International Organization for Migration and UNICEF, and LAWA Ghana, Inc., which implemented the project.

To commence the project, we engaged the services of Social Work students at the University of Ghana to collect data on children who worked in the streets of Accra during school hours. Over 400 children were identified in three days. Although most of them were domestic servants living in households that were unrelated to them, some lived with immediate relatives including parents or grandparents, but had to engage in petty trading to support household incomes. The majority of the participants were survivors of what we call "soft"[3] trafficking and had

---

[3]   Trafficking may be defined as hard or soft depending on the level of coercion and physical abuses in the processes of "recruitment." Soft trafficking exists when the victims do not experience any forms of torture or hazardous conditions as they are

been removed from their villages by teachers, acquaintances, relatives, or fellow townsmen and women to go live in the cities.

We discovered further that many domestic servants were enrolled in school. However, visits to some public schools disclosed that the conditions of domestic servants were similar to those who were never enrolled or school dropouts. In the first school we worked with, we interviewed 72 girls and boys who lived as servants, came to school late after approximately four hours of work, and performed poorly when in school. Based on that, we selected children whose parents were believed to reside in parts of the Central Region to commence the removal of the children from servitude but with parental permission. Interviews were conducted in the presence of social welfare staff, a legal practitioner from the implementing agency, LAWA, Inc., the police, or teachers, following strict international standards of ethics (Powell et al., 2013).

We had several meetings with the parents, interviewing them, and crosschecking the validity of their responses through discussions at subsequent meetings. We also had discussions with staff from the Department of Social Welfare — during and after the project. We aimed at ensuring that their children had experienced, at a minimum, what we defined as soft trafficking and lived in servitude. We also discussed the living conditions of the children while they were away from their parents and investigated factors that drove parents to send their children into servitude. We interacted with participants and stakeholders.

Discussions with Social Welfare indicated that there were three categories of beneficiaries in the current LEAP programme. These were (a) orphans 17 years old and younger, (b) persons who suffer severe disability, and (c) persons who are 65 years and older. In addition to being one of the above categories, a major limiting factor for LEAP was that the recipients had to also be living in extreme monetary poverty. In 2016, the amounts paid out per month differed from what the literature established earlier: one-member households received C32 (approximately $9); two-member households received C36 (approximately $11); and three person households received C44 (approximately $13). Households that had four members or more were paid C53 (approximately $15). Households received the equivalent of two-month payments every other month.

---

moved from one location to another. Typically, they are deceived with promises of good paying jobs and improved living conditions.

We collected both qualitative and quantitative data at several stages of the project. After direct beneficiaries (rescued children) were enrolled in schools or apprentice training, our visits to the communities monitored and evaluated progress to determine effectiveness of our strategies and to develop new approaches if determined necessary. We strengthened the internal validity of our observations through several practices, which included triangulation of techniques, replication of questions in all communities, verification with community members and leaders, and direct interaction with and observation of child beneficiaries at their homes, in schools, and at training centres. The number of interviews conducted throughout the project led to extensive saturation of the data. We exceeded the initial stage of saturation in order to select direct beneficiaries of the project. Interviews with participants including community leaders, parents, and the survivors and regular observations of activities such as classrooms or apprentice centres further solidified our data.

Furthermore, we applied the grounded theory approach to analyse our data (Charmaz, 2014; Glaser, 1978; Glaser and Strauss, 1967; Strauss, 1987). We also used the constant comparative approaches (Fram, 2013; Hewitt-Taylor, 2001) so that for the most part, new participants or visits to newer communities did not require repeating previously administered interview questions, but comprised the application of themes observed in previous studies. This approach further served as our technique of ensuring that our conclusions from previous iterations of our analyses were valid and depicted what participants and direct beneficiaries identified as causes of their migration or trafficking.

RESULTS: QUALITATIVE ANALYSIS OF THE SITUATION OF CHILDREN IN SERVITUDE

As we analysed the evidence, several themes emerged. These themes were categorized for more nuanced concepts on child labour, particularly in terms of those recruited or trafficked for domestic servitude. For the purpose of this chapter, we focus on a framework that conceptualizes: (a) contemporary child domestic servitude in Ghana; (b) abuses and injustices prevalent within child labour exploitation; (c) factors that sustained child labour exploitation; and (d) disconnections between child protection and social protection programmes, and child labour exploitation. This section outlines the first three parts of the framework, while the last is presented under the discussion section.

Contemporary child domestic servitude in Ghana

Survivors of domestic servitude who participated in this project were recruited to child labour through diverse means. None of them went through a formal recruitment agency but rather through relatives or fellow village men and women who had migrated to the cities. For some of the participants, visitors to their villages asked parents to permit them to migrate to the cities with the children. While no money changed hands, parents believed permitting their children to migrate to the cities would be beneficial; they hoped the children would have access to quality education, healthcare, and improved quality of life.

Child domestic servants performed three main tasks, namely babysitting, household chores including cleaning, laundry and cooking, and hawking. According to our participants, domestic servants were the first to wake up but typically the last to go to bed. They generally woke up between 4 a.m. and 6 a.m., depending on the chores and instructions by their "madams" or how the households were structured and organised. They swept the entire house, dusted windows and living rooms, mopped kitchen and living room floors, prepared breakfast and had the younger children in the family ready for school. Depending on the age of the domestic servant, they might not be assigned some of these chores, and for that matter, might not be required to wake up very early. After breakfast and when all the children and adult workers had left for school and work, domestic servants could be free to nap, watch television, or just sit and wait. For the most part, however, they were required to do the laundry every day, and to continue with the cleaning of the entire house. Prior to finishing these chores, they probably were required to prepare lunch for the children and adult household members who may not be working or those who came home for lunch. Before they were able to take a break, it was usually time to prepare dinner for the family. When that was completed, they cleaned the dishes and prepared the younger family members for bed. They sometimes were required to iron and complete the laundry by folding them.

Domestic servants who engaged in hawking had to do so very early in the morning and throughout the day, depending on whether the household had other domestic servants to cover the other chores, or if the servant was recruited primarily for selling. Otherwise, when they woke up in the mornings, they performed general house cleaning duties and then set off to sell for the household. They might return home to continue with their work by cleaning, babysitting, and cooking. One 9-year-old girl had to keep selling liquor for the pastor she lived with.

Servants who were enrolled in schools had to put in approximately two to four hours of work before going to school every day. They performed household chores and or hawked convenience items prior to school. When the children returned home, they continued with chores and hawking and had limited time to finish their homework or to read. In a particular case, a 15-year-old girl who was still in the third grade had to walk the 3-5 miles to sell purified sachet water. She made three trips a day to sell the water at the same location. At the end of the third trip, she had dinner and spent the rest of the night keeping her madam's shop. By the time she was allowed to leave, she would be too tired, and it would be too late, to complete her homework.

Abuses and Violations of Rights Prevalent within Child Domestic Servitude

Some of the domestic servants who participated in the study were enrolled in schools, a new phenomenon that resembled the traditional practice of placing children to serve in the household of relatives or other adults in exchange for protection, education, and the promise of a better future than with their own family (e.g. if they lived in marginalized or distant areas). The difference, however, was that the children in contemporary domestic servitude spent more time completing their chores than attending school or completing school related assignments (Darby, 2012). They went to school late because of the chores assigned to them in the mornings, missed classes for the same reason, and sometimes went to school on empty stomachs. One of the participating head teachers indicated in an interview that she was able to determine students who lived in servitude because of their consistent tardiness, unkempt appearances, tattered uniforms, and their lack of school supplies. Some of them came to school merely to sleep because it was the only place they could rest without constant verbal abuse. The authors observed that they had to rush from school as soon as the bell went for closing; they were afraid of being punished if they got home later than usual. The head teacher further specified that there were instances where while school was in session, she could see a particular student carting loads across campus for the household he served.

From the ongoing discussions on child domestic servitude, we observe the ineffectiveness of the laws aimed at protecting Ghana's children. Children exposed to labour exploitation through domestic servitude endure physical and emotional abuse, neglect, dehumanizing practices, and isolation, all of which violate their rights. Physical abuse comprised of child rape, flogging with canes and other household objects, hitting with bare hands, and shoving.

Cases of rape

Our participants were vulnerable to sexual exploitation within the household and outside. Some of the girls were raped by male members of the households they served. Even where girls lived and served biological relatives, the likelihood of rape or sexual abuse remained significant. Because of poor supervision as they run errands outside their homes, some of the girls also stood the risk of rape by outside men. In one of the cases that we dealt with, the domestic servant, 14 years-old, was provided the opportunity of formal education. Her interactions with us, and our discussions with her teachers, suggested she was an excellent student. She lived with a female military officer — whom she referred to as her sister – and the officer's husband. One night while the officer was away on an official assignment, the "sister's" husband raped her. He repeated the crime every time his wife was away. The girl indicated she developed a kind of sexually transmitted disease and got concerned about her madam's health because there were other women whom her husband brought to their matrimonial home whenever she travelled. She was, however, scared of the repercussions should she report her abuse. She ultimately decided to discuss the rape with her madam's best friend for advice and possibly to make the former aware of her husband's infidelity. Unfortunately, she suffered secondary victimization because of the verbal abuse she had to endure and her subsequent dismissal from that household, a place she believed had been protective of her in some ways (despite the rape). She was blamed for the dissolution of the marriage; her madam, who had otherwise treated her with much kindness, severed ties with her.

Another domestic servant was raped under similar circumstances. The wife of the abusive husband came to his defence, chastised the domestic servant for attempting to tarnish his reputation, and denigrated her at every opportunity. Consequently, this girl decided to run away from servitude. She found herself working in a roadside cooked food bar. By this time, she had been reported missing. Months into her escape, her mother's neighbour found her at the bar and informed her family. She was soon removed from that location.

Other victims of such instances of sexual abuse never reported their encounters to anybody because of fear and secondary victimization. They would rather resort to secrecy, running away, or abortion. At one of the schools we worked at Accra, we learned of a 15-year-old girl who kept a journal of her sexual abuse and being forced to have illegal abortions. She informed her best friend in school about these abuses and indicated she was pregnant again but was afraid she might not survive another abortion. She showed the friend where she kept the journal. Tragically, she died in the subsequent abortion procedure, and the friend brought out the journal. Reports suggest the abuser was arrested, but there was no evidence of conviction for the crimes of rape, illegal abortions, and murder.

Secondary victimization sometimes affected not only the child servant, but also their immediate family members, who might be similarly economically challenged. One of the girls the authors of this chapter removed was pregnant, and we discovered she was impregnated while still in servitude. Fruitless efforts were made to contact the abuser who lived near the house she worked in. As we endeavoured to support this girl and to locate the culprit for potential prosecution, her mother was blamed for poor parenting and failure to monitor her daughter, despite the fact that she lived hundreds of miles away from the girl and never made any contact while she was in servitude.

Neglect

Child neglect in this context comprised actions and inactions that eventually stripped the child servant of their rights and protection. Once they moved out of their parents' homes and became identified as maidservants or houseboys, they had limited access to quality education, healthcare, and healthy relationships. They were excluded from many normal childhood activities. They were denied play, or they were simply too busy. Their households were uninterested in their welfare or education. Hence, the educated members of the receiving households hardly assisted them with their schoolwork. As a result, we met a number of 15- to 18-year-olds who were still in the first through third grades in school. One girl we spoke to believed that the household's primary goal of her free labour inhibited her academic performance and future career. She stated, "I get angry because they treat me as if I am not a human being."

We could sometimes identify domestic servants by their clothing.[4] They were typically dressed in oversized clothes relative to other children in the same household (probably hand-me-downs or other second-hand clothes). The other children were normally well-dressed. Even when we met them at church, we noticed some of them wore flip-flops when the other kids had more appropriate dress shoes on.

Normally, households would not deny healthcare to domestic servants living with them. When such children were ill, if they were assertive enough to make it known, they would at least be given painkillers and later sent to see the doctor. Participants rarely went to see the doctor though. Nevertheless, we were in a head teacher's office when a student who had symptoms of leprosy came in for money to go and see a doctor. The household he lived in had virtually abandoned him. We were informed that day about children who relied on the head teacher and staff for healthcare, food, and uniforms. We also learnt of one fatality involving a student who was denied healthcare by the household he lived in. The teachers found out third grade children were making donations to purchase over-the-counter medicine and food for their domestic servant classmate, a boy, who had missed school for being sick. This prompted the head teacher to visit the boy's house, only to find out that he had passed away that morning. She believed if there had been prompt intervention, the boy could have been saved.

Restricted contact with parents

Some of the parents never contacted their children or did so very rarely. The most fortunate of the children who remained in constant contact with their parents lived with relatives, friends, or acquaintances of relatives or neighbours. In some of those instances, parents were in contact with the children because there were family meetings or special occasions such as funerals, or when the parents travelled to the cities to purchase needed

---

[4]   Thus corroborating what the teacher had told us about her pupils (see above)

items or sell foodstuff. They might come into contact with their children who petty traded for their "madams" on the same market. Some children sold water and other foodstuffs at bus stations, giving them better access to transport and information exchange. Local commercial bus drivers sometimes carried messages from the children to the parents.

In other cases, contact was never maintained with children once they had left. A 15-year-old girl in one of the primary schools we visited indicated her grandmother had sent her to the city to live with a madam who the grandmother knew through trading at the market. Since she was brought to the city, the grandmother never visited her nor sent any message to her. The girl had no way of finding her, as the madam maltreated her and refused to let her go back to her hometown.

Factors that challenge efforts to eliminate child labour exploitation

Discussions with law enforcement agencies, and an NGO specializing in responding to violence against women, concluded there were practically no reports on violations of the law in relation to domestic servitude, and they did not have any special programmes for children living in servitude. They admitted, nevertheless, that while laws such as the Children's Act existed to protect children in general, they were knowledgeable of the poor and abusive treatments of domestic servants. They expressed concern and further acknowledged failure on the part of the government or relevant agencies to fight it. By implication, law enforcement agencies have failed to put the law into practice or protect the children. In addition, many NGOs have also failed to advocate on behalf of these children, to expose these practices, or to try to prosecute cases of child servitude. Two representatives of an NGO shared with the researchers that the practice of child servitude was extremely entrenched in Ghanaian society; no one ever perceived it as a form of child labour exploitation, although servants encountered numerous injustices that violated their basic rights. This section outlines some of the factors responsible for the exclusion of domestic servitude from mainstream programmes and the social policy debate in Ghana.

Denial of the problem

We observed in this project that unless there were reported cases of multiple abuses — such as busload of children being trafficked — children continued to suffer slavery-like conditions in servitude, farming, and other exploitive occupations. Driving through the major streets of the cities of Ghana, one found several children hawking, running errands, or just loitering about during school hours. This evidence notwithstanding, it was difficult for some of those stakeholders who participated in this project to admit the existence of child domestic servitude. The following subsections outline some of the instances where stakeholders supposedly in charge of children's welfare, protection, and law enforcement vehemently denied the existence of domestic servitude. Some participants who denied child domestic servitude lived with underage servants themselves; they probably refused to acknowledge the problem of exploitation because of the personal and household benefits they derived from the everyday practice.

Denial through labels

When the State Department sponsored project was commenced in 2010, a number of prominent Ghanaian officials advised the project team to stop identifying the phenomenon as domestic servitude or the girls as domestic servants. A multiple award winner and founder of a NGO, as well as several professional women who seemed to champion the cause of women and children in Ghana, were among those who appeared more concerned about the label rather than the abuses the child servants were forced to endure. These stakeholders argued the label was derogatory. They recommended a more "classy" identity like "house helps" and thought the research was being insensitive and disrespectful by refusing to deny the girls their true identities. In other words, they expected the relabelling would "re-classify" them as doing something good or worthwhile, thus avoiding the recognition that these children are being exploited and require the attention of child protection activists.

Denial and justification of child labour by law makers of Ghana

At a presentation to the Gender Committee of Ghana's Parliament, one of the authors was heckled for adopting an ILO definition that distinguished positive and negative children's work. The first reaction came from a ranking member of the committee who pointed out that they did not welcome definitions from the United Nations and the ILO. However, considering the country's ratification of the CRC and the subsequent promulgation of the Children's Act, this sounded contradictory and demonstrated ignorance and a lack of commitment to both international conventions and local legislative instruments. Subsequent comments from members at the meeting sought to vehemently deny child domestic servitude in the country. References were made to its historical practice, which contrary to current "foreign" attempts to "mischaracterize" it, was originally positive and served an important function. We agreed with them that traditional fosterage was an old practice. Still it was equally exploitative - even if in the past some children could increase their access to education. In today's practice, most of the children spent significantly more time running errands, petty trading, or performing other household chores and so could not devote adequate time to school.

The Members present seemed to justify this exploitative labour while overlooking the abuses and injustices the girls and boys suffered. A female parliamentarian claimed she lived with a 13-year-old girl from her constituency purposely to keep watch of her home. She emphasized she did not require the girl to perform any chores besides keeping watch over the house while she was gone. Obviously, this MP did not consider the role of keeping watch over her house as a form of domestic servitude. She did not consider other things the child had a right to be doing, such as learning or playing. She further argued it was part of her contribution to her constituency because, as she stated emphatically, the girl was the beneficiary. Surprisingly, other members of parliament present concurred with her. It was notorious that the MP managed to overlook the fact that this child needed protection rather than a grown-up's job.

Denial of domestic servitude by "humanitarian" Rotarians

The level of defensiveness exhibited in parliament was repeated when we received an invitation to discuss issues of domestic servitude at a meeting of a Rotary Club chapter in Accra. Like parliamentarians, the members present denied domestic servitude, felt insulted, and even pointed out it was not their responsibility to address child domestic servitude in Ghana. An issue that drove them to be angry was that the presentation employed the first person plural, using "we" in discussing the role Ghanaians played in domestic servitude. They could not understand the analogical usage of the pronoun and felt extremely offended; it roused unusual amounts of anger. Analyses of notes made at the meeting suggested elitism somehow determined their membership in the club and drove them to disconnect themselves from the realities facing the poor Ghanaian child. They focused more on the display of wealth and influence, either at their meetings or through print and electronic media publications.

The most vocal person at the meeting, a bank worker, admitted she had seen children working in the streets, but questioned how that was supposed to be her problem (even though she was a Rotarian), or what she could do if that was what their parents demanded of them. She was sure there was never domestic servitude in Ghana, and that poor parents exploited their own children, as if such children did not deserve the support of such a humanitarian organisation. Later, the first author received several calls from executives of the club, apologizing for the unruly behaviour of other members, and confirming child domestic servitude was a problem that needed everybody's attention. Other members spoke to her immediately after the meeting, citing instances where they had observed abuses of underage children in domestic servitude. Such children were vulnerable to physical attacks and labour.

Denial by a television producer
Several media outlets were contacted. The response was generally positive, with the exception of one television show. However, when we eventually spoke to the producer, we had to answer several questions, which unmasked the animosity and prejudices of the show producer. She wanted to know why we perceived domestic servitude in exploitive terms because it was beneficial to the children, and in her opinion, the servants were fortunate to have been removed from the villages. She stated specifically that most of their viewers would not perceive the phenomenon as problematic. Hence, she refused to schedule us for an interview.

It should be emphasized that, as the two NGO representatives intimated, domestic servitude was a common practice and unfortunately entrenched in mainstream Ghanaian culture, hence the non-existent records of any reporting even when the servants were seriously abused. From parliamentarians to the television producer, we observed people who benefited from the practice, and thus they failed to perceive it as abusive or a type of modern slavery. This corroborated the NGO conclusion that the very people who were responsible for the protection of the children were the perpetrators of the abuses, hence their exclusion from protective programmes and their attempts to avoid the use of concepts as servitude or trafficking in reference to the children's situation.

DISCUSSION: OPTIONS TO DESIGN SOCIAL PROTECTION TO ADDRESS CHILD PROTECTION

Since 2003, there has been a significant change in the educational status of domestic servants (Derby, 2009, 2010). This is because currently, many more domestic servants in the cities — compared to those from previous research — are enrolled in schools (Derby, 2012). That has been a positive and major outcome of social policies such as Ghana's Free Compulsory Universal Basic Education (FCUBE), the provision of school uniforms, and school feeding (which is part of social protection). That notwithstanding, as we observed in this study, domestic servants who were enrolled in schools performed poorly because they had to spend more time working than studying. Such persistent exploitation of children's labour through trafficking and for purposes of domestic servitude in Ghana shows that there is still a lot of work to do.

In particular, newer or expanded social protection programmes are needed to prevent some of the conditions that perpetuate domestic servitude. This conclusion stems from the framework that such programmes could empower socially and economically excluded populations (Kaplan and Jones, 2013; Pino and Confalonieri, 2014). We maintain that irrespective of quantitative reports praising the numbers who have benefited from social protection programmes such as cash transfers, there are still too many households which remain extremely impoverished and lack their basic needs. Social protection programmes are not ends in themselves; they must effectively address issues that prevent access to formal education, healthcare, safety, and economic security. For instance, school enrolment should not only be perceived as an end in itself, because children do have a right to education (Ananta, 2012). School enrolment is also a means towards long-term security and empowerment. Therefore, in order to help protect poor rural children from trafficking, domestic servitude, and other forms of child labour exploitation in urban areas, social protection should be complemented with other social services. In particular, quality education that empowers children should be expanded and should be coordinated with child protection activities (what is known as "social protection plus").

This section highlights the constraints rural families face, which are the reasons many children end up going alone to urban areas. Parents in the project provided detailed descriptions of their reasons for permitting their children's migration to other parts of the country. Some of them blamed it on poverty[5], while others believed city lives were key to social mobility and security for their children. They complained about their village schools, poor structures, inadequate numbers of teachers, and poor academic performance among the children. Annually, most of those schools score close to 0 percent in the final external examinations when the students are supposed to be graduating with a basic education. Their academic advancements are curtailed with such grades, and the cycle of poverty continues, despite costly social protection programmes.

These and other reasons are why they permit their children to work in other households, expecting some advantages for the children, as was the case in the past. They expected children living with older relatives to have access to formal education and in exchange, perform minimal chores that would not interfere with their school participation (Derby, 2009; 2010; 2012). Some children had to endure abuses in the past, but unless they were primarily recruited for hard labour exploitation, such as working on cocoa farms, children who went through traditional fosterage were typically successful in education. In the past, children's ability to participate sufficiently in formal education while performing some amount of household chores that did not inhibit their physical and psychological development, or training as an apprentice, was deemed appropriate and socializing (as recognized by the ILO Conventions). Traffickers and the households they serve manipulate such perceptions of reciprocity and deceive poor and deprived families to believe their children would be better off living in the cities as servants.

If support for poor and disadvantaged communities is key (Kabeer, 2008), then in Ghana, there is a gap. We recommend an integrated social protection system, with programmes that can address the root causes of

---

[5]   Although usually people refer to monetary poverty in this context, the lack of adequate social services (in particular health and education), which are comprised under multidimensional child poverty, is also a major part of the problem, as it is explained below.

trafficking and servitude. Social protection programmes consisting of measures mitigating risks and providing support to families could help keep their children, allowing them to grow up in loving households as stipulated by the Children's Act. Children must enjoy their childhoods - and they must be protected from exploitive and hazardous work that interfere with their growth and childhoods.

Ghana has been commended for its social assistance programmes. Its cash transfers, provision of school uniforms (even if they are oversized and do not always fit properly), school feeding programmes, and the national health insurance schemes, are all relatively uncommon in Sub-Saharan Africa. Nevertheless, while those programmes are sufficiently child sensitive, two issues remain vital if they are to effectively address problems emanating from child poverty. These are the need to expand coverage, and the need for additional programmes. Social protection interventions should be complemented in two mutually reinforcing ways. One is to expand investment in basic social services. Thus, when families approach (or surpass) the monetary poverty line (or receive incentives or assistance to attend health or education services), services of acceptable quality should be available to them near their residences.

The relevance of programmes that simultaneously keep children in loving households, prevent them from child labour, and keep them in schools cannot be overemphasized. As Guarcello, Lyon, and Rosati (2014) observed, child labour often prevents formal educational participation by working children, may reduce attention span, increase absenteeism, and prevent proper homework completion. According to Zibagwe et al. (2013) and Pino and Confalonieri (2014), social protection programmes should contribute to reduce child poverty, promote safe childhoods, and facilitate access to education, healthcare, and nutrition. Many underprivileged parents prefer and hope that their children would escape the vulnerabilities of childhood in villages; hence, they accept offers to let their children migrate even when they are aware the outcomes could be exploitive labour. Therefore, social protection programmes in Ghana should consider this state of desperation among rural parents. Ghana's school feeding and cash transfer programmes could and should be combined with other investments, for instance child healthcare and high-quality education in rural areas.

Secondly, social protection programmes should be accompanied with child protection interventions that can, for instance, identify children at risk of being trafficked. Integral components of such child intervention programmes must be capable of follow-up procedures when there are signs of possible exploitation or abuse. This kind of complementarity could be accomplished through collaborations among stakeholder agencies. For instance, they may share databases on recipients of social protection benefits. Schools may also work with social welfare departments to facilitate access to commonly needed data.

The exploitation in servitude, as perceived in the number of hours worked, poor participation in formal education, neglect, and physical and sexual abuse, constitutes a denial of children's rights. These have prevailed irrespective of Ghana's prolific ratification and promulgation of laws. These encounters of children living in servitude violate Ghana's Children's Act, which includes: the right of children to live with their parents and in a loving household; the right to education; the right to social activities; and the right to protection from exploitive labour, torture, and degrading treatment.

LIMITATIONS AND FUTURE RESEARCH

Numerous limitations were encountered throughout the project and the development of this manuscript. Specific among them was accessibility to current data on social protection projects in Ghana, in spite of the existence of several reports and many academic articles using public data on access to cash transfers. Relevant offices supporting the success of social protection programmes could not readily provide the information. We were able to analyse only limited information on the various social protection programmes. Therefore, while participants in the project emphasized the lack of social amenities and educational facilities, we could not assess if improved facilities would actually deter parents from sending their children to the cities as domestic servants.

For future research, we recommend longitudinal and comparative studies of beneficiary communities of the social protection programmes to examine the impact both qualitatively and quantitatively. Additionally, the acquisition of supportive data on the ability of households to successfully invest the sums they receive will be helpful for purposes of advocacy and policy generation. Ghana recently implemented a programme of free senior high school. It would be excellent if future data on child domestic servitude examines the impact of this major educational project with so much potential for child protection. The new free senior high school — particularly if it has a good reputation in rural areas — can reduce the potential of child labour and urban migration, and both qualitative and quantitative studies to substantiate the relationship would be useful.

REFERENCES

Abebrese, J. (n.d.) *Social Protection in Ghana, An overview of existing programmes and their prospects and challenges.* [Online] Available at: http://library.fes.de/pdf-files/bueros/ghana/10497.pdf [Accessed on January 15, 2016]

Ananta, A. (2012) 'Sustainable and Just Social Protection in South East Asia', *ASEAN Economic Bulletin*, 29(3): 171-183.

Bailey, C. (2010). 'Social Protection in Communities Vulnerable to Criminal Activities', *Social Protection in the Caribbean*, 59(1/2): 211-242.

Barrientos, A. (2010) 'Vulnerability and Social Protection in Small Island States: The Case of Grenada', Social & Economic 59(1/2): 3-30.

Berhane, G., Gilligan, D. O., Hoddinott, J., Kuma, N. & A. S. Taffesse (2014) 'Can Social Protection Work in Africa? The Impact of Ethipia's Productive Safety Net Programme' in *Economic Development and Cultural Change*, 63(1): 1-26.

Browne, E. (2015) 'Social Protection' *Applied Knowledge Services* [Online] Available at: http://www.gsdrc.org/topic-guides/social-protection/types-of-social-protection/ [Accessed on August 13, 2016].

Charmaz, K. (2014). *Constructing Grounded Theory.* Sage Publications.

Conway, T., de Haan, A. and A. Norton (2000) 'Social Protection: New Directions of Donor Agencies', [Online]. Available at: https://www.odi.org/'sites/odi.org.uk/files/odi-assets/publications-opinion-files/2233.pdf [Accessed on July 8, 2016]

Debrah, E. (2013). 'Alleviating Poverty in Ghana: The Case of Livelihood Empowerment against Poverty (LEAP)'. *Africa Today. 69* (1) 41-67

Devereux, S. and Sabates-Wheeler, R. (2004) 'Transformative social protection', IDS Working Paper 232, IDS: Brighton, Sussex

Derby, C. N. (2012) 'Are the Barrels Empty? Are the Children any Safer? Child Domestic Labor and Servitude in Ghana' in M. Ensor (Ed.) *African Childhoods: Education, Development, Peacebuilding, and the Youngest Continent,* New York, NY: Palgrave, pp. 10-32.

Derby, C. N. (2010) 'Enslavement and Human Trafficking: the Supple Swimmers of Fishing at Yeji, Ghana', in Shechory, M., Soen, D., S. Ben-david (Eds.). *Who Pays the Price? Foreign Workers, Society, Crime and the Law,* Hauppauge, NY: Nova Publishers, pp. 191 – 200.

Derby, C. N. (2009) *Contemporary Slavery: Researching Child Domestic Servitude*, Lanham, Maryland: University Press of America.

Fram, S. M. (2013) 'The Constant Comparative Analysis Method Outside of Grounded Theory' in *The Qualitative Report* 2013 Volume 18, Article 1, 1-25. [Online] Available at: http://www.nova.edu/ssss/QR/QR18/fram1.pdf [Accessed on July 8, 2016]

Guarcello, L., Lyon, S., and F. Rosati (2014) 'Child Labour and Out-Of-School Children: Evidence from 25 Developing Countries' in *Understanding Children's Work (UCW) Programme* [Online]

Available at: http://allinschool.org/wp-content/uploads/2015/01/OOSC-2014-Child-labour-final.pdf [Accessed on July 8, 2016]

Handa, S., Park, M., Osei Akoto, I., Darko Osei, R., Davis, B., & Diadone, S. (2013). Livelihood Empowerment against Poverty Programme Impact Evaluation. Chapel Hill: University of North Carolina, Carolina Population Center. Available at: http://www.unicef.org/ghana/gh_resources_LEAP_Quant_impact_evaluatio n_FINAL_OCT_2013.pdf

Harvey, P., Holmes, R., Slater, R. and Martin, E. (2007) 'Social Protection in Fragile States'. London: ODI.

Hewitt-Taylor, J. (2001) 'Use of constant comparative analysis in qualitative research' in *Nursing Standard*. 15, 42, 39-42. [Online] Available at http://citeseerx. ist.psu.edu/viewdoc/download?doi=10.1.1.130.6954&rep=rep1&type=pdf [Accessed on July 8, 2016]

International Labour Organization. (2015). 'Rationalizing social protection expenditure in Ghana' [Online]. Available at: http://www.social-protection.org/gimi/gess/ RessourcePDF.action?ressource.ressourceId=50738 [Accessed on January 16, 2016]

Jones, N. and Holmes, R. (2010). 'Gender-sensitive Social Protection and the MDGs'. ODI Briefing Paper 61. London: Overseas Development Institute (ODI)Kabeer, N. (2008) 'Gender mainstreaming in Social Protection for the Informal Economy' London: Commonwealth Secretariat.

Kaplan J. and N. Jones (2013), 'Child-Sensitive Social Protection in Africa: Challenges and Opportunities' in *The African Child Policy Forum* [Online]. Available at: http://resourcecentre.savethechildren.se/sites/default/files/documents/child-sensitive_social_protection_systems_nov11.pdf [Accessed on July 8, 2016]

Laiglesia, J. R. (2011) 'Coverage Gaps in Social Protection', [Online]. Available at: https://www.oecd.org/dev/pgd/47588850.pdf [Accessed on July 8, 2016]

Long, G. T. (2012) 'Delivering Social Protection to the Poor and Vulnerable Groups in Vietnam: Challenges and the Role of the Government' *ASEAN Economic Bulletin*, 29(3): 245-258.Mochiah, E., Darko, R. D., & Akoto, I. O. (2014). The impact of conditional cash transfer programmes on household work decisions in Ghana. Retrieved from https://www.econstor.eu/bitstream/10419/107972/1/797 370579.pdf

Mkandawire, T. (2004) "Social Policy in a Development Context: Introduction ", in T. Mkandawire (ed.) *Social Policy in a Development Context*, Palgrave Macmillan.

Norton, A., Conway, T., & M. Foster (2001) 'Social Protection Concepts and Approaches: Implications for Policy and Practice in International Development' [Online]. Available at: https://www.odi.org/sites/odi.org.uk/files/odi-assets/publication s-opinion-files/2999.pdf [Accessed on 10 March 2016].

Oduro, D. A. (2010) 'Formal and Informal Social Protection in sub-Saharan Africa', Paper presented for the European Report on Development.

Ofori-Addo, L. (n.d.) *Social Protection Landscape in Ghana*. www.inter-reseaux.org/ IMG/pdf/Presentation_SOCIAL_PROTECTION_LANDSCAPE_IN_GHANA.pdf [Accessed on January 15, 2016]

Phukon, D. (Oct – Dec 2008) 'Gender Development Approach and Social Protection: Understanding the Case of Assam', *The Indian Journal of Political Science, 69(4): 771-785*.

Pino and Confalonieri (2014) 'National social protection policies in West Africa: A comparative analysis', *International Social Security Review*, 67(3/4): 127-152.

Powell, M. A.; Nicola Taylor; Robyn Fitzgerald; Ann Graham; Donnah Anderson (2013) *Ethical Research Involving Children*, Innocenti Publications, UNICEF, Florence, Italy.

Sepulveda, M. and C. Nyst (2012) 'The Human Rights Approach to Social Protection'. Available at: http://www.ohchr.org/Documents/Issues/EPoverty/HumanRight sApproachToSocialProtection.pdf [Accessed on January 15, 2016]

Standing, G. (2007) 'Social Protection' *Development in Practice*, 17(4/5): 511-522.

Zibagwe, S., Nduna, T. and G. Dafuleya (2013) 'Are Social Protection Programs Child Sensitive', *Development Southern Africa*, 30(1): 111-120.

Zin, R. H. (2012) 'Towards a Social Protection in an Advanced Equitable Society', *ASEAN Economic Bulletin*, 29(3): 197-217

CHAPTER 11

BENEFIT INCIDENCE OF PUBLIC SPENDING ON SOCIAL SERVICES AND CHILD POVERTY RATES IN NIGERIA

Robert C. Asogwa

INTRODUCTION

The use of fiscal policy for child poverty reduction in Nigeria and other Sub-Sahara African countries is rarely addressed in academic literature. Most existing empirical studies on the determinants of child poverty and child labour ignore the government transfers and social sector expenditures variables (Adeoti and Olufemi, 2012; cf. Rufai et al., 2016 for Nigeria; Makhalima et al., 2014 for South Africa; Okpukpara et al., 2006 for Nigeria). A recent exception is a UNICEF (2009) study for Mali, Senegal and Congo. The story is, however, different for several developed countries where there are large amounts of literature surveying the impact of fiscal policy on child poverty reduction. Eurostat (2010) finds that social transfers in European countries had a significant impact on reducing the risk of poverty among children (under the age of 18). The transfers removed 39.4 percent of children from the risk of poverty in the EU27 in 2007, more than that of all the age groups (34.6 percent). Longford and Nicodemo (2010), and Papatheodorou et al. (2016), find that the impact of social transfers on poverty are more effective in the north and west of Europe than in the south and in the former Soviet republics.

The objective of this chapter is therefore to assess whether or not government expenditure on the social sector (education and health) affect child poverty rates across Nigerian regions. The key question is: to what extent can the regional disparities in child poverty (especially severe deprivations in health and education) be attributed to the benefit incidence of public spending on education and health in the same locations? In other words, are Nigerian regions with more progressive benefit incidence of public spending on education and health (in favour of poorer and younger persons) also likely to have reduced child poverty rates?

Analytically, we adopt the incidence approach, which determines the benefit incidence of fiscal policy (public spending, taxes and transfers) on particular age cohorts and household groups. In the literature however, several other methods have been used to assess the impact of fiscal policy (i.e. expenditures on social sector, transfers and taxes) on child poverty rates and they include: the impact evaluation approaches using experimental and observational techniques to isolate the poverty reduction effects of social and cash transfers (see Del Carpio and Marcous, 2010; Barrientos et al., 2013); the relative efficiency approach with both vertical and horizontal efficiency scores (Atkinson, 1995; Barrientos and Dejong, 2006); and the 'before and after approach', also called the 'with and without approach' (Longford and Nicodemo, 2010; Gabos, 2010; Levine et al., 2009); the policy impact approach (used in EU Task-Force, 2008 and Gabos, 2010), which first estimates poverty rates before transfers and then adds specific transfers to evaluate the poverty reduction effect of income supports.

Specifically, we use the incidence approach to determine who benefits more (especially the poor and the young) from public expenditure on education and health across the different regions in Nigeria. Measuring the benefit incidence of public spending is not new in Nigeria as both Alabi (2010) and Amakom (2013) have done so using the 2003/4 Nigerian Living Standards Survey (NLSS). Apart from using an updated data set (2009/10 NLSS), we move a step further to investigate who benefits more across the different age groups from public spending on education and health. We also explore the linkages between benefit incidence estimates for the different age groups in the regions and the child poverty rates in the regions (measured as percentage of severe child deprivations in education and health as computed from the 2007 Nigeria Multiple Indicator Cluster Survey (MICS). The results can be useful for the design and targeting of public expenditure on social sector and transfers.

PUBLIC EXPENDITURE ON SOCIAL SECTOR AND CHILD POVERTY TRENDS IN NIGERIA

Public expenditure trends

An important part of the theory of public finance is how government spending can affect the economic position of individuals and households. Generally, government expenditures affect the wellbeing of individuals and households through direct cash transfers and the benefits generated by the provision of goods and services. As Davoodi et al. (2003: 21) note, "although other categories of government expenditures are important for individual welfare, social services such as education, health care and social safety net programmes are normally regarded as being the most important for enhancing the long-run earning potential of the population, particularly the poor." This has however not been the case in many developing countries, as the fiscal space for expanding more redistributive (and progressive) social transfers is constrained by large expenditures on regressive sectors, which benefit only the middle and upper income households such as free residence for higher paid public functionaries (Coady, 2010).

Recent public expenditure trends in Nigeria seem to suggest that its focus has been to support growth and promote macroeconomic stability rather than to redistribute income or to ensure improved access and equality of opportunity for different income or age groups. A careful look at the 2014-2106 Medium Term Expenditure Framework and Fiscal Strategy Paper in Nigeria shows that the focus of fiscal policy is still largely on growth and stabilization (Asogwa, 2015). The history and trend of fiscal policy in Nigeria beginning from the pre-independence era, the post-independence era up to the period before the current democratic governance era are well documented in other literature (Anyafo, 1996).

In Tables 1 and 2, we compare public expenditure on a key poverty reduction and income redistribution sector (social and community services) with other sectors over two distinct periods in Nigeria: The era of low Gini coefficient, i.e. before 1985; and the era of high Gini coefficient as from 2004.

Table 1:   Breakdown of public capital expenditure in Nigeria - % of total expenditure (era of low Gini coefficient in Nigeria)

	1976	1977	1978	1979	1980	1981	1982	1983
Administration	18.8	18.6	19.0	15.0	15.3	12.6	9.6	11.6
Economic Services	52.6	57.4	56.8	58.1	64.9	62.3	38.2	41.1
Social and Community Services	21.2	15.2	21.0	12.7	15.8	24.2	17.6	15.6
Transfers	7.4	8.8	3.2	13.3	4.0	0.9	34.6	31.7

Note: Administration includes general administration, defence and internal security. Economic Services includes agriculture, manufacturing, transport, housing, roads and other priority projects. Social and Community Services is comprised of education, health and other sectors including social welfare. Transfers includes financial obligations, capital repayments, and capital supplementation.
Source: Central Bank of Nigeria (CBN) Statistical Bulletin, 1991

Table 2:   Breakdown of public capital expenditure in Nigeria - % of total
expenditure (era of high Gini coefficient in Nigeria)

	2006	2007	2008	2009	2010	2011	2012	2013
Administration	33.5	29.8	29.8	25.3	29.4	25.2	21.7	25.5
Economic Services	47.4	47.2	52.4	43.8	46.6	42.0	36.7	45.6
Social and Community Services	14.2	19.8	15.8	12.5	17.7	10.1	11.3	13.9
Transfers	4.76	3.03	1.80	18.2	6.7	22.5	30.3	14.8

Source: CBN Statistical Bulletin 2013

It is clear from Tables 1 and 2 that expenditures on social and community services was second to economic services for the period 1976 to 1983, an era characterized by low Gini coefficient. In contrast, during the period 2006 to 2013, social and community services was the category receiving the least amount of public annual expenditure, lagging behind all other sectors.

Why has administration and transfers in recent years suddenly received greater attention than social and community services, and what implications does this have for income redistribution and poverty reduction? Can the high Gini coefficient during this period be attributed to the declining expenditures on social and community services as compared to other sectors? The poverty incidence rate, which by 1985 was 46.3 percent, has by 2010 moved to 69 percent. Similarly, both the income inequality trend and the human development indicators have worsened between 2004 and 2010, and further worsened between 2010 and 2013. (UNDP 2016).[1]

A second aspect of the trend of public expenditure on social and community services is the breakdown of spending across the three tiers of government in Nigeria (Federal, State and Local Governments). A sectoral representation of the recent public expenditure trends in Nigeria for the three tiers of government is shown in Figure 1, comparing social and community services, and in Figure 2 for transfers. It is normal that the combined spending by all States is much higher than that of the Federal and Local Governments for social and community services. What is surprising is the low levels of spending by the local governments, which are ordinarily responsible for primary education as well as primary health care.

---

[1]   The OECD (2011) reports that for each year between 1985 and 2005, fiscal policy reduced the Gini Coefficient in 25 OECD member counties by an average of around 15 percentage points. In contrast, as Bastalgi et al. (2012) note, low transfers greatly limit the redistributive impact of fiscal policy in developing economies.

Figure 1:   Public expenditure trend in Nigeria (social and community services 2009-2013, Naira' Billion)

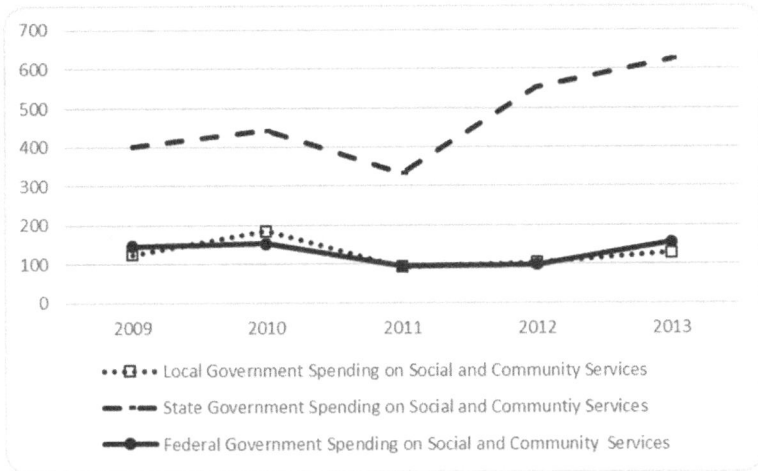

Source: Computed from Central Bank of Nigeria Economic Report, 2013

While State governments have a jump in spending on social and community services between 2009 and 2013 compared to the Federal and Local Governments, the reverse is the case for the expenditures on transfers.

Figure 2:   Public expenditure trend in Nigeria (transfers 2009-2013, Naira' Billion)

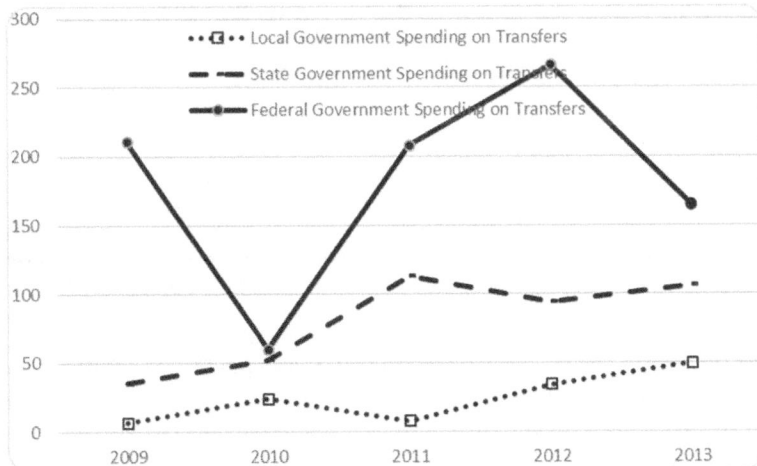

Source: Computed from Central Bank of Nigeria Economic Report, 2013

In Tables 3 and 4, we specifically examine recent public spending on education and health (for both Federal and State governments), which are significant determinants of an individual's earning potential and thus income redistribution capacity. It is clear that capital expenditures on both education and health are on the decline for both Federal and State governments but the recurrent expenditures for the Federal level increased only marginally.

Table 3:   Education and health expenditure for Federal and State Governments 2009-2013 (% of total capital expenditures)

	2009	2010	2011	2012	2013
Education					
Federal	3.7	9.9	3.8	5.4	3.1
State	7.2	6.6	5.9	6.6	6.6
Health					
Federal	4.5	3.9	4.3	5.1	2.9
State	5.6	4.2	3.1	4.3	4.3

Table 4:   Education and health expenditure for Federal and State Governments 2009-2013 (% of total recurrent expenditures)

	2009	2010	2011	2012	2013
Education					
Federal	6.4	5.4	10.1	10.4	10.5
State	9.8	9.3	6.3	8.5	8.5
Health					
Federal	4.2	3.1	6.9	5.9	4.8
State	5.4	4.5	3.6	4.5	4.5

Source (for tables 3 and 4): Computed from Central Bank of Nigeria Economic Report, 2013

Apart from the low size and scale of these public expenditures on education and health, the critical question is; who really benefits from it — the poor and young, or the rich and elderly? Evidence from Davoodi et al. (2010) and ADB (2014) indicate that aggregate spending on education and health care has been regressive in developing countries, with the lowest 40 percent of the population receiving less than 40 percent of the benefits. This is because some components are regressive. While primary education can be progressive, benefit from total education spending is dominated by the regressive nature of secondary and tertiary education.

Child poverty trends in Nigeria

There are recent measures of child poverty in Nigeria computed mainly using the multiple dimension deprivation approach and lately a modified approach by UNICEF (Multiple Overlapping Deprivation Analysis-MODA). These include: Gordon et al. (2003); UNICEF (2009); Global Study on Child Poverty and Disparities (based on 2007 Nigeria MICS); Adeoti and Olufemi (2012), based on the NPC (2008) Nigeria Demographic and Health Survey-NDHS; Rufai et al. (2016), based on the NPC (2013) NDHS; and Cid Martinez (Chapter 4 in this volume).

Table 5:   Change in prevalence of severe child deprivations in Nigeria (2000 survey and 2007 MICS)

	Percent of children deprived in 2000	Percent prevalence of 'severe' child deprivation in 2007	Percentage change in 2007 from 2000
Shelter	45	50	+11.1
Sanitation	26	28	+7.7
Water	44	37	-15.9
Information	35	18	-48.6
Food	16	24	+50.0
Education	22	30	+36.4
Health	40	27	-32.5

Source: 2000 data is taken from Gordon et al. (2003) Child Poverty in the Developing World. 2007 data is taken from UNICEF (2007) Global Study on Child Poverty and Disparities

Using data from two such sources and comparing two time periods (Table 5), it is clear that while the prevalence of child deprivation increased for shelter, sanitation, food and education between 2000 and 2007, it decreased for water, information and health. Based on the 2007 data, there seems to be huge disparities across Nigerian geopolitical zones especially for education, health and shelter (Table 6). On average the southern regions (South-East, South-South and South-West) have less severe child deprivations than the northern regions (North-Central,

North-East and North-West). For sanitation and water however, the North East and North West regions look better than the southern regions.

Table 6: Prevalence of seven severe child deprivations by region (percent) using 2007 MICS

	Shelter	Sanitation	Water	Information	Food	Education	Health
North Central	33.91	54.63	53.79	21.41	28.47	11.26	18.97
North East	64.03	22.91	58.17	38.30	27.18	77.95	66.17
North West	57.96	17.99	25.17	19.65	35.16	47.99	60.12
South East	28.35	24.78	58.86	15.90	25.13	2.22	10.19
South-South	29.22	21.94	54.21	26.87	19.33	2.13	15.21
South West	21.49	57.67	46.79	25.87	23.12	1.30	8.56

Source: UNICEF Global Study on Child Poverty and Disparities

A critical question is therefore whether the scale of severe child deprivation (in education and health for instance) is affected by the average benefit children derive from government spending on health and education? Can this lower prevalence of child deprivations in education and health for the South-East, South-South and South-West regions be attributed to the higher benefits by children from public expenditure in education and health? This is the focus of the next sections.

BENEFIT INCIDENCE ANALYSIS (BIA) OF PUBLIC SPENDING ON EDUCATION AND HEALTH IN NIGERIA

In calculating the benefit incidence of public spending on education, we adopt a method similar to Demery (2000), Davoodi et al. (2003), Amakom (2013), and Asogwa (2015) which includes[2];

a) Identification of households that benefited from public service in education and health care based on the 2009/2010 NLSS.

b) Ranking all households (recipients and non-recipients alike) by level of welfare (total household consumption per capita).

---

[2] The widely used method of benefit incidence analysis used in this study is explained in Appendix 1 at the end of this chapter.

c) Aggregating individuals/households into five income quintiles using the NLSS and further into regions, States, age cohorts.

d) Accounting for households' direct spending on education or health (such as out-of-pocket expenditures to gain access to subsidized government services). This is the value on services received.

e) Estimating unit cost of providing education defined as total government spending on education or health (net of out-of-pocket expenses and cost recovery fees by users) divided by the total number of users of the service (for example, total primary education spending per primary enrolment).

f) Defining the average benefit from government spending on education or health as the average unit cost of providing education or health as computed in (e) above.

We focus only on public expenditure on education and health (primary, secondary and tertiary) and apply the traditional Benefit Incidence Analysis methodology described in Appendix 1 (at the end of this chapter) to first compute the benefits across five income groups (poorest, poor, average, rich and richest).

Two types of data are necessary for benefit incidence analysis: household-level data on participation in public goods or services, and information on the unit costs (or benefits) of those services. For the first type of data on household utilization of public services, we use the 2009/2010 Harmonized NLSS conducted by the National Bureau of Statistics. The welfare approach component of the survey (Part A) was conducted in 77,400 households which is an average of one hundred households per Local Government area. The consumption/expenditure component (Part B) was conducted on 38,700 households that are subset of the 77,400 households selected for Part A and covered 50 households per Local Government area.

The principal questionnaire used for the 2009/10 NLSS covered a wide scope of data including: demography; health; fertility behaviour; education; training; employment; time use; housing condition; social capital; agriculture; household income; consumption; and expenditure. Additional information obtained by the survey include: household assets; production and consumption from own produce; access to basic facilities; household expenditures on food and non-food items; expenditures and revenues from non-farm enterprises; expenditure on key services; and transfer payments (out and in transfers). The health and education questionnaire included questions on the use of health facilities, and on enrolment in schools at all levels.

For the second type of data required for benefit incidence analysis (i.e. information on the unit cost of service provision), we use data on expenditures on education and health care across States sourced from Central Bank of Nigeria Publications and State reports. We also obtain additional information from some sector-based reports. For education, we also use the Nigerian Education Data (NED) survey implemented by the National Population Commission (NPC, 2010) in collaboration with the Federal Ministry of Education and with data on Household Expenditure on schooling during the 2009-2010 school year. The NED survey contained information on per pupil household expenditure on primary and secondary school for each income quintile, as well as the school attendance for each quintile for each State. For healthcare, we obtain additional information from National Health Accounts of Nigeria. With both sets of data, we can reliably compute the unit subsidy in education in 2010 for all States, and Federal (dividing government expenditures in 2010 by enrolment figures). We can also calculate the per user unit subsidy for health services (by dividing government expenditures with utilization of health services).

RESULTS AND DISCUSSION

Benefit incidence across household income groups

The various income groups (poorest to richest) are based on the 2009/10 NLSS using the mean per capita household expenditure approach, which the National Bureau of Statistics preferred for purposes of consistency with the 2003/2004 NLSS rather than the adult equivalent approach. The results are presented in Table 7 for education and Table 8 for health.

Education

Table 7:   Benefit incidence of public spending on primary, secondary and tertiary education in Nigeria using NLSS 2009/2010 (poorest to richest in Nigerian Currency - Naira)

		1 (poorest)	2 (poor)	3 (average)	4 (rich)	5 (richest)
Primary Education	Share (in Naira)	6346	5341	4879	3457	2841
	Comment	Absolutely Progressive				
Secondary Education	Share (in Naira)	4442	4500	4587	4599	4603
	Comment	Mildly Regressive				
Tertiary Education	Share (in Naira)		10345	14356	19123	21675
	Comment	Absolutely Regressive				

Source: Authors computation from NBS NLSS 2009/2010

The results in Table 7 show that benefit incidence was absolutely progressive for primary education, mildly regressive for secondary education but absolutely regressive for tertiary education. The differences in share of primary education is high to the advantage of the poorest as compared to the other quintiles. This pro-poor targeting of primary education spending has been noted in several other African countries, as spending on primary education is often regarded as an important tool for ensuring universal access to a formal education system. The preference of private primary schools by the average, rich and richest income quintiles may have also increased the benefits share for the poorest, given that all government expenditures on public primary education accrue the poor who attend such schools.

For secondary education, the poorest seem to benefit less, even though the differences are only mild. The results show that benefit incidence is mildly regressive and not pro-poor, since it appears that the distribution is more equitable across all income groups when compared to primary education. For tertiary education, the richest benefit much more than other quintiles. This finding corroborates some earlier studies which show that spending on secondary education and tertiary education primarily benefits the non-poor and there is strong evidence of middle-class capture.

We compare the benefit incidence results based on the 2003/2004 NLSS (Amakom, 2013; and Alabi, 2010—see Appendix 2) with this study using 2009/2010 NLSS (Table 7). An a priori expectation is that benefit incidence should improve with the latest data set considering the changes in educational characteristics between the two time periods. For instance, while the number of public primary and secondary schools increased between 2005 and 2009, the total enrolment for both categories declined within the same period[3]. The large decreases in enrolment is partly attributed to the increases in enrolment in private secondary schools and also the withdrawal of free secondary education policy in many States in Nigeria.

The changes in the incidence of spending between 2004 and 2010 show that secondary education has moved from being "mildly progressive in 2004" to "mildly regressive in 2010" considering the share of total expenditures that each group received based on the 2004 and 2010 NLSS. The reasons for the stronger benefit incidence for primary education may be related to the abolition of primary school fees in many more States prior to and after the 2007 elections. In addition, with the intervention of the Universal Basic Education Scheme in building additional public schools, the mean walking time to the nearest primary school reduced in 2010 as compared to 2004. By contrast, public expenditures on tertiary education is absolutely regressive in 2010 and appears to have become even more pro-rich in 2010 compared to 2004. It is important to note that the benefit incidence for secondary education moved from mildly progressive in the 2003/2004 NLSS (Amakom, 2013) to mildly regressive using the 2009/2010 NLSS.

Health

The benefit incidence for public spending on health care shows that it is mildly progressive for primary healthcare but mildly regressive for secondary healthcare (Table 8). This is similar to Amakom's study using

---

[3]   The number of public primary schools increased from 60,189 in 2005 to 68,715 in 2009, but the total enrollment declined from 22,115,432 in 2005 to 18,818,544 in 2009. The number of public secondary schools also increased from 10,913 in 2005 to 18,238 in 2009 but the enrollment also declined from 6,279,462 in 2005 to 2,505,473 in 2009 (NBS, 2010).

the 2003/2004 NLSS. In Alabi's study using 2003/2004 NLSS, the benefit incidence is mildly regressive for vaccination, pre-natal consultation and postnatal consultation showing that the richest quintiles benefited more than the poorest quintiles. Some authors argue that the poor in Nigeria evade secondary healthcare citing reasons as distance and request for registration.[4]

Table 8:   Benefit incidence of public spending on primary and secondary healthcare in Nigeria using NLSS 2009/2010 (poorest to richest in Nigerian Currency - Naira)

		1 (poorest)	2 (poor)	3 (average)	4 (rich)	5 (richest)
Primary Healthcare	Share (in Naira)	1968	1783	1657	1555	1457
	Comment	Mildly Progressive				
Secondary Healthcare	Share (in Naira)	1579	1620	2120	2135	2235
	Comment	Mildly Regressive				

Source: Authors computation from NBS NLSS 2009/2010

Benefit incidence across household income groups by age cohorts

How are different age groups affected by public spending on education and health? Sometimes, there are just claims that either the young or the old are receiving too much or too little from government expenditure at any point in time. The fact is that household income groups are not categorized based on children, but rather on the whole population; this will sometimes bias results, especially for primary education and primary health care with most results looking progressive. As such, it will be good to access how the different age groups benefit even within the different income groups. This is the key for this research, given that our main interest in this study is to find out how children benefit from public spending. An important step therefore is to estimate the age profiles of

---

[4]   Most secondary health care facilities including the "referral clinics" are located in urban areas. As such poor households in the rural areas complain of travelling distances from their rural residences to the urban areas and also the "patient user registration cost" usually charged by the secondary health care facilities.

public expenditures on education and health care which will enable us to compare the child benefits from public spending on education and health with the child poverty trend.

Recent attempts at estimating the benefit incidence of public transfers across age cohorts (Turra et al., 2011; Shen and Lee, 2014) follow the Generational Accounting Framework of Auerbach, Kotlikoff and Leibfritz (1999). In the People's Republic of China, Shen and Lee (2014) report that total public spending favoured elderly people as spending per person 65 years and older was twice that per child younger than 19.

In order to estimate the age profile of public education consumption in Nigeria, we combine data from the NED survey 2010 and the Federal Ministry of Education Report of Sub-National Education Financing, 2010 to get the cost per student enrolled by level of education, and the 2009/2010 NLSS to estimate the age-specific enrolment rates education (primary and secondary) and for each household group. The NED survey shows the age specific enrolment rates for each income group. It is clear that enrolment in education increases with income group. Among children aged 5-10, only about 30 percent are currently enrolled for the poorest quintiles, as compared to more than 70 percent for the richest quintiles.

Education

We estimate the benefit incidence of public spending on education for the different age cohorts across the five income groups. The question we seek to answer is first whether younger children benefit more than older ones in the combined education public spending; and second, whether children of the poorest quintile benefit more than the children of the richest quintile in public education spending.

Figure 3:   Benefit incidence for education to different age groups by income quintile

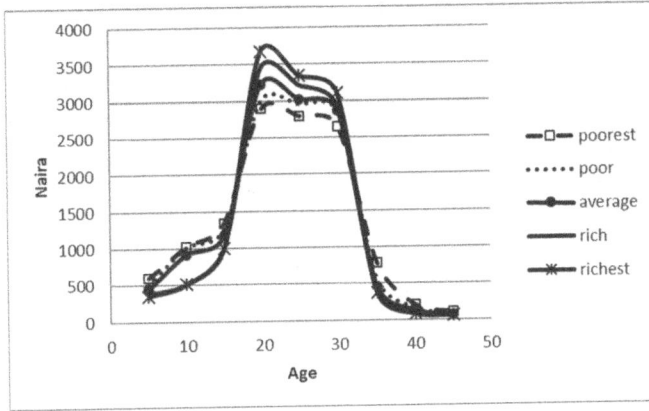

From Figure 3, it is clear that most of the benefits for public spending on education go to ages 20-25, more than for ages 5-15. At this age cohort 20-25, the richest quintiles benefit more. For early ages 5-15, children in the lower income groups benefit more than the higher income groups, but the bulk of education spending accrue to ages 20-25 where the richer income group dominates. This finding suggests that public education spending may be progressive at the early ages (5-15) but becomes regressive at later ages (20-25) where the rich benefit and the greater resources accrue to this age group. There may be several reasons for this finding. First, many poor households have children aged 5-15 attending primary school. The 2010 NED survey shows that 30 percent of 14-year-old male children attend primary school, while 24 percent of 14-year-old female children attend primary school and most of the over-age pupils in primary school are from the lowest economic quintile. The fact that the average benefit incidence for public spending on education peaks at age 20 can be either as a result of delayed enrolment rates, or more resources being allocated to secondary education (and higher) where the number of pupils are still limited and in favour of higher income quintiles. The 2010 NED survey also shows that the number of pupils enrolled in school declines gradually between ages 20 to 25. Generally, the average benefit incidence when education spending is combined is regressive in favour of the rich and the middle age children, as compared to being progressive when primary education spending alone is considered.

Health

Estimating the age profile for public health care participation is more difficult than that of education participation since health care usage is not reported by age cohorts, unlike the education enrolment. We therefore adopt a proxy for age participation/usage in healthcare. This is again similar to the approach used in China by Shen and Lee (2014) requiring calculating the age profile of out-of-pocket medical expenditures. The NLSS 2010 has information on the distribution of household out-of-pocket health expenditure by geo-political zone, household head and age. We use out-of-pocket expenditures for each age group as a substitute for utilization rates with the assumption that medical expenditures for each age group are proportional to utilization rates and thus age profile of public health consumption. In several cases, the age profile of reimbursed health consumption is the same as the age profile of out-of-pocket medical expenditures.

Figure 4:   Benefit incidence for healthcare to different age groups by income quintile

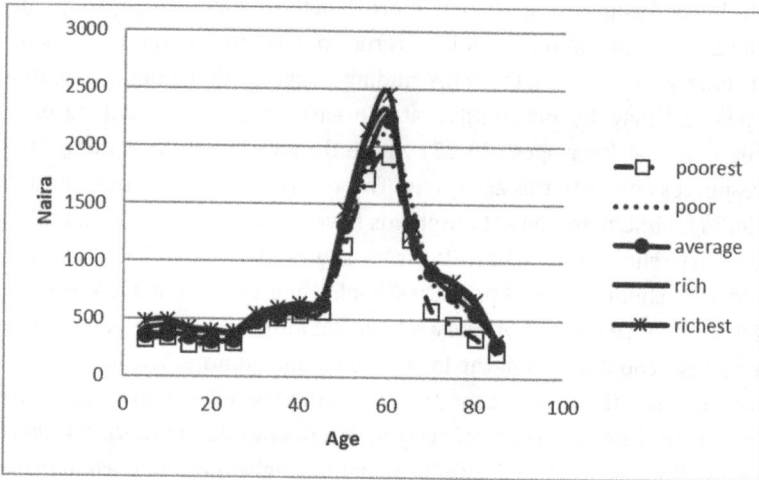

There are two things easily noticeable in Figure 4. First, the benefits rise sharply at around age 55 but also declines sharply around age 65. Second, children aged 5-10 benefit slightly more than children around 15-20. Moreover, the fact that the richest quintile seems to dominate the other quintiles in the size of benefit except at ages 65-70 corroborates earlier findings of regressive incidence especially for secondary and tertiary healthcare in Nigeria. The somewhat higher benefit for ages 5-10 may be attributed to the larger amount of subsidized health care such as vaccinations for these age group. There may also be possible explanations for the larger benefits received by the richest quintiles at this early age cohort. Alabi (2010), notes that while 51 percent of the children from the richest quintile participated in vaccination, only 44 percent of eligible children from the poorest quintiles participated in vaccination programmes. The reasons for non-participation in vaccine according to NBS (2004) relate to ignorance about the vaccination, distance of vaccination centre, short supply of vaccines and cost. This finding, which is similar to Chen and Lee (2014) for China, contrasts with Turra et al. (2011) finding in Brazil and Chile, which suggest that the poor make intensive use of public healthcare services, more than the rich at all ages, simply because the rich are usually inclined to use the private health services.

Benefit incidence by regions

We estimate how benefits of education and health spending are distributed within each of the six regions in Nigeria. Even though the regions are not autonomous financial authority zones, the distribution of benefits across them has often generated huge political interest. A very useful analysis will be to have the distribution of benefits assessed across the 36 States in Nigeria, to enable a comparison with the child poverty rates across these States. This would however require massive data sets and additional space for analysis. As such, we restrict ourselves to the benefit incidence analysis for the six regions (North Central, North East, North West, South East, South-South, and South West).[5] The NLSS also publishes the poverty and inequality data across the six regions as well as the respective states in Nigeria. In most regions, there is an average of six states which often have similar characteristics.

Appendix 3 shows the results of the benefit incidence on education and health care for the different regions based on the NLSS 2009/10. As expected, primary education is still progressive in all the regions with the

---

[5]   In Amakom's (2013) study using the 2003/2004 NLSS, the results of the benefit incidence analysis for the States are similar to the ones for computed for their respective regions.

poorer quintiles receiving larger average shares in Naira as compared to the richer quintiles. Secondary education is still mildly regressive with the richest quintiles benefitting more than the poorest quintiles. On the regional disparities, for primary education, the South West leads in terms of average benefit size followed by the South-South and South East respectively. For secondary education, the South West also leads followed by the South-South and the South East respectively. This pattern of regional disparities was also observed in Alabi (2010) and Amakom (2013), using the previous NLSS (2003/2004). The average benefit for primary healthcare is mildly progressive for most of the regions with the poorer quintiles benefitting more than the richer quintiles. In secondary healthcare, the benefits are mildly regressive, with the richer quintiles benefitting more than the poorer quintiles. Even though the average benefits for the quintiles within the regions seems identical, the South-South leads for primary health care, while the South West leads for secondary health care.

Additionally, we estimate the age profiles of public expenditures benefits across regions using data from NLSS 2009/10 into regions. The age profile for education beneficiaries in each region is derived from the age-specific enrolment rates. Within the regions, there are differences in both total enrolments and age-specific enrolment status. The Southern zone (South East, South West and South-South) have more people enrolled in each age group than the Northern zones, but pupil concentration for the Northern zone (North East, North West and North Central) is less for ages 0-5 and 6-10, which may be an indication of over-age pupils in the northern primary schools. We also calculate the age profile of health beneficiaries using as proxy — the out-of-pocket health expenditures which is available in the 2009/2010 NLSS by geo-political zone and for age groups. The mean distribution of out-of-pocket health expenditures from the 2009/10 NLSS shows that the South East has the highest, which is even double that of the third zone (North East).

The results in appendix 3 show that for combined public education spending, age cohorts 0-5 and 6-10 benefited somewhat closely to age cohorts 11-15, 16-20 and 20-25 in South West, while age cohorts 16-20 and 21-25 benefitted more in other regions. The size of the benefit for ages 16-20 and 21-25 is sometimes twice that for the others.

For health care spending, appendix 3 also show that adults at ages 56-60 and 61- 65 have higher average benefits than the other age groups, but children at 0-5 still benefit more than age cohorts 6-10, 11-15 and 16-20 for most of the regions. The average benefit for ages 5-10 and 11-15 is higher for the southern states than the northern states.

SUMMARY

The objective of this chapter is to analyse how fiscal policy, measured as government spending on education and health, affects children's poverty status in Nigeria. We use the standard non-behavioural benefit-incidence method which adapts to readily available and less rigorous data requirements and enables an isolation of who really benefits amongst the different groups and stratification (income, gender, age, residence, location etc.). We combine household data based on the latest Nigerian Living Standards Survey – NLSS 2009/10 – with Federal and State level expenditure data. Since our main interest is on the impact of education and health spending on children, then the stratification of the household beneficiaries of education and health spending in the different age cohorts is particularly important, despite the technical challenges we faced.

Several interesting results emerge from the analysis of both trend and benefit incidence of public expenditure on education and health. In terms of trend, it is clear that public annual capital expenditures on social and community services (education, health, and social welfare) now lag behind other sectors (up to 2014). Also, capital expenditures on both education and health for the Federal and State governments have been on the decline.

In terms of the benefit incidence, it is clear from the analysis that the poorer quintiles benefit more than the richer quintiles in both primary education and primary healthcare (mildly progressive). However, the richer quintiles benefit more than the poorer quintiles in secondary education and health care (mildly progressive). When education spending is combined (primary plus secondary) and health care spending is combined (primary plus secondary), the richer quintiles get the larger size of benefits. For benefit distribution across age groups, it is clear that most of the benefits for public spending on education go to ages 20-25 which is sometimes twice the average benefits for ages 5-15. For health care, the benefits are also unevenly distributed, with ages 50-60 dominating. Even though, there appears to be a fair distribution of benefit for ages 5-30, the age cohort 5-10 have marginal advantage over ages 11-15 and 16 to 20.

These results have important implications for child poverty rates given the close linkage between differences in child deprivation across the regions especially in education and health, and the computed average benefit incidence on education and health spending for age cohorts 5-10, 11-15 and 16-20. The key policy recommendation is that improving the average benefit of public spending on education and health by perhaps fiscal expansion and better targeting can reduce severe child deprivation and poverty.

REFERENCES

Adeoti A and P. Olufemi (2012) 'Determinants of Child Poverty in Rural Nigeria: A Multidimensional Approach' *Global Journal of Human Social Science, Arts and Humanities*, Vol 12. No 12

Alabi R.A (2010) 'Marginal Benefit Incidence Analysis of Public Spending in Nigeria' PEP Research Paper, PMMA1.

Amakom U (2013) Public Spending and Poverty Reduction in Nigeria: A Benefit Incidence Analysis in Education and Health. AERC Research Paper 254, Nairobi.

Anyafo A.M.O (1996) Public Finance in a Developing Economy: The Nigerian Case. UNEC Publications, Enugu.

Asian Development Bank –ADB (2014) 'Fiscal Policy for Inclusive Growth' Outlook for 2014,

Asogwa R.C (2015) 'Inclusive Growth Impact of recent Fiscal Policy Trends in Nigeria: An Incidence Analysis' Conference Paper, Nigerian Economic Society, 2015, Abuja.

Atkinson A. B (1995) Incomes and the Welfare State. Cambridge University Press, UK.

Auerbach A. J, L. Kotlikoff and W. Leibriftz (1999) Generational Accounting around the World. Chicago: The University of Chicago Press.

Barrientos A., J Byrne, J Villa and P Piers (2013) 'Social Transfers and Child Protection' Working Paper 2013-05, UNICEF Office of Research, Florence. 9-38

Barrientos A and J Dejong (2006) 'Reducing Child Poverty with Cash Transfers: A sure thing? Development Policy Review, 24:537-552

Bastalgi F, D Coady and S. Gupta (2012) Income Inequality and Fiscal Policy. IMF Discussion Note SDN/12/08.

Central Bank of Nigeria- CBN (1991) Statistical Bulletin, 1991

Central Bank of Nigeria- CBN (2013) Statistical Bulletin, 2013

Central Bank of Nigeria –CBN Economic Report, 2013

Coady D (2010) 'The Distributional Impacts of Indirect Tax and Public Policy Reforms: A Review of Methods and Empirical Evidence' IMF Review of Methodology and Selected Evidence' IMF

Davoodi H.R, E Tiongson and S. Asawanuchit (2003) 'How useful are Benefit Incidence Analyses of Public Education and Health Spending? IMF Working Paper WP/03/227

Del Carpio X.V and K Macours (2010) 'Impact of Conditional Cash Transfers on Child Labour Allocation in Nicaragua' Research in Labour Economics, Volume 31:259-295

Demery. L (2000) 'Benefit Incidence: A Practitioners Guide' Poverty and Social Development Group, Africa Region, World Bank.

Eurostat (2010) Combating Poverty and Social Exclusion: A Statistical portrait of the European Union.

Eurostat Statistical Books, Luxembourg

EU Task Force (2008) 'Child Poverty and Child Well-being in the EU' Brussels: European Commission.

Gabos A. (2010) 'Determinants of Child Poverty and Policy Responses in the European Union' Conference on Social Policy and the Global Crisis: Budapest September, 2010.

Gordon D, Nandy S, Pantazis C, Pemberton S and Townsend P (2003) 'The Distribution of Child Poverty in the Developing World' University of Bristol.

Heltherg, R, K. Simler and F. Tarp (2003) "Public Spending and Poverty in Mozambique" IFPR FCNDP Discussion Paper, No 167.

Kruse I, M Pradhan and R. Sparrow (2003) 'Marginal Benefit Incidence of Public Spending: Evidence from Indonesian sub-national data' HEFPA Working Paper, Rotterdam.

Levine S, S van der Berg and Derek Yu (2009) 'Measuring the Impact of Social Cash Transfers on Poverty and Inequality in Namibia' Development Southern Africa 14/4

Lanjouw P and M. Ravallion (1999) 'Benefit Incidence, Public Spending Reforms and the Timing of Programme Capture' World Bank Economic Review, Vol 13 pp 257-73.

Longford N.T and C. Nicodemo (2010) 'The Contribution of Social Transfers to the Reduction of Poverty' IZA Discussion Paper Series No 5223

Makhalima J L, M. B Sekatane and S. H Dunga (2014) 'Determinants of Child Poverty in a South African Township: A Case of Boipatang Township' Mediterranean Journal of Social Sciences, Vol 5 No, 1 235-241.

Meerman J (1979) Public Expenditures in Malaysia: Who Benefits and Why? New York: Oxford University Press for the World Bank.

National Bureau of Statistics, (NBS), Nigeria (2004) NLSS, and Poverty Profile, 2003/2004

National Bureau of Statistics, (NBS), Nigeria (2010) NLSS and Poverty Profile, 2009/2010

National Population Commission-NPC (2008) 'Nigeria Demographic and Health Survey-2008

National Population Commission-NPC (2010) 'Nigeria Education Data-NED Survey, Abuja.

National Population Commission-NPC (2013) 'Nigeria Demographic and Health Survey-2013

Organization for Economic Cooperation and Development –OECD (2011) 'An Overview of Growing Income Inequalities in OECD Countries: Main findings, 'divided we start, why inequality keeps rises' Paris

Okpukpara C. B, Chine P, Uguru F.N, Chukwuone N (2006) 'Child Welfare and Poverty in Nigeria' PEP Disseminations Workshop, Addis Ababa, October 2006.

Papatheodorou, C, S. Papanastasiou and M. Petmesidou, (2016) "Child Poverty and Intergenerational Poverty Transmission in the EU: Assessing the Impact of Social Protection and Labour Market Institutions", in Child Poverty, Youth (Un)Employment, and Social Inclusion, edited by Maria Petmesidou, Enrique Delamonica, Christos Papatheodorou, and Aldrie Henry-Lee (Ibidem-Verlag, Suttgart, 2016)

Ravallion M (1999) 'Is More Targeting Consistent with less Spending?' International Tax and Public Finance' Vol 6. Pp 411-19.

Rufai A.M, Yusuf S. A, Awoyemi TT, Salman K.K and Oyekale A.S (2016) 'Child Poverty in Rural Nigeria' Journal of Poverty, Investment and Development' Vol 20: 40 - 51.

Selowsky M (1979) Who Benefits from Government Expenditure? A Case study of Columbia. New York: Oxford University Press.

Shen Ke and Lee Sang-Hyop (2014) Benefit Incidence of Public Transfers: Evidence from the People Republic of China. Manila: Asian Development Bank.

Turra C. M, M Holz and D Cotlear (2011) 'Who Benefits from Public Transfers? Incidence Across Income Groups and Across Generations in Brazil and Chile' in D. Cotlear ed. Population Aging in Latin America Ready? Washington DC World Bank

Younger S.D (2001) 'The Relative Progressivity of Social Services in Ecuador' Public Finance Review, vol 27, No 3 PP. 310-352.

UNDP (2016) 'Human Security and Human Development in Nigeria' NHDR, Nigeria.

UNICEF (2007) 'National Report, Nigeria- Global Study on Child Poverty and Disparities'

UNICEF (2009) 'Child Poverty: A Role for Cash Transfers? West and Central Africa. Report 3 S van de Walle, D and K. Nead (1995) Public Spending and the Poor: Theory and Evidence. Baltimore Md USA John Hopkins University Press

APPENDIX 1: METHOD OF BENEFIT INCIDENCE ANALYSIS

The methodology of Benefit Incidence Analysis (BIA) was first introduced in two separate studies focused on developing countries: Selowsky (1979) for Colombia and Meerman (1979) for Malaysia. The two studies have been replicated in various country case studies, sometimes involving several refinements of the original methodology. There are excellent surveys on the Benefit Incidence Analysis by Demery (2000) and Younger (2001). In this study, we estimate the average benefit using the non-behavioural social benefit incidence approach (van de Walle and Nead, 1995). This means that data on costs of service provision are combined with user information to assess how costs are distributed among the various population subgroups. The main advantage of the non-behavioural benefit incidence method is its simplicity and the relatively modest data requirements. A potential problem occurs when quality of the service varies systematically with the level of welfare. For instance, if poorer individuals receive lower quality services, the results will be biased in the direction of finding progressive results (Heltberg et al., 2003). This applies to the case of Nigeria, where quality of public service delivery often varies extensively across the regions and States. We however address this potential problem as in other studies by ensuring that data for unit costs of service provision are as disaggregated as possible. Some other authors, however, argue in favour of marginal benefit incidence incorporating behavioural responses to changes in public spending (Lanjouv and Ravallion, 1999; Ravallion, 1999; Kruse et al., 2003).

Two recent studies in Nigeria have tested both approaches. Alabi (2010) used the marginal benefit incidence approach, while Amakom (2011) used the average benefit incidence approach, but with the same Nigerian Living Standard Survey (NLSS) 2003/2004 data set. Both studies show interesting and somewhat similar results.

Following Demery (2000) and others, we focus on government spending on social sector (education and health), which can be formally written as:

$$X_1 \equiv E_{1p} [S_p/E_p] + E_{1s}[S_s/E_s] + E_{1t}[S_t/E_t], \text{------}(1)$$

Where X_1 is the amount of the education or health spending that benefits group 1. S and E refer respectively to the government spending on education or health and the number of people expected to benefit from them (school enrolments for education and users of health facility for health), and the subscripts p, s and t denote the level of education or health service (primary, secondary and tertiary, respectively).

The benefit incidence of total education spending accruing to group 1 is given by the number of primary enrolments from group (E_{1p}) times the unit cost of a primary schooling [Sp/Ep], plus the number of secondary enrolments times the secondary unit cost, plus the number of tertiary enrolments times the unit cost of tertiary education. Similarly, the benefit incidence of total health spending accruing to group 1 is given by the number of users of primary health care from group (E_{1p}) times the unit cost of a primary healthcare [Sp/Ep], plus the number of users of secondary healthcare times the secondary healthcare unit cost, plus the number of users of tertiary healthcare times the unit cost of providing tertiary healthcare.

This can easily be re-written as:

$$X_j \equiv \sum_{i=1}^{3} E_{ij} \frac{S_i}{E_i} \equiv \sum_{i=1}^{3} \frac{E_{ij}}{E_i} S_i \text{--------(2)}$$

Where:

- X_j is the benefit incidence of spending on education or healthcare to group j
- E_{ij} is the number of enrollments from group j at education level i or users from group j at healthcare i
- E_i is the total number of enrollments at level i and number of users of health facilities at level i
- S_i is the net spending by the government on education or health at level I (i=1to 3 representing primary, secondary and tertiary)
- (S_i/E_i) is the mean (average) unit subsidy of an enrollment at education level i or unit spending of usage of a health facility at a health level i.

The share of total education spending to group j (Xj) is then;

$$X_j \equiv \sum_{i=1}^{3} \frac{E_{ij}}{E_i} \left(\frac{S_i}{S} \right) \equiv \sum_{i=1}^{3} e_{ij} s_i \; \text{-------} \; (3)$$

Equation 3 depends on two determinants:

- The eij's which are the shares of the group in total service (enrolments in education and users of health facilities). These reflect household behavior.
- The si, which is the share of public spending across the different types of service, reflecting government behavior.

In view of the usual differences across the States and regions, this disaggregation is further incorporated in equation 4 below:

$$X_j \equiv \sum_{k=1}^{n} \sum_{i=1}^{3} \frac{E_{ijk}}{E_i} \left(\frac{S_{ik}}{S} \right) \equiv \sum_{k=1}^{n} \sum_{i=1}^{3} e_{ijk} s_{ik}$$
$$\text{-------} \; (4)$$

I's is levels of education or health, j's for the different quintiles and k's for the disaggregated levels (region, state, age).

APPENDIX 2: BENEFIT INCIDENCE RESULTS USING NL22 2003/2004 FOR EDUCATION

Benefit incidence of public spending on primary and secondary education in Nigeria (Alabi's Study using NLSS 2003/2004)

Quintile		1 (poorest)	2 (poor)	3 (average)	4 (rich)	5 (richest)
Primary Education	Share participation	0.596	0.723	0.789	0.854	0.773
	Share by group	0.154	0.187	0.204	0.221	0.234
	Comment	Regressive				
Secondary Education	Share participation	0.393	0.523	0.565	0.685	0.717
	Share by group	0.136	0.182	0.196	0.238	0.249
	Comment	Regressive				

Benefit incidence of public spending on primary, secondary and tertiary
education in Nigeria (Amakom's Study using NLSS 2003/2004)

		1 (poorest)	2 (poor)	3 (average)	4 (rich)	5 (richest)
Primary Education	Share (Nigerian Naira)	3707	3465	2925	2413	2095
	Comment	Absolutely Progressive				
Secondary Education	Share (Nigerian Naira)	3806	3856	4020	3804	3789
	Comment	Mildly Progressive.				
Tertiary Education	Share (Nigerian Naira)	8585	9159	10249	11263	11525
	Comment	Absolutely Regressive				

APPENDIX 3: BENEFIT INCIDENCE ON EDUCATION AND HEALTH BY REGIONS AND ACROSS INCOME GROUPS (NIGERIAN NAIRA)

Primary education

Region	Poorest	Poor	Average	Rich	Richest
North Central	1214	1089	1054	1008	976
North East	1012	1011	1005	985	935
North West	1089	1023	1009	985	954
South East	1300	1254	1200	1103	1084
South West	1535	1407	1383	1276	1134
South-South	1421	1317	1289	1143	1076

Secondary education

Region	Poorest	Poor	Average	Rich	Richest
North Central	1103	1643	2011	2093	2114
North East	878	1011	1689	1764	1806
North West	983	1203	1713	1838	1915
South East	1008	1537	1984	2013	2089
South West	1726	1910	2102	2412	2562
South-South	1331	1802	2089	2264	2314

Primary health care

Region	Poorest	Poor	Average	Rich	Richest
North Central	1341	1210	1073	1000	985
North East	1005	895	825	757	901
North West	1101	985	910	898	876
South East	1211	1110	1005	987	965
South West	1523	1412	1165	1089	1015
South-South	1611	1576	1281	1179	1108

Secondary health care

Region	Poorest	Poor	Average	Rich	Richest
North Central	1076	1421	1765	1985	2005
North East	735	1100	1210	1411	1535
North West	811	1221	1510	1723	1875
South East	1325	1675	1896	2005	2021
South West	1412	1982	2011	2089	2431
South-South	1011	1372	1652	1896	1985

APPENDIX 4: BENEFIT INCIDENCE ON EDUCATION AND HEALTH BY REGIONS AND ACROSS AGE GROUPS

Education

Ages	North Central (Naira)	North East (Naira)	North West (Naira)	South East (Naira)	South West (Naira)	South-South (Naira)
0-5	423	210	332	645	1251	754
6-10	663	340	495	1100	1291	1243
11-15	794	416	562	1320	1421	1368
16-20	1342	724	835	1542	1765	1610
21-25	1465	814	910	1612	1982	1725
26-30	541	421	475	765	1011	976
31-35	360	205	310	545	825	643
36-40	21	13	15	25	41	32
41-45	11	10	15	16	30	13

Health care

Ages	North Central (Naira)	North East (Naira)	North West (Naira)	South East (Naira)	South West (Naira)	South-South (Naira)
0-5	347	240	260	508	700	628
6-10	298	190	210	400	628	598
11-15	276	170	172	380	573	536
16-20	256	166	165	377	570	552
21-25	260	170	147	365	525	503
26-30	274	183	133	353	501	472
31-35	350	211	160	307	498	435
36-40	389	235	183	300	488	445
41-45	400	310	211	298	620	440
46-50	412	320	260	393	815	580
51-55	623	415	281	610	850	775
56-60	658	470	342	670	800	780
61-65	594	436	301	690	680	662
66-70	498	411	298	545	570	512
71-75	387	303	254	411	427	400
76-80	360	297	222	393	401	397
81-85	321	217	178	301	375	321

Source: Author's computation

CONCLUSION

Gustave Nébié, Chinyere Emeka-Anuna, Felix Fofana N'Zue, and Enrique Delamonica

The first Sustainable Development Goal (SDG) requires countries to eradicate poverty in all its dimensions and for all age groups, including children, according to national definitions. The implementation of nationally appropriate social protection systems for all is mentioned explicitly in the SDGs as a paramount strategy in this endeavour. In this book, policy recommendations contributing to achieve these goals are provided, combined with practical ideas and steps on how to implement them. Some chapters also review child poverty trends and disaggregation. These could be used directly or as examples, as baselines to track the SDGs.

This concluding chapter summarizes the main ideas and policy recommendations from the chapters[1]. The book covers a lot of ground; our authors emphasise the importance of mapping child poverty and associated vulnerabilities; the need to plan for emergencies and their impact on child health and child poverty; the level and equity of public spending on health and education; the importance of universal approaches to social protection; and the need to address the underlying, larger inequities in society leading to child poverty[2]. In addition, based on the authors' recommendations, guidelines on some specific issues pertaining how to estimate multi-dimensional child poverty are offered.

IMPORTANCE OF MAPPING

As explained by Nébié, Central and Western African countries vary extensively in terms of levels of economic and social development. It is therefore important to better understand the underlying dynamics of this

---

[1] Methodological issues, although very important, are not emphasized here. Suffice to say that the chapters cover much ground: from primarily quantitative to participatory and qualitative analysis, through single country as well as inter-country comparisons, and covering a range of disciplines (Economics, Sociology, etc.).

[2] Obviously, these issues are connected, and the different chapters deal with more than one of them.

variegated situation, in order to adapt interventions and recommendations accordingly. Thus, policies will be more efficient and equitable. In this analysis countries are classified into relatively homogeneous sub-groups, based on the most recent key economic and social indicators. Operational lessons in terms of strategic planning and priority areas of interventions regarding social protection are offered for each group.

Violating the children's right to be with their parents, a non-material shortcoming, is explored by Skelton and Plaisir, who map the relationship of unwarranted family separation to poverty in general and child poverty in particular, as well as ways in which social protection can promote family reunification. With examples from Burkina Faso, Central African Republic, and Democratic Republic of Congo, the authors give practical recommendations that include: 1) making it possible for extended families to renew relationships with children who have left home; 2) reinforcing efforts of young people in low-income communities to look after and protect younger children; and 3) following the lead of children themselves who can play an active role in strengthening their communities and all the families there.

EMERGENCIES

Various types of emergencies have been addressed by different authors: economic crises, the Ebola epidemic, and natural disasters such as floods. On the latter, in the context of the growing literature relating disaster risk reduction and sustainable development, there is abundant evidence that poor women, the elderly and people living with disabilities are disproportionally affected by disasters through the pernicious combination of exposure, socio-economic vulnerability factors and reduced capacities to recover from shocks. However, a good analysis about the impact of disasters on children often seems to be missing. Thus, Gregr show how child poverty measurements can capture essential dimensions of vulnerability to shocks of girls and boys in different age groups as well as both adaptive capacities and responses of households. They also discuss how this type of analysis was used for disaster risk reduction and emergency preparedness in Mauritania.

Regarding Ebola in Sierra Leone, Abdu explains how the government (with the support of other stakeholders) extended the social safety net programme to cover households with people affected by or survivors from Ebola. The crisis and its aftermath put pressure on an already weak social protection and welfare system. However, qualitative evidence showed that households with cash transfers did spend more on food and sending their children back to school, as well as improving health seeking behaviour. The experience in Sierra Leone demonstrates it is possible to set up quickly social protection interventions in an emergency, even in low income countries.

In response to the 2008-2009 world-wide financial, food and fuel prices crises, the Togolese government implemented a set of measures to offset the negative effects of the crisis on the rural population. These measures have also had an impact on poverty and on child poverty. Kielem combines information on monetary and child (multi-dimensional) poverty to argue that not all households were worse off by the crisis, as changes in relative prices benefited some groups, such as those working in agriculture. Nevertheless, many households did suffer, and the government's social protection efforts mitigated some negative impact.

UNIVERSAL APPROACHES

Around the developing world, social protection contributes increasingly to reduced child poverty, inclusive social development, and equitable economic growth. The associated impacts depend vitally on critical policy choices driving the design and implementation of social protection policies and programmes. Gaps in the evidence base continue to create challenges for how evidence-informed policy design builds appropriate, effective, and sustainable social protection systems. No design choice creates greater challenges or raises more difficult questions than the issue of poverty targeting. As policymakers increasingly recognise the high administrative, private, social, economic, political, and psycho-social costs associated with administrative processes that aim to direct benefits only to the poor, decision-makers progressively opt for more universal approaches. One of the most important trends in social protection design today is the shift towards universalism. Moving toward entirely universal programmes, however, is not always initially feasible in many country contexts; limited resources, capacity, and funding often dictate the rollout of targeted programmes that focus on selected groups. Yet, programmes can adopt more universal approaches, when deciding between the nature of targeting design, in terms of heavier or lighter means of selection and implementation.

Clearly, for universality to be effective, it is important than there be no "invisible children." Social protection is conceptualized as encompassing programmes that create safety nets, enhance risk-coping capabilities, and mitigate vulnerabilities and insecurities among populations. Social protection programmes would be considered effective if they contribute to generate opportunities of choice, survival, and independence for all, and in particular among otherwise impoverished households. Based on the experience of a programme that reunited over 450 children in domestic servitude with their families (and enrolled them in schools or apprentice training) in Ghana, Derby, Okposin, Adetunde, and Okposin address the need to ensure not only that social protection interventions assist these children, but also that they directly address the conditions that push children into child labour. This would require coordinating social protection with social policy writ large — meaning the provision of quality health and educational facilities in rural villages as well as strong systems to protect children from abuse, exploitation, neglect, and trafficking.

ADDRESSING UNDERLYING INEQUALITIES

Social protection is part and parcel of addressing persistent child poverty. However, less than a third of the poorest African children are covered by social protection, posing a formidable challenge for policymakers. Yet, as argued by Vandemoortele, if social protection is seen merely as a technical response to poverty, it is unlikely to yield much impact — no matter how well the programmes are designed. Technical aspects are important and need to be discussed in detail, but this must be done within the right analytical framework. It is of utmost importance to frame social protection within the context of growing inequality. Inequality has become a major obstacle to reducing child poverty in most countries. Yet, inequality seldom features prominently in the clash of narratives regarding poverty reduction. The dominant narrative is that poverty must be addressed through economic growth, accompanied by interventions such as social protection. Reducing inequality is seen as noble but not essential for reducing poverty. As long as policymakers and development practitioners stick to the belief that poverty reduction is mostly growth-mediated and keep negating that future progress will be either equity-mediated or elusive, the impact of social protection on child poverty will remain marginal at best.

In line with this argument, Hague, Cook and McKay scrutinize the impact of changes in income inequality on monetary poverty in Ghana; the country is often cited as a good regional example of stable governance, high economic growth, and gradual social development. However, increasing levels of inequality and recent economic crises have jeopardised its positive progress in recent years. Having achieved the millennium development goal (MDG) target of halving monetary poverty, more than one in four children continue to be poor and increasing inequality and stalling progress have significantly reduced the rate of poverty reduction. Using the new data from Ghana's 2013 Living Standards Survey, they highlight the correlation between monetary and child (multidimensional) poverty. The authors also examine the possibility that not only are children more likely to be poorer than adults, but that the progress made in reducing their poverty has also been slower, constrained by income inequality.

PUBLIC SPENDING EQUITY

A fundamental tool all governments have to use when addressing inequities and inequalities is fiscal policy. Asogwa utilizes empirical data from the 2009/10 Nigerian Living Standards Survey (NLSS) to carry out a benefit incidence analysis of public expenditures on education and health. The results indicate that public spending on education benefits more young persons (aged 20-25) than children (5-15), and that the richer quintiles benefit more than poorer quintiles. Also, public spending on health care benefit older persons between ages 50 and 60 more than the younger persons, and in addition the richer quintiles benefit more than the poorer quintiles. Interestingly, the differences in average benefit of education and health spending for the age groups in the different regions are similar to the differences in severe child deprivations for education and health for the regions. The key policy suggestion is, then, that improving the average benefit of public spending on education and health can reduce severe child deprivation and poverty. One, a way to achieve this, without impacting the groups already enjoying health and education, is to expand fiscal revenue.

ESTIMATE MULTI-DIMENSIONAL CHILD POVERTY

Beyond contexts, institutions and policies, it is important also to estimate and lay out the distribution and characteristics of child poverty and other violations of child rights. While all the authors used the same methodlogy to estimate child (multidimensional) poverty, a couple of them introduced interesting extensions and innovations. Nandy and Pomati present an application and adaptation of the Consensual Approach to poverty measurement (which has already been used successfully in a succession of low-, middle- and high-income countries) to estimate child poverty in Benin and Mali.

Cid Martinez examines child wellbeing and child poverty in Cameroon, Côte d'Ivoire, and Nigeria since the turn of the century. In addition, he explores the impact of including material deprivation associated with a violation of a child's right to play. A methodology for capturing severe, moderate, and mild deprivation in this dimension with available survey data is provided. Sensitivity analysis concludes that while the depth of child poverty is not affected, severity of poverty becomes slightly higher. In addition, a novel way to present all combinations of deprivations simultaneously in one graph is introduced. It should be pointed out that these innovations do not invalidate the basic approach to child poverty measurement. On the contrary, they strengthen it. In these, and all the other chapters, the authors apply the same methodology (first find deprivations in each dimension, then aggregate/count across dimensions) with no weights, a cut-off of one dimension to be considered poor, and a selection of dimensions based on rights constitutive of poverty.

This approach is not only technically sound but also consistent with a human rights approach. Moreover, it is holistically focused on the experience of poverty by the individual child (i.e. it measures the actual deprivation suffered by each child), and uses strictly material deprivations (leaving for cross-tabulation and correlation analysis the non-material deprivations and other child rights violations). Moreover, it is simple to understand both by policy makers and lay persons.

As the Communique of the Conference (reproduced in the Annex) mentions, it is important for countries to estimate child poverty periodically in order to track progress towards the SDGs. Also, combined with policies to address income inequality and expansion of quality social services, the progressive realization of a universal Social Protection Floor is the only way to strengthen families and create inclusive societies in which children grow up happy, healthy, safe, and thriving.

COMMUNIQUÉ OF THE INTERNATIONAL CONFERENCE ON CHILD POVERTY AND SOCIAL PROTECTION, 23-25 May 2016, ABUJA, NIGERIA

The Participants to the meeting (consisting of academia, social policy advocates and practitioners) commend ECOWAS, UNICEF, CROP, Equity for Children, and ILO for successfully organizing the International Conference on Child Poverty and Social Protection. The participants stand resolute on our position that child poverty should be eradicated and social protection be provided to all children specifically in West and Central Africa;

The participants would like to express our sincere appreciation to the Federal Government of Nigeria for the hospitality extended to all the participants during their stay in the country. Our appreciation also goes to the CROP, ILO, UNICEF, Equity for Children, and ECOWAS for the financial support provided to make this conference a reality.

THE ORGANISING INSTITUTIONS (ECOWAS, UNICEF, EQUITY FOR CHILDREN, AND CROP)

1. Note with satisfaction the presentations and fruitful discussions based on research work conducted on child poverty and social protection in West and Central Africa;

2. Recognize that economic growth does not automatically translate into improvements for the population; thus, child poverty and social protection remain critical and need to be addressed in a holistic and integrated manner;

3. Unanimously note with deep concern that children in the region and especially the girl child continue to suffer several deprivations that affect their lives, imperil their wellbeing, and consequently will surely impact the region's future human capital and hence its prospect of sustainable development if nothing is done to halt it;

4. Take note of the seriousness of child poverty with a special attention to girl child poverty in West and Central Africa even in countries classified as middle-income countries;

5. Mindful that without a conducive environment in which children's needs are properly catered for, the future of the region could be jeopardized, for the simple reason that today's children are tomorrow's leaders;

6. Based on the above and on the studies presented at the workshop showing the proven feasibility of taking the following steps;

7. Recommend that in order to design, implement, and evaluate polices to eliminate child poverty, it must be measured routinely, combining the use of census and household surveys to disaggregate along geographic, gender, and socio-economic axes of disparities

8. Recommend the schedule of population censuses be adhered to in all countries;

9. Recommend that in order to contribute to tracking the SDGs, child poverty be estimated using a multi-dimensional perspective and rights-based approach, that monetary measures of poverty be disaggregated by age, and that the two measures be presented in simple ways to be understood by wide-audiences, including civil society organizations and policy-makers;

10. Recommend Policy makers of West and Central Africa to endeavour to design and implement policies targeting the eradication of child poverty and providing social protection for all in West and Central Africa. These policies should be clearly spelled out in the vision and strategic documents of the region;

11. Recommend the widespread sharing of knowledge, efforts and resources within the region, development partners and the scientific community to develop the capacities of countries to monitor and evaluate the impacts of policy implementation on the eradication of child poverty and the extent of social protection coverage in West and Central Africa;

12. Recommend that social protection policies be based on the Social Protection Floor framework, which has been estimated to be affordable for all counties, even in low income ones;

13. Recommend that social protection be considered as more than small-scale anti-poverty programmes;

14. Recommend that social protection be based on principles of non-discrimination and universality with due consideration of progressive realization when resources are constrained in the short run;

15. Recommend that development partners consider their role and commitments vis-à-vis contributing to the well-being of the populations in poorer countries as well as their duty and obligation in terms of realizing the rights of children in these countries;

16. Encourage collaboration between Member States and the wider development community in addressing child poverty and social protection in a coordinated manner, even in countries with relatively higher per capita income but with lagging social development.

17. Express our deep appreciation once again to the stakeholders who made this conference a reality i.e. The Federal Government of Nigeria, ECOWAS, UNICEF, CROP, Equity for Children, and ILO.

CONTRIBUTOR BIOGRAPHIES

Maryam Onyinoyi Abdu was the Chief of Social Policy Planning and M&E at UNICEF Sierra Leone. She is currently the Chief of Social Policy Monitoring and Evaluation in UNICEF in Lao People's Democratic Republic.

Christiana Olufunke Adetunde works in the Department of Sociology, Covenant University, Nigeria. Her research endeavours focus on retirement, the aged, and modern-day slavery.

Robert Chikwendu Asogwa is a Macroeconomist at the African Development Bank Group, Regional Office for Nigeria. His research interests include poverty, unemployment and inclusive growth analysis; macroeconomics; finance and monetary economics as well as public sector and institutional economics.

Ismael Cid-Martinez is a Ph.D. Candidate in the Economics Department at The New School for Social Research and a research assistant for UNICEF's Division of Data, Analysis, Planning and Monitoring. His published research focuses on development theory, the capability approach, stratification economics, public finance, and child poverty.

Edgar Cooke is a lecturer in the Business Administration Department at Ashesi University in Ghana. His research interests are in the areas of poverty, inequality, economic growth and international trade.

Enrique Delamonica is senior statistics specialist focusing on child poverty and gender equality at UNICEF Headquarters, New York. He has held senior positions in social policy in UNICEF Nigeria and the Latin America and Caribbean Regional Office. He was a CROP fellow, and holds a Ph.D. in economics from the New School for Social Research, New York.

C. Nana Derby is Professor and Chair of the Department of Sociology and Criminal Justice at Virginia State University. She primarily focuses her research on child labor, contemporary slavery, and human trafficking. She also studies other criminological issues including prisons and gangs.

Chinyere Dorothy Emeka-Anuna is the Senior Programmes Officer for International Labour Organisation (ILO), Abuja Country Office, covering Nigeria, Ghana, Liberia, Sierra Leone and the Liaison Office for ECOWAS.

Daniela Gregr works for the Ministry of Foreign Affairs of her native Luxembourg. Daniela spearheaded the Child Poverty and Vulnerability Analysis as Chief of Social Policy with UNICEF Mauritania.

Sarah Hague is Chief of Policy for UNICEF Lebanon where she leads a team working on child poverty, social protection and public finance. Prior to UNICEF she headed Save the Children's research team, where she established the first global measure of child poverty.

Aristide Kielem is Programme Analysis expert with the Government of Quebec in Canada, while leading independent researches on child poverty. In this capacity, he also works as a consultant for UNICEF on child poverty and gender.

Andy McKay has been Professor of Development Economics at the University of Sussex since 2006. He specialises in research on poverty and in labour/ gender issues, with a particular focus on sub-Saharan Africa.

Shailen Nandy is Reader in Social Policy at Cardiff University's School of Social Sciences. He has collaborated with UNICEF for nearly 20 years on understanding, measuring and tackling international child poverty.

Gustave Nébié is a Senior Expert on social protection in Burkina Faso within the Permanent Secretariat of the National Council for Social Protection in the Prime Minister office. He holds a PhD in Economics from Paris Dauphine, France, as well as a degree in Public Administration from the French National School of Administration (ENA).

Felix Fofana N'Zué is Principal Programme Officer in charge of Research, Knowledge Management and Economic Policy Analysis with the ECOWAS Commission. He holds a Ph.D. in Agricultural Economics from Oklahoma State University. His current research focuses on Fiscal Policy (debt and growth) and climate change.

Samuel Okposin is the MBA director at the Economics and Development Studies Department of Covenant University, Nigeria.

Shelley Okposin works for a non-government organisation to increase the quality of education in schools across West Africa. Her professional interests include developing strategies to assist overage students in Liberia and improving outcomes for girls.

Jacqueline Plaisir is one of All Together in Dignity/ATD Fourth World's regional directors for Africa and has been based in Dakar since 2017, where her work focuses on education, solidarity, and sharing knowledge.

Marco Pomati is Lecturer in Social Sciences and Research Methods at Cardiff University's School of Social Sciences.

Diana Skelton served on the International Leadership Team of All Together in Dignity / ATD Fourth World for nine years. Currently, she is a national coordinator of ATD Fourth World UK and a member of the Global Coalition to End Child Poverty.

Jan Vandemoortele has served in several capacities with various parts of the United Nations (UNICEF, UNDP, ILO, World Bank) for over 30 years. He is the co-architect of the Millennium Development Goals (MDGs). He holds a PhD in Development Economics.

ibidem.eu